WORKPLACE PRIVACY

Employee Testing, Surveillance, Wrongful Discharge, and Other Areas of Vulnerability

2nd Edition

By
Ira Michael Shepard
Robert L. Duston
Karen S. Russell

D1231459

Copyright © 1989
The Bureau of National Affairs, Inc.
1231 25th St., N.W.
Washington, D.C. 20037

International Standard Book Number: 1-55871-137-6

Library of Congress Cataloging-in-Publication Data

Shepard, Ira Michael, 1947-
　　Workplace privacy.

　　　(A BNA special report)
　　　Includes bibliographical references.
　　　1. Employee rights—United States.　2. Privacy,
Right of—United States.　3. Confidential communications
Personnel records—United States.　I. Duston, Robert
Lewis.　II. Russell, Karen S.　III. Bureau of National
Affairs (Washington, D.C.)　IV. Title.　V. Series.
KF3455.S54　1989　　　344.73'012596　　　89-22353
ISBN 1-55871-137-6　　　347.30412596

Table of Contents

Appendices

Introduction/Highlights

Workplace privacy rights of public and private-sector employees is the most dynamic and volatile area of employment law in the United States.

The advent of drug and alcohol abuse testing, computer monitoring of employees, employer liability for negligent hiring and for defaming employees, and erosion of the common-law doctrine of employment-at-will have spawned a revolutionary change in employment law, workplace attitudes, and practices. A substantial new array of complex and novel legal theories have developed under which employees are attempting to redress what they see as a decline in their privacy rights. The United States is forging the cutting edge of employee privacy rights. These developments will establish the limits on enlightened management's ability to effectively compete internationally while dealing with the difficult societal developments which all too often invade the workplace.

Workplace privacy, an issue that had been dormant since the passage of the federal Privacy Act and similar state laws in the mid-1970s, gained national attention in 1987 with the Reagan Administration's recruitment of employers to help fight the war on drugs, concerns over the transmission of acquired immune deficiency syndrome (AIDS), and the debate surrounding polygraphs. These events focused attention on the broader questions of employers' involvement in their employees' private lives.

In one of its most important decisions on this subject, *O'Connor v. Ortega*, the U.S. Supreme Court in 1987 addressed, for the first time in a civil case, the privacy rights of public sector employees. Since Justice William O. Douglas' majority opinion in the 1965 decision, *Griswold v. Connecticut*, which announced a right of privacy protected by the U.S. Constitution, the court had been slow to develop the general concept of a constitutional right of privacy. In *Ortega*, the court decided that public employees have the right to sue their employer in an attempt to prove that the employer's policies led the employee to have the expectation of privacy in the workplace. The Supreme Court in *Ortega* went far beyond the vaguely described constitutional right of privacy in having access to contraceptives recognized in *Griswold*.

The court in 1989 applied its decision in *Ortega* to drug testing in *National Treasury Employees Union v. Von Raab* and in *Railroad Labor Executives Association v. Skinner*, stimulating further debate over the balancing of employer and employee rights.

Workplace Privacy, published by BNA in 1987, was among the first publications devoted exclusively to the various issues often called "employee privacy problems." An exclusive survey of jury verdicts conducted by the Washington, D.C., management law firm of Schmeltzer, Aptaker & Sheppard revealed that workplace privacy-case jury verdicts averaged $316,000 during 1985-87 and verdicts for the plaintiffs increased 20-fold. Major newspapers and national magazines said the survey revealed an outbreak of privacy and wrongful discharge issues. A new survey conducted by the same law firm reveals that privacy issues are continuing to grow in importance.

The survey reveals that employees won 72% of workplace privacy trials between 1985 and 1988. The average jury award in 1988 was $375,307, and the median verdict was $97,000.[1] The cases surveyed did not even involve wrongful discharge claims, where, according to an earlier survey by the law firm, jury verdicts average $602,302, with a median verdict of $158,800.[2]

Under Supreme Court workplace privacy decisions—which affect public employers and private employers acting under government requirements—employees have a right to bring an action based on their "expectation of privacy" based on their employers' policies and practices. If the law continues to develop along these lines, employers should have at least partial control over the number and types of employee actions in the field of workplace privacy, because they can adopt and enforce policies and practices that ensure reasonable privacy but are limited by legitimate business concerns and considerations. Courts probably will defer to employer policies and practices that strike a reasonable balance between employees' legitimate workplace privacy rights and employers' legitimate business concerns. In other areas, such as employees' off-duty conduct, employer policies will be challenged increasingly as an invasion of privacy, especially where they cannot be directly related to legitimate business interests.

Privacy issues will be the labor law issue of the 1990s. As employees become increasingly concerned about what they feel are employer intrusions into their private lives, they will seek relief from Congress, state legislatures, and state and federal courts. Workplace privacy-case damage awards totaling hundreds of thousands of dollars probably will spawn more lawsuits in this field. At the same time, employers will be increasingly involved in their employees' backgrounds and personal lives—in such areas as day care, flexible leave, and remedial education—as a result of their efforts to recruit and retain qualified workers in a shrinking labor market. Employers forced to interview and hire marginally qualified job applicants they previously would have rejected will continue to try to identify and reject workers who are dishonest or who abuse substances that can hinder their ability to perform their jobs. The increased recruitment of women and minorities will increase concerns about sexual harassment and discrimination. As employer benefits expand, new questions will arise about access to employee records and personal information and the confidentiality of such data.

Although these are national issues, they seldom have been regulated only at the federal level. Employers must deal with a panoply of federal and state laws and court decisions that regulate their activities. Several state constitutions exceed the U.S.

Constitution in guaranteeing the right to privacy. In many states, employers are subject to vague common-law doctrines that have not been applied to the privacy issues they will face in the 1990s, so they must learn how courts have applied these doctrines in other fields.

This second edition of BNA's *Privacy in the Workplace* special report is an up-to-date guide to workplace privacy that discusses the practical and legal concerns of employers and employees. It is greatly expanded and reorganized to make it a more convenient resource. This report guides the user through the various theories being tested in the courts as a result of employee litigation, and it describes the various legislative proposals concerning worker privacy protection being considered in Congress and in state legislatures. This report enables corporate executives, human relations professionals, employment law practitioners, and employees to understand the current rights and responsibilities of employers and employees in the privacy area.

The report addresses practical problems and permissible parameters of employer activity against the backdrop of the workplace privacy law that is developing. The report describes preventive measures that employers can take with regard to each area of litigation in the privacy field. No text, however, can substitute for sound legal counsel when confronting particular problems. The advice of counsel is especially important in the rapidly developing area of privacy rights, where new decisions and legislation affecting individual rights in the workplace must be monitored closely.

HIGHLIGHTS

Chapter I of this BNA Special Report outlines the U.S. Supreme Court's landmark decision in *Ortega* and the recent decisions in *Von Raab* and *Skinner* and explains how these decisions will affect the right of privacy.

Chapter II describes the history of the right to privacy under the common law, and how it has been applied to the workplace.

Chapter III discusses employers' increasing use of drug and alcohol tests on job applicants and employees, and challenges to this practice.

Chapter IV updates restrictions on the use of polygraphs, including a comprehensive analysis of the Employee Polygraph Protection Act of 1988.

Chapter V analyzes problems employers can encounter when they investigate job applicants, including reference and credit checks.

Chapter VI explains the debate surrounding honesty tests and other psychological tests given to applicants and employees.

Chapter VII covers issues involving AIDS in the workplace, including restrictions on testing for AIDS, and legal protections for people with AIDS, including the issue of confidentiality.

Chapter VIII focuses on medical screening of workers, including the controversial issues of genetic testing of employees and the legality of fetal protection policies.

Chapter IX deals with several areas of employee investigations, including searches of employees' offices or personal belongings.

Chapter X deals with federal and state limits on electronic monitoring, surveillance, and bugging.

Chapter XI reviews the legal restrictions against sexual harassment, the standards for determining employer liability, and how employers can communicate their policies and minimize their liability.

Chapter XII analyzes employer restrictions on their employees' personal relationships, including no-spouse rules, limits on intra-company dating, discrimination based on sexual

preference, and disciplining employees for their off-duty sexual
behavior.

Chapter XIII addresses the issues of access to employee information and their confidentiality, including security reports
and personnel files.

Chapter XIV examines the need for employers to protect
the personal and confidential medical information they receive
about their employees through employee assistance programs
(EAPs).

Chapter XV provides a capsule summary of the major
statutory and common-law exceptions to the employment-at-
will doctrine and how these exceptions have been used to support breach of privacy claims.

Chapter XVI outlines how employee privacy claims of
defamation and civil wrongs are being brought in cases involving discharges and job references.

The principal appendix is a comprehensive state-by-state
compilation of laws and court decisions that affect workplace
privacy. Other appendices to the report include the text of the
two Supreme Court drug testing cases, sample corporate
policies, and a selected bibliography.

ABOUT THE AUTHORS

Ira Michael Shepard is a partner in the Washington, D.C.,
law firm of Schmeltzer, Aptaker & Sheppard, P.C. He heads
the firm's labor law section, representing management in all
areas of labor and employment law. Before he joined the firm,
Mr. Shepard served as counsel to the Republican members of
the Senate Labor and Human Resources Committee. He is a
graduate of the Cornell University School of Industrial and
Labor Relations and the Cornell Law School, and is a member
of the bars of New York, the District of Columbia, and the
U.S. Supreme Court. Mr. Shepard and Robert Duston co-
authored the BNA Special Reports *Workplace Privacy* (BNA
1987); *Thieves at Work: An Employer's Guide to Combating*

Workplace Dishonesty (BNA 1988); and *Without Just Cause, An Employer's Practical and Legal Guide to Wrongful Discharge* (BNA 1989) (with Paul Heylman).

Robert L. Duston is an associate in Schmeltzer, Aptaker & Sheppard. He represents management in all areas of labor and employment law, with an emphasis on wrongful discharge, employment discrimination, and employee benefits litigation. Prior to joining the firm, Mr. Duston served as a law clerk to Judge Jackson L. Kiser of the U.S. District Court for the Western District of Virginia. Mr. Duston is a graduate of George Mason University and the University of Virginia School of Law, and is a member of the bars of the Commonwealth of Virginia and the District of Columbia.

Karen S. Russell is an associate in Schmeltzer, Aptaker & Sheppard, where she represents management in all areas of labor and employment law. She is a graduate of Oklahoma State University and the University of Oklahoma School of Law, where she was an editor of the law review. Ms. Russell is a member of the bars of Oklahoma and the District of Columbia. She assisted in the preparation of the first edition of *Workplace Privacy*.

ACKNOWLEDGMENTS

The authors wish to thank the researchers and assistants who worked on this second edition, including Michelle Amber, Stephen Born, Richard Heffner, David Newman, Jarnitha Woodson, and Schmeltzer, Aptaker & Sheppard associates Catherine Werner and and Scott Robins. The authors particularly thank Carole Connolly for her patience and skill in typing the manuscript of this report.

This special report is published by the Special Projects Unit of The Bureau of National Affairs, Inc. Drew Douglas, managing editor, served as project manager. Roger Feinthel, staff editor, served as copy editor. Gwen Moulton, staff editor, served as production editor. Loretta Kotzin, staff researcher, compiled the appendices. Karen Cargill, editorial assistant, also contributed to the preparation of this report, as did BNA researchers Brian Broderick and Anthony Owens.

ENDNOTES

[1] Based upon data collected and analyzed by Jury Verdict Research Inc., Solon, Ohio.

[2] See *Without Just Cause: An Employer's Practical and Legal Guide on Wrongful Discharge* (BNA 1989).

* * *

Privacy and the Constitution

The Declaration of Independence states that people have certain "inalienable rights." While no agreement seems to exist among legislators, judges, or philosophers about what "privacy" comprises and which privacy interests are entitled to protection from the government or other people, the "right to privacy" is considered by many to be one of those inalienable rights.[1]

The principal concern of employers and employees is which privacy rights have been recognized and protected, and how those rights apply in the workplace. An analysis of workplace privacy rights should begin with a review of their major sources: (1) the U.S. Constitution, which places limits on the government; (2) common law torts, which create liability for certain acts one person commits against another; and (3) state constitutions and laws, which provide additional rights and protections against specific intrusions into areas of personal privacy.[2] This chapter focuses on the right of privacy under the U.S. Constitution.

GRISWOLD AND ITS PROGENY

The Constitution contains no express privacy provision. In 1928, U.S. Supreme Court Justice Louis D. Brandeis wrote in a dissenting opinion in *Olmstead v. United States*[3] that the Fourth Amendment protection against unreasonable searches and seizures extends beyond physical invasions of protected space to include "the right to be let alone." Later cases recognized several specific constitutional rights relating to personal privacy, but it was not until *Griswold v. Connecticut*,[4] a 1965 case involving access to contraceptives by married couples, that the Supreme Court recognized, within the Constitution, an implied privacy right that applies to the states through the 14th

Amendment. This constitutional right of privacy has been developed through subsequent case law. Although the scope of the right is not well-defined, its existence is recognized.

Justice William O. Douglas' majority opinion in *Griswold* relied on several cases which suggested that the specific guarantees in the Bill of Rights create "zones of privacy." For example, the freedom to associate with other people is not mentioned in the Constitution or the Bill of Rights. The right to educate a child in a school of the parent's choice—public, private, or parochial—also is not mentioned, nor is the right to study any particular subject or any foreign language. Yet the First Amendment has been construed to include these rights.[5] *Pierce v. Society of Sisters*[6] upheld parents' right to educate their children as they choose, and *Meyer v. Nebraska*[7] recognized the right to study the German language in a private school. Similarly, the Supreme Court has protected the "freedom to associate and privacy in one's associations," noting that freedom of association is a peripheral First Amendment right.[8]

Douglas noted that other guarantees, like those protected by the First Amendment, had been recognized as protecting "zones of privacy." The Fourth Amendment affirms the "right of the people to be secure in their persons, houses, papers, and effects, against unreasonable searches and seizures." The Fifth Amendment, in its Self-Incrimination Clause, enables citizens to create a zone of privacy that government may not force them to surrender to their detriment. The Fourth and Fifth Amendments have been described as providing protection against all governmental invasions "of the sanctity of a man's home and the privacies of life."[9] In *Mapp v. Ohio*, the court referred to the Fourth Amendment as creating a "right to privacy, no less important than any other right carefully and particularly reserved to the people."[10]

After reviewing these decisions, Douglas concluded in *Griswold* that "[t]hese cases bear witness that the right of privacy which presses for recognition here is a legitimate one."[11] The court found that the concerns of the marital relationship are within the zone of privacy created by several fundamental constitutional guarantees, and that a state, by forbidding the use of contraceptives, impermissibly intruded on that relationship.

In the 24 years since *Griswold*, the Supreme Court has been presented with many cases seeking to define and expand the right of privacy. The leading cases have been in the area of personal relationships and procreation. Justice William J. Brennan's majority opinion in *Eisenstadt v. Baird*,[12] one of several cases striking down limits on access to contraceptives, observed that if "the right of privacy means anything, it is the right of the individual, married or single, to be free from unwanted governmental intrusions into matters so fundamentally affecting a person as the decision whether to bear or beget a child."[13]

Subsequent decisions have stated that the right of privacy is founded in the 14th Amendment's concept of personal liberty and restrictions on state action.[14] The court has noted that the right of privacy protects two kinds of interest. These are individuals' interest in:

- Independence in making certain kinds of important decisions; and
- Avoiding disclosure of personal matters.

The court also has noted a third interest, directly protected by the Fourth Amendment, of individuals to be free from governmental surveillance and intrusion in their private affairs.[15]

The court explained the right of privacy in avoiding disclosure of personal matters in *Whalen v. Roe*, a case that involved a New York statutory scheme for maintaining computerized records on prescriptions for certain dangerous drugs. The court upheld the law, finding that the required disclosures of private information to the New York Department of Health were not meaningfully distinguishable "from a host of other unpleasant invasions of privacy that are associated with many

facets of health care, such as the disclosure of private medical
information to doctors, hospital personnel, insurance companies, and to public health agencies." However, Justice John
Paul Steven's majority opinion went on to discuss the privacy
interests in personal information:

> We are not unaware of the threat to privacy implicit in the ac-
> cumulation of vast amounts of personal information in com-
> puterized databanks or other massive government files .... The
> right to collect and use such data for public purposes is typically
> accompanied by a concomitant statutory or regulatory duty to
> avoid unwarranted disclosures. Recognizing that in some cir-
> cumstances that duty arguably has its roots in the Constitution,
> nevertheless the New York statutory scheme, and its implementing
> administrative procedures, evidence of proper concern with, and
> protection of, the individual's interest in privacy.[16]

PRIVACY IN THE WORKPLACE

The Supreme Court first confronted the issue of privacy in
the workplace in cases involving search and seizure. The court
recognized prior to 1987, in the context of criminal litigation,
that employees sometimes may have a reasonable expectation
of privacy within the workplace. In *Mancusi v. De Forte*,[17] the
court concluded that a union official had a personal right
under the Fourth Amendment to object to an allegedly unreasonable police search and seizure of union records from a
union office shared with other union officials. The court found
that the union official, who spent considerable time in the office, had custody of records at the time of the seizure and
could reasonably have expected that such records would not be
touched except with the permission of other union officials. In
another criminal case, *Oliver v. United States*,[18] where the court
found no legitimate expectation of privacy in open fields, that
is, farm land or park land, the court noted in a footnote that
legitimate expectations of privacy may exist in offices and commercial buildings.

These cases foreshadowed the possible extension of the
right to privacy into the workplace, depending on whether

employees have a reasonable expectation of privacy in their place of employment from searches of desks, lockers, and personal belongings. The extent to which the Fourth Amendment provides a right to privacy in a governmental workplace was finally presented to the Supreme Court in the case of *O'Connor v. Ortega.*[19]

In *Ortega*, the court addressed the issue of whether the search of a state employee's desk, without prior notification or his approval, constituted an unreasonable search and seizure in violation of the employee's reasonable expectation of privacy in the workplace. This case is the first civil action of this kind to have reached the Supreme Court.

Ortega, a psychiatrist employed by a state hospital in California for 17 years, had primary responsibility for training physicians in the psychiatric residency program. Hospital officials became concerned about possible improprieties in Ortega's management of the residency program, particularly his acquisition of a computer possibly financed through coerced contributions and charges that he had sexually harassed female hospital employees and had taken inappropriate disciplinary action against a resident.

While Ortega was on administrative leave pending investigation of the charges, hospital officials, allegedly to inventory and secure state property, searched Ortega's office and seized several personal items from his desk and file cabinets—a Valentine's Day card, photographs, and a book of poetry from a former resident—that were used later in administrative proceedings resulting in his discharge. No formal inventory of the property was made; all of the other papers in the office were placed in boxes for storage. Ortega sued hospital officials, alleging that the search of his office violated the Fourth Amendment.

The Supreme Court addressed two issues: (1) whether Ortega, as a public employee, had a reasonable expectation of privacy in his office, desk, and file cabinets at his place of work, and if so, (2) whether the search was reasonable under the Fourth Amendment.

The Fourth Amendment protects the "right of the people to be secure in their persons, houses, papers and effects, against unreasonable searches and seizures."[20] The Fourth Amendment applies, through the Due Process Clause of the 14th Amendment, to the conduct of state and local government officials, including searches and seizures by government employees or supervisors of the private property of their employees. Fourth Amendment rights are implicated only if the conduct of the governmental officials infringe on "an expectation of privacy that society is prepared to consider reasonable."[21] Courts use several factors to determine what expectations are considered reasonable, including the intention of the framers of the Fourth Amendment, the uses to which the individual has put a location, and societal understanding that certain areas deserve protection from the government.[22]

Drawing on *Oliver* and other decisions, the Supreme Court in *Ortega* held that public employees may have a reasonable expectation of privacy against intrusions in the workplace. As with the expectation of privacy in a person's home, this expectation of privacy at a person's place of work is "based on societal expectations that have deep roots in the history of the Amendment."

The court, noting that a wide variety of work environments exist in the public sector, held that the reasonableness of an expectation of privacy must be decided on a case-by-case basis. An office seldom is a private enclave free from entry by others. Because of the nature of government, many people — fellow employees, supervisors, consensual visitors, and the general public — may have frequent access to government employees' offices. While "constitutional protection against unreasonable searches by the government does not disappear merely because the government has the right to make reasonable intrusions in its capacity as employer,"[23] some government offices may be so open to fellow employees or to the public that no expectation of privacy is reasonable.

The undisputed evidence disclosed that Ortega did not share his desk or file cabinets with any other employees. Ortega had occupied the office for 17 years and he kept many materials in his office, including personal correspondence, medical files, correspondence from private patients unconnected to the hospital, personal financial records, teaching aids and notes, and personal gifts and mementos. The files on physicians in residency training were kept outside Ortega's office. On these findings, the court agreed that Ortega had a reasonable expectation of privacy in his desk and file cabinets. Five justices also agreed that Ortega had a reasonable expectation of privacy in the office itself.

The court then considered whether the search was reasonable under the Fourth Amendment. What is reasonable depends on the context within which a search is conducted.[24] The standard of reasonableness applicable to different types of searches involves "balancing the nature and quality of the intrusion against the important governmental interest alleged to justify the intrusion."[25] In the case of searches conducted by a public employer, courts must balance the invasion of employees' legitimate expectations of privacy against the governments' needs for supervision, control, and efficient operation of the workplace.

The Supreme Court found little case law on the appropriate standard of reasonableness for a public employer's work-related search of its employees' offices, desks, or file cabinets. The lower courts that had addressed this issue usually had ruled that any work-related search by an employer satisfies the Fourth Amendment reasonableness requirement.[26] Recognizing that the legitimate privacy interests of public employees in the private objects they bring into the workplace may be substantial, the Supreme Court balanced the realities of the workplace and rejected a proposed standard of reasonableness that would have required a warrant before a search could occur. In the court's view, requiring a public employer to obtain a warrant whenever it wants to enter an employee's office, desk, or file cabinet for a work-related purpose would seriously disrupt the routine conduct of business and would be unduly burdensome.

The court also considered whether probable cause was an appropriate standard for public employer searches of their employees' offices. Although recognizing that searches usually must be based on probable cause, the court held in *Ortega* that a probable cause requirement would place intolerable burdens on public employers confronted with a need to correct employee misconduct or incompetence.[27] The court concluded that for legitimate, work-related, noninvestigatory intrusions as well as investigations of work-related misconduct, a standard of reasonableness should be applied. This standard, the court held, would neither unduly burden the efforts of government employers to ensure the efficient and proper operation of the workplace nor would it authorize arbitrary intrusion on the privacy of public employees.

Under the standard adopted in *Ortega*, a search of an employee's office must be "justified at its inception," as where reasonable grounds exist for suspecting that the employee is guilty of work-related misconduct, or where the search is necessary for another record-related purpose, such as retrieving a file. The search that is conducted also must be reasonable, not excessively intrusive, and the procedures used must relate to the objective of the search. The court remanded *Ortega* so that the lower court could apply these standards.

Justice Antonin Scalia concurred in the reversal, but he favored a more explicit holding in favor of the employer. Scalia suggested that the reasonableness formula used by the plurality of justices in the ruling is "so devoid of content that it produces rather than eliminates uncertainty in this field." Endorsing a supervisor's unrestricted right of access, Scalia suggested that Fourth Amendment protections are limited in light of the government's "special" needs:

> [T]he government, like any other employer, needs frequent and convenient access to its desks, files, and offices for work-related purposes. I would hold that government searches to retrieve work-related materials or to investigate violations of workplace rules — searches of the sort that are regarded as reasonable and normal in the private employer context — do not violate the Fourth Amendment.[28]

The balance struck in *Ortega* will have a significant impact on the development of privacy rights in the workplace. Experts view the court's recognition that the government may do certain acts in its role as an employer that it could not do to other citizens as a victory for employers. At the same time, the court's statement that employees may have a legitimate expectation of privacy in the workplace, while applying directly only to searches by public employers under the Fourth Amendment, sets the stage for future litigation over employee privacy rights.

WORKPLACE PRIVACY 1989

The Supreme Court next addressed the application of the right of privacy in the workplace in two 1989 decisions involving drug testing. In *National Treasury Employees Union v. Von Raab*[29] and *Skinner v. Railway Labor Executives Association,*[30] the Supreme Court continued to develop the standards to be applied in workplace privacy cases.

In *Skinner*, the court held, 7-2, that the Fourth Amendment was applicable to drug and alcohol testing mandated or authorized by Federal Railroad Administration (FRA) regulations. The court ruled that the tests were reasonable under the Fourth Amendment, even though neither a warrant nor a reasonable suspicion that any employee might be impaired was required, due to the compelling governmental interest served by the regulations, which outweighed employees' privacy concerns.

The court concluded that any compelled intrusion into the body for a blood sample to be analyzed for alcohol content constitutes a "search," and infringes an expectation of privacy that society is prepared to recognize as reasonable. The ensuing chemical analysis of the sample to obtain physiological data is a further invasion of the employee's privacy interest. The court extended to drug tests its previous holdings regarding blood tests, holding that chemical analysis of urine also can reveal a host of private medical facts about an employee. The court also recognized that the process usually used to collect urine samples for testing implicates privacy interests.[31]

The court then applied the balancing test outlined in *Ortega*, finding that the government's interest in regulating the conduct of railroad employees to ensure safety, "like its supervision of probationers or regulated industries, or its operation of a government office, school or prison, likewise presents special needs beyond normal law enforcement that may justify departures from the usual warrant and probable cause requirements" for a search.[32]

As in *Ortega*, the court rejected a warrant requirement or a requirement of probable cause. It held that "where the privacy interests implicated by the search are minimal, and where an important governmental interest furthered by the intrusion would be placed in jeopardy by a requirement of individualized suspicion, a search may be reasonable despite the absence of such suspicion." The court went on to find that the intrusions on privacy under the FRA regulations were limited:

> ...to the extent transportation and like restrictions are necessary to procure the requisite blood, breath and urine samples for testing, this interference alone is minimal given the employment context in which it takes place. Ordinarily, an employee consents to significant restrictions in his freedom of movement where necessary for his employment, and few are free to come and go as they please during working hours .... Any additional interference with a railroad employee's freedom of movement that occurs in the time it takes to procure a blood, breath or urine sample for testing cannot, by itself, be said to infringe significant privacy interests.[33]

The court also found that the expectation of privacy of the employees was diminished because they worked in an industry that is regulated pervasively to ensure safety, and that most railroads require periodic physical examinations for many employees. On balance, the court found that the governmental interests involved outweighed the employees' privacy interests.[34]

In *NTEU v. Von Raab*, the court applied a similar analysis in upholding, 5-4, a drug testing program by the U.S. Customs Service of employees applying for promotion to positions involving interdiction of illegal drugs or requiring them to carry firearms. The court ruled that requiring the government to procure a warrant for every work-related intrusion "would conflict with the common sense realization that government offices could not function if every employment decision became a constitutional matter." The court noted that under the Customs Service program, no discretion was involved because every employee who sought a transfer to a covered position had to be tested. The court also rejected a probable cause or individualized reasonable suspicion requirement, claiming that the government's need to conduct suspicionless searches required by the program outweighed the privacy interests of employees engaged directly in drug interdiction, and of those who otherwise are required to carry firearms.[35]

The court held that "certain forms of public employment may diminish privacy expectations even with respect to personal searches." For example, the court noted that employees of the United States Mint should expect to submit to certain routine personal searches when they leave the workplace every day, and that employees joining the military or intelligence services may be required to give extraordinary assurances of trustworthiness and expect intrusive inquiries into their physical fitness for such jobs. The court held that the Customs Service employees, unlike most private citizens or government employees, reasonably should expect an inquiry into their fitness for duty.[36]

Scalia, in his dissent in *Von Raab*, found a total absence of any governmental justification for the intrusion in the privacy of Customs Service employees. Scalia concluded that the only plausible explanation for the regulations was the one articulated by the commissioner of the Customs Service, to set an important example in the nation's struggle against drugs. Scalia concluded that "I think it is obvious that this justification is unacceptable; the impairment of individual liberties cannot be the means of making a point; that symbolism, even symbolism for so worthy a cause as the abolition of unlawful drugs, cannot validate an otherwise unreasonable search."[37]

STATE ACTION AND SECTION 1983

Most of the protections for individual rights and liberties contained in the Constitution apply only to the actions of the state or federal governments. Thus, when a suit is brought against private individuals alleging that they have taken actions which have violated the civil or political rights of another person, a court must determine whether the defendant's actions constitute governmental or "state" action of a type regulated by the appropriate constitutional provision.

When a legislature, executive officer, or a court takes some official action against an individual, that action is subjected to review under the Constitution, because the official act of any governmental agency is direct governmental action and therefore subject to the restraints of the Constitution. The first issue addressed by the Supreme Court in *Skinner* was whether a search conducted by a private railroad complying with regulations promulgated by the FRA implicated the Fourth Amendment. The court noted that the Fourth Amendment does not apply to a search and seizure conducted by a private party on its own initiative, even if it is arbitrary, but the amendment protects against such intrusions if the private party acted as an instrument or agent of the government. The FRA regulations made post-accident testing mandatory. The court found that because railroads were required to conduct such testing under the requirements of the federal agency, the Fourth Amendment was applicable. A separate part of the regulations authorized railroads to require covered employees to submit to breath or urine tests on a "for-cause" basis. Although the government did not compel railroads to perform these searches, the court found that the regulations were intended to pre-empt state laws and any provisions of collective bargaining agreements or arbitration awards, and that government employees who refused their employers' requests to take these tests were fired. The court concluded that the government's removal of all legal barriers to testing and its strong preference for testing, as well as the government's desire to receive the results of the tests, was sufficient evidence of the government's encouragement, endorsement, and participation to implicate the Fourth Amendment.

The legal basis used most frequently by public employees and those injured by state or other governmental action is Section 1983, a federal law codified at 42 USC 1983 that was modeled after the Civil Rights Act of 1866 .[38] Section 1983 provides a cause of action for the deprivation "under color of state law" of any right secured by the U.S. Constitution. Individual federal officials and agencies can be sued, and states can be sued when their sovereign immunity has been waived. Municipalities and other local government units can be sued for constitutional deprivations caused by customs, policies, ordinances, or regulations. Thus, many decisions of public employers that act under color of state law are subject to challenge under Section 1983. Private employers cannot be sued under this law unless they are acting as agents of the government.[39]

Many Section 1983 suits allege a deprivation of the due process protections of the 14th Amendment. In procedural due process cases, public employees allege that they had a property interest in their employment that could not be taken away from them without due process. Federal courts frequently look to a combination of an agency's policies and procedures and applicable state law to determine whether an employee has a property interest in a job. If a court finds that a covered employee has a property interest in the job, the employee is entitled at least to notice of the reason for discipline or discharge and an opportunity for a hearing. If the employer's policies provide additional protections, those must be followed.[40]

Another class of Section 1983 cases comprises substantive due process claims, which operate as federal "public policy" exceptions. Many such cases involve public employees fired for exercising their free speech rights, their voting rights, or their privacy rights.

Although the constitutional right of privacy applies only to the actions of the federal government and the states, and usually does not restrict the acts of private employers, the protections afforded public employees are nevertheless important to private employees. As later chapters illustrate, some courts and arbitrators look to the protections provided by the Constitution for guidance on the type of privacy interests that deserve protection.

ENDNOTES

[1] Tribe, *American Constitutional Law* § 15-3 (New York: The Foundation Press Inc.) 1978.

[2] Common law torts and state constitutions and laws as sources of privacy rights are discussed in detail in Chapter II.

[3] 277 U.S. 438, 471, 48 S. Ct. 564, 570 (1928) (Brandeis, J., dissenting).

[4] 381 U.S. 479, 85 S. Ct. 1678 (1965).

[5] 381 U.S. at 482, 85 S. Ct. at 1680.

[6] 268 U.S. 510, 45 S. Ct. 571 (1925).

[7] 262 U.S. 390, 43 S. Ct. 625 (1923).

[8] *NAACP v. Alabama*, 357 U.S. 449, 78 S. Ct. 1163 (1958).

[9] *Boyd v. United States*, 116 U.S. 616, 6 S. Ct. 524 (1886).

[10] 367 U.S. 643, 656, 81 S. Ct. 1684, 1692 (1961).

[11] 381 U.S. at 485, 85 S. Ct. at 1682.

[12] 405 U.S. 438, 92 S. Ct. 1029 (1972).

[13] *Id.* at 453. This line of decisions includes the abortion case, *Roe v. Wade*, 410 U.S. 113, 93 S. Ct. 705 (1973), which extended the right of privacy to a woman's decision to terminate her pregnancy.

[14] *Whalen v. Roe*, 429 U.S. 589, 598 n.22, 97 S. Ct. 869, 876 (1977), *citing, Roe v. Wade*, 410 U.S. at 13, 93 S. Ct. at 727 (1974).

[15] *Whalen v. Roe*, 429 U.S. at 599 n.24, 97 S. Ct. at 876.

[16] *Whalen v. Roe*, 429 U.S. at 605, 97 S. Ct. at 879.

[17] 392 U.S. 364, 88 S. Ct. 2120 (1968).

[18] 466 U.S. 170, 178, 104 S. Ct. 1735, 1741 (1984).

[19] 480 U.S. 709, 107 S. Ct. 1492, 1 IER 1617 (1987).

[20] U.S. CONST. amend. IV.

[21] *Ortega*, 107 S. Ct. at 1497, *citing, United States v. Jacobsen*, 466 U.S. 109, 113, 104 S. Ct. 1652, 1656 (1984).

[22] *Ortega*, 107 S.Ct. at 1497.

[23] *Ortega*, 107 S.Ct. at 1505 (Scalia, J., concurring).

[24] *New Jersey v. T.L.O.*, 469 U.S. 325, 337, 105 S. Ct. 733, 740 (1985).

[25] *See United States v. Place*, 462 U.S. 696, 703, 103 S. Ct. 2637, 2642 (1983); *Camara v. Municipal Court*, 387 U.S. 523, 536-37, 87 S. Ct. 1727, 1734-35 (1967).

[26] *See United States v. Nasser*, 476 F.2d 1111, 1123 (7th Cir. 1973) (work-related searches and seizures are reasonable under the Fourth Amendment); *United States v. Collins*, 349 F.2d 863, 868 (2d Cir. 1965), *cert. denied*, 383 U.S. 960, 86 S. Ct. 1228 (1966) (upholding search and seizure of a government agent's office and desk pursuant to "the power of the Government as defendant's employer, to supervise and investigate the performance of his duties as a Customs employee"); *United States v. Bunkers*, 521 F.2d 1217 (9th Cir.), *cert. denied*, 423 U.S. 989, 96 S. Ct. 400 (1975)(work-related search of a locker tested under reasonable cause standard).

[27] *T.L.O.*, 469 U.S. at 351, 105 S. Ct. at 747-48.

[28] *Ortega*, 480 U.S. 709, 107 S.Ct. at 1505-1506 (Scalia, J., concurring).

[29] 109 S. Ct. 1384, 4 IER Cases 246 (1989).

[30] 109 S. Ct. 1402 (1989).

[31] *Skinner*, 109 S. Ct. at 1412-13.

[32] *Id.* at 1414.

[33] *Id.* at 1417.

[34] *Id.* at 1418-19.

[35] *Von Raab*, 109 S. Ct. at 1391-92.

[36] *Id.* at 1393-94.

[37] *Id.* at 1401.

[38] A good summary of Section 1983 is contained in Richey, *Manual on Employment Discrimination Law and Civil Rights Actions in the Federal Courts*, (Clark Boardman 1987) § D.2.

[39] *Sanders v. A.J. Canfield Co.*, 635 F. Supp. 85, 45 FEP 1504 (N.D. Ill. 1986).

[40] *Cleveland Bd. of Education v. Loudermill*, 470 U.S. 532, 546, 105 S. Ct. 1487, 1495, 1 IER Cases 424 (1985); *Matthews v. Eldridge*, 424 U.S. 319, 335, 96 S. Ct. 893, 903 (1976).

* * *

Common Law and Statutory Rights

The erosion of the doctrine that employment is at will, and that employees may be discharged for any reason, has been paralleled by an increase in employee claims alleging invasions of privacy. Employees have used many theories in trying to create an enforceable right of privacy in the workplace. State laws concerning specific issues have been one source of privacy rights. Other chapters in this report detail legislative efforts in areas such as polygraph testing, electronic monitoring, and the confidentiality of employee records. This chapter details three other sources of privacy rights: 1) the common law tort of "invasion of privacy"; 2) state constitutional provisions and laws that deal with individual privacy rights; and 3) tort claims of wrongful discharge in violation of public policy.

DEFINITION OF COMMON LAW
RIGHTS OF PRIVACY

To understand the different ways the right of privacy has been applied to the workplace, it is helpful to understand the difference between common law and statutory law. Common law is primarily law made by judges. Over many centuries, the courts of England developed rules governing the relationships between people—property rights, enforcement of agreements, and recovery for injuries. These "laws" were not enacted by Parliament, but evolved from judicial opinions that were then summarized and restated by legal scholars. This "common law" includes the law of contracts and the law of "torts"—a broad class of civil wrongs comprising any non-contractual breach of duty that gives rise to an action for damages.

English common law was brought to America by the earliest English settlers, and it became the basis for most U.S. jurisprudence. In many states, some of the rights established in common law have been codified by the legislature, but many theories of liability and remedies cannot be found in state laws, codes, or rules of civil procedure. To determine the "law" of a state, employers must review its courts' decisions that apply different common law theories to particular sets of facts, and then generalize those decisions into rules that they can use to guide their business decisions. Because common law rights and remedies were created by courts, they also can be restricted or broadened by the courts. Judges rely heavily on judicial precedent in interpreting common law theories and remedies. As a result, most courts are reluctant to create entirely new rights or remedies not previously recognized by other courts in their state.

TYPES OF COMMON LAW RIGHTS OF PRIVACY

Prior to 1890, no English or U.S. court had ever expressly granted relief based on an individual right of privacy, although a noted commentator on the law of torts articulated a concept of "the right to be let alone."[1] In 1890, Samuel D. Warren and Louis D. Brandeis argued in a now-famous article in the *Harvard Law Review* entitled "The Right To Privacy," that implicit in many common law cases dealing with defamation and property rights was a broader principle, the right to privacy, that should receive separate recognition as a distinct tort action. They stressed that the press was overstepping the bounds of propriety and decency and that "while solitude and privacy has become more essential to the individual; ... modern enterprise and invention have, through invasions on his privacy, subjected him to mental pain and distress, far greater than could be inflicted by mere bodily injury."[2]

The tort of invasion of privacy was included in the *Restatement of Torts* in the 1930s, and in some form it has been accepted by the courts or established by statute in every state.[3] In a 1960 law review article analyzing how the right to privacy had developed, legal commentator William Prosser contended that four torts—not one—exist:

> The law of privacy comprises four distinct kinds of invasion of four different interests of the plaintiff, which are tied together by the common name, but otherwise have almost nothing in common except that each represents an interference with the right of the plaintiff, in the phrase coined by Judge Cooley, 'to be let alone.'[4]

Prosser's four-part analysis of the right to privacy was adopted by the *Restatement (Second) of Torts* in 1977. It has become accepted by nearly all courts, and some states have adopted this description of the right of privacy by law.[5] All four of the privacy torts identified by Prosser have been used in the workplace context. They are:

- Appropriation of the name and likeness of another person;
- Unreasonable intrusion into the seclusion of another person;
- Unreasonable publicity given to another person's private life; and
- Publicity that unreasonably places a person in a false light before the public.

Any person who commits one of these torts may be held liable to the injured person for compensatory and possibly punitive damages.

Appropriation

The privacy right recognized earliest by the courts involves the appropriation of the name or likeness of another person, without permission, for commercial use.[6] This tort involves individuals' interest in not seeing their name or face used by another person, and a property interest in their name. It is sometimes described as the "right of publicity," and many celebrities have sued to prevent other people from using their names. The tort of appropriation occasionally has been used in the workplace. For example, a company cannot use photographs of its employees to advertise products without obtaining their consent and a release. However, it has not been the focus of most privacy suits by employees.

Intrusion

Anyone who intentionally intrudes on the solitude or seclusion of other individuals or on their private affairs or concerns is subject to liability if the intrusion would be highly offensive to a reasonable person.[7] The intrusion can be a physical one, such as breaking into a person's home. But the principle extends to eavesdropping on private conversations by means of wire-tapping or looking into the windows of a person's home. The intrusion also may comprise some other type of investigation or examination into the other person's private concerns, such as opening private and personal mail or searching a person's handbag or wallet.[8] The place, item, or entity intruded on must be private and entitled to privacy. For example, it has been argued that no legal right exists to be let alone on a public street and therefore it is not an invasion of privacy to follow and watch a person on the street.[9]

The tort is based on the psychological distress caused by the intrusion itself. It is not necessary that the defendant learn anything embarrassing or private about the plaintiff or that the defendant wrongfully disclose that information. In the employment setting, intrusion cases have been brought as a result of an employer's surveillance or investigation of its employees,[10] searches of an employee's personal belongings contrary to the employer's policies and practices,[11] and where employers have taken action based on an employee's private affairs, such as a discharge for socializing with or dating employees of a business competitor.[12]

Public Disclosure of Private Facts

This tort is based on making public those matters that concern the private life of another where the publicity is highly offensive to a reasonable person and is not of legitimate concern to the public. Liability can be imposed even though the information is true and the plaintiff would not be able to sue for defamation.[13] The focus of this tort is on the publicity given to private facts concerning an individual. "Publicity" in this context means that the matter is made public by communicating it to a large number of people. Courts usually hold that it is not an invasion of the right of privacy to communicate a fact concerning the plaintiff's private life to a single person or to a small group of people. However, the same statement made in an address to a large audience can be sufficient.[14] For example, it can be an invasion of an individuals' rights to publish in a newspaper that they do not pay their debts, but it is not an invasion to communicate that same information to their employer.[15]

The facts that are made public must involve private matters. These include sexual relations, family quarrels, many types of illnesses, and other intimate details of the individual's life. In the workplace, cases have been brought when a supervisor disclosed an accurate medical diagnosis of AIDS or past psychiatric treatment, without the employee's knowledge or permission. The outcome of these cases often depends on the extent of the publicity and the state where the claim is brought.[16]

False Light

The "false light" tort involves publicity that places the plaintiff in a false light in the public eye. It requires a showing that the false light in which the individual is placed would be highly offensive to a reasonable person.[17] The tort is similar in many respects to defamation, but it is not necessary that the plaintiff be defamed. The classic example was a suit by Lord Byron to enjoin the circulation of a bad poem that had been attributed to him.[18] Another example would be a published photograph that depicts a group of wildcat strikers, but includes a person who was merely passing by when the picture was taken.[19] In the workplace context, false light claims have been brought — in conjunction with a defamation claim — in situations where an employee has been wrongfully accused of dishonesty or other negative acts.[20]

Defenses

Warren and Brandeis argued in their article that any action that would be privileged under the law of defamation also should be privileged under the law of privacy.[21] As discussed in detail later, the law recognizes a qualified privilege where a statement is made in good faith regarding a subject in which the person communicating has an interest, and the communication is made to a person who has a corresponding interest. This privilege can apply to employer communications.[22] The qualified privilege of employers to protect or further their own legitimate interests has appeared in some privacy cases where employers have been allowed to monitor telephone calls or conduct time and motion studies of employees.[23]

STATE-PROVIDED PRIVACY RIGHTS

Most state constitutions have provisions similar to the Fourth Amendment of the U.S. Constitution. These state constitutional provisions, which often are cited in workplace search or testing cases, sometimes have been interpreted more liberally than the Fourth Amendment.[24] Several states also have constitutional provisions that specifically recognize and protect the right of privacy. For example, Article 1, Section 22 of the Alaska Constitution states: "[t]he right of the people to privacy is recognized and shall not be infringed."[25] Some of these provisions apply only to the government. Florida's constitution similarly provides that:

> Every natural person has the right to be left alone and free from governmental intrusion into his private life except as otherwise provided herein. This section shall not be construed to limit the public's right of access to public records and meetings as provided by law.[26]

Other provisions are more general. For example, the California Constitution recognizes that:

> [a]ll people are by nature free and independent and have inalienable rights. Among those are enjoying and defending life and liberty, acquiring, possessing and protecting property, and pursuing and obtaining safety, happiness, and privacy.[27]

This clause has been interpreted to apply to both public and private employers.[28] Although no direct right of action exists for violations of the California Constitution, an employee may be able to use these provisions as an example of public policy that should be enforced through the law.

Several other states also have some form of privacy guarantee in their constitutions.[29] If a state constitution extends to private employers, employees have an additional theory to challenge invasions of privacy. Where the constitution applies only to public employees, it can be cited to demonstrate the "public policy" importance of the right to privacy.

In February 1989, the Alaska Supreme Court in *Luedtke v. Nabors Alaska Drilling, Inc.*[30] emphasized that although the right of privacy exists under many states' constitutions, including Alaska's, the right to privacy under the Alaska Constitution does not extend to the actions of private persons. In *Luedtke*, two employees of Nabors who worked on drilling rigs in Alaska were terminated after they refused to submit to urinalysis screening for drug use. The plaintiffs challenged their discharge on several grounds, including 1) violation of right to privacy guaranteed by Article I, Section 22 of the Alaska Constitution; 2) violation of the implied covenant of good faith and fair dealing; 3) wrongful discharge; and 4) violation of the common law tort of invasion of privacy.

In rejecting the plaintiffs' claims of a violation of privacy under the Alaska Constitution, the court stated that they failed to produce evidence that Alaska's constitutional right to privacy was intended to bar private action, such as Nabors' drug testing program. The court also rejected the plaintiffs' claim of a violation of the common law right to privacy because they were not aware that the urine tests to which they voluntarily submitted were conducted as part of the company's drug testing program. The plaintiffs were aware that the test results would be reported to their employer. As to the urinalysis that the plaintiffs refused to take, the court held that no invasion of privacy claim could succeed because no intrusion took place.

The broadest law allowing relief to private employees for "constitutional violations" is a Connecticut law[31] which provides that:

> [A]ny employer ... who subjects any employee to discipline or discharge on account of the exercise by such employee of rights guaranteed by the First Amendment to the U.S. Constitution, or Section 3, 4 or 14 of Article I of the constitution of the state, provided such activity does not substantially or materially interfere with the employee's bona fide job performance or the working relationship between the employee and the employer, shall be liable to such employee for damages caused by such discipline or discharge, including punitive damages, and for reasonable attorneys fees as a part of the cost of any such action for damages.

The states also are at the forefront in protecting workplace privacy through legislation. Where common law torts are not applicable, private employees often have few remedies against their employers except through legislative initiatives. That is why developments in polygraph testing and other privacy issues have focused most often on legislation rather than court decisions. The development of the law under state statutes has varied among the states, but it probably will increase as issues of workplace privacy become more prominent.

PUBLIC POLICY TORT CLAIMS

Private employers usually are not liable under federal or state law for violations of an employee's constitutional rights. However, a few states have expanded employer liability by law, and some employees have claimed that the federal and state constitutions embody "public policies" that can be enforced through a wrongful discharge tort claim.

A public policy claim based on constitutional principles cannot be made in most states. Many states that have adopted a public policy exception to the at-will rule also have declared that the exception applies in only a limited number of circumstances, such as engaging in a statutorily protected activity or refusing to commit an illegal act. Courts in a few states have said a public policy claim might be based on provisions in the federal or state constitution but only a few cases have expanded on that idea. For example, the Maryland Court of Appeals has observed that Maryland courts have not always confined themselves to legislative enactments, prior judicial decisions, or administrative regulations when determining public policy, but the appeals court has indicated its reluctance to encroach on the responsibilities of the Maryland legislature:

> We have always been aware, however, that recognition of an otherwise undeclared public policy as a basis for a judicial decision involves the application of a very nebulous concept to the facts of a given case, and that declaration of public policy is normally the function of a legislative branch.[32]

In the same decision in which it recognized the public policy exception, the state appeals court cautioned lower Maryland courts to "act only with the utmost circumspection in pronouncing such undeclared public policy."[33] Most lower courts have taken this caution to heart and have sustained a public policy claim only when an employer has violated a state law or an employee was exercising a statutory right when fired.[34]

Public policy claims are being made in an increasing number of situations based on free speech and privacy interests, but few have been successful.

Free Speech Claims

It is well established that public employees have First Amendment rights under the U.S. Constitution. The U.S.

Supreme Court has established a test that balances the interest
of a public employee as a citizen who has a right to comment
on matters of public concern, against the interest of government as an employer with a right to require employee efficiency. In the leading case of *Connick v. Myers,*[35] the Supreme
Court recognized that "for at least fifteen years, it has been
settled that a state cannot condition public employment on a
basis that infringes the employee's constitutionally protected
freedom of expression."[36] In *Connick,* the court upheld the
discharge of an assistant district attorney who claimed the discharge was motivated by his exercise of his First Amendment
right to circulate an inter-office questionnaire regarding office
policy and morale. The court found that most of the questions
did not involve matters of "public concern" and that, balancing
the interests involved, the employee's discharge was proper
where the employee was undermining the authority of his supervisor. In many cases, however, courts have overturned discharges based on a public employee's exercise of free speech,
including a police employee and union representative discharged for publicly criticizing a decision not to give police officers an annual raise,[37] and a computer operator who said "I
hope they get him" after an assassination attempt on President
Reagan.[38]

The courts have not been as receptive to free speech claims
asserted by private employees. Private employers are not
directly restricted by the U.S. Constitution in matters involving
their employees. The constitutional guarantee of due process
limits federal and state action, not the acts of private individuals or companies. Some employees, however, have tried
to have constitutional restrictions on public employers incorporated into public policy claims. One case in Wisconsin involved an employee who was fired after publication of a
lengthy letter he wrote to a local newspaper sharply criticizing
his employer.[39] Wisconsin recognizes a public policy exception
when an employee's discharge is contrary to a fundamental and
well-defined public policy as evidenced by existing law. How-

ever, applying the analysis used in *Connick v. Myers*, and recognizing that a private employer need not tolerate actions that undermine authority or discipline or otherwise disrupt the office routine or employment relations in the name of a limited free speech interest, a Wisconsin court rejected the employee's free speech claim. The Supreme Court of Wisconsin subsequently ruled in *Bushko v. Miller Brewing Co.*[40] that a private sector employee's claim that he was wrongfully discharged for complaining about plant safety, hazardous waste, and honesty was insufficient, even if the complaints were expressions of free speech.

The most expansive recognition of a private sector public policy claim in the area of freedom of expression may be *Novosel v. Nationwide Insurance Co.*[41] Nationwide Insurance sent a memorandum to all of its employees soliciting their participation in an effort to lobby the state legislature against no-fault auto insurance legislation. The plaintiff claimed that the only reasons he was fired were his refusal to participate in the lobbying effort and his private opposition to the company's position on the issue. The U.S. Court of Appeals for the Third Circuit, applying Pennsylvania law, held that even though Nationwide was not a governmental employer, Novosel had stated a cognizable claim for wrongful discharge in breach of public policy.

The court looked to the landmark Pennsylvania Supreme Court decision that recognized the tort of wrongful discharge, which stated:

> It may be granted that there are areas of an employee's life in which his employer has no legitimate interest. An intrusion into one of these areas by virtue of the employers' power of discharge might plausibly give rise to a cause of action, particularly where some recognized facet of public policy is threatened.[42]

The federal appeals court in *Novosel* went on to rule that the protection of an employee's freedom of political expression would appear to involve a no-less compelling societal interest than jury duty or filing a worker's compensation claim.

The court looked at the extensive case law concerning the First Amendment rights of government employees and concluded that an important public policy is implicated when the power to hire and fire is used to limit employees' political activities. The court remanded the case for trial, stating that the lower courts in Pennsylvania should apply to private sector employees the same type of test set forth in public employee speech cases.[43]

Decisions like *Novosel* to date have been rare. Even Pennsylvania courts have not sustained all private sector free speech claims.[44]

Similarly, a federal court in Maryland recognized that private employees may state a wrongful discharge claim based on the state constitution and laws embodying public policies. In *Ring v. River Walk Manor, Inc.,*[45] Ring filed suit against her former employer, River Walk, for violation of her constitutional rights of free speech and free association, and alleged that she was wrongfully terminated for speaking with a former employee of River Walk and for refusing to talk to her supervisor about the incident. The former employee was a union organizer, but no evidence indicated that the conversation was union-related.

Ring also contended that her discharge by River Walk was against the public policy of the state of Maryland in that it violated her right to free speech and her right to associate with whom she pleased outside of her employment. The court acknowledged the possibility that a state court could find that Maryland has a public policy against the violation of free speech rights of private individuals. The court then stated that if Maryland has a discernible public policy requiring private individuals, or privately owned, privately run businesses, to respect other individuals' rights of free speech, Ring could assert her claim of wrongful discharge in the state court.

Where these claims are recognized, a distinction probably will be drawn between acts of public importance, such as comments regarding the competency of a candidate for president, and acts that have a direct impact on job performance, such as public criticism of an employer's practices. Courts will allow employers more discretion when a legitimate business reason is involved in their actions, and they will apply constitutional protections more narrowly where employees' speech or privacy interests interfere with their ability to do their jobs. In these situations, public policy claims by private employees probably will be more limited than the public employees' rights that are enforceable under Section 1983.

Search and Seizure

The Fourth Amendment, incorporated by the 14th Amendment, applies to the conduct of state government officials, including searches and seizures by government employees or supervisors of the private property of their employees. The U.S. Supreme Court held in *O'Connor v. Ortega* that public employees may have a reasonable expectation of privacy against intrusions in the workplace.

Ortega is strongly influencing the development of privacy rights in the workplace. The court's recognition that the government, in its role as an employer, may conduct certain activities that it could not conduct with other citizens gives employers wide latitude and much discretion in their dealings with their employees. However, the court's statement that employees may have a legitimate expectation of privacy in the workplace sets the stage for possible application of similar protections to private employees.

No court has applied the principle of legitimate expectation of workplace privacy embodied in the U.S. Constitution directly to private employers under the public policy exception. A similar claim has been made, however, under state constitutions. A trial judge in California issued a preliminary injunction prohibiting a private employer's drug testing policy on the grounds that it might violate the state constitution's limits on unreasonable searches and seizures. The employer, Times Mirror Books, argued that the state constitution's privacy provisions do not pertain to the private sector. A California appeals court issued an order in July 1988 overturning the injunction.[46] Similar claims are being made in other states. (See Chapter III.)

ENDNOTES

[1] William Prosser, *Law of Torts*, § 117, at 802 (4th ed. 1971), *citing* Cooley, *Torts*, at 29 (2d ed. 1888).

[2] Warren and Brandeis, "The Right To Privacy," 4 *Harv. L. Rev.* 193, 196 (1890).

[3] States that have recognized the right of privacy by law include New York, McKinney's Consol. Laws of New York, Civil Rts. § 51 (West 1976), Oklahoma (Okla. Stat. Ann. tit. 21, § 839 (West 1982)), Utah (Utah Code Ann. § 49-3-1 (Allen Smith 1982)), and Virginia (Va. Code Ann. § 18.2-216.1 (Michie 1982)).

[4] Prosser, "Privacy", 48 Calif. L. Rev. 383, 389 (1960). A version of this article appears in Chapter 20 of Prosser's treatise, *Law of Torts*.

[5] J. Thomas McCarthy, *The Rights of Publicity and Privacy*, (New York: Clark Boardman Co., Ltd.) 1987 § 1.5. *See, e.g.*, R.I. Gen. Laws § 9-1-28.1 (1980).

[6] *See Restatement (Second) of Torts* § 652C (1977).

[7] *See Restatement (Second) of Torts* § 652B (1977).

[8] *Restatement (Second) of Torts* § 652D, comment d (1977); Prosser, § 117 at 807-808.

[9] Prosser, *Law of Torts* § 117 at 808; *Cf. Prosser and Keeton on Torts*, § 117 at 855-56 (5th ed., 1984).

[10] *Pemberton v. Bethlehem Steel Corp.*, 66 Md. App. 133, 502 A.2d 1101 (1986), *cert. denied*, 306 Md. 289, 508 A.2d 488 (1986); *cert. denied*, 479 U.S. 984, 107 S.Ct. 571 (1986).

[11] *K-Mart Corp. Store No. 7441 v. Trotti*, 677 S.W.2d 632 (Tex. Ct. App. 1984), *error refused n.r.e.*, 686 S.W.2d 593 (Tex. 1985).

[12] *Rulon-Miller v. International Business Machine Corp.*, 162 Cal. App. 241, 208 Cal. Rptr. 524, 1 IER Cases 405 (1984).

[13] *Restatement (Second) of Torts*, § 652D (1977).

[14] *Restatement (Second) of Torts*, § 652D, comment a (1977).

[15] Prosser, § 117 at 810.

[16] *Compare Cronan v. New England Telephone Co.*, No. 80332, 1 IER Cases 651 (Mass. Sup. Ct. 1986), where an invasion of privacy was found,

with *Eddy v. Brown*, 715 P.2d 74 (Okla. 1986), where the court found insufficient publicity.

[17] *Restatement (Second) of Torts* § 652E (1977).

[18] Prosser, § 117 at 812.

[19] *See, Restatement (Second) of Torts* § 652E, comment b (1977).

[20] *Ledl v. Quik Pik Food Stores, Inc.*, 133 Mich. App. 583, 349 N.W.2d 529, 117 LRRM 2971 (1984).

[21] Warren and Brandeis at 216.

[22] *See* Chapter XVI.

[23] Prosser, § 117 at 818; *Schmukler v. Ohio-Bell Tel. Co.*, 116 N.E.2d 819 (Ohio C.P. 1953)(monitoring of telephone calls to ensure proper service); *Thomas v. General Electric Co.*, 207 F. Supp. 792 (W.D. Ky. 1962)(time and motion studies), *City of University Heights v. Conloy*, 20 Ohio Misc. 112, 252 N.E.2d 198 (1969)(spying on suspected thief).

[24] *See In The Matter of Patchogue-Medford Congress of Teachers v. Board of Education of the Patchogue-Medford Union Free School District*, 133 A.D.2d 823, 520 N.Y.S.2d 399 (1987).

[25] ALASKA CONST. art. I, § 22 (1972).

[26] FLA. CONST. art. I, § 23.

[27] CAL. CONST. art. I, § 1 (1972).

[28] *See Porten v. University of San Francisco*, 64 Cal. App. 3d 825, 829 n.2, 134 Cal. Rptr. 839 (1976).

[29] *See* ALASKA CONST. art. I, § 22; ARIZ CONST. art. II, § 8 (1982) CAL. CONST. art. I, § 1 (1972); FLA. CONST. art. I, § 23; HAW. CONST. art. I, § 6 (1978); ILL. CONST. art. I, § 6; LA. CONST. art. I, § 5 (1975) MONT. CONST. art. II, § 10 (1972); S.C. CONST. art. I, § 10 (1971); WASH. CONST. art. I, § 7.

[30] 768 P.2d 1123, 4 IER Cases 129 (Alaska 1989).

[31] CONN. GEN. STAT. § 31-51q (West 1972 & Supp. 1984).

[32] *Adler v. American Standard Corp.*, 291 Md. 31, 432 A.2d 464, 472, 115 LRRM 4130 (1981).

[33] *Id.* at 472, *quoting Patton v. United States*, 281 U.S. 276, 306, 50 S. Ct. 253, 261 (1930).

[34] *See Moniodis v. Cook*, 64 Md. App. 1, 494 A.2d 212, 119 LRRM 3556, 1 IER Cases 441, *cert. denied*, 304 Md. 631, 500 A.2d 649 (1985) (violation of state law prohibiting employers from giving polygraph tests).

[35] 461 U.S. 138, 103 S. Ct. 1684 (1983).

[36] *Id.* at 142 S. Ct. 1687.

[37] *McKinley v. City of Elox*, 705 F.2d 1110 (9th Cir 1983).

[38] *Rankin v. McPherson*, 483 U.S. 378, 107 S. Ct. 2891 (1987).

[39] *Schultz v. Industrial Coils Inc.*, 125 Wis.2d 520, 373 N.W.2d 74 (Wis. Ct. App. 1985).

[40] 134 Wis.2d 136, 396 N.W.2d 167 (1986).

[41] 721 F.2d 894 (3d Cir. 1983).

[42] *Id.* at 897, *quoting Geary v. United States Steel Corp.*, 456 Pa. 171, 184, 319 A.2d 174, 180, 115 LRRM 4665 (1974).

[43] *Id.* at 901.

[44] *Martin v. Capital Cities Media Inc.*, 354 Pa. Super. 199, 511 A.2d 830 (1986) (the discharge of a newspaper employee who placed an advertisement in a competing newspaper did not violate public policy).

[45] 596 F. Supp. 393 (D. Md. 1984).

[46] *Times Mirror Books v. Wilkinson*, No. A042567 (Cal. Ct. App.), *cert. granted* (1988). See "California Judge Prohibits Publisher from Using Pre-Employment Drug Testing," 112 DLR A-8 (BNA) (June 10, 1988); "California Court Overturns Injunction Prohibiting Pre-Employment Drug Testing; 131 DLR A-8 (BNA) (July 8, 1988).

* * *

Drug and Alcohol Abuse

Employee alcohol and drug abuse lowers productivity and increases absenteeism, accidents and injuries, and the use of medical benefits. A 1980 Research Triangle Institute study found that alcohol abuse cost $71.5 billion annually in lost productivity and absenteeism and drug abuse cost $34 billion.[1] A 1986 study by the Employee Assistance Society of North America estimated alcohol-related productivity losses at $39.1 billion a year, and drug-related losses at $8.3 billion.[2]

A survey by the National Institute on Drug Abuse (NIDA) released in mid-1989 revealed declines in casual drug use and alcohol consumption, but it showed that substance abuse is still a major nationwide problem.

The results of a 1988 household survey by NIDA reveal that:

- 11.6 million people used marijuana at least once a month, down from 18 million in 1985;
- 2.9 million people used cocaine at least once a month in 1988, down from 5.8 million in 1985;
- The number of people who use cocaine at least once a week or more increased one-third, to 862,000, and 484,000 people used crack at least once a month;
- 65 million people have tried marijuana, and 21 million have tried cocaine.

NIDA Director Charles Schuster estimates that between 500,000 and 750,000 people use heroine regularly and that approximately 17 million people are alcoholics. "There's no question about it, alcohol remains the number one drug problem in the United States, " Schuster said.[3]

In addition to the economic losses, substance abusers expose their employers to legal liabilities. Employers repeatedly have been held responsible for injuries to third parties when their intoxicated employees have had automobile accidents while on company business.[4] Many states require employers to use reasonable care in the selection of employees, and employers who do not may be held liable if an employee later injures a member of the public or a fellow employee. One employer was held liable for the sexual assault of a guest at the employer's inn by an employee whose alcoholism and tendency toward violence were known by the employer.[5] Employers also have been found liable for negligent supervision of employees, as in a case where a supervisor escorted an intoxicated employee to his car, accepted the worker's assurance that he could make it home safely, and the employee had an auto accident in which he and several other people were killed.[6]

EMPLOYER POLICIES, TESTING

Most employers are well aware of the problems caused by substance abuse, and many have responded by instituting drug and alcohol policies. These policies vary widely, and may include a prohibition of drugs and alcohol on the job, rehabilitation or employee assistance programs (EAPs) for addicted employees, and penalties, including termination, for use of illegal substances or impairment at work due to drug or alcohol abuse.

The most controversial component of these policies is drug and alcohol testing.

Workplace substance abuse testing is increasing in both the public and private sectors. The President's Commission on Organized Crime report issued March 6, 1986, *America's Habit: Drug Abuse, Drug Trafficking, and Organized Crime*, recommended that all employers screen applicants and employees for drugs and adopt a policy of zero tolerance. Executive Order 12564 issued by President Reagan Sept. 15, 1986, required all federal agencies to adopt drug testing programs for employees in "sensitive positions." The order also authorized the agencies to test applicants and to test employees in non-sensitive positions (a) on reasonable suspicion of drug use; (b) in investigations of accidents or unsafe conditions; and (c) as part of a follow-up to a drug rehabilitation program. On 60-day notice, employees found to be using illegal drugs are to be disciplined unless they voluntarily identify themselves, obtain counseling, and remain drug-free. Any employee testing positive who refuses counseling or rehabilitation or does not remain drug-free is to be discharged.[7]

The federal government has proposed testing about 400,000 of its 2.2 million civilian workers and some 50,000 workers had been tested by mid-1989. More than 2 million people in the armed forces have undergone random drug tests for several years. White House officials publicly have expressed their hope that random testing of federal workers will induce private industry to increase the use of drug tests. In one briefing, White House Press Secretary Marlin Fitzwater stated:

> The issue for the federal government is one of leadership in providing random drug testing as a means of insuring a clean workplace .... The evidence about the effectiveness of random drug testing is widespread and legion and well-known ... in curbing drug use.[8]

In 1986, the Federal Railroad Administration (FRA) implemented pre-employment, post-accident, and probable-cause testing and treatment for the railroad industry. Although positive test results are down, 5 percent of 759 employees involved in accidents tested positive for drugs or alcohol in 1987, prompting calls for random drug testing.[9] The House of Representatives passed a bill in August 1988 to require random drug testing of all railroad employees in safety-sensitive positions, and legislation was pending in the Senate in July 1989 to require random drug and alcohol testing of employees in the railroad, aviation, and trucking industries.[10]

Testing in the private sector also has grown. Experts estimated in 1985 that 20-25 percent of *Fortune* 500 companies had or were planning to conduct drug tests. By 1987, the number was more than 33 percent.[11] A 1988 survey by the Gallup

Organization commissioned by Hoffman-LaRoche, Inc., revealed that 76 percent of large companies with drug testing programs have had their programs in place for less than three years. A comprehensive study conducted by the U.S. Department of Labor's Bureau of Labor Statistics (BLS) between the summer of 1987 and 1988 found that 43 percent of the nation's employers with 1,000 or more workers had drug testing programs, but only 2 percent of employers with fewer than 50 workers had such programs. Because small workplaces comprise the majority of the nation's employers, BLS estimates that only 3 percent of employers nationwide had drug testing programs. BLS found that fewer than 1 million employees on private payrolls—about 1 percent of all such workers—are actually tested for drugs. The BLS study also showed that:

- Eighty-five percent of employers with testing programs targeted job applicants, while 64 percent focused on current employees.

- Of those employers who tested their current employees, 67 percent tested those suspected of drug use, while approximately 25 percent had programs for mandatory or random testing. BLS concluded that most of those programs were random programs because only 9 percent of all workers in those companies were actually tested.

- Employers in mining, communications, public utilities, and transportation industries are the most likely to have testing programs. The employers least likely to have drug testing programs included those in the retail trade, services, and construction industries.

- Of the 953,000 employees tested, about 8.8 percent tested positive. Of the 3.9 million job applicants tested, 11.9 percent had positive results.[12]

Several other surveys have confirmed the results of the BLS study.[13]

Formal policies and programs regarding drug use by employees are much more numerous than testing. BLS found that 13 percent of all employers had formal written policies regarding drug use, including 83 percent of those with 5,000 or more employees. A comprehensive poll of larger Washington, D.C., area employers revealed that more than 67 percent have programs to monitor or alleviate illicit drug use, a rise from 30 percent in 1985.[14]

Some employers report significant results from testing. The U.S. Navy says that the percentage of its members reportedly using illegal drugs declined from 47 percent in 1980 to 4 percent in 1989. The Southern Pacific Transportation Co. reports that since it started a drug and alcohol testing program in 1983 the percentage of positive test results dropped from 22.9 percent to 5.5 percent in 1988. During the same period, train accidents attributable to human failure dropped from 911 to 96, and personal injuries per 200,000 employee hours dropped from 15.6 to 6.5.[15]

Despite these reported successes, drug and alcohol testing remains highly controversial, and it is challenged as an invasion of employees' privacy. Critics object that the usual procedure for drug testing — collecting a urine sample for chemical analysis — is extremely intrusive and embarrassing, often requiring an employee to perform a private bodily function in the presence of an observer. Critics also charge that the tests are inaccurate and even the best chemical tests can measure only the presence of drugs, not impairment. Nevertheless, a 1986 *New York Times* public opinion poll showed that nearly 75 percent of all full-time workers feel that drug testing in the workplace would be the most effective way to curb drug abuse.[16]

The controversial nature of drug testing has led to numerous privacy challenges. As these cases progress through the courts, additional guidance is being provided on the types of substance abuse policies that are permissible. The most significant factor in the reported cases is whether the employer is a public entity, subject to constitutional restrictions, or a private employer, not restrained by the U.S. Constitution, and

whether the testing is random, universal, or conducted as a
result of "reasonable suspicion."

CONSTITUTIONAL LIMITS ON TESTING

The Fourth Amendment's prohibition on unreasonable
searches and seizures is "designed to protect the personal
privacy and dignity of the individual against unwarranted
intrusions" by the government.[17] The restriction applies to the
police, all government officials, and to any private individual
acting as an instrument or agent of the government.[18]

In the leading case of *Schmerber v. California*, the U.S.
Supreme Court held that the Fourth Amendment restricted
the circumstances in which a person could be "searched"
through the use of a blood test.[19] Despite strenuous arguments
to the contrary by federal and state agencies, nearly every
court considering the question has determined that drug testing constitutes a "search." In accepting the argument that a
person has a legitimate expectation of privacy in the collection
of urine samples for drug tests, the Court of Appeals for the
State of New York, that state's highest court, found:

> The act of discharging urine is a private, indeed intimate, one and
> the product may contain revealing information concerning an
> individual's personal life and habits for those capable of analyzing
> it. There is no question that requiring a person to disrobe and ex-
> pose his body or body cavities, or to empty the contents of his
> pockets, involves a sufficient intrusion on privacy to constitute a
> search.[20]

Recognition that drug tests are covered by the Fourth
Amendment is only the first step of the inquiry. The difficult
question is knowing when a blood or urinalysis test for drugs
or alcohol—as a search—is "reasonable." The reasonableness
standard of the Fourth Amendment usually requires that
public officials have probable cause and obtain a warrant
before conducting a search. However, the Supreme Court has
developed many exceptions to these requirements in criminal
cases that apply equally to civil claims brought by public

employees to enjoin testing programs. In *Bell v. Wolfish*, the court stated:

> The test of reasonableness under the Fourth Amendment is not capable of precise definition or mechanical application. In each case it requires a balancing of the need for the particular search against the invasion of personal rights that the search entails. Courts must consider the scope of the particular intrusion, the manner in which it is conducted, the justification for initiating it, and the place in which it is conducted.[21]

Many courts have applied the "special needs" exception of *O'Connor v. Ortega*,[22] because government agencies have different needs in their role as employers than in other roles. A few courts have applied exceptions for heavily regulated industries. The results have been mixed. Substantial agreement exists among the courts that testing based on individualized reasonable suspicion of impairment or of unlawful drug use is acceptable under the Fourth Amendment. But substantial disagreement exists over whether drug testing programs that test employees on a random or universal basis may be conducted absent individualized suspicion.

Special Needs and Reasonableness

The special needs exception of *O'Connor v. Ortega* requires that for a warrantless search to be reasonable under the Fourth Amendment, it must be justified at its inception—the governmental interest must outweigh the employee's privacy interest. Courts' views of the "intrusiveness" of a drug test often have been related to the particular procedures used by a testing program. The presence of an examiner during urination is a factor considered by some courts. In *Capua v. City of Plainfield*,[23] the court, in enjoining mass drug testing of city fire fighters, noted that:

> The requirement of surveillance during urine collection forces those tested to expose parts of their anatomy to the testing official in a manner akin to strip search exposure. Body surveillance is considered essential and standard operating procedure in the ad-

ministration of urine drug tests ... thus heightening the intrusiveness of these searches.[24]

Several factors may reduce an employee's expectations of
privacy. Where the tests are part of a routine, reasonably required, annual medical examination[25] or where random testing
had been conducted in the past, courts have found the tests
less intimidating and embarrassing than other testing
programs.[26] The nature of the job also has led courts to find
that employees also have less expectation of privacy, especially
in safety or security positions such as police officers and FBI
agents.[27]

Courts analyze the governmental interests on a case-by-case
basis. The value assigned to a particular governmental goal is
often subjective. In public safety cases, the governmental interest is very high. In *Jones v. McKenzie*,[28] the U.S. Court of Appeals for the District of Columbia Circuit found that "a
governmental concern is particularly compelling when it involves the physical safety of the employees themselves or of
others." There, the court held that school bus attendants'
privacy interests were outweighed because "the School
System's mission of safely transporting handicapped children
cannot be ensured if employees of the Transportation Branch
are allowed to work under the influence of illicit drugs." Other
courts have found, for example, that "employees in dangerous
and/or highly visible occupations, which involve the safety,
well-being, and integrity of the public, are and should be held
to a higher standard of care than other less conspicuous, non-
safety-related positions."[29]

The scope of warrantless searches also must be reasonably
related to the circumstances cited to justify them. For drug
testing plans, this means that "[w]here there is no relationship
between what a search is expected to produce and the
governmental interest asserted to support the search, the
search cannot be justified."[30] This requirement is sometimes
addressed in courts' discussions of the accuracy of drug testing.
In *National Federation of Federal Employees v. Carlucci*,[31] the

court found that "urinalysis is not 'reasonably' related to the justification because, as the technology now stands, it fails to show whether an employee is impaired on the job."

Results of the Balancing Test

Courts have been nearly uniform in holding that consideration of the physical safety of employees and the public justifies testing public transit employees who are not suspected of using drugs.[32] Similarly, the security and physical safety of high government officials also have been held to constitute compelling government interests,[33] while courts usually have refused to allow suspicionless, random testing of civilian employees of the military.[34]

The courts are divided over whether suspicionless random testing should be allowed for police and fire fighters. In some cases courts have refused to allow random testing of city fire fighters and police absent "some evidence of a significant department-wide drug problem or individualized suspicion,"[35] while in others random testing has been allowed.[36]

General national security considerations often have been insufficient to support random, suspicionless testing in the absence of specific concern for the physical safety of employees or the public. Lower courts have rejected random testing of employees in "sensitive" positions at the Department of Justice [37] and the Department of the Interior.[38]

The Regulated Industry Exception

The regulated industry/administrative search exception is a separate justification for government-mandated, warrantless, suspicionless substance testing in private industries subject to heavy government regulation. In *Shoemaker v. Handel*, the U.S. Court of Appeals for the Third Circuit applied a two-part test: "First, there must be a strong state interest in conducting an unannounced search. Second, the pervasive regulation of the industry must have reduced the justifiable privacy expectation of the subject of the search."[39] In that case, the court found that heavy regulation of horse racing had reduced jockeys' privacy expectations through daily breathalyzer tests, warrantless searches of stables, and licensing of all employees in the industry. Consequently, the state satisfied the administrative search exception, and no individualized suspicion was required.[40]

Some courts have applied the regulated industry/administrative search exception to certain types of government employees. In *Rushton v. Nebraska Public Power Dist.*[41] the U.S. Court of Appeals for the Eighth Circuit applied this exception to urinalysis testing of employees of a state-owned nuclear power plant and in *Policeman's Benevolent Association of N.J., Local 318 v. Township of Washington,*[42] the U.S. Court of Appeals for the Third Circuit extended the administrative search exception to random drug testing of police officers. Other courts have refused to find police officers part of a heavily regulated "industry."[43]

Random Testing

Some courts indicate they are confused about the role that randomness of a drug testing program should play in determining its constitutionality. When properly conducted, a random program leaves no discretion with the tester regarding who is selected for testing. A truly random test is one that subjects everyone in a group to an equal possibility of testing. Tests are conducted on only a percentage of the group, selected at random. The constitutionally significant factor in a random program is the absence of any individualized suspicion of drug use. However, some courts have referred to randomness itself, rather than the lack of individualized suspicion, as a constitutional infirmity. Thus, in *Thomson v. Weinberger,*[44] the court chastised the Army for doing "nothing to minimize the intrusiveness or the randomness of their program."

Reasonable Suspicion Testing

While mandatory or random drug and alcohol testing programs by some public employers have been upheld, especially in safety-related jobs, several courts have held that the agency must first have a "reasonable suspicion" concerning a particular employee to test that employee. In *Capua v. City of Plainfield*,[45] all city firefighters and police officers were ordered to submit to a surprise urinalysis. Those who tested positive were discharged or asked to resign. A U.S. district court recognized that the particular testing program subjected the employees to a high degree of bodily intrusion in an area where the employees have a legitimate expectation of privacy. The court noted that tests conducted under the surveillance of government officials are likely to be very embarrassing and humiliating. While recognizing the city's interest in a drug-free workplace, the court held that the "mere possibility" of discovering that some firefighters might be using drugs and might be impaired in the future was not a sufficient justification for the tests.

The Court of Appeals for the State of New York Court reached the same conclusion in *Patchogue-Medford Congress of Teachers v. Board of Education*.[46] The court recognized that teachers in New York are required to submit to physical examinations to determine their fitness for duty, and thus have a diminished expectation of privacy. No dispute existed that if school authorities have reason to suspect a teacher is unfit for teaching duties, that teacher could be compelled to submit to a further examination, including drug testing. But the court struck down the mandatory testing of all employees as unreasonable where no evidence existed that drug abuse was a problem among teachers generally or in that school district.

THE 1989 SUPREME COURT DECISIONS

In March 1989, the U.S. Supreme Court addressed public sector testing in two companion cases: *Skinner v. Railway*

Labor Executives Association[47] and *National Treasury Employees Union v. Von Raab.*[48] A third decision, *Consolidated Rail Corp. v. RLEA,*[49] sheds further light on the Supreme Court's attitude toward drug testing in the private sector.

Skinner v. RLEA

Skinner involved FRA regulations requiring private railroads to collect blood and urine samples from railroad crews after certain serious accidents and conduct breath or urine tests after other accidents, rule violations, or where a supervisor has reasonable suspicion that an employee is under the influence of alcohol or drugs. The Railway Labor Executives Association (RLEA) and others challenged the constitutionality of the regulations, and the U.S. Court of Appeals for the Ninth Circuit struck down the regulations, finding that warrantless drug testing requires individualized reasonable suspicion of illegal drug use or impairment.[50] The court also found the program failed the second criterion of the reasonableness test. "Blood and urine tests intended to establish drug use other than alcohol are not reasonably related to the stated purpose of the tests, because the tests cannot measure current drug intoxication or degree of impairment."[51]

The U.S. Supreme Court, in a 7 to 2 decision written by Justice Anthony M. Kennedy, reversed the appellate court decision, relying primarily on the balancing of interests of the special needs exception. The Supreme Court found the railroad employees' expectations of privacy minimal because as employees in an industry with pervasive government safety regulations, they had diminished expectations of privacy.[52] The court found that the government had a compelling interest in testing without a showing of individualized suspicion, due to the damage that impaired employees could cause, the regulations' potential deterrent effect, and the value of testing in determining the cause of railway accidents.[53]

The Supreme Court took issue with the Ninth Circuit's conclusion that blood and urine tests "cannot measure current drug intoxication or degree of impairment."[54] The court found instead that the FRA's regulations served the dual purpose of deterring use as well as detecting on-the-job impairment, for which blood and urine tests taken together are a "highly effective means."[55] The court noted FRA's policy statement[56] that "blood is the only available body fluid that can be drawn from the living subject that can provide a clear indication not only of the presence of alcohol and drugs but also their current impairment effects."[57]

Because the Supreme Court found the railroad employees' privacy expectations minimal and the government's interest in testing compelling, it found the suspicionless testing program reasonable under the Fourth Amendment. Justice John Paul Stevens, concurring in the judgment, found "the public interest in determining the causes of serious railroad accidents adequately supports the validity of the challenged regulations," but the perceived deterrent effect was not a valid justification.[58]

NTEU v. Von Raab

Von Raab involved a mandatory "urinalysis drug screening program for applicants tentatively selected to engage in three kinds of jobs: positions that either directly involve the interdiction of illicit drugs, require the carrying of a firearm, or involve access to classified information."[59] The union challenged the program and a U.S. district court permanently enjoined all drug testing, both of employees and applicants for employment at the U.S. Customs Service.

The U.S. Court of Appeals for the Fifth Circuit reversed, finding that (a) the Customs Service tried to minimize the search's intrusiveness, (b) the Customs Service tried to remove discretion in selecting subjects for testing, (c) illegal drug use is a pervasive problem posing special problems for customs officers, (d) the search was to be conducted in private, (e) because it was limited to voluntary job applicants the test was partially consensual, (f) test results were not used for criminal investigatory purposes, and (g) the employees may have a diminished expectation of privacy because of the nature of the Customs Service.

The court found the program reasonable and therefore constitutional for all three job categories.

The Supreme Court, in a 5 to 4 decision, again written by Kennedy, affirmed that testing of people applying for jobs involving the interdiction of drugs or that require carrying a firearm was reasonable, but remanded the case for further consideration of the scope of testing Customs Service employees with access to classified information.[60] The court found that the government has a compelling border-security interest in preventing employee drug use because of potential resulting "indifference to the Service's basic mission or, even worse, [a drug user's] active complicity with the malefactors ...."[61] Similarly, the government has a compelling public safety interest with regard to employees who carry firearms on the job. The court noted, "that the public should not bear the risk that employees who may suffer from impaired perception and judgment will be promoted to positions where they may need to employ deadly force."[62] The court concluded that the government need not demonstrate an existing drug problem in the Customs Service because: "It is sufficient that the Government have a compelling interest in preventing an otherwise pervasive societal problem from spreading to the particular context."[63]

With respect to the third category of Customs Service employees, the court recognized "that the Government has a compelling interest in protecting truly sensitive information..." but could not determine from the record whether the Customs Service's program was tailored to encompass "only those Customs employees likely to gain access to sensitive information."[64] Consequently, the court remanded the case to clarify the scope of this category of employees subject to testing.

Justice Antonin Scalia, joined by Stevens, dissented in *Von Raab* because, unlike *Skinner*, no demonstrated history of drug abuse by the targeted class of employees existed. Scalia found no nexus between employee drug use and any increased potential for accepting a bribe or any decreased zeal in drug enforcement.[65] Justice Thurgood Marshall, joined by Justice William Brennan, dissented in *Skinner* and concurred in Scalia's dissent in *Von Raab*. Marshall berated the majority for continuing incrementally to abandon the probable-cause requirement of the Fourth Amendment.

Unresolved Issues

In *Von Raab*, the Supreme Court recognized compelling government interests or "special needs" in border security (direct drug interdiction), public safety (gun-carrying employees), and, presumably, in protecting "truly sensitive information." After *Von Raab*, challenges to programs that test police officers or other public employees who carry guns on the job are unlikely to be successful. Prior decisions that have enjoined random testing of police officers are probably no longer good law.

Skinner recognizes a compelling government interest in public safety, at least with respect to activities potentially hazardous to a large number of people; in this case, railroad accidents. *Skinner* also may stand for a license for non-criminal, investigational testing of entire working units, absent individualized suspicion, where a drug problem and a threat to public safety exist. This may allow the use of random or mandatory testing of workers in the transportation, nuclear energy, and chemical industries.

In limiting testing of the third category of employees in *Von Raab* to only those "employees likely to gain access to sensitive information,"[66] the Supreme Court may have implied a nexus requirement between the government's interest and the security risks attendant to an individual's position. The scope of this nexus requirement probably will be decided in future cases.

The Supreme Court's analysis in *Skinner* and *Von Raab* focuses on whether the government has a compelling interest in performing a drug test. Once such an interest is found, testing programs probably will be upheld if they are no more intrusive than the testing procedures used in these cases.

These decisions do not directly affect the ability of private employers to administer drug tests. Most legal experts advise that where testing is allowed under the Fourth Amendment, employers have a strong argument that similar programs should be upheld against challenges under state constitutions or common-law claims. However, courts in several states have interpreted state constitutional provisions analogous to the Fourth Amendment more liberally than the U.S. Supreme Court did.

The immediate impact of *Skinner* and *Von Raab* probably will be on the perception of other courts that legitimate reasons exist to test employees for substance abuse. In this regard, the Supreme Court's discussion in a relatively little-noticed decision under the Railway Labor Act (RLA), *Consolidated Rail Corp. v. RLEA*,[67] may prove more beneficial in defending private-sector testing than *Skinner* or *Von Raab*.

Conrail

In *Consolidated Rail Corp.*, the court held, 7 to 2, that the issue of whether Conrail's drug screening program was allowed under the collective bargaining agreement was a "minor dispute" under RLA and within the exclusive jurisdiction of the Railway Adjustment Board (RAB), and therefore could be unilaterally implemented by Conrail pending arbitration. The standard utilized by the Supreme Court to determine whether the dispute was "major" or "minor" was whether the proposed change was arguably justified by the terms of the parties' collective bargaining agreement and whether the employer's claims were frivolous or obviously insubstantial.

Although careful to note that it was not deciding the merits of the case, the Supreme Court found that Conrail's contractual arguments were not insubstantial. Since 1976, Conrail routinely has required its employees to undergo physical examinations. This was an implied term of the collective bargaining agreement, and was a longstanding past practice acquiesced in by the union. In the past, examinations had included periodic physical examinations, return-to-duty physical examinations, and follow-up physical examinations for employees with certain disabilities. Drug screening had been performed as part of return-to-duty physical examinations of employees taken out of service for drug-related problems and whenever the examining physician thought the employee may have been using drugs. In 1987, Conrail proposed implementing drug testing as part of all its periodic and return-to-duty physicals. Employees who tested positive would not be returned to service unless they provided a negative drug test within 45 days. Such employees also would be allowed to go through Conrail's EAP. If addicted employees entered treatment, they would be given another 125 days to test negative for drugs.

The union argued that this proposal was not covered by the parties' past practice because drug testing had been limited to circumstances where cause existed to believe the employee was using drugs; that the proposed testing program provided a fixed time limit in which the employee could provide a negative test before being fired; and that the proposed program regulated an employee's private, off-duty conduct.

The Supreme Court rejected these arguments. The court held that the parties need not agree on the details of drug testing methods or confidentiality standards for Conrail's program arguably to be justified by the party's contract. The court noted that Conrail's claim that drug testing was an area in which the employer retained a degree of discretion had some support, and that the union had not previously intervened in or challenged the procedural details of Conrail's medical testing.

The court found on the basis of Conrail's past practice that it had treated drug testing as part of its medical program and that this weakened the union's claim that Conrail was implementing testing merely to inquire into an employee's private, off-duty conduct. The court found that "the fact that medical testing often detects physical problems linked to off-duty behavior makes it difficult to draw a bright line for jurisdictional purposes between testing which does and that which does not reflect on private conduct."[68]

The court did recognize that a difference existed between Conrail's past practice of testing for cause and its new policy of mandatory drug tests and routine physical examinations, and noted that this distinction could be important to arbitrators trying to determine whether a program was covered by the parties' collective bargaining agreement. Nevertheless, the court found that Conrail's claim of a contractual right to change its medical testing procedures was not obviously insubstantial on this point:

> As Conrail pointed out and urged at its oral argument, 'particularized suspicion' is not an accepted prerequisite for medical testing. (Tr. of Oral Arg. 21.) A physician's decision to perform certain diagnostic tests is likely to turn not on the legal concept of 'cause' or 'individualized suspicion,' but rather on factors such as the expected incidence of the medical condition in the relevant population, the cost, accuracy, and inherent medical risk of the test, and the likely benefits of detection. In designing diagnostic-testing programs, some employers establish a set of basic tests that are to be administered to *all* employees, see generally, M. Rothstein, Medical Screening of Workers 16-19 (1984), regardless of whether there is cause to believe a particular employee will test positive. It is arguably within Conrail's range of discretion to alter its position on drug testing based on perceived changes in these variables.[69]

The court also noted that because Conrail was not claiming a right under its medical policy to discharge an employee because of a single positive drug test, and because Conrail gave employees the option of requesting a period of rehabilitation, it was at least arguable that Conrail's use of drug testing in physical examinations had a medical rather than a disciplinary goal. Thus, this was consistent with the parties' past practice.[70]

All of these comments are non-binding observations and it was not necessary for the court to decide whether Conrail's interpretation of its powers under the collective bargaining agreement was correct. The court was deciding only whether Conrail's arguments were "not insubstantial." Nevertheless, *Conrail* indicates the Supreme Court's current view about the legitimate uses of drug testing by private-sector employers.

THE DRUG-FREE WORKPLACE ACT OF 1988

The Drug-Free Workplace Act of 1988,[71] applies to all federal contracts and grants awarded on or after March 18, 1989. It is designed to reduce illegal workplace drug use by requiring contractors and grant recipients to adopt drug-free workplace programs, to discipline and/or rehabilitate offenders, and to report drug-related workplace convictions to the federal agency administering the contract or grant. The act neither requires nor prohibits drug testing.

The act covers organizations receiving federal contracts of at least $25,000; all federal contracts awarded to individuals, regardless of amount; and all recipients of federal grants.

The act is directed at all employees "engaged in the performance" of a federal contract; that is, all employees, hourly or salaried, who work directly or indirectly on a contract.

Requirements Under the Act

The act requires grantees and contractors to adopt a drug-free workplace policy and to give copies of it to employees working on covered contracts and grants. The policy must:

- Prohibit the unlawful manufacture, distribution, dispensation, possession, or use of a controlled substance in the workplace;
- Specify the personnel action the contractor will take against employees who violate the prohibition, such as a mandatory rehabilitation program approved by

federal, state, or local health-law enforcement
agency, and/or appropriate disciplinary measures, up
to and including termination; and

- Include a notice to all employees working on covered
contracts or grants that, as a condition of
employment, each employee must abide by the policy
and must notify the contractor within five days of any
conviction for a violation of any criminal drug law
that occurs in the workplace.

Contractors also must establish an ongoing drug awareness
program that explains to employees on covered contracts and
grants the dangers of drug abuse in the workplace; the
contractor's policy to maintain a drug-free workplace; the
availability of drug counseling, rehabilitation, and EAPs; and
the penalties that may be imposed on an employee for
workplace drug law violations.

Employers must notify the federal contracting or granting
agency within 10 days after learning of a covered employee's
conviction for a workplace violation of any criminal drug law.
Within 30 days of learning of a conviction, the contractor must
take appropriate personnel action against the employee. Sanctions range from satisfactory participation in a drug abuse
rehabilitation program to discharge.

Individuals who are direct contractors must certify that they
will not engage in the unlawful manufacture, distribution, dispensation, possession, or use of a controlled substance during
the performance of the contract.

The act requires contractors to "make a good faith effort to
maintain a drug-free workplace" by complying with its requirements. The federal contracting or granting agency may use the
reported number of employee convictions for workplace drug
activity to determine the good faith of an employer in complying with the act, but it does not provide a numerical standard
for how many convictions are sufficient to determine that the
employer is not making a good faith effort.

The act does not require or prohibit drug testing of employees. Moreover, it does not require that the contractor pay for rehabilitation, if that is determined by the contractor to be the appropriate sanction. The violating employee can be told to bear the cost. However, some employee benefit plans cover such programs.

Sanctions

Sanctions can be imposed if:

- The employer falsely certifies that it will comply with the act's requirements;
- The certification that the employer will comply with the act by taking the steps outlined above is violated; or
- If the number of employees convicted for criminal drug activity in the workplace is large enough to indicate the contractor has failed to make a good-faith effort to maintain a drug-free workplace.

The federal granting or contracting agency decides which sanction or sanctions to impose, if any, including suspension of payments under the contract or grant, termination of the contract or grant, and debarment from participation in any federal contract or grant for up to five years. False certifications also are punishable under the criminal provisions of the *U.S. Code*.[72] Conviction carries a penalty of up to five years in prison and a $10,000 fine.

The act allows these penalties to be waived if the head of the contracting or granting agency determines that in the case of a contract, the penalty would severely disrupt the operation to the detriment of the federal government or the general public or, in the case of a grant, the penalty would not be in the public interest.

Interpretations

On Jan. 31, 1989, the Office of Management and Budget (OMB) issued interim guidelines to federal agencies for implementing the act. The guidelines articulate OMB's position that the act applies to any contract or grant that is modified on or after March 18, 1989, if it would be considered a new commitment by the contracting agency, and the act does not apply to contracts awarded with non-appropriated funds or any contracts not subject to the Federal Acquisition Regulation (FAR). The proposed regulations also would make clear that neither the act nor its implementing regulations require or prohibit drug testing.

The act has been cited in several recent court decisions, notably *Georgia Power Co. v. IBEW, Local 84,*[73] in which a U.S. district court was faced with an employer's challenge to an arbitrator's award reinstating an employee discharged for failing a drug test. The arbitrator had awarded reinstatement even though he found that: (1) the company found marijuana in the employee's car in the company parking lot; (2) the employee was a chronic heavy drug user and probably was under the influence of marijuana at work; and (3) his job was to monitor temperature and pressure gauges at the power plant. On appeal, the court overturned the arbitrator's award as a violation of public policy, and sustained the discharge. The court found that the Drug-Free Workplace Act and other laws make it clear that a well-defined and dominant public policy exists against illegal drug use in the workplace.

Practical Tips

Covered employers should consider extending their drug-free workplace policies to all employees. The act does not require testing; it is a limited, relatively non-intrusive means to try to decrease drugs in the workplace. The cost and effort necessary to comply would not increase significantly by expanding the program to cover all employees because most of the cost and effort are in establishing the education programs, developing policies and procedures for correcting problems through rehabilitation and/or discipline. Extending these to additional employees would avoid any dispute with the government over who is and who is not a covered employee, and it would enhance the perception among the employees and the contracting agency that the employer is committed to a drug-free workplace.

Covered employers should structure the rehabilitation and disciplinary facets of their programs carefully, especially in jurisdictions where drug use or addiction is viewed as a protected handicap. The regulations allow taking into account how long the offender has worked for the company, the nature of the offense and the drug involved, plus other mitigating factors. For example, the act allows workplace sales of heroin by a probationary employee to be treated more harshly than workplace possession of a small amount of marijuana by a long-time employee. The act allows employers to decide what punishment to impose, and this may be appropriate to take into account.

DOD, DOT REGULATIONS

Department of Defense Regulations

The Department of Defense (DOD) issued a rule on Oct. 31, 1988, designed to eliminate drugs in the workplace by compelling defense contractors to establish programs to ensure that employees in "sensitive" positions do not possess and do not use illegal drugs. All employers seeking or entering into a DOD contract are subject to a contract clause that outlines the steps that must be followed by such a contractor. The rule applies to any contract involving workers in "sensitive" positions. Employees in sensitive positions are defined under the interim rules as those who are granted access to classified information, are treated with a high degree of trust and confidence, or

whose duties involve national security, health, or safety.
Employers are responsible for determining the criteria and the
extent of testing based on the:

- Type of work being performed under the contract;
- Duties of each contract employee;
- Efficient use of the contractor's resources; and
- Risks to public health and safety or national security
  concerns that could result from the failure or inability
  to perform contract tasks properly.

The DOD's Office of General Counsel has stated that random drug testing of employees in sensitive positions is required under the interim rule. DOD has not addressed the
possibility that such rules pre-empt state and local laws. The
interim rules regarding drug testing do apply to the extent they
are inconsistent with state or local law.

DOD also has indicated that it might defend or assume the
costs of defending contractors who are sued by employees
challenging such testing, although this is not a legally enforceable commitment by the department.

The DOD rules are designed to require defense contractors
to institute programs and policies to eliminate drug abuse from
the workplace. Such programs must include testing for the use
of illegal drugs of employees in sensitive positions or where
individuals show signs of drug abuse on the job. The rules give
employers broad discretion in deciding whether to test individual employees. Further, employers must establish and
publicize policies to discipline employees who are found to be
using illegal drugs. Employer policies also must include
provisions for drug-free workplace training, EAPs, and
rehabilitation programs, or "appropriate" alternatives.

Finally, the regulations require that if the clause is in violation of an existing union contract, the employer must make a
good-faith effort to renegotiate such clause at the next collective bargaining session. The regulations are unclear as to
whether employers are required to insist on the clause to the

point that their insistence creates a bargaining impasse or spawns a strike.

A recent survey by the Corporation Against Drug Use of drug testing by corporations in the Washington, D.C., area[74] found that defense contractors were more than twice as likely to test as companies that have no government contracts.[75]

Department of Transportation Requirements

On Nov. 21, 1988, the Department of Transportation (DOT) issued a final rule requiring that all employers operating commercial motor vehicles implement drug education and testing programs for their drivers.[76] The rule covers employers that have 50 or more drivers who at least occasionally cross state lines and whose cargoes are of certain types and sizes. It covers regular employees and independent contractors hired for extended periods. Drivers of vehicles covered by the rule are subject to random testing, and they must be tested before they are hired, when they undergo the mandatory biennial physical examination required by DOT's Driver Qualification Regulations, after accidents, and whenever reasonable cause exists to believe that the driver is using drugs.

The DOT regulation requires motor carriers to phase in testing on the basis of the number of drivers involved and to conduct an educational program for covered drivers and their supervisors.

These programs must include information on the employer's drug policy, the dangers of illegal drug use, signs of drug abuse, and available drug counseling services.

UNIONS' ROLE IN TESTING PROGRAMS

The most extensive challenges to substance abuse testing in the private sector have involved unionized companies. This is because of such employers' legal obligation to bargain over changes in working conditions and the fact that disciplinary action taken against an employee who refuses to take or fails a test often can be appealed to a neutral arbitrator.

Significant changes in work rules that involve discipline affect the terms and conditions of employment in ways that can make them mandatory subjects of bargaining. It is generally accepted that drug testing of employees is a mandatory subject of bargaining under the National Labor Relations Act (NLRA). The National Labor Relations Board (NLRB) in 1989 issued companion decisions defining the circumstances under which a drug testing program is a mandatory subject of bargaining. The NLRB held that testing of job applicants is not subject to mandatory bargaining because (1) applicants are not "employees" under the Labor Management Relations Act (LMRA), and (2) such testing does not vitally affect the terms and conditions of bargaining unit members' employment.[77]

The NLRB held that management may not unilaterally impose a drug/alcohol testing requirement on active employees without providing the union an opportunity to bargain.[78] In one of the definitive NLRB cases, the employer had instituted a program under which employees who required medical attention for work injuries were also tested for drug and alcohol use. The NLRB found such a program to be germane to the work environment, and not an entrepreneurial decision reserved to management. In reaching its decision, the NLRB compared drug/alcohol testing to employers' use of the polygraph, relying heavily on that analogy in deciding that drug/alcohol testing of existing employees, like polygraph testing, is a mandatory subject of bargaining.[79]

Unless the union waives its right to bargain about workplace substance testing, employers must give prior notice to the union of any proposed testing policy and to bargain with the union about it. The NLRB reconfirmed that it will not easily infer a waiver of the right to bargain and that waivers must be clear and unmistakable.[80] Thus, a failure by management to give notice to the union and to bargain with it would be an unfair labor practice in violation of the NLRA.[81]

Courts have ruled on several cases brought by unions alleging that the unilateral adoption of these programs by private employers violates collective bargaining agreements or the duty to bargain. In *Stove, Furnace and Allied Appliance Workers International Union v. Weyerhaeuser Paper Co.*,[82] the court found that the invasion of privacy caused by the drug test and the stigma on union members' work records and reputations were injuries that could not be redressed if the testing were not enjoined pending arbitration, and that no irreparable harm would come to the company if the injunction were issued.

A contrary result was reached in the District of Columbia, where a U.S. district judge issued a temporary restraining order against a unilaterally implemented drug testing plan at Potomac Electric Power Co., finding the program "draconian" and "almost unheard of in a free society." Several days later, another U.S. district judge dissolved the restraining order and refused to grant a preliminary injunction based on a finding that any temporary loss of employment by some employees could be remedied through the arbitration process.[83]

These decisions caution against the unilateral implementation of drug policies in unionized companies. The U.S. Chamber of Commerce also advises all employers to discuss the implementation of drug and alcohol tests with unions, to try to develop cooperative programs,[84] and not to refuse to bargain over drug abuse prevention programs.

The parties are not always required to reach agreement where notice to the union and bargaining are required. When testing programs are proposed during negotiations for a new agreement, the parties are required only to bargain in good faith. If the employer and union bargain to an impasse, the employer may implement unilaterally a substance abuse policy it proposed to the union prior to impasse. However, this rule does not allow unilateral implementation of testing when a collective bargaining agreement prohibiting such activity is in effect.

Union waiver of the right to bargain about such proposals may occur through a failure to request bargaining after notice, explicit contract language, or acquiescence in the employer's position in contract negotiations after full discussion.[85] The NLRB, arbitrators, and courts do not favor non-specific, unwritten waivers and consents. Arbitrators may void written waivers if employers administer them poorly. In *Union Plaza Hotel*,[86] a woman who worked as a waiter's helper at a restaurant was ordered by her supervisor to undergo a drug test at an independent medical clinic after she exhibited bizarre behavior during her early morning shift. Although the woman signed a consent form, she became reluctant to take the urine test after learning that she would be required to urinate in the presence of a female nurse. The employee asked to be allowed to take the test in a room without a water source with which she could contaminate the sample. This was denied. She then asked the nurse for a robe. This was also denied. Ultimately, the employee refused to submit to the test and was discharged.

The arbitrator found that the employer properly required the grievant to submit to the urine test while being observed by the nurse. He concluded, however, that the nurse's refusal to provide the employee with a robe made the conditions of the test "unnecessarily onerous," and the employer exceeded its rights by requiring the employee to take the test in an unusually embarrassing manner, which violated the employee's privacy expectations. According to the arbitrator, an agreement by a union to allow drug testing does not represent a waiver of its member's rights to preserve a reasonable amount of privacy and dignity.

Unions and their members also have challenged substance abuse testing programs under state laws protecting privacy. Such challenges usually fail, with most being dismissed on the ground that Section 301 of the LMRA[87] pre-empts any state law privacy claims arising in the context of a collective bargaining agreement. To create a uniform body of national labor law and to ensure that unions and their members use agreed-upon grievance procedures, the courts have held that if a state-law claim depends on interpretation of a collective bargaining agreement, the state law is pre-empted and federal labor law must be used to resolve the dispute.[88] The pre-emption rule has been applied to defeat claims of privacy under the Massachusetts Constitution and privacy laws,[89] to dismiss privacy claims under Oregon common law,[90] and to defeat allegations involving the California constitutional right to privacy.[91] The effect of pre-emption is to force the union or employee to resort to the remedies available under the collective bargaining agreement, which usually comprise arbitration.

STATE LAW CLAIMS

The Fourth Amendment of the U.S. Constitution does not apply to private employers, except under very limited circumstances when they act at the direction of, or in concert with a government agency.[92] Some state constitutional provisions parallel to the Fourth Amendment may protect privacy interests, and a few arguably cover actions by private employers. The privacy clause of the California Constitution, for example, has been construed to apply to private action.[93] Conversely, the privacy clause of the Alaska Constitution has not been extended to the actions of private parties.[94] Constitutional standards have been cited by some employees trying to show that their discharges violated public policy.[95] However, claims against private employers alleging that drug testing violates federal or state constitutions usually fail because no government or state action is involved.[96] In public-sector cases, the courts focus on the "reasonableness" of the intrusion into personal privacy under the Fourth Amendment, but in private sector cases the focus is on whether any protectable privacy interest exists.

State Laws and Proposed Legislation

Numerous state laws have been proposed to regulate private employers' use of drug and alcohol testing procedures. As of July 1989, Connecticut, Iowa, Louisiana, Maine, Maryland, Minnesota, Montana, Nebraska, Rhode Island, Utah, and Vermont had passed laws governing employers' use of substance abuse testing. Vermont's Act 61 was one of the first such laws passed. It prohibits drug and alcohol testing unless the employer has probable cause to believe that the employee is using drugs or alcohol on the job. The law also prohibits termination based on the results of the drug test unless the employee completes a drug assistance program and thereafter tests positive.[97]

In contrast, Utah passed legislation protecting the right of employers to conduct drug tests to determine if individual workers are impaired, investigate accidents, maintain safety, productivity, quality of products and services, or for security reasons. Employers that adopt procedural safeguards are allowed to fire employees or refuse to hire job applicants who fail a drug test or refuse it.[98] New Jersey enacted a similar law in 1987. Maryland and Nebraska laws provide that employers that want to implement drug testing must follow certain procedures and maintain certain safeguards.

Nineteen other state legislatures in 1988 considered drug testing bills that would have affected employers. According to the U.S. Chamber of Commerce, 12 state legislatures were considering bills in March 1989 that would substantially either limit or increase employers' ability to implement drug testing. The debate over when and how drug and alcohol testing can be used is expected to continue in most state legislatures for the next several years. The approaches vary, but even the bills that favor employers usually require that employers use minimally intrusive techniques, institute procedures for proper labeling and handling, and administer tests designed to check the original test results.

Public Policy Wrongful Discharge Claims

A few employees have tried to bring wrongful discharge claims against private employers on the grounds that a discharge based on the results of an unreasonable search (a drug test) or based on off-duty conduct violates public policy. Most of these claims have been rejected on the grounds that public policies also oppose the use of illegal substances, but several of these claims are pending in late 1989.

In *Wilkinson v. Times-Mirror*,[99] the California courts are determining for the first time whether the California Constitution protects an individual's right of privacy from drug testing by a private employer. Three applicants for employment were rejected for refusing to undergo drug tests. The lower court granted them a preliminary injunction prohibiting the employer from continuing its pre-employment drug testing pending trial. The judge felt that the drug testing program violated the applicants' constitutional right to privacy because it was not based on individualized suspicion and because the job did not involve significant public safety risks or hazards. The injunction was overturned on appeal, however, and the employer was allowed to continue its testing program pending trial on the merits. California Superior Court Judge Michael Ballachey threw out two causes of action filed by the plaintiffs, leaving only the constitutional issue and the issue of whether the testing is an unfair business practice.[100]

In *Hennessey v. Coastal Eagle Point Oil Co.*,[101] the New Jersey Superior Court rendered one of the first findings that an employee's discharge after a positive drug test was a violation of public policy. The employee had been employed at an oil refinery for 13 years. He had never been disciplined or observed as being under the influence of alcohol or drugs. The company established a drug abuse policy in 1985 that allowed employees who tested positive for drugs to remain employed if they sought rehabilitation. Six months later, the firm distributed a memorandum to its managers which ended that practice and required that employees who tested positive for drugs be terminated. The memorandum was not given to employees. The plaintiff later tested positive for marijuana and Valium during a random drug test and was discharged.

The court held that criminal decisions interpreting the New Jersey constitutional provisions on search and seizure and similar decisions regarding drug testing of public employers had established a general public policy that drug testing is inappropriate without individualized reasonable suspicion. The court found an absence of individualized reasonable suspicion in this case, and it expressed concern that the test had been implemented in an unreasonable and intrusive manner without discussion of alternative or less-intrusive means of enforcing company policy. The court concluded that the employee had stated a cause of action for wrongful discharge. The decision was being appealed in late 1989.

Common Law Tort Claims

The U.S. Court of Appeals for the First Circuit in *O'Brien v. Papa Gino's of America*,[102] upheld a common law privacy challenge to a polygraph test where an employee was suspected of using drugs outside work. A jury found that the company's allegations of drug use and its use of a polygraph test violated the employee's common law right of privacy, and awarded him $398,200. The issue presented to the jury was not whether the employer was justified in terminating an employee for off-duty drug use, but whether the methods used to investigate allegations of such use were highly offensive to a reasonable person and invaded the employee's privacy.

Employees have alleged in several pending cases that a drug test is an equally intrusive method of investigating off-duty conduct.

One employee sued to enjoin her employer from implementing random voluntary drug tests, arguing that they would be an unwarranted invasion of her privacy.[103] The court denied the injunction, finding "implied consent" by the employee because she continued to work at the job after the drug testing program was implemented. This theory is important because consent is an absolute defense in any tort action based on invasion of privacy.[104]

The court said:

> The plan therefore assumes, respects, and depends on the central element of the right of privacy and its attendant public policy: the individual's exclusive right to determine the occasion, extent, and conditions under which he will disclose his private affairs to others.

Employees also have used the tort of defamation to challenge employer drug testing. In *Houston Belt & Terminal Railway Co. v. Wherry*,[105] an employee was discharged after an accident because urinalysis revealed apparent traces of methadone, a substance commonly used to treat heroin addiction. A physician consulted by the discharged employee undertook further urinalysis and discovered that the urine sample contained a compound that is similar to methadone but was not methadone. Although advised of this result, the employer refused to reconsider the discharge decision. An internal accident report and a letter from the employer's director of labor relations repeated the allegation that the discharged employee was a recovering heroin addict. A jury awarded the former employee $200,000 in damages for defamation. This employer could have avoided litigation by not announcing the "medical" conclusions and by establishing a policy of having an independent laboratory re-examine positive test results.

Common-law tort theories relied on in challenging drug testing programs also include intentional and negligent infliction of emotional distress. The U.S. Court of Appeals for the First Circuit affirmed a jury award of $125,000 in damages to an employee who challenged his employer's drug testing policy.[106] The employer, a drilling rig owner, administered surprise urine tests, and representatives of the employer watched as employees urinated to provide the urine samples. The plaintiff's urine had traces of marijuana and he was discharged on that basis. The jury decided that the employer acted unreasonably in implementing the drug test and that the drug test caused foreseeable emotional distress to the employee. The court held that under Louisiana law, an employer may be held liable for the tort of negligent infliction of emotional distress if a drug testing procedure would foreseeably cause serious emotional injury to a reasonable person.

THE REHABILITATION ACT, STATE HANDICAP LAWS

Alcoholism and drug addiction are considered handicaps under the Rehabilitation Act of 1973,[107] which prohibits discrimination against an "otherwise qualified individual" who is handicapped.[108] The Rehabilitation Act covers federal contractors or subcontractors receiving $2,500 or more in federal contracts, and all employers that receive federal funds. The law was amended in 1978 to exclude from the definition of "handicapped persons" people currently using drugs or alcohol if that use impairs job performance.[109] Forty-one states have similar laws prohibiting discrimination on the basis of handicap or disability. (See Chapter VII.)

Employees must first establish that they are handicapped by alcoholism or drug addiction. Courts have indicated that casual or "recreational" users of illegal drugs do not meet this definition.[110] To claim protection, employees also must prove that their current usage does not impair their performance. Some courts have indicated that this definition limits the act to addicts whose problems are under control or who are undergoing rehabilitation.[111] This requirement, and the provision of the law that the person be "otherwise qualified" for the position, enable employers to fire or refuse to hire employees and job applicants whose current use would directly threaten the property or safety of others, or would interfere with job performance.[112] Because employers may reject applicants on these grounds, a testing program designed to identify current alcohol and drug users would not violate the law.

Where applicants or employees are covered, the Rehabilitation Act requires both non-discrimination and a "reasonable accommodation" of the handicap.[113] Several cases involving federal agencies have interpreted the act to require offering treatment rather than termination when substance abuse is discovered.[114] While no case has imposed a similar burden on private employers, a regulation promulgated under Section 503 of the act imposes an analogous duty of reasonable accommodation on federal contractors.[115]

ARBITRATORS' VIEWS

Drug testing is seldom, if ever, conducted without some prior consideration of what an employer intends to do with the test results. The many approaches and policies implemented in the private sector usually include rehabilitation, discipline, or discharge. If an employer can show that drug or alcohol use impaired the employee on the job, the discharge decision usually will be upheld. However, surveys of arbitration decisions reveal that arbitrators usually do not uphold discharges based on off-the-job drug use.[116]

Even in cases where public safety is at risk, arbitrators have refused to uphold a discharge in favor of giving the employee another chance.[117]

A leading text on arbitration states that the right of management to discharge an employee for conduct away from the plant depends on the effect of that conduct on plant operations, as where the behavior damages the employer's product or reputation, renders the employee unable to perform job duties or to come to work, or affects other employees' morale or willingness to work with the employee.[118] Where drug or alcohol tests are conducted based on reasonable suspicion of substance abuse on the job and to confirm those suspicions of impairment, a termination usually will be upheld based on reasonable suspicion and positive test results, even in the absence of direct proof of actual use of drugs on the job. Random or mandatory drug tests can reveal the presence of certain drugs, including marijuana, days after use. Because of this, employers that base a discharge solely on this evidence may find it difficult to prove to an arbitrator that good cause existed for a firing based on off-duty drug use without evidence of impairment or substandard job performance.

Arbitrators usually have applied a relaxed standard in determining whether the employer had sufficient grounds (reasonable suspicion) to order testing of an individual employee. They have recognized the special concern for safety associated with hazardous workplaces and with jobs that involve public safety. For example, testing of petroleum refinery employees has been sustained where drug use was rumored and other employees tested positive for drugs,[119] and where the employee was absent and suffered seizures.[120] A similar modest standard for reasonable cause has been applied to bus drivers, due to the safety implications of the job.[121] One arbitrator offers the following rule for determining whether an employer has reasonable cause to order a drug screen:[122]

> All they (the arbitrators) want to know is that the employer has some rational grounds for testing the employee, not whim or caprice, not unfounded suspicion or discriminatory motive, not ancient superstitions or old wives' tales. In short, is the employer acting like a reasonable man, seeking to protect his business and recognizing that the employees also have rights which are entitled to protection?

Random testing of employees, as opposed to testing of a particular employee based on individualized suspicion, raises substantial privacy issues. However, heightened public awareness of drug problems in the late 1980s is not lost on arbitrators. Thus, in *Dow Chemical Co.*[123] the arbitrator upheld the company's random program over strong union opposition. The decision points out that Dow operates the largest chemical manufacturing facility in North America, producing 11 million pounds of chlorine a day and storing 1 billion pounds of toxic chemicals on any given day. The record also showed serious drug problems among the 7,500 employees at the plant where the complainant worked, including a cocaine distribution network operated from the machine shop. The arbitrator balanced the interests, using the nature of the industry and work involved, and the seriousness of the drug problem as the important factors weighing in favor of the random testing program.

Arbitrators usually disallow what they perceive to be onerous testing techniques. One technique that has been criticized is the observed test, where the employee is observed by the tester while providing a urine sample.[124] However, arbitrators make exceptions to the general rule in especially dangerous work environments, such as nuclear power plants.[125]

The U.S. Supreme Court has held that the role of the courts in reviewing arbitration awards is extremely limited, and an arbitrator's interpretation of a collective bargaining agreement is entitled to great deference. However, courts can refuse to enforce an arbitrator's interpretation where the contract, as interpreted, would violate some explicit public policy.[126] The U.S. Court of Appeals for the Fifth Circuit in 1987 considered two arbitration decisions involving off-duty activities by two employees of Union Oil of California, Inc. Both employees were discharged for use of illegal drugs. The discharge of one employee for use and sale of drugs was sustained because he presented a safety risk. A different arbitrator overturned the second discharge and ordered reinstatement of the other employee after finding that the other employee was drug-free. The court held that the competing public policies against drug use and favoring rehabilitation were questions for the arbitrator, not the court, and that reinstatement did not violate public policy.[127]

Other courts, however, have overturned arbitrators' decisions ordering reinstatement of employees in safety positions. In one case, an airline pilot was discharged for operating a passenger plane while seriously intoxicated, in violation of company rules and federal regulations. The arbitrator ordered reinstatement because the pilot had not been offered rehabilitation. The court found that this decision would violate clearly established public policy.[128]

APPLICANT TESTING

Testing of job applicants for substance abuse poses fewer problems than testing employees. No serious legal challenge to the right of private employers to test applicants for drugs has been decided by the courts. The prevailing view is that applicants choose to take a test to obtain a job. However, two federal laws could apply. First, Title VII of the Civil Rights Act of 1964 and the Equal Employment Opportunity Commission's (EEOC) Uniform Guidelines on Employee Selection Procedures might apply if drug tests disproportionately exclude minorities. In one case, the U.S. Supreme Court allowed the New York City Transit Authority to refuse employment to individuals on a methadone maintenance program, even though a majority of those excluded were minorities, because the narcotics use was related to the legitimate interest in safety and efficiency.[129] It is unclear whether this decision, which involved employees in public safety positions, could be applied in other contexts. Second, the Rehabilitation Act and some state laws may prohibit discrimination against people with a history of subtance abuse who are not current users. Covered employers should be cautious in making pre-employment inquiries about job applicants' past use of alcohol and drugs.[130] However, this would not restrict the use of testing to determine current use.

AN EFFECTIVE SUBSTANCE ABUSE POLICY

Testing Procedures, Problems

The Mandatory Guidelines for Federal Workplace Drug Testing Programs published on April 11, 1988, by the Department of Health and Human Services (HHS)[131] were tacitly approved in *Von Raab* as those that the Customs Service would use.[132] The guidelines provide detailed procedures that are likely to protect public employers from claims challenging the techniques used for drug tests. They also serve as a useful guide for private employers.

Under the HHS collection procedures, subjects are to produce their urine specimens in private unless a designated "collection site person" has reason to believe the employee will alter the specimen or substitute another one for it. To guard further against substitution or adulteration, toilet water in the collection enclosure is colored blue, the subject employee has no access to water, soap, or any garment or purse that may conceal substances which could be used to tamper with the specimen, and the temperature and quantity of the specimen provided are measured and recorded after it is collected.

The HHS security and chain-of-custody procedures provide for photographic identification of the person giving the specimen before the specimen is collected. The collected specimen is kept in view of the subject employee and the collection site person until it is sealed and labeled. A chain-of-custody form is executed by the collection site person, and it accompanies the specimen throughout the process. The collection site person enters all information identifying the specimen, its temperature, and any unusual behavior by the subject employee in a permanent record book that the subject employee is asked to read and sign.

The specimen is subjected to an initial screening immunoassay test at a laboratory to determine whether any of five classes of drugs is present. Specimens initially testing positive are then subjected to a second, confirmatory test using a gas chromatography/mass spectrometry (GC/MS) technique. The HHS guidelines list levels above which the results are considered positive for both the immunoassay and the GC/MS tests.

The guidelines require that all confirmed positive results be investigated by a medical review officer, who must be a licensed physician with knowledge of substance abuse disorders, before the subject worker's employer is informed. The medical review officer may order reanalysis of the specimen and may examine alternative medical explanations for the test result. Medical review officers may decide to take no further action if they determine that the result is consistent with legal drug use. The HHS guidelines do not include a frequently recommended procedure that allows test subjects, before their specimens are collected, to explain things they may have done or to describe substances they may have consumed that might make the test result erroneously positive, such as prescription and over-the-counter medicines and certain foods.

Employers that are interested in establishing drug testing programs should be as careful in selecting laboratories as they are in selecting other professionals to help conduct the tests. Several firms have prepared guidelines for employers on this subject. (See Appendix D.) The HHS guidelines establish a procedure for certification of drug testing laboratories, and employers should determine whether laboratories they plan to use have been certified by HHS.

The most widely used group of drug screening tests are the Enzyme Multiplied Immunoassay Technique (EMIT) tests manufactured by Syva Co. of Palo Alto, Calif. Each test is designed to react with the metabolites of a particular class of drugs. The HHS guidelines call for testing for five classes of drugs: marijuana, cocaine, opiates, phencyclidine (PCP), and amphetamines.[133] Studies have shown the EMIT tests to be more than 98 percent accurate.[134] Syva Co. has for years encouraged confirmatory testing of positive EMIT results.[135] The HHS guidelines require that federal agencies use the GC/MS technique. However, GC/MS is less sensitive for certain drugs than EMIT or other confirmatory techniques, and it may produce some false negatives.[136] Many courts have commented on the accuracy and effectiveness of using both EMIT and GC-MS.[137] Properly conducted two-step testing programs produce only a negligible number of false positive results.[138] However, because accurate laboratory techniques are crucial to obtaining correct results, testing laboratories should be chosen with great care.[139]

A significant problem in any drug testing program is the difficulty of measuring degrees of impairment with the technology available today. Justice Kennedy noted in *Skinner v. Railway Labor Executives Association*[140] that "the metabolites of some drugs ... may enable the Agency to estimate whether the employee was impaired by those drugs at the time of a covered accident ...."[141] Present medical evidence does not appear to support this conclusion. It is well established that a link exists between levels of alcohol in a person's bloodstream and degrees of impairment. Thus, impairment can be inferred from tests that measure blood alcohol levels. No similar relationship has been established between the levels of metabolites or drugs in a urine or blood sample and impairment. The higher the measured level, the greater is the likelihood that an illegal substance was used, but that does not prove impairment.[142]

Another problem inherent in drug testing is cross-reactivity. Some legitimate substances are indistinguishable from certain illicit drugs under both EMIT and GC/MS. Poppy seeds, frequently found in food, break down into metabolites identical to those of illegal opiates. The explanation for this is readily apparent—opium and heroin are also extracted from poppy plants. These problems do not require employers to forego substance abuse testing. Employers should be cautious, however, in how they use the results of positive urinalysis tests.

Policy Guidelines

It is readily apparent from the controversial nature of mandatory employee drug testing that privacy challenges to proposed or implemented drug and alcohol screening are likely to increase. The law with respect to substance abuse policies is not well-developed and provides less than complete guidance to employers. The permissibility of a given policy will probably be determined on a review of the following factors:

- **The Type of Position Covered.** Courts and juries can more easily understand the importance of detecting drug and alcohol use among employees involved in public safety (airline pilots, truck drivers, police officers) and dangerous jobs involving electricity and machinery. Uniform testing of all employees and executives may also be viewed more favorably than testing that excludes management.

- **Standard for Testing.** Random testing without notice has caused the greatest concern among most authorities. Mandatory testing, such as during an annual physical, is seen as less intrusive and less arbitrary. Testing that is limited to situations involving an individualized reasonable suspicion of on-the-job impairment is most likely to withstand challenge.

- **Written Policies and Notice.** Employers that have a carefully worded, comprehensive, written substance abuse policy and that have given full notice of that policy to job applicants and employees have greater latitude than employers that act on the basis of ad hoc unwritten policies. These statements should explain the employer's policy on drug and alcohol use, state when and how testing will be conducted, and the penalties for negative results.

- **Procedural Protections.** Employers that use qualified, experienced laboratories, careful labeling and chain-of-custody procedures, and provide appropriately sophisticated secondary tests to confirm results have a better chance of defending actions taken on positive results.

- **Confidentiality of Results.** Employers that ensure that test results do not convey other private medical information, that no results are released or announced without confirmation testing, and that all

results are conveyed only on a need-to-know basis
can limit the risk of defamation claims.

- **The Standard That Triggers Action.** Employers can
  more easily justify adverse action for the on-the-job
  possession of quantities of an illicit drug than they
  can for only trace amounts of alcohol or marijuana in
  a urine sample.

- **Type of Adverse Action.** Employers that offer
  voluntary rehabilitation programs can more easily
  defend their substance abuse policies than employers
  that have no rehabilitation programs and
  automatically terminate employees for a first offense.

ENDNOTES

[1] NIDA, *The Economic Cost of Drug Abuse,* citing Harwood, et al,
"Economic Costs to Society of Alcohol and Drug Abuse and Mental Illness:
1980," Research Triangle Institute: Research Triangle Park, N.C., 1984.

[2] *Alcohol & Drugs in the Workplace: Costs, Controls and Controversies*
(BNA 1986) at 7.

[3] "Casual Use of Drugs Found to Drop Sharply," *The Washington Post,*
Aug. 1, 1989, at A-1, A-7; "Highlights of the 1988 Household Survey on
Drug Abuse," NIDA, August 1988.

[4] *See, e.g., G. & H. Equipment Co. v. Alexander,* 533 S.W.2d 872 (Tex. Civ.
App. 1976)(employer liable for damage when employee who was on errand
was involved in automobile accident after having two beers at lunch).

[5] *Pittard v. Four Seasons Motor Inn, Inc.,* 101 N.M. 723, 688 P.2d 333 (Ct.
App. 1984).

[6] *Otis Engineering Corp. v. Clark,* 688 S.W.2d 307 (Tex. 1983); see also
Brockett v. Kitchen Boyd Motor Co., 264 Cal. App. 2d 69, 70 Cal Rptr. 136
(1968)(plaintiffs state cause of action against employer whose employee injured them in car accident. Employee was intoxicated from office Christmas
party).

[7] Exec. Order No. 12564, 50 FR 32889 (1986).

[8] "White House Favors Expanding Random Drug Testing," *The Denver
Post,* April 9, 1989, at 3-A.

[9] 68 DLR A-12 (BNA), April 10, 1987.

[10] 148 DLR A-1 (BNA), Aug. 3, 1989; 115 DLR A-13 (BNA), June 16,
1989.

[11] NIDA, "Facts About Drugs in the Workplace," 1986.

[12] *Survey of Employer Anti-Drug Programs*, U.S. Department of Labor, Bureau of Labor Statistics, January 1989, Report No. 760.

[13] "Surveys Show Surprisingly Few Employers Use Drug Testing," *ABA Journal*, June 1989 at 38, 40; "Survey Shows Little Use of Random Test Programs," 179 DLR A-7 (BNA), Sept. 17, 1987.

[14] "Poll Says Most Area Employers Have Programs to Fight Drugs," *Washington Post*, Feb. 9, 1989, at E-1.

[15] "Corporate Drug Testing Programs Effective, Companies Tell Conference," 144 DLR A-12 (BNA), July 28, 1989.

[16] *N.Y. Times*, Sept. 16, 1986, at A-16, col. 3.

[17] *Schmerber v. California*, 384 U.S. 757, 767, 86 S. Ct. 1826 (1966).

[18] *Skinner*, 109 S.Ct. 1402, 1411, 4 IER Cases 224 (1989).

[19] *Schmerber*, 384 U.S. at 767-68.

[20] *Patchogue-Medford Congress of Teachers v. Board of Education*, 70 N.Y.2d 62, 67, 510 N.E.2d 325, 329, 517 N.Y.S.2d 456, 461, 2 IER Cases 198 (1987).

[21] 441 U.S. 520, 559 (1979).

[22] *O'Connor v. Ortega*, 480 U.S. 709, 107 S. Ct. 1492, 1497, 1 IER Cases 1617 (1987).

[23] 643 F. Supp. 1507, 1 IER Cases 625 (D.N.J. 1986).

[24] *Id.* at 1514.

[25] *Jones v. McKenzie*, 833 F.2d 335, 2 IER Cases 1121 (D.C. Cir. 1987), vacated, 109 S. Ct. 1633, 4 IER Cases 352 (1989), *aff'd on reconsideration*, 4 IER 842 (D.C. Cir. 1989); *American Federation of Government Employees v. Dole*, 670 F.Supp. 3445, 448, 2 IER Cases 841 (D.D.C. 1987).

[26] See *Dozier v. New York City*, 519 N.Y.S.2d 135, 142 (A.D.2 Dept. 1987).

[27] *Mack v. United States*, 653 F. Supp. 70, 75 (S.D.N.Y. 1986), *aff'd on other grounds*, 814 F.2d 120 (2d Cir. 1987).

[28] 833 F.2d at 340 (D.C. Cir. 1987).

[29] *Mullholland v. Department of Army*, 660 F. Supp. 1565, 1570, 2 IER Cases 1565 (E.D. Va. 1987). *See also American Federation of Government Employees v. Dole*, 670 F. Supp. 445, 2 IER Cases 841 (D.D.C. 1987).

[30] *Harmon v. Meese*, 690 F. Supp. 65, 69 (D.D.C. 1988).

[31] 680 F. Supp. 416, 434 (D.D.C. 1988). *See also Harmon* at 69-70.

[32] See *Burka v. New York City Transit Authority*, 680 F. Supp. 590, 3 IER Cases 186 (S.D.N.Y. 1988) (mandatory testing of all Transit Authority employees and job applicants); *Amalgamated Transit Union v. Cambria County Transit Authority*, 691 F. Supp. 898 (W.D. Pa. 1988) (bus drivers and mechanics tested as part of annual physical examination).

[33] *Mulholland v. Army*, 660 F. Supp. 1565, 2 IER Cases 868 (E.D. Va. 1987); *Uniformed Div. Officers Assn., Local 17 v. Brady*, No. 88-3377, 1988 WESTLAW 142378 (D.D.C. 1988) (uniformed secret service agents).

[34] *See Thompson v. Weinberger*, 682 F. Supp. 829, 3 IER Cases 7 (D. Md. 1988) (civilians in "critical" jobs; specifically with access to toxic chemicals); *NFFE v. Carlucci*, 690 F. Supp. 46 (D.D.C. 1988) (civilians on "critical" jobs), *same case* at 680 F. Supp. 416 (because testing for off-duty use is not reasonably related to on-the-job impairment), 690 F. Supp. at 50; *Egloff v. New Jersey Air National Guard*, 684 F. Supp. 1275, 3 IER Cases 509 (D.N.J. 1988) (individual reasonable suspicion required).

[35] *Lovvorn v. City of Chattanooga*, 846 F.2d 1539, 1547 (6th Cir. 1988); *see also Guiney v. Roache*, 686 F. Supp. 956, 3 IER Cases 598 (D. Mass. 1988).

[36] *Wrightsell v. City of Chicago*, 678 F. Supp. 727 (N.D. Ill. 1988). *See also, City of East Point v. Smith*, 258 Ga. 111, 365 S.E.2d 432, 3 IER 157 (1988).

[37] *Harmon v. Meese*, 690 F. Supp. 65 (D.D.C. 1988).

[38] *Bangert v. Hodel*, 705 F. Supp. 643, 4 IER Cases 12 (D.D.C. 1989).

[39] 795 F.2d 1136, 1142, 1 IER Cases 814 (3rd Cir. 1986), *citing Donovan v. Dewey*, 452 U.S. 594, 101 S. Ct. 2534, 69 L. Ed. 2d 262 (1981).

[40] At least one jurisdiction has declined to follow *Shoemaker* on nearly identical facts. *Horsemens Benevolent and Protective Association v. Massachusetts Racing Commission*, 403 Mass. 692, 532 N.E.2d 644, 4 IER Cases 147 (Mass. Jan. 9, 1989) (drug testing program held to violate Mass. statute and, in dicta, Fourth Amendment).

[41] 844 F.2d 562, 3 IER Cases 768 (8th Cir. 1988).

[42] 850 F.2d 133 (3rd Cir. 1988).

[43] *See Guiney v. Roache*, 686 F. Supp. 956, 963, 3 IER Cases 598 (D. Mass. 1988) (express rejection of application of *Shoemaker* rationale to police); *Lovvorn v. City of Chattanooga*, 846 F.2d 1539, 1545 (6th Cir. 1988) (rejection of administrative search as justification for suspicionless testing).

[44] 682 F. Supp. 829, 3 IER Cases 7 (D. Md. 1988).

[45] 643 F. Supp. 1507, 1 IER Cases 625 (D.N.J. 1986).

[46] 70 N.Y.2d 62, 510 N.E.2d 325, 517 N.Y.S.2d 456, 2 IER Cases 198 (1987).

[47] 109 S. Ct. 1402, 130 LRRM 2666 (1989).

[48] 109 S. Ct. 1384 (1989).

[49] 109 S. Ct. 2477, 131 LRRM 2601 (1989).

[50] 839 F.2d 575, 584, 46 FEP Cases 43 (9th Cir. 1988).

[51] *Id.* at 588.

[52] 109 S.Ct. at 1417.

[53] *Id.* at 1419-1420.

[54] *Id.* at 1420, *quoting* 839 F.2d at 588.

[55] *Id.* at 1421.

[56] 49 FR 24291 (1984).

[57] The accuracy of this conclusion is discussed at the end of this chapter.

[58] 109 S.Ct. at 1422.

[59] 816 F.2d 170, 173, 2 IER Cases 15 (5th Cir. 1987).

[60] 109 S. Ct. 1384, 1392 (1989).

[61] *Id.* at 1393.

[62] *Id.*

[63] *Id.* at 1394, n.3.

[64] *Id.* at 1396-97.

[65] *Id.* at 1399.

[66] *Id.* at 1397.

[67] 109 S. Ct. 2477, 131 LRRM 2601 (1989).

[68] 131 LRRM 2609 (1989).

[69] *Id.*

[70] Justice Brennan noted, in his dissent, that under this reasoning the outcome of the case should be different if an employer's policy were indeed to discharge an employee because of a single positive test.

[71] 41 U.S.C. 701-707.

[72] 18 U.S.C. 1001.

[73] 707 F.Supp. 531, 130 LRRM 2419 (N.D. Ga. 1989).

[74] 29 DLR A-2 (BNA), Feb. 14, 1989.

[75] 42 percent of the defense contractors had a policy including testing while only 18 percent of the non-contracting companies had a policy including testing.

[76] 49 CFR Pt 391; 394, 53 FR 47134.

[77] *Star Tribune*, 117 DLR E-1 (BNA), June 20, 1989.

[78] *Johnson-Bateman Company*, 117 DLR E-1, F-1 (BNA), June 20, 1989.

[79] *Id.* at F-2. *See Medicenter, Mid-South Hospital*, 221 NLRB 670, 678, 90 LRRM 1576 (1975).

[80] *Johnson-Bateman Company, supra*, at F-3.

[81] *NLRB v. Katz*, 369 U.S. 736 (1962).

[82] 650 F. Supp. 431, 433, 126 LRRM 2184 (S.D. Ill. 1986).

[83] *International Brotherhood of Electrical Workers, Local 1900 v. Potomac Electric Power Co.*, 634 F. Supp. 642, 121 LRRM 3071 (D.D.C. 1986).

[84] M. de Bernardo, *Drug Abuse in the Workplace: An Employer's Guide For Prevention* (U.S. Chamber of Commerce 1987) at 17, 30.

[85] C. Morris, *The Developing Labor Law*, v. 1, 640-48 (2d ed. 1971).

[86] 88 LA 528 (1986)(McKay).

[87] 29 U.S.C. 185.

[88] *Lingle v. Norge Division of Magic Chef*, 108 S. Ct. 1877, 1881 (1988).

[89] *Jackson v. Liquid Carbonic Corp.*, 863 F.2d 111, 130 LRRM 2143 (1st Cir. 1988).

[90] *Association of Western Pulp and Paper Workers v. Boise-Cascade Corp.*, 644 F. Supp. 183, 123 LRRM 3097 (D. Or. 1986).

[91] *Laws v. Calmat*, 852 F.2d 420, 3 IER Cases 785 (9th Cir. 1988).

[92] *United States v. Jacobson*, 466 U.S. 109, 113, 104 S.Ct. 1652, 1656 (1984); *See, United States v. McGreecry*, 652 F.2d 847 (9th Cir. 1981)(off-duty police officer working as a private security guard in a drug search is not "state action" for purposes of the Fourth Amendment); *United States v. Gumerlock*, 590 F.2d 794 (9th Cir.)(en banc), *cert. denied*, 441 U.S. 948 (1979)(Fourth Amendment does not apply to search by a private individual motivated by desire to assist law enforcement effort if government is neither involved in nor encouraged the search).

[93] *See, e.g., Chico Feminist Women's Health Center v. Butte Glenn Medical Society*, 557 F. Supp. 1190, 1202-03 (E.D. Cal. 1983).

[94] *Luedtke v. Nabors*, 768 P.2d 1123, 4 IER Cases 129 (Alaska 1989).

[95] *See, e.g., Novosel v. Nationwide Insurance Co.*, 721 F.2d 894, 114 LRRM 3105 (3d Cir. 1983), discussed in Chapter VII.

[96] *Monroe v. Consolidated Freightways*, 654 F.Supp. 661, 3 IER Cases 1185 (E.D. Mo. 1987).

[97] Title 21, Secs. 511-520, as enacted by Act 61, L. 1987 or IERM 587:4.

[98] HR 145, reported in 64 DLR A-15 (BNA), April 6, 1987.

[99] Cal. Ct. App., 1st Dist., No. A042567, June 24, 1988.

[100] 131 DLR A-8 (BNA), July 8, 1988.

[101] Docket Number W-003611-86, April 28, 1989.

[102] 780 F.2d 1067, 121 LRRM 2321 (1st Cir. 1986).

[103] *Jennings v. Minco Technology Labs, Inc.*, 765 S.W.2d 497 (Tex. Ct. App. 1989).

[104] *Restatement (Second) of Torts* § 752F (1977). *See also Texas Employment Commission v. Hughes Drilling Fluids*, 746 S.W.2d 796, 799-800, 3 IER Cases 451 (Tex. Ct. App. 1988).

[105] 548 S.W.2d 743 (Tex. Civ. App.), *cert. denied*, 434 U.S. 962 (1977).

[106] *Kelley v. Schlumberger*, 849 F.2d 41, 3 IER Cases 696 (1st Cir. 1988).

[107] 29 U.S.C. 793 & 794.

[108] *Rodgers v. Lehman*, 869 F.2d 253 (4th Cir. 1989) (alcoholism); *Crewe v. Office of Personnel Mgmt.*, 834 F.2d 140 (8th Cir. 1987) (alcoholism); *Wallace v. Veterans Administration*, 683 F. Supp. 758 (D. Kan. 1988) (drug

abuse); *National Treasury Employees Union v. Reagan*, 685 F. Supp. 1346 (E.D. La. 1988) (alcoholism & drug abuse).

[109] 29 U.S.C. 706(8)(B). *See* HRConfRep. No. 1780, 95th Cong., 2d Sess. 65, 102, *reprinted in* 1978 *U.S. Code Cong. & Admin. News* 7375, 7413.

[110] *Burka v. New York City Transit Authority*, 680 F. Supp. 590, 600 note 18 (S.D.N.Y. 1988) ("[V]oluntary drug use should not become a handicap until it reaches the stage of an involuntary impairment, presumably at addiction.").

[111] *Burka v. New York City Transit Authority*, 680 F. Supp. 590 (S.D.N.Y. 1988), 2 IER Cases 1625; *Railway Labor Executives' Association*, 839 F.2d at 591 (Act only covers addicts whose problems are under control).

[112] *Copeland v. Philadelphia Police Department*, 840 F.2d 1139, 2 IER Cases 1825 (3rd Cir. 1988), *cert. denied*, 109 S. Ct. 1636 (1989) (police officer under drug addiction was not "otherwise qualified"); *Lemere v. Burnles*, 683 F. Supp. 275, 46 FEP Cases 845 (D.D.C. 1988) (two year pattern of unscheduled absences resulted in alcoholic employee's loss of "qualified handicapped employee" status).

[113] 29 CFR 1613.704; 29 U.S.C. 791.

[114] *Rodgers v. Lehman*, 869 F.2d 253, 49 FEP Cases 351 (4th Cir. 1989) (Navy and Army employees must be given an opportunity for inpatient treatment before being discharged); *Ferguson v. Department of Commerce*, 680 F. Supp. 1514, 46 FEP Cases 241 (M.D. Fla. 1988) (agency had a duty of accommodation where it should have known, but did not, that employee was an alcoholic); *Calicotti v. Carlucci* 698 F. Supp. 944 (D.D.C. 1988) (agency did not reasonably accommodate alcoholic where it terminated her after only one unsuccessful attempt at treatment).

[115] 41 CFR 60-741.6(d); 29 U.S.C. 793.

[116] Geidt, "Drug and Alcohol Abuse in the Work Place: Balancing Employer and Employee Rights," 11 *Employee Rel. L. J.* 181, 193 (Autumn 1985).

[117] *Northwest Airlines*, 89 LA 943 (Nicolau 1984); *Delta Air Lines*, 89 LA 408 (Kahn 1987). In both cases the employee was a pilot who was intoxicated while flying.

[118] Elkouri and Elkouri, *How Arbitration Works*, 4th ed. 1985 (BNA) at 656-58.

[119] *Marathon Petroleum*, 89 LA 716 (Grimes 1987).

[120] *Ashland Oil*, 89 LA 795 (Flannagan 1987).

[121] *Metropolitan Transit Authority, Houston, Texas*, 89 LA 129 (Baroni 1987); *Southeastern Pa. Transportation Authority*, 89 LA 1280 (DiLauro 1987).

[122] *Warehouse Distribution Centers*, 90 LA 979, 982 (Weiss 1987).

[123] 91 LA 1385 (Baroni 1989).

[124] *Transportation & Packing Authority*, 88 LA 492 (Harr 1986); *Union Plaza Hotel, supra.*

[125] *Arkansas Power & Light Co.*, 88 LA 1065 (Weisbrod 1987).

[126] *United Paper Workers International Union v. Misco, Inc.*, 484 U.S. 29, 108 S. Ct. 364, 373, 126 LRRM 3113 (1987).

[127] *Oil, Chemical and Atomic Workers, International Union, Local No. 4-228 v. Union Oil Co. of California*, 818 F.2d 437, 126 LRRM 2630 (5th Cir. 1987).

[128] *Delta Air Lines v. Air Lines Pilots Ass'n, Int'l*, 686 F. Supp. 1573 (N.D. Ga. 1987), *aff'd*, 861 F.2d 665 (11th Cir. 1988); *see also Georgia Power Co. v. IBEW, Local 84*, 707 F. Supp. 531 (N.D. Ga. 1989).

[129] *New York City Transit Authority v. Beazer*, 440 U.S. 568, 19 FEP Cases 149 (1979).

[130] *See, e.g., Davis v. Bucher*, 451 F. Supp. 791 (E.D. Pa. 1978) (ban on hiring all former drug users violated Rehabilitation Act).

[131] 53 FR 11970 (1988).

[132] 109 S. Ct. at 1388 n.7.

[133] 53 FR. 11983 (1988).

[134] Brief for Amici Curiae PharmChem Laboratories, Inc. and Syva Co. at 13-14, *National Treasury Employees' Union v. Von Raab*, __U.S.__, 109 S. Ct. 1384 (1989) (summary of 16 studies involving 30,126 urine samples). *See also*, Kelly, *The Accuracy and Reliability of Tests for Drugs of Abuse in Urine Samples*, 8 Pharmacotherapy, no. 5, 263, 273 (1988) ("[I]n the crudest of analyses the confirmation rate of initial tests [including test other than EMIT] appears to be approximately 98.3%").

[135] *See* Brief for Amici Curiae at 15, note 17, *NTEU v. Von Raab.*

[136] Kelly, *supra* note 136, at 268.

[137] *Lovvorn v. City of Chattanooga*, 846 F.2d 1539, 1541 (6th Cir. 1988) ("virtually 100 percent accurate"); *Brotherhood of Maintenance of Way Employees v. Burlington Northern R.R.*, 802 F.2d 1016, 1019, 1 IER Cases 789 (8th Cir. 1986) (GC/MS test is "the most accurate available"); *Taylor v. O'-Grady*, 669 F. Supp. 1422, 1430 (N.D. Ill. 1987) ("EMIT/GCMS testing procedure is an accurate and reliable procedure for detecting the presence of metabolites of cocaine, marijuana and heroin ... "); *National Treasury Employees Union v. Von Raab*, 816 F.2d 170, 174 (5th Cir. 1987), *aff'd in part*, __U.S.__, 109 S. Ct. 1384 (1989) ("Both parties agree that GC/MS provides a highly accurate test for the presence of drugs ... ").

[138] Brief for Amici Curiae at 23, *NTEU v. Von Raab, quoting*, Staff of House Subcomm. on Civil Service, (Report on Drug Testing in the Federal Government, at 42, June 20, 1986).

[139] R. Decresce, A. Mazura, M. Lifshitz & J. Tilson, *Drug Testing in the Workplace*, 70 (1989); Kelly, *supra* note 136, at 272-73. (Both cite a Centers for Disease Control study finding a wide variation in different laboratories' error rates.) Hansen, Caudill & Boone, *Crisis in Drug Testing: Results of CDC Blind Study*, 254 J.A.M.A. 2382 (1985).

[140] 109 S. Ct. 1402, 4 IER Cases 224 (1989).

[141] *Skinner*, 109 S. Ct. at 1416, *citing*, 49 FR 24291 (1984) (Federal Railroad Administration regulations).

[142] Consensus Development Panel, *Consensus Report: Drug Concentrations and Driving Impairment*, 254 J.A.M.A. 2618 (1985).

* * *

Polygraphs

No workplace privacy issue has undergone as much change in recent years as the use of polygraphs and other mechanical lie detectors by employers. It was estimated in 1987 that 1.8 million polygraph tests were conducted by private employers each year. Three out of every four of those tests were administered to job applicants.[1] More than 30 percent of the Fortune 500 companies and at least half of all retail firms reportedly used polygraphs in 1985, either in lieu of background checks or to enhance them.[2] Although the use of polygraphs had declined in recent years as a result of concerns over their validity and state law restrictions, their use was still widespread in 1987. However, use probably has declined dramatically since June 1988, when President Reagan signed the Employee Polygraph Protection Act of 1988 (EPPA). Under the act (PL 100-347), the use of polygraphs as a job-applicant screening device is generally banned for private employers in all but the pharmaceutical and security industries, and their use on current employees is severely curtailed throughout private employment.

NATURE AND VALIDITY OF LIE DETECTORS

For the past 60 years, proponents and opponents have argued about the legal, ethical, and constitutional implications of polygraph testing. The debate focuses on the balancing of employers' interests in the cost-effective screening of applicants, insuring a secure workplace, and maintaining a profitable business and productive workforce, against employees' concerns with privacy, false accusations, job security, fair and impartial investigations, and maintenance of an accurate and non-prejudicial personnel record. Privacy concerns include the intrusive nature of a test designed to measure thoughts and emotions, the questions that are asked by the examiner, often probing into employees' personal lives, the accuracy of the test, and the confidentiality of the results.

Every form of mechanical lie detector operates on the principle that people have different physiological responses when they are lying and under stress than when they are telling the truth. The best-known and most often-used mechanical lie detector is the polygraph. The psychophysiological basis for the polygraph has been described as follows:

> Stress associated with the fear of a lie being detected activates a portion of the nervous system, that, in turn, causes a series of physiological changes to take place. Some of these are measured and recorded in the form of tracings on a moving polygraph chart. From the variations and the responses related to truthfulness and lying, the examiner can deduce with some degree of accuracy the veracity of each person examined. He is not, however, measuring lying per se, but changes in the person's body reactions related to the stress associated with deception.[3]

Most polygraphs comprise receptors that measure three neurological responses to stress: respiration, galvanic skin response, and blood volume and pulse rate. People taking the test are asked control questions where they are instructed to lie, and substantive questions for which the examiner seeks a response.

The other major type of mechanical lie detector is the voice stress analyzer, also referred to as a "psychological stress evaluator" (PSE). The voice stress analyzer is based on the theory that when subjects believe they are in danger of punishment or are engaging in deception, they will have stressful reactions that suppress certain normal frequency modulations in their voices. The voice stress analyzer comprises a spectrum analyzer that measures frequency modulations in a subject's voice. Like the polygraph, the voice stress analyzer detects stress, not deception.[4]

Studies of pre-employment screening devices have found that polygraphs are a very unreliable way to determine general honesty. The Office of Technology Assessment (OTA) concluded in a 1983 report that the available research studies did not establish the validity of the polygraph as a general screening technique.[5] The American Psychological Association concluded in 1986 that the evidence of polygraph validity is "particularly poor concerning polygraph use in employee screening."[6] Experts attribute the inaccuracy of pre-employment polygraphs to:

- The increased number of false results that accompanies a large testing population;

- The increased likelihood that the subject's response arises from something other than falsehood when testing goes beyond a pre-determined group of suspects about a particular incident; and

- The fact that the broadness of questions typically asked in pre-employment screening, such as "Have you ever stolen anything?" are more likely to arouse stress in an honest person trying to answer the question truthfully but unsure of its scope, than in a dishonest person.

Most polygraph exams administered to current employees are conducted in connection with criminal investigations or other probes into incidents of theft or misconduct. Some employers also administer polygraphs periodically to detect or deter theft. Periodic, generalized examinations have the same flaws as tests used for pre-employment screening. However, evidence shows that polygraphs are useful in investigations of specific incidents.

The OTA report found that previous reviews of field studies had estimated polygraph accuracy to be between 64 percent and 98 percent. Of the studies reviewed by OTA, correct guilty rates averaged 86.3 percent in field studies and 63.7 percent in analog studies. False-negative rates (guilty people the polygraph found to be not deceptive) averaged 10 percent. However, false-positive rates (innocent people the polygraph said were deceptive) ranged from zero percent to 75 percent in field studies (averaging 19.1 percent) and from 2 percent to

50.7 percent in analog studies (averaging 14.1 percent).[7] In other words, polygraphs do much better than chance at detecting deception, but they also incorrectly identify a large percentage of innocent people as liars.

Despite these findings, some private employers insist that polygraphs can be a useful tool. The U.S. Chamber of Commerce argues that the polygraph is a quick and inexpensive way to screen out high-risk employees and that it is especially valuable for investigations, with an effectiveness rate of up to 90 percent. The chamber and other polygraph proponents note that polygraph screening is a central feature of programs for national defense and security agencies, including the Central Intelligence Agency and the Department of Defense.[8] Many polygraph proponents maintain that polygraph testing also offers innocent suspects an opportunity to clear their names.

Polygraph accuracy is limited by the quality of the examiner. Even proponents of polygraph testing concede that polygraphs are not a useful tool in the hands of an untrained or unqualified examiner. The instrument itself cannot detect deception; its effectiveness is based on the examiner's interpretation of different physiological reactions to different questions prepared and used by the examiner. A majority of states have laws that establish polygraph examiner qualifications and licensing requirements, ranging from completion of a polygraph course and a six-month internship to completion of a baccalaureate, investigative experience, plus a polygraph course and internship.[9]

One measure of the accuracy of polygraph results is the degree to which those results are accepted into evidence by the courts. The standard applied by courts is whether the polygraph test is "sufficiently established to have gained general acceptance" by the scientific community.[10] At the federal level, most judges have rejected polygraph results, ruling that they are inaccurate, not generally accepted, overly prejudicial because juries give them too much weight, or because the time necessary to show the scientific basis outweighs the value of the tests.[11] State courts also have tended to exclude polygraph results in the absence of written stipulations by the parties, and some courts exclude results regardless of such stipulations.[12]

Concerns over accuracy have led many states and the federal government to limit or ban the use of polygraphs in the workplace. Courts and arbitrators also consider accuracy in reviewing employers' decisions to fire employees for refusing to take the tests or for "failing" them.

PRIVACY CHALLENGES
IN THE PUBLIC SECTOR

The EPPA exempts federal, state, and local governments from its restrictions, as well as certain classes of federal contractors who are required to administer polygraphs. Therefore, the legality of polygraph use on public employees must take into consideration constitutional claims, state laws restricting the use of polygraphs, and various common law theories that have been used to attack polygraph testing.

The U.S. Supreme Court has never decided whether public employees can be required to take polygraphs. Lower courts usually have held that as long as the questions asked relate narrowly and specifically to the performance of official duties and employers do not require employees to waive their constitutional right against self-incrimination, public employees may be required to submit to polygraph testing on threat of dismissal.[13]

The right of public employers to require polygraph examinations is limited by law in many states, and may also be limited by state constitutions. For example, a California law forbidding compulsory polygraph testing for private employees and public safety officers, but allowing testing of all other public employees, has been found to violate the state's constitutionally protected right to privacy. The state supreme court found that requiring an employee to submit to such a test vio-

lated that person's basic right to privacy because the test, unlike ordinary verbal questioning, intrudes continuously into the
minds of the employees and records physiological functions
against the employees' wills even when they refuse to respond
verbally.[14]

A similar conclusion was reached by the Texas Supreme
Court, which found that requiring employees at the state
Department of Mental Health and Mental Retardation to submit to mandatory polygraph testing violated the employees'
rights of privacy under the Texas Constitution. The court distinguished the governmental interest that might exist in testing
police officers and members of other quasi-military organizations, from the interest to be served by testing employees
working in the mental health field. The trial court found, and
the state supreme court affirmed, that the polygraph's intrusion
is highly offensive to the average person and, in light of its
unreliability, a polygraph test is not a reasonable way to identify "miscreant employees."[15]

Testing by public employers also has been challenged in
federal court on constitutional privacy grounds. In *Hester v.
City of Milledgeville*, the U.S. Court of Appeals for the 11th
Circuit considered a privacy challenge to using mandatory
polygraphs to discover substance abuse among firefighters.[16]
The court held that the city could, without violating the Fifth
Amendment, order firefighters to take polygraph tests if the
employees were not required to waive any constitutional right
of self-incrimination. The court also concluded that use of
"control questions" in the polygraph examination was not a
violation of the constitutional right to privacy. The tested
firefighters were asked whether they had ever done anything
that, if revealed, would result in their dismissal or discredit the
department. These questions are designed to evoke deceptive
or nervous responses from everyone tested.

The city's interest in using control questions to improve the
accuracy of the polygraph testing was important, the court
noted, and the control questions were only a limited intrusion

into the sphere of confidentiality. Although potentially embarrassing, the questions avoided issues related to marriage, family, and sexual relations.[17]

Applicants for public employment also have challenged the use of polygraph testing for pre-employment screening under the due process and equal protection clauses of the U.S. Constitution. These employees' procedural due process argument is that they are deprived of a "property interest" without due process of law. The courts that have considered these claims usually have rejected the argument, finding that applicants for employment do not have a vested property interest in that employment. The courts have taken the due process "liberty interest" claims somewhat more seriously.

Courts have stated that polygraph results might be viewed as stigmatizing plaintiffs or damaging their reputations, but no liberty interest claim exists unless the results are made public. Where the results are kept confidential and undisclosed, and are not published or otherwise disseminated by the government employer to the public, applicants and employees cannot claim that they have been deprived of a liberty interest without due process.[18]

The equal protection claims are based on arguments that the polygraph does nothing to help select the best possible employees such as law enforcement officers, has been found periodically to be invalid or unreliable, and produces an unacceptably high percentage of false-positive results. The U.S. Court of Appeals for the Third Circuit rejected this claim, finding that the use of such screening by the National Security Agency (NSA), the Central Intelligence Agency (CIA), and about 50 percent of the police departments throughout the nation demonstrated that it is rational and reasonable to use polygraphs. The court said no basis existed for finding that a better selection device than a polygraph was available, so it was rational for the police department to use it as a follow-up to questionnaires completed by applicants.[19]

Challenges to the polygraph testing issue have arisen frequently in cases involving law enforcement officials. The reason most often cited for treating police differently is the special need for public confidence in them. As the court wrote in *Richardson v. City of Pasadena*, "by accepting public employment as a police officer [the plaintiff] subordinated his right of privacy as a private citizen to the superior right of the public to an efficient and credible police department."[20] Yet in several states, such decisions have been overturned by higher courts or the legislature. The Illinois Supreme Court overturned several appellate court decisions and forbade the use of polygraphs, concluding that polygraphs are not sufficiently reliable to justify an outright invasion into the officer's privacy expectations or to serve as a basis for disciplinary action.[21]

COMMON LAW CLAIMS
AND OTHER CHALLENGES

Forty-two states and the District of Columbia regulate the use of lie detectors. Many of these laws comprise licensing requirements or restrictions on examiners and the questions they may ask. Almost half of the states prohibit employers from demanding or requiring, directly or indirectly, that employees take lie detector tests, but do not prohibit employees from taking them voluntarily. Tennessee prohibits employers from basing any personnel action solely on the outcome of a polygraph test. Delaware, Hawaii, Massachusetts, Michigan, Minnesota, Oregon, and Rhode Island prohibit any use of polygraphs in private-sector employment. In Massachusetts, all job applications must note that it is unlawful "to require or administer a lie detector test as a condition of employment." These laws have been upheld as a permissible regulation of commercial speech.[22]

Employers' failure to comply with these laws can be costly. In *Moniodis v. Cook*,[23] the Maryland Court of Special Appeals upheld an award of $1.3 million to a drugstore employee who was fired for refusing to take a polygraph examination. The court held that the employer violated the state's Polygraph Protection Act when it fired or transferred employees in retaliation for refusing to take a polygraph examination. The court, agreeing with the trial judge, felt that the employer's conduct was extreme and outrageous. The former employee's discharge for refusing to submit to a polygraph examination violated the clear mandate of the law prohibiting lie detector tests as a condition of employment, the appeals court found.

The National Labor Relations Board has ruled that polygraph testing, like drug testing, is a mandatory issue of collective bargaining.[24] Employers are required to negotiate with unions over the use of polygraphs.[25] Failure to do so can be an unfair labor practice. Where polygraphs are used, the overwhelming weight of arbitral authority is that employees may not be disciplined for refusing to take a polygraph examination because it is an unwarranted invasion of privacy. Most arbitrators also usually disregard the results of polygraph tests. One arbitrator declared, after surveying decisions regarding polygraphs, "the conclusion is compelling that no matter how well qualified educationally and experientially may be the polygraphist, the results of the lie-detector tests should routinely be ruled inadmissible."[26]

Before EPPA was enacted, courts in states without polygraph laws frequently held that such examinations were a valid exercise of the employer's rights, in upholding discharges of at-will employees who refused to submit to polygraph tests or took them and failed. These courts reasoned that the at-will employee's status allowed the employer to discharge the employee for any reason or for no reason.[27] For example, in *Zaccardi v. Zale Corp.*,[28] an employee was fired after he refused to sign a form acknowledging that he was taking a polygraph test without duress or coercion. He had asked to take the test to help clear himself of alleged wrongdoing. The test was not administered because signing the form was a company prerequisite to giving the exam. The court found that because mandatory polygraph examinations did not violate any contractual provision or New Mexico public policy, the company's warnings that it would fire the employee if he did not consent to the test did not constitute duress or coercion, and did not render his willingness to be tested involuntary.

Other courts have found that requiring a polygraph is an unreasonable invasion of privacy. In *O'Brien v. Papa Gino's of America, Inc.*,[29] the employer required an employee to take a polygraph when he was suspected of using drugs outside of work, and was required to answer questions that were unrelated to his employment. The jury awarded $450,000 to the employee and determined that the supervisor's investigative techniques, which included the use of polygraph examinations, would be highly offensive to a reasonable person and constituted an invasion of the employee's privacy.

Similarly, the Supreme Court of West Virginia found—even before the state legislature limited the use of polygraphs—that the public policy of protecting privacy rights was sufficient to allow a wrongful discharge claim where employees refused to take a polygraph exam.[30] Other states have refused to recognize any such "public policy" in the absence of a specific law. The result of each case frequently depends more on whether the state recognizes exceptions to the at-will rule, rather than the positive or negative features of polygraph testing.[31]

Where employers are allowed to use polygraphs, they must exercise care when they conduct such examinations and when they distribute the results. Invasion of privacy claims have been made when examiners have inquired into the personal lives of employees, and the disclosure of false or inconclusive test results has led to suits for defamation. While employers have many defenses to these claims,[32] the potential for litigation stemming from inaccurate results is great.

Employers and polygraph examiners also have been challenged under negligence theories. In these cases the employee alleges that the polygraph was administered in a negligent manner resulting in injuries ranging from defamatory statements to discharge. Most employees are asked to sign releases before they take polygraph tests, but many courts have stated that where the employee does not receive additional consideration for the release, the release is not effective against the examiner's subsequent negligence.[33]

Workers also have challenged polygraph testing under intentional or negligent infliction of emotional distress doctrines. Courts in these cases usually find that the mere administration of a polygraph examination or requests that employees take a polygraph on pain of discharge do not constitute the extreme, outrageous, or atrocious conduct necessary to sustain claims for intentional infliction of emotional distress.[34]

The tort of intrusion can apply to certain areas of questioning. In one public-sector case, the court found that questions concerning a police officer's sexual activities were an invasion of his privacy.[35] In another case, an employer was penalized because its polygraph examiner sexually harassed female job applicants.[36]

The Equal Employment Opportunity Commission (EEOC) has issued a policy statement saying that polygraph testing in the workplace is not discriminatory, but discrimination can occur if the tests are administered disparately with regard to race, sex, national origin, or age. EEOC said no conclusive evidence existed that performance on polygraph exams differed significantly on the basis of race, sex, national origin, or age, so claims concerning the discriminatory use of polygraphs should focus on the disparate impact theory to determine whether the employer administered the exam in an unlawful discriminatory manner.[37]

EPPA

The Employee Polygraph Protection Act of 1988 represents a legislative compromise between polygraph opponents who wanted a complete ban on the use of such devices in the workplace and people who wanted to preserve their use where they have shown that they are most effective, such as specific-incident investigations. The Department of Labor (DOL) issued interim final regulations implementing the act Oct. 21, 1988, and it went into effect Dec. 27.[38] The final regulations were to be published in September 1989.

Governmental Exemptions

EPPA covers only private employers; Section 7(a) exempts federal, state, and local governments. Section 7(b)(1) comprises a "national defense and security exception" that allows the federal government to test—in the performance of its counterintelligence operations—private contractors and their employees under contract to the Department of Defense (DOD) and Department of Energy (DOE) atomic energy defense programs, plus applicants to, employees of, and contractors of NSA, CIA, the Defense Intelligence Agency, and any other agency where the contractor would have access to top secret information [§7(b)(2)]. An "FBI contractors exemption" allows the federal government to administer polygraph tests to employees of FBI contractors [§ 7(c)]. These exemptions are designed to allow these agencies to require government contractors to administer lie detector tests to their employees as part of the security clearance process.[39]

Prohibited Devices

The act is designed to cover a variety of lie detectors, including polygraphs, voice stress analyzers, psychological stress evaluators, deceptographs, and "any similar device (whether mechanical or electrical) that is used, or the results of which are used, for the purpose of rendering a diagnostic opinion regarding the honesty or dishonesty of an individual" [§ 2(3)].[40] The conference report states that the conferees "do not intend to include written or oral tests (commonly referred to as 'honesty' or 'paper and pencil' tests) within the definition of lie detector."[41]

The Senate bill also included "chemical" devices in its definition of lie detector, but this was not part of the House definition and it was omitted from the act.[42] The conference report states that the conference committee intended that the term "lie detector" not include medical tests to determine the presence or absence of controlled substances or alcohol in bodily fluids.[43] The legislative history does not indicate whether narcoanalysis or other forms of "truth serum" are prohibited by the act, but deletion of the term "chemical" probably excludes such drugs from it.[44]

The act distinguishes among the various types of lie detectors. Its general prohibition applies to all lie detectors [§ 8(1), (2) and (3)]. The various governmental exemptions apply to all mechanical lie detectors, but those covering private investigations and the security and drug industries allow the use of polygraphs only [§ 7(d), 7(e)(1) and 7(f)(1)]. This distinction was made, according to the Senate committee, because polygraphs have some validity for specific-incident investigations and therefore a total ban on them was unwarranted.[45]

Limits on Pre-Employment Screening

EPPA prohibits every private employer from using lie detectors to screen job applicants, with two narrow exceptions. The act provides that private employers may not directly or indirectly require, request, suggest, or cause prospective employees to take a lie detector test [§ 3(1)]. It also prohibits employers from inquiring into, using, referring to, or accepting the results of any lie detector test taken by prospective employees [§ 3(2)]. Private employers also are prohibited from refusing to hire or otherwise discriminating against prospective employees based on the results of any lie detector test or because of their refusal to submit to such a test [§ 3(3)]. Finally, the act prohibits employers from retaliating against prospective employees for suing under the act, for testifying in a proceeding under the act, or for exercising any rights granted by the act [§ 3(4)].

These prohibitions essentially ban the use of polygraphs as a pre-employment screening device by private employers. They also prohibit private employers from refusing to hire applicants because of the results of polygraph examinations administered by previous employers. Therefore, employers conducting background checks should avoid eliciting information indicating that applicants took polygraphs.

The act contains narrow exceptions for polygraph testing of job applicants by the pharmaceutical industry and by employers that provide security services. Employers whose primary business is providing security alarm systems or security personnel may administer pre-employment polygraphs if the applicant's job will involve protection of (1) facilities, materials, or operations that have a significant impact on health and safety or national security, including power plants, nuclear plants, public water supplies, radioactive or toxic waste, and public transportation [§ 8(e)(1)(A)], or (2) currency, negotiable securities, precious commodities or instruments, or proprietary information [§ 8(e)(1)(B)].

Sen. Don Nickles (R-Okla), co-author of the security amendment, referred to the amendment as the armored car or security guard amendment, and cited Brinks, Wells Fargo, and Rollins Protective Services as companies that would be covered.[46] Nickles argued that security firms need polygraphs to prevent terrorists or other criminals from infiltrating nuclear plants, armored cars, and home security alarm installation services.[47] He also said the amendment was needed to cover guards at airports that use private security services.[48]

Rep. Marge Roukema (R-NJ), author of a similar amendment in the House, said the measure covered both uniformed and plainclothes guards, and was designed to cover armored car company employees who transfer money each day and to deter terrorists from infiltrating nuclear plants or local water treatment facilities. She noted that "private firms that perform a policing function of protection of certain types of property and facilities would have the same ability to use the polygraph as public police forces."[49]

The interim final DOL regulations take a restrictive view of the security exemption, holding, for example, that it did not apply to security guards or security alarm firms protecting private homes or to businesses that are not engaged primarily in handling, trading, or storing currency, negotiable securities, precious commodities, or proprietary information. Roukema, the American Polygraph Association, and others criticized the restrictive nature of the interim final regulations.[50]

To fall within this exception, security services must be the employer's "primary business purpose." The interim final regulations define this term to mean at least 50 percent of an employer's annual volume is derived from the covered security activities. Thus, a private company that has security guards on its payroll could not test those guards. Nor does a general exemption exist for all employees of nuclear power plants. The conferees deleted the exemption for nuclear power plants, finding that the current requirement that all unescorted personnel must be fingerprinted and checked by the U.S. attorney general provides sufficient protection.[51]

The pharmaceutical industry exemption covers employers that manufacture, distribute, or dispense a "controlled substance." The regulations incorporate the Controlled Substances Act (CSA) [21 USC 802] definitions of these terms. That act requires such employers register with the Drug Enforcement Administration (DEA). EPPA allows these employers to test prospective employees who will have "direct access" to the manufacture, storage, distribution, or sale of any of these substances [§ 8(f)]. The scope of this exemption is not clear. This definition probably encompasses all drug manufacturing companies, research laboratories, and pharmacies or hospitals that sell controlled substances. Rep. Bill Richardson's (D-NM) amendment creating this exemption was designed to cover the pharmaceutical industry, including manufacturers and drug stores, as a way to prevent the diversion of drugs into the black market. Richardson explained during the House floor debate on EPPA that the amendment did not cover truck drivers who transport drugs because they do not have "direct access" to drugs, but includes warehouses that are registered with DEA, and anyone else involved in the "channel of controlled substances."[52] DOL's interim final EPPA regulations state that a prospective employee would have "direct access" if the position has responsibilities that include packaging, ordering, licensing, shipping, receiving, taking inventory, providing security, prescribing, and handling controlled substances.

The amendment conceivably could cover medical personnel in doctors' offices, nursing homes, or other facilities that "store" controlled substances. A nursing home amendment was rejected, with opponents noting that it was opposed by the American Medical Association and the American Nursing Association as an invasion of the rights of health care workers. But the conference report describes this exemption as covering employers engaged in manufacturing, distributing, or dispensing controlled substances.[53] EPPA's legislative history and the interim final regulations do not answer the question of whether the pharmaceutical industry exemption covers hospitals, nursing homes, and other health care facilities.

Even if an employer is covered by one of the exemptions that allow pre-employment lie detector testing, the employer must comply with restrictions imposed by state and local laws and any applicable collective bargaining agreements. In addition, the act's numerous procedural safeguards for current employees requiring advance notice, applicants' right to terminate the test at any time, and restrictions on the manner in which the test is administered and scored, apply to the testing of prospective employees in the exempted industries [§ 8(c)].

The final restriction on the pharmaceutical and security services industries exemption is that no employer can deny employment or discriminate against a prospective employee if the polygraph test results are the only reason for the rejection

[§ 8(b)(2)]. In these industries polygraphs can be used only as one component in the pre-employment screening process.

The Specific-Incident Exception

EPPA bans using lie detectors on current employees in the private sector except when employers are investigating specific incidents. The act contains a somewhat broader incident exception for the pharmaceutical industry, but no such exception for security firms to test current employees. The act allows private employers to ask current employees to take a polygraph test (but not any other type of lie detector) if these four requirements are met:

- The test is administered as part of an ongoing investigation involving economic loss or injury to the employer's business. The examples given in the act are theft, embezzlement, misappropriation, industrial espionage, and sabotage [§ 7(d)(1)].
- The employee must have had "access" to the property that is the subject of the investigation [§ 7(d)(2)].
- The employer must have a "reasonable suspicion" that the particular employee to be tested was involved in the incident or activity being investigated [§ 7(d)(3)].
- The employer must execute a statement identifying the specific economic loss or injury, the employee's access, and the basis for the employer's reasonable suspicion that the employee was involved in the incident or activity.

Injury and Access Requirements

The specific-incident exception is derived from the Senate version of the act. The Senate committee report explained that the investigation must involve a specific economic loss or injury to the employer's business. The committee defined "injury" to include certain activities that could provide a short-term gain to the company, such as check-kiting, money laundering, or the misappropriation of insider information.[54] This explanation was included in the conference report.[55]

House-Senate conferees on EPPA noted that they did not want all losses, such as an unintentional loss stemming from a truck crash or workplace accident, to serve as a pretext for requiring employees to take polygraph tests.[56] The conferees also said economic-loss incidents involving lawful union or employee activity, such as strikes, could not be cited to require workers to take polygraph exams.

The act does not say whether the "injury" must be to the employer's property or if it can include theft from co-workers, vendors, or customers. During the Senate debate, Sen. Orrin Hatch (R-Utah) cited as an example of indirect loss or injury a building repairman who steals from tenants, and the conference report included a statement that theft from property managed by employers would satisfy the injury standard.[57] The legislative history thus indicates that injury to others is sufficient to satisfy the first part of the exemption, at least in situations where the employer may be liable for the loss under contract or the doctrines of agency or respondeat superior. The interim final regulations state that because the business of the employer must suffer, a theft by one employee from another would not satisfy the injury requirement.

The conference report does not discuss the "access" requirement in detail. The "access" provision refers to specific property, a term in which the Senate committee intended to include other items of value such as security codes and computer information.[58] It is not clear whether this definition extends to all forms of intellectual property, ideas, or trade secrets. Theft or misappropriation of confidential documents is covered. The conference committee's specific reference to misappropriation of confidential information indicates that the term "property" extends to intellectual property.[59]

Many types of misconduct such as discrimination or sexual harassment could cause employers economic loss or injury. Although the conference report contains no expressed intent to exclude these types of misconduct, Congress' intent to exclude them can be inferred from the requirement that the employee must have "had access to the property that is the subject of the investigation" [§ 7(d)(2)]. Investigations of sexual harassment or personal injury could be brought within the scope of the specific-incident exception only if the access requirement were found to be inapplicable to certain types of misconduct, or read to mean "access to the person or property" that is under investigation. Each of these interpretations requires the courts to change the statutory language, which they are unlikely to do in the absence of legislative history on this point. Congressional intent also can be inferred from the fact whereas that the pharmaceutical industry investigation exception uses the phrase "person or property," the general exception does not.

The extent to which investigations of drug and alcohol use or other forms of "injury" are covered also is unclear. An employer may be able to argue that these activities involve direct or indirect injury to the company. As with sexual harassment, the access requirement presents a hurdle if it is mandatory that the "subject of the investigation" be "property." The interim final regulations state that the exemption does not allow the use of polygraph tests to learn whether an employee has used drugs or alcohol, even where such possible use may have contributed to an economic loss to the employer, through an accident or otherwise.

Reasonable Suspicion

EPPA outlaws random testing of current employees to detect possible dishonesty and dragnet testing of employees when a specific incident of theft has been discovered but the employer has no basis to suspect any individual employee. Instead, the employer must have "a reasonable suspicion that the employee was involved in the incident or activity under investigation" and must put the basis for such suspicion in writing [§ 7(d)(3) and § 7(d)(4)(D)(iii)]. Reasonable suspicion will be the most important facet for employers to show to use this exception, and it probably will be the focus of most litigation, but it is almost ignored in the act's legislative history. In their report, the conferees stated that the term "reasonable suspicion" refers to "some observable, articulable basis in fact beyond the predicate loss and access required for any testing."[60] It usually is not sufficient that a loss occurred and that the employee had access to the property—an employer cannot give polygraph tests to all employees who knew the combination to the safe.

The conference report cites the following as factors that could comprise "reasonable suspicion":

- The employee's demeanor;
- Discrepancies arising during the course of an investigation; and
- The totality of circumstances involved in an employee's access to certain property under investigation, such as whether the access was unauthorized or unusual.

The fact that an employee was the only person with the safe's combination, or the only person who acted evasively when interviewed, may be a sufficient basis for a reasonable suspicion of involvement. However, beyond these few comments, the legislative history contains little guidance regarding the meaning of the term "reasonable suspicion."

The interim final regulations state that information from a co-worker may be a factor in the employer's basis for reasonable suspicion. The act and its legislative history do not indicate whether information submitted to employers anonymously would be sufficient. Similarly, the interim final regulations state that inconsistencies among facts, claims, or statements that appear during investigations may be sufficient. Ultimately, the proposed test is whether an "observable, articulable basis in fact which indicates that a particular employee was involved in, or responsible for, an economic loss" exists.

The Senate committee stated that the reasonable suspicion standard is considered less stringent than the standard afforded criminal suspects yet far more stringent than the current standards in the employment context.[61] The term "reasonable suspicion" appears in criminal law and throughout the law of search and seizure as the least demanding end of a spectrum of the quantity of proof of wrongdoing necessary to take a particular act. "Reasonable suspicion" is a less stringent standard than "probable cause," which in turn is less stringent than "beyond a reasonable doubt." Reasonable suspicion also has been used in cases since *O'Connor v. Ortega* that involved searches of public employees in the workplace. Finally, the term "reasonable suspicion" has been used in several post-*Ortega* cases involving the constitutionality of drug testing programs.

Some attorneys have argued that application of the term "reasonable suspicion" in all of these cases is irrelevant to the interpretation of EPPA because the constitutionally required standard of "reasonable suspicion" applied to searches by public employers does not apply to private employers. This argument has merit—the courts should be reluctant to incorporate constitutional standards into legislation covering only private employers. Nevertheless, plaintiffs' attorneys are likely to argue that Congress has the power to look to standards developed for public employers in drafting new laws, and that the choice of a term that has an established meaning in analogous contexts (searches of employees) is evidence of congressional intent. Until the courts resolve this issue, employers should be cautious before requesting polygraphs during any investigation. They should have the facts of each incident reviewed by counsel to see if they satisfy the standards of "reasonable suspicion" established by the courts in other contexts, because the safest course for employers is to act on the basis of the highest standard that the courts can apply.

Drug Industry Investigations

EPPA gives the pharmaceutical industry more latitude than other private employers to test current employees. Such employers are allowed to test in connection with investigations of criminal conduct or other misconduct "involving or potentially involving" loss or injury to the manufacture, distribution, or dispensing of controlled substances by that employer if the employee had access to the "person or property" that is the subject of the investigation [§ 7(f)(2)(B)]. This exemption is broader than the ongoing-investigation exemption given to other employers because pharmaceutical industry employers need not show that a loss or injury involving controlled substances has occurred, only that loss could occur. In addition, if the subject of the investigation is a person who was involved in some loss, another employee with access to that person can be given a polygraph. The employee need not have had direct access to the controlled substance. The security industry, unlike the pharmaceutical industry, has no specific exemption that applies to examinations of current employees.

Procedural Requirements

Even if the testing falls within the ongoing-investigation exception, the employer must comply with extensive procedural safeguards, including submitting questions in advance to the people to be tested. The procedural safeguards for current employees governing notice to the employee concerning the test and the manner in which the test is administered and scored also apply to the testing of prospective employees in the few situations where such testing is allowed. A private employer may not administer a polygraph test under any circumstances unless the test satisfies these conditions:

- The employee to be tested must have had access to the property that is the subject of the investigation [§ 7(d)(2)];

- The employer has reasonable suspicion before the test that the employee was involved in the incident under investigation [§ 7(d)(3)];

- The employer provides a legally binding signed statement to the employee before the test identifying the loss under investigation, showing that the employee had access to the subject of the investigation, and outlining the basis for the employer's reasonable suspicion that the employee was involved in the incident or activity under investigation [§ 7(d)(4)]. The interim final regulations require that this statement be provided at least 48 hours before the examination and that it state "with particularity" the basis for the reasonable suspicion;

- The employee is informed of the right to terminate the test at any time, and is allowed to do so [§ 8(c)(1)(A) and (2)(E)];

- The employee is not asked degrading or intrusive questions, or questions about religious or political beliefs and affiliations, racial matters, sexual behavior, or attitudes or affiliations concerning labor unions [§ 8(c)(1)(B) and (C)];

- The employee is given reasonable written notice of: the time and place of the examination; the employee's right to consult with counsel or an employee representative before each phase of the test; the conditions of the test; and the nature and characteristics of the instruments involved, including whether any two-way mirrors, video or tape recorders, or other devices will be used to monitor the employee [§ 8(c)(2)(A) through (C)];

- The employee is told of tested employees' right to record the proceeding on film or tape [§ 8(c)(2)(C)(iii)];

- The employee is given an opportunity to review all questions to be asked during the test and is not asked any relevant questions that have not been submitted in writing to the employee in advance [§ 8(c)(2)(E) and 8(c)(3)];

- The examiner is licensed, if required by the state in which the test is conducted, and is bonded or insured for not less than $50,000 [§ 8(d)(1)] or more if required by law in the state where the test is to take place;[62]

- The test lasts at least 90 minutes and the examiner administers no more than five tests in the same day [§ 8(c)(5)];

- The employee reads and signs a written notice stating that the examinee cannot be required to take the test as a condition of employment; statements made can be used against the employee as evidence for later discipline or discharge; and the applications, limitations, and legal rights and remedies of the employee under the act [§ 8(c)(2)(D)];

- No written evidence by a physician exists that the employee suffers from a medical or psychological condition or requires treatment that could cause abnormal test results [§ 8(c)(1)(D)]; and

- Before any adverse action is taken, the employee must be interviewed by the employer regarding the test results and provided a copy of the questions and answers [§ 8(c)(4)].

The requirement that questions be submitted to the test subject in advance may eliminate polygraph testing's usefulness. The effectiveness of polygraph testing depends greatly on creating anxiety in the test subject about being caught lying during the test. Learning in advance what questions will be asked may eliminate this spontaneous anxiety reaction. The OTA report said mental preparation for test questions can enable test subjects to lie and escape detection during polygraph tests.[63]

The employer's statement required under the investigation section is a legally binding statement of its reasonable suspicion for conducting the polygraph examination, and it must be kept on file for at least three years. Employees to whom employers plan to give polygraphs will know most of the details about the investigation soon after they are asked to take the test [§ 8(c)(2)(A)], as a result of the requirements that they be given the questions and a detailed written statement before they take the test. Therefore, polygraph exams should be given only as a last resort at the conclusion of investigations. They also are best suited for employees who want to clear themselves of suspicion after investigations have begun.

The legislative history of the act suggests that while employees have a right to consult with counsel before each phase of the test, employees' attorneys do not have a right to be in the room during the examination. In fact, attorneys may be barred because of the potential for disruption.[64] However, under Labor Management Relations Act case law, union employees' *Weingarten* rights may allow them to have a union representative present during polygraph interrogations.[65]

Disclosure of Results

The new polygraph act prohibits disclosure of polygraph results by examiners or private employers to anyone other than the examiner, people designated by the examiner in writing, people or agencies exempt from the act under the government and national security exceptions, or a court, government agency, arbitrator, or mediator pursuant to a court order [§ 9]. This latter provision allows disclosure of results, under appropriate protections, to parties who are in arbitration or mediation over a wrongful discharge claim.[66] However, an employer who discharged an employee based in part on the results of a polygraph is not allowed to convey that information in an employment reference.

Basis for Discharge

An employer may not base an adverse employment action solely on the results of a polygraph or polygraphs, even if they are administered in accordance with the act. Additional supporting evidence is required. This can comprise the evidence that established the reasonable suspicion necessary to require the test or admissions or information elicited from the subject before, during, or after the test [§ 8(b)(1)].

Among the written statements that employers must give to employees to be tested is one that says "the examinee cannot be required to take the test as a condition of employment." The Senate committee report notes that a refusal to take a polygraph test may result in an adverse employment action if the employer has satisfied all other provisions of the act.[67] Hatch explained during the Senate debate that an employee who refuses to take a polygraph is treated the same as one who took it and failed—the employer is free to take any action it deems appropriate. The reason is that, before employers may ask employees to take polygraphs they must have a sufficient evidentiary basis for giving the test; that is, reasonable suspicion and access. Any adverse employment action can then be based on the established evidence plus the employee's refusal to take the test.[68]

Tested employees also must be told that they have the right to terminate the test at any time. The legislative history of the act does not indicate whether employees can be discharged after they stop a polygraph exam. Employers will contend that these employees can be treated the same as employees who refuse to take a test—they can be fired based on other evidence, and the interim final regulations support this interpretation. However, many plaintiffs may contend that the reason they were fired was not the reasonable suspicion that they engaged in wrongdoing, but for exercising their statutory right to end the test. Employers faced with this situation should avoid terminating an employee for failing to cooperate in the investigation, and base its decision to fire the worker on the existing evidence of wrongdoing.

Enforcement, Remedies Under the Act

EPPA is administered by DOL. The secretary of labor can assess civil penalties of up to $10,000 against employers for a violation of the act [§ 6(a)]. The interim final regulations establish an extensive administrative procedure for assessing these civil monetary penalties. Employers are required to post a notice prepared by DOL that explains the act, but a separate penalty for failure to post notices was deleted.[69] DOL can ask a federal court to issue injunctions against violators. The department also can seek legal and equitable relief for employees, including employment, reinstatement, promotion, and lost wages and benefits [§ 6(b)]. The secretary of labor's enforcement powers over the act are similar to the secretary's powers to enforce other wage and hour laws. The polygraph act's legislative history does not indicate whether suits by the secretary of labor preclude subsequent suits by individual employees. A comment in the conference report that employees or job applicants "may bring an action as well"[70] gives little guidance on this question.

The act also creates a private civil right of action for job applicants and current employees whose rights under the act are violated. An applicant or employee, individually or on behalf of all other similarly situated applicants or employees, may sue an employer in either federal court or state court for violations of the act [§ 6(c)(2)]. The act provides for a three-year statute of limitations, which is the deadline for an employee to sue. The remedies available to a successful plaintiff include a wide variety of legal and equitable relief, including employment of applicants rejected on the basis of polygraph results, reinstatement or promotion of an employee denied a position

or discharged based on the results of any test given in violation of the act, and the payment of lost wages and
benefits [§ 6(c)(1)]. The reference to "equitable relief"
presumably includes injunctive relief, if appropriate.

In addition, EPPA provides that a court, in its discretion,
may allow a prevailing party, except the federal government,
reasonable costs, including attorney's fees [§ 6(c)(3)]. Unlike
Title VII of the Civil Rights Act of 1964, attorney's fees under
EPPA are not mandatory.

EPPA does not expressly provide for compensatory
damages for emotional distress or for punitive damages.
Employee advocates had urged that this point be clarified, but
it was not.[71] EPPA, unlike Title VII, is not limited on its terms
to equitable relief. "Legal relief" normally encompasses a
variety of money damages, including compensatory and punitive damages. EPPA says the examples of employment,
reinstatement, promotion, and payment of lost wages and
benefits do not constitute an exclusive list of legal and equitable remedies. However, employers may want to argue that
legal relief in the form of monetary damages is limited to back
pay. This will be a major issue for the courts to resolve [§ 6(c)].

The act also does not state that employees or employers
have a right to a jury trial. Parties usually have no right to a
jury trial in lawsuits that claim "equitable" relief such as in-
junctions and reinstatements. Plaintiffs and defendants usually
are entitled, under the U.S. Constitution and common law, to a
jury trial on "legal" claims. This is another issue that will have
to be resolved through litigation.

In addition, the act apparently invalidates releases signed by
job applicants waiving causes of action against prospective
employers arising from pre-employment polygraph examinations, and written releases by employees that often are requested by polygraph examiners. The act states that the rights
and procedures provided under it may not be waived, by contract or otherwise, unless in settlement of an action under the

act. The provision does not exempt waivers or releases signed by job applicants [§ 6(d)].

Pre-Emption and Existing State Laws

EPPA does not pre-empt any state or local law, or any provision in a collective bargaining agreement that is more restrictive concerning polygraph tests. Sections of the act that allow polygraph testing of current employees during investigations do not affect the laws in 22 states and the District of Columbia that restrict polygraph testing of current employees. However, if a state law allows employers in certain industries to test employees, those exemptions are superseded by EPPA law. Where a state law regulating polygraph examiners is more restrictive than the act, or imposes licensing requirements, those laws must be followed. Indeed, they are incorporated into the act [§ 8(d)(1)]. The security and pharmaceutical industries and all public employers that are allowed to test applicants under the act cannot do so in any state where such testing is banned.

It is unclear whether the act pre-empts common-law tort claims. Private employers that use tests in compliance with the act will want to argue that the act serves as employees' exclusive remedy. The legislative history indicates that Congress' primary focus was state laws, but similar language in ERISA has been interpreted to encompass common-law claims. Public employees, however, can argue that neither the act nor its pre-emption provision apply to public employers, and that public employees retain all common-law claims.

ENDNOTES

[1] HRep 100-208, *Employee Polygraph Protection Act*, 100th Cong., 1st Sess. 3 (July 9, 1987) to accompany HR 1212.

[2] HRep 416, *Employee Polygraph Protection Act of 1985*, 99th Cong., 1st Sess. 7 (1985).

[3] L. Taylor, *Scientific Interrogation* 201 (Charlottesville, Va.: The Michie Co. 1984).

[4] *Id.* at 324-26.

[5] *Scientific Validity of Polygraph Testing: A Research Review and Evaluation—A Technical Memorandum*, 99-100 Washington, D.C.: U.S. Congress, Office of Technology Assessment, OTA-TM-H-15 (November 1983) ("OTA Report").

[6] *Polygraph Testing in the Private Workforce*, Hearings Before the Subcomm. on Employment Opportunities of the House Committee on Education and Labor, 100th Cong., 1st Sess. 67 (1987) ("House Hearings").

[7] OTA Report at 97.

[8] *Polygraphs In the Workplace*, Hearings before the Senate Committee on Labor and Human Resources, 100th Cong., 1st Sess. 63 (1987) ("Senate Hearings") (testimony of William Zierdan).

[9] *See, e.g.*, ALA. CODE § 34-25-1 (Michie 1985); ILL. ANN. STAT. ch. 111, § 2401 to 2432 (West 1978 and Supp. 1987); LA. REV. STAT. ANN. § 37.2831 to 2854 (West Supp. 1987); TENN. CODE ANN. §§ 62-27-101 to 27-124 (Michie 1986).

[10] *Frye v. United States*, 293 U.S. 1013 (1923).

[11] *See, e.g., United States v. Earley*, 657 F.2d 195 (8th Cir. 1981).

[12] *Polygraphs and Employment* BNA 1985 at 43-45.

[13] *See Gulden v. McCorkle*, 680 F.2d 1070 (5th Cir. 1982) (holding that public works employees in Texas were properly discharged for refusing to take polygraphs on a matter related to their employment where employees were warned that refusal could cost them their jobs and "this was a permissible requirement"). *See also Brown v. State of Tennessee*, 693 F.2d 600, 30 FEP Cases 459 (6th Cir. 1982) ("when polygraph testing is a lawful method for determining employment-related questions, ... the failure to submit to an examination ... may be a legitimate nondiscriminatory reason for dissimilar treatment").

[14] *Long Beach City Employees Ass'n v. City of Long Beach*, 41 Cal. 3d 937, 719 P.2d 660, 1 IER Cases 465 (1986).

[15] *Texas State Employees Union v. Texas Dept. of Mental Health and Mental Retardation*, Tex., 746 S.W.2d 203, 2 IER Cases 1077 (1987).

[16] 777 F.2d 1492 (11th Cir. 1985).

[17] *Id.* at 1497.

[18] *Anderson v. Philadelphia*, 845 F.2d 1216, 3 IER 353 (3d Cir. 1988).

[19] *Id.* at 358-59.

[20] 500 S.W.2d 175 (Tex. Ct. App. 1973), *rev'd* 513 S.W.2d 1 (Tex. 1974), *appeal after remand*, 523 S.W.2d 506 (Tex. Ct. App. 1975).

[21] *Kaske v. City of Rockford* and *Collura v. Board of Fire and Police Commissioners of the Village of Itasca*, 96 Ill. 2d 298, 450 N.E.2d 314, *cert. denied* 464 U.S. 960 (1983).

[22] *See State v. Century Camera, Inc.*, 309 N.W.2d 735, 741 (Minn. 1981) (Minnesota law upheld as constitutional on ground that it regulates commercial speech, not free speech).

[23] 64 Md. App. 1, 494 A.2d 212 (1984), *cert. denied* 304 Md. 631 (1985).

[24] *See Medicenter, Mid-South Hospital*, 221 NLRB 670, 90 LRRM 1976 (1975).

[25] *Glover Bottled Gas Corp. v. Local Union 282*, 711 F.2d 479, 113 LRRM 3211 (2d Cir. 1983).

[26] *See* Elkouri and Elkouri, *How Arbitration Works* 315 (4th ed. 1985). *See, e.g., Glen Manor Home for the Jewish Aged*, 81 Lab. Arb. 1178 (1983).

[27] *Cipov v. International Harvester Co.*, 134 Ill. App. 3d 522, 481 N.E.2d 22 (1985).

[28] 856 F.2d 1473, 3 IER Cases 1249 (10th Cir. 1988).

[29] 780 F.2d 1167 (1st Cir. 1986).

[30] *Cordle v. General Hugh Mercer Corp.*, 325 S.E.2d 111 (W.Va. 1984). *See also Ambroz v. Cornhusker Square Ltd.*, 226 Neb. 899, 416 N.W.2d 510, 2 IER Cases 1185 (1987).

[31] *Hamblen v. Danners, Inc.*, 478 N.E.2d 926, 119 LRRM 3470 (Ind. Ct. App. 1985). See Chapter XV, for a discussion of exceptions to at-will employment.

[32] See Chapter XVI.

[33] *Johnson v. Delchamps, Inc.*, 846 F.2d 1003, 3 IER 560 (5th Cir. 1988); *Mechanics Lumber Co. v. Smith*, Arkansas, 752 S.W.2d 763, 3 IER 891 (1988).

[34] *See Buffolino v. Long Island Savings Bank, FSB*, N.Y. 510 N.Y.S. 2d 628, 2 IER 894 (1987).

[35] *Schuman v. City of Philadelphia, 470 F. Supp. 449 (E.D. Pa. 1979).*

[36] *People by Abrams v. Hamilton, 125 A.D.2d 1000, 511 N.Y.S.2d 190, 42 FEP Cases 1069 (1986).*

[37] EEOC Compliance Manual; *Brown v. State of Tennessee*, 693 F.2d 600, 30 FEP Cases 459 (6th Cir. 1982); *Ramirez v. City of Omaha*, 693 F.2d 600, 30 FEP Cases 477 (8th Cir. 1981); and *United States v. City of Miami*, 614 F.2d 1322, 22 FEP Cases 846 (5th Cir. 1980).

[38] *Daily Labor Report* (BNA), No. 204, at E-1.

[39] HRep 659, Conference Report, *Employee Polygraph Protection Act of 1988*, 100th Cong., 2d Sess. 12 (May 26, 1988) ("Conf. Rep.").

[40] All references in the text are to the sections of HR 1212 as passed by both houses of Congress and signed by President Reagan.

[41] Conf. Rep. at 11. See also HRep 100-208 at 11. SR 100-284, 100th Cong., 2d Sess. 47 (Feb. 11, 1988).

[42] *See* SR 100-284 47, 51.

[43] Conf. Rep. at 11.

[44] For a good discussion of the validity of narcoanalysis as a truth-detection device, see Taylor, *Scientific Interrogation*, where the effect of chemical truth serums is compared with the consumption of bourbon.

[45] SR 100-284 at 47.

[46] 134 *CR* S1702-08 (daily ed. March 2, 1988) (remarks of Sen. Nickles and others).

[47] *Id.* at S1708.

[48] *Id.* at S1712.

[49] 133 *CR* H9560 (daily ed. Nov. 4, 1987) (remarks of Rep. Roukema).

[50] *Daily Labor Report* (BNA) No. 62, April 3, 1989, at D-1.

[51] Conf. Rep. at 13.

[52] 133 *CR* H9576 (daily ed. Nov. 4, 1987) (remarks of Rep. Richardson).

[53] Conf. Rep. at 13.

[54] SR 100-284 at 48.

[55] Conf. Rep. at 12.

[56] Conf. Rep. at 12.

[57] 134 *CR* S1646 (daily ed. March 1, 1988) (remarks of Sen. Hatch).

[58] SR 100-284 at 48.

[59] Conf. Rep. at 12.

[60] Conf. Rep. at 13.

[61] SR 100-284 at 48-49.

[62] Conf. Rep. at 15.

[63] OTA Report at 89.

[64] 134 *CR* §1646 (daily ed. March 1, 1988) (remarks of Sen. Hatch).

[65] *Consolidated Casinos Corp.*, 226 NLRB No. 172, 113 LRRM 1081 (1983).

[66] 134 *CR* S1655, (daily ed. March 1, 1988) (remarks of Sen. Hatch).

[67] SR 100-284 at 53.

[68] 134 *CR* S1642 (daily ed. March 1, 1988) (remarks of Sen. Hatch).

[69] Conf. Rep. at 14.

[70] Conf. Rep. at 14.

[71] Testimony of Robert B. Fitzpatrick, Fitzpatrick & Verstegen, on behalf of the Plaintiff Employment Lawyers Assoc., House Hearings at 73-74.

* * *

Applicant Investigations

The use of pre-employment screening and background investigations is widespread among employers. One recent survey indicated that 90 percent of employers use one or more pre-employment screening techniques.[1] Employers have a compelling need to conduct investigations of potential employees to determine if applicants are trustworthy and capable of performing the work. Background checks can reveal whether applicants have the proper credentials for the job and can determine whether applicants have been honest about their experience and performance. Background investigations also may reveal facts that applicants omitted—such as a criminal record or a discharge for cause.

In recent years, applicant investigations have become more important as a result of employer concerns about liability for "negligent hiring" where the employee subsequently injures a fellow employee, customer, or member of the public. In a growing number of cases, injured parties are winning suits against employers on the basis that facts in an employee's past, such as a criminal record, should have alerted the employer that the employee probably would injure someone. Liability is often based on the employer's failure to perform reference checks or to verify past employment. In one case, parents of a child who was sexually assaulted on hotel premises by an employee sued the hotel for negligent hiring and negligent retention of the employee. The court held that the hotel management's prior knowledge of the employee's alcoholism and tendency toward violent behavior was sufficient to submit a claim of negligent hiring to the jury.[2] In another well-publicized case, the Supreme Court of Minnesota imposed liability on the owner of an apartment complex for hiring an apartment manager who later raped a tenant, where the owner did not investigate the employee's prior criminal record.[3] The potential liability faced by employers for the negligent acts of their employees also is one of the reasons employers test job applicants for drugs and alcohol.

Because negligent hiring liability is increasing, employers are conducting more thorough job applicant background investigations and legal experts are advising them to look for incidents in applicants' pasts, such as criminal convictions or psychiatric treatment, that might indicate the applicant has a potential for violence. Other chapters in this report discuss such screening tools as drug testing, polygraphs, and honesty tests. This chapter outlines some of the practical and legal considerations connected with more-commonly used techniques for investigating applicants.

LEGAL ISSUES

All screening techniques are subject to challenge under anti-discrimination laws and privacy theories. The constitutional right of privacy also has been interpreted to give protection to job applicants.

Disparate Impact After Wards Cove Packing

Every stage of the hiring process—applications, interviews, background checks, and testing—is subject to scrutiny under Title VII of the Civil Rights Act of 1964[4] and the Age Discrimination in Employment Act.[5] Employment criteria that disproportionately screen out members of minority groups, members of one sex, or members of other protected classes, that is, have a "disparate impact" on those members, are unlawful unless they are reasonably related to successful job performance or are justified by "business necessity."

The basic analysis set down in 1971 by the U.S. Supreme Court in *Griggs v. Duke Power*[6] remains in effect, although its scope must be reconsidered in light of several recent decisions. The court held in *Griggs* that the requirement of a high school diploma for being hired for the job in question violated Title

VII because the requirement disqualified black applicants at a substantially higher rate than white applicants, and it could not be shown, based on the past experience of the employer, to be significantly related to successful job performance. Subsequent decisions have applied disparate impact analysis to all scored tests, including psychological tests, honesty tests, and polygraph tests; to non-scored "objective" criteria, including prior arrests, convictions, credit ratings, and references from past employers; and to subjective evaluations such as interviewers ranking applicants after conducting interviews.

Several courts have applied two general principles that have been adopted by the Equal Employment Opportunity Commission (EEOC):

- If an inquiry is made or a screening technique is used prior to employment, it presumptively played some role in the hiring decision;[7] and

- The use of any individual procedure that has an adverse impact is discriminatory unless the procedure has been "validated" in accordance with the EEOC Uniform Guidelines on Employee Selection Procedures.[8]

Many courts have upheld the EEOC's position that arguing that the employer's overall recruitment and selection process does not have a discriminatory impact is not an acceptable defense for using a discriminatory selection device.[9]

The Supreme Court addressed the application of *Griggs* and the uniform guidelines to subjective criteria and certain "objective" criteria in June 1988 in *Watson v. Fort Worth Bank & Trust*.[10] *Watson* involved a bank's subjective practices for promotion to supervisory positions, especially subjective performance ratings by supervisors. The lower court held that the disparate impact model could not be applied to subjective procedures, and that the claims of the plaintiffs, female employees passed over for promotion, could be analyzed only for disparate treatment; that is, each rejected applicant had to show that she was denied a promotion for discriminatory reasons, and that the supervisors' evaluations were a pretext for discrimination. The Supreme Court reversed the lower court's decision and concluded that disparate impact analysis could be applied to a subjective or discretionary promotion system. Disparate impact analysis was held to be an appropriate remedy and necessary to deal with the problem of subconscious stereotypes and prejudices. In a plurality opinion, Justice Sandra Day O'Connor also significantly increased the proof plaintiffs needed to establish that a subjective procedure violated Title VII.

The court resolved the issue of whether *Watson* would become a binding precedent in June 1989 in *Wards Cove Packing Co. v. Atonio.*[11] Writing for the majority in the 5-4 decision, Justice Byron White relied extensively on O'Connor's plurality of opinion in *Watson* in setting out guidelines for disparate impact cases. White analyzed the evidentiary standards that apply to all disparate impact cases, and held that plaintiffs must do more than identify statistical disparities in the employer's workforce. They must identify the criteria being challenged, and offer statistical evidence sufficient to show that the criteria caused the disproportionate exclusion of job applicants because they are members of protected groups. In other words, plaintiffs must show that particular hiring practices have a disproportionate impact. Title VII plaintiffs cannot show that a particular procedure has a disparate impact simply by showing that at the "bottom line" a racial imbalance exists in the workforce.

Watson had stressed that statistical disparities must be sufficiently high to raise an inference of causation, and O'Connor noted in a footnote that the four-fifths rule of the uniform guidelines and other mathematical formulas were not binding. That opinion also noted that plaintiffs' statistical evidence had to be reliable, and could not be based on small numbers or incomplete data. *Wards Cove* did not clarify this issue.

The Supreme Court in *Wards Cove* also concluded that, contrary to widespread interpretation of earlier opinions, the ultimate burden of proof never shifts to employers in disparate impact cases. If a defendant satisfies its burden of producing evidence that its employment practices are based on legitimate business reasons, the plaintiff must show that other tests or selection devices without disparate impacts would serve the same purposes, and the court should consider the costs and burdens of those alternatives. The court also held that although a mere insubstantial justification will not suffice, the employer need not show that the challenged practice is essential or indispensable to the employer's business for it to be acceptable. Rather, it is the employer's burden to show that the challenged practice serves, in a significant way, the legitimate employment goals of the employer.

Watson and *Wards Cove* are a mixed blessing for employers. The court has held that subjective hiring and promotional practices can be challenged on a class-wide basis by demonstrating statistical disparities. Thus, it does not matter whether an employer's hiring decisions are based on objective factors such as a past criminal record or falsification on an employment application, or more subjective factors such as evaluations of an employee's performance in a job reference. Any selection device can be challenged. However, employers have several ways to defeat these claims, and *Wards Cove* makes it clear in disparate impact cases that the employee has the burden of proof to demonstrate that a particular hiring criterion results in a disparate impact.

Constitutional Privacy Issues

Even when a public employer has what it believes to be a legitimate need for personal information, it must weigh that need against the applicant's right to privacy under the U.S. Constitution. An example is the job application questionnaire for a special investigations unit that was established by the Philadelphia Police Department to deal with narcotics, prostitution, gambling, internal corruption, and complaints against members of the department. The questionnaire, which had to be answered by any employee who wanted to be transferred to the unit, asked for information on the arrest records of family members, including in-laws; a list of physical defects and any extended time spent in the hospital for any reason; use of prescription drugs; any treatment for mental or psychiatric conditions; gambling and use of alcoholic beverages; a list of each loan or debt over $1,000; and the salary and wages of applicants, their spouses, and their children. These questions were challenged by the employees' union as an unconstitutional invasion of privacy.

A U.S. district court ruled against the city in *Fraternal Order of Police, Lodge 5 v. City of Philadelphia*,[12] stating that all the information requested was protected information within the applicant's "zone of privacy," and that the intrusion by the police department was not justified because of the lack of adequate safeguards against subsequent non-disclosure, the ambiguity of the questions, and the vagueness of the information sought.

The U.S. Court of Appeals for the Third Circuit reversed the district court on nearly all issues. The appeals court recognized that individuals have a constitutional right to privacy that protects their interest in avoiding disclosure of personal matters, but the court explained that the protection was not absolute. Disclosure may be required if the government's interest in disclosure outweighs the individual's privacy interest. The court found that while the medical information sought was within the officers' expectation of privacy, the police department's interest in determining the officers' fitness for stressful positions outweighed that interest. Moreover, similar medical information had historically been requested of all police department applicants, so their justifiable privacy expectations were lower.

A second group of questions sought personal financial information that implicated some privacy interests, particularly when subject to public disclosure.[13] The court held that the applicant's expectations of privacy were reduced because financial data also had been sought from all police department applicants and the public interest in avoiding corruption among these officers outweighed the police officer's limited privacy expectations.

A third group of questions sought information about the applicant's personal life, including gambling, use of alcoholic beverages, and the arrest records of the applicant's family. The court concluded that no privacy interest was present in disclosing arrest records, because arrests are by definition public, and that the request for information on drinking and gambling habits was reasonable based on the purpose of a special investigatory unit. The appeals court agreed only that the city should be enjoined from asking these questions until it developed written, explicit, and binding rules containing adequate safeguards against unnecessary disclosure of the confidential information elicited by the questionnaire.[14]

Common Law Privacy Issues

Although some states have enacted laws restricting employers' inquiries into certain areas such as arrest records, in the absence of specific state constitutional or statutory protections, private employers usually may require disclosure of a broad range of information from job applicants that in the public sector might be protected by a right to privacy. Most states follow the philosophy that employers may ask any personal questions that do not violate state fair employment laws, and job applicants may choose whether to answer them. While in theory an invasion-of-privacy claim or intrusion claim could be raised simply because an employer asked certain questions, such a claim probably would not succeed if the applicant refused to answer. One court has held that where employees refused to answer confidential questions, the questioning constituted at most an attempted invasion of privacy.[15] While this decision implied that employers might be liable for discharging employees for their refusal to answer questions not related to business purposes, no court has held that an employer can be liable for rejecting a job applicant who refuses to answer non-discriminatory questions.

The danger of liability is limited for private employers that seek information directly from applicants if the questions are job-related. Potential employers should ask applicants to consent to additional investigations, including reference checks. If the results of those investigations are kept confidential and access is limited to personnel involved in the hiring process, the risk of a lawsuit based on the public disclosure of private facts or other invasions of privacy is minimal.

ARREST AND CONVICTION INQUIRIES

The best-known disparate impact cases dealing with screening applicants involve the use of arrest and conviction records. In a case involving applicants for an apprenticeship program, the U.S. District Court for the District of Columbia held that all inquiries into arrest records had to be eliminated because no attempt had been made to determine that the inquiries were job-related.[16] EEOC's 1981 "Guide to Pre-Employment Inquiries"[17] codified judicial and EEOC decisions on the use of arrest records, conviction records, and other criteria as pre-employment screening devices. The EEOC guide states that because members of some minority groups are arrested substantially more often than whites in proportion to their numbers in the population, making personnel decisions on the basis of arrest records involving no subsequent conviction has a disproportionate effect on the employment opportunities of these groups. EEOC concluded that without proof of business necessity, an employer's use of arrest records to disqualify job applicants is unlawful. The commission also stated that a conviction for a felony or misdemeanor may not, by itself, constitute a bar to employment because such a bar would have a disparate impact on minorities.

Employers frequently are advised on the basis of the EEOC guide and several early court decisions that it is discriminatory to ask applicants about arrest records, but it is permissible to ask about the number and kinds of convictions for felonies. By implication, inquiries concerning past criminal activity that did not result in a felony conviction are impermissible.[18] Although this usually is sound advice, in a few circumstances, especially where successful applicants will be handling large sums of money, employers may make limited inquiries into past behavior that did not result in a conviction.

One of the leading cases on this subject is *Gregory v. Litton Systems, Inc.*[19] Litton had a policy of disqualifying applicants who had been arrested "on a number of other occasions" for acts other than minor traffic offenses. A U.S. district court found no evidence to support a claim that people who have been arrested but have suffered no criminal convictions can be expected to perform less honestly than other employees. But the court issued an injunction allowing the employer to inquire into the underlying facts concerning the prosecution and trial of any prospective employee, even if the proceeding eventually resulted in an acquittal. Under *Litton*, employers could ask an applicant: "Have you ever been prosecuted and tried for any crime other than minor traffic offenses?" Employers also would be allowed to ask applicants about any pending indictment or prosecution that could lead to their conviction. Employers considering an applicant who is under indictment for a crime that is relevant to the job should delay consideration of that applicant until the charge is resolved.

The judicial decisions in this area suggest that certain inquiries can be made into illegal activity that did not result in a conviction. One line of questions sometimes asked in interviews is whether an applicant has ever engaged in unlawful conduct on the job. The focus of these questions is not on arrest, but on actual conduct.

Such questions may include:

- Have you ever stolen any property from a previous employer?

- Has any supervisor ever accused you of theft, fraud, or embezzlement?

- Have you engaged in shoplifting, fraud, theft, or embezzlement in the last 10 years?

- Have you ever lied to a previous employer?

- Have you ever signed a written statement admitting that you engaged in any type of theft?

An applicant would have difficulty demonstrating that answers to these questions have a disparate impact on minorities. Even if they do have such an effect, the questions are related to past job performance. Employers that use questions like these should limit the period covered—for example, to the last five or 10 years—and should define the unlawful conduct that is significant based on the job. Limiting the questions in this way reduces the risk that an applicant can charge a rejection was based on outdated, irrelevant acts.

The more difficult issue is the permissibility of questions regarding arrests at the request of a previous employer ("Have you ever been arrested for fraud, theft, or embezzlement from a previous employer?") or arrests for certain types of larcenous crimes ("Have you ever been arrested for theft or embezzlement?"). It may be permissible to ask applicants for positions as financial officers, treasurers, or other positions with access to large sums of money narrowly tailored questions regarding arrests, followed by questions concerning the circumstances of the arrest and the disposition of the case. Answers to these questions then can be used, in combination with a background check, to determine whether the applicant engaged in unlawful conduct or was accused wrongfully. Investigations always should focus on the applicant's past conduct, not on arrests.

In some states these inquiries are illegal. Illinois law, for example, makes it discriminatory to base any employment decision on an arrest from which no conviction resulted.[20] In addition, EEOC interpretive decisions of Title VII are more restrictive than the existing judicial decisions. The EEOC tends to be very strict on employers' use of arrest and conviction records in screening job applicants. The majority of the commission's interpretive decisions find the employer's practices unlawful unless a strong business justification existed.[21] It is unclear how much weight the courts will give to these decisions and other EEOC guidelines in cases brought after *Wards Cove*.

Employers that inquire about job applicants' past illegal acts, arrests, or convictions, must stress to them that the mere fact that they have been convicted or have engaged in illegal conduct will not alone disqualify them. Judicial decisions on the use of conviction records indicate that convictions should be cause for rejection only if their number, nature, and recentness would cause the applicant to be unsuitable for a position. The EEOC recommends that a statement to this effect be included on the job application. The following sample statement is taken from the commission's guidelines on pre-employment inquiries:

> This information will not necessarily be a bar to employment. Factors such as the age and time of the offense, the seriousness and nature of the violation, any rehabilitation, and your subsequent employment history, will be taken into account.

JOB APPLICATIONS AND INTERVIEWS

Job applications are the first tool most employers use in screening applicants. Employers should view job applications as the primary source of information for the rest of the applicant investigation. Applications should provide enough space to enable job applicants to discuss in detail why they left previous positions. Although applicants frequently have more than one supervisor who is familiar with their work, most applications ask for only one supervisor's name. If applicants are asked to list only one supervisor, they will pick the one they think will give them the best reference. To combat this tendency, the application should ask applicants to list all supervisors who evaluated their job performance, including immediate and second-level supervisors, plus all people who supervised them at any time while they were employed at each previous employer.

Many corporations rely on resumes prepared by applicants when filling many higher-level management and professional jobs. Although this is considered an advantage in recruiting professionals and managers, it can be a costly mistake. Many job applications require applicants to put in writing a great deal of information that they would not put on a resume, such as having been fired from a previous job.

Job applications also can be used, in addition to interviews or in place of them, to ask difficult questions about applicants' histories or illegal conduct. This way, any false or deceptive statements made by the applicant are preserved in writing, and they cannot be denied in subsequent litigation. If the inquiries are job-related, their appearance on an application, when combined with a statement that all information will be verified, may result in a high number of admissions of previous misconduct. Employers also may want to adopt policies that disqualify applicants if they give any false information. Firms that adopt such policies should state them clearly on their job applications.

Much of the information on which employers base their hiring decisions is obtained in the initial interview. Good interviews offer many advantages. It has long been recognized that each person communicates at several levels, and much more communication occurs at the non-verbal level through gestures, posture, and eye contact than through spoken words. An observant, trained interviewer also can detect evasive responses or uneasiness regarding certain areas of inquiry, and these should be investigated further.

The final step in any job application or initial interview should be to obtain the applicant's consent, in the form of a waiver or release, for the employer to conduct a subsequent investigation. All waivers should be in writing, either at the end of the application itself, or on a separate document signed when the application is signed. Waivers should include:

- Information about the entire pre-employment screening procedure;

- If any testing is to be conducted, a statement to that effect, along with the applicant's consent to be tested as a condition of employment, and disclosure of any absolute disqualifying factors, such as the detection of certain illegal substances during a confirmed drug test;

- A statement that the employer will conduct background checks to verify information on applications;

- Language making clear that the applicant gives the company permission to make more detailed inquiries to present or past employers, and will consent to the release of information by those employers; and

- A statement that gives the employer permission to discuss the results of the investigation with the people who conduct the investigation and those responsible for hiring. This may protect the employer from any claims that it republished defamatory remarks made by a prior employer.

The increase in defamation claims by former employees has made it more difficult for prospective employers to obtain honest references. (See Chapter XVI.) One possible solution is to have applicants execute a release and covenant not to sue, stating that their previous employers can give a reference without being liable for defamation. It is unclear whether previous employers could enforce this type of release.[22] Factors that affect the validity of any release include whether the parties negotiated at arm's length and whether the agreement was knowingly and truly voluntary. It also must be shown that job applicants who sign such releases understood that they were agreeing to release any claim of defamation, regardless of what the previous employer might say.[23] These are legitimate concerns of previous employers that could be subject to defamation claims. For prospective employers (who will be receiving defamatory statements, not making them), job applicants' signatures on covenants not to sue may help overcome reluctance of applicants' previous employers to provide complete and accurate references and job evaluations.

BACKGROUND CHECKS

Ninety-six percent of all employers conduct some type of background check of job applicants.[24] At a minimum, applicants' current or immediate-past employers usually are asked to provide information on the applicants' abilities and performance. Background investigations can show that applicants are honest and dependable, or that they have lied about every significant aspect of their background. Background checks sometimes are time-consuming and expensive. The process of obtaining accurate information also is made more difficult by the fact that most applicants name references who will provide only favorable information, and by previous employers' desires to help former employees obtain a new job, either out of altruism or a desire to reduce the risk that the employee will sue for wrongful discharge. The increase in defamation actions also has led many companies, on the advice of counsel, to limit responses to verification of the names of former employees, their positions, and their years of employment. One recent survey found that prospective employers do not check references of many job candidates because they think former employers will not cooperate because they are afraid they will be sued.[25]

Despite these obstacles, employers should not abandon background investigations. The process of verifying information on applicants' resumes or job applications, such as dates of employment, education, and other credentials, can reveal that applicants have lied to prospective employers. Mis-representation of education and work history is increasing, and is detected by more than 25 percent of corporate executives who recruit new employees.[26] Falsified applicant information is a valid reason not to hire an applicant, and thus prevent a dishonest job seeker from becoming a potentially dishonest employee.

Background investigations comprise at least these three stages:

- First, verifying all information on applicants' resumes or job applications;

- Second, checking applicants' criminal and/or civil records; and

- Third, conducting interviews with personal and professional references, including prior employers, in an effort to determine whether applicants have engaged in misconduct or dishonest behavior at previous jobs, and to determine whether they exhibited positive traits like loyalty and honesty.

Many investigations, such as verification of educational background, can be conducted by the company's personnel officer without paying agency fees or hiring outside investigators. According to National Employment Screening Services, 97 percent of all higher education institutions will verify job applicants' degrees and/or dates of attendance, and almost 85 percent will confirm this information over the phone if they are given information on individuals such as their Social Security number, dates of attendance, or other information usually contained on a job application.[27] Nearly every company will verify whether applicants were employed, their positions, job duties, and the dates of employment. This type of verification can reveal any discrepancies in job titles or positions that applicants claimed they held, padding of job descriptions, and gaps in employment not obvious on the application or resume.

A recent survey by New York placement expert Ward Howell revealed that only 14 percent of human relations executives will "comment candidly" about past employees without the consent of the employee.[28] Employers can increase their chances of obtaining comprehensive, honest references in an increasingly litigious society by contacting the person best suited to provide them. In most cases, these are applicants' immediate supervisors. Recruiters have found that even at companies where personnel departments will verify only limited information about ex-employees, supervisors are willing to be much more open. This is because supervisors, who are responsible for hiring good candidates, need the same candor when they obtain references. Applicants' co-workers also may be good sources of information.

Employers can take several steps to increase the likelihood they will obtain valid information from previous employers:

- If you have obtained releases from applicants, tell their previous employers.

- Let references know that you already have learned a great deal from applicants concerning the circumstances of their departure from the reference's firm, implying that you are trying only to verify that information. If the information is false, the reference is more likely to say so.

- Focus your first questions on factors for which the previous employer should have documentation, such as annual performance evaluations ratings and promotions or demotions.

- Seek opinions on applicants' personal characteristics—"Was this a loyal, trustworthy employee?" A reluctance to answer or evasive answers to such open-ended questions may indicate the applicant caused problems.

- Use narrow, specific questions. They usually achieve better results than broad, open-ended questions because most people will not volunteer negative information, but if they are asked a specific question they will answer it.

Which information is most useful to a prospective employer depends on the industry and type of job for which applicants are applying. Questions tailored to fit the job for which the worker is applying are best, whether they deal with past job performance or specific types of misconduct. Because of this, employers should not use standard form interview checklists designed for all positions. Their convenience usually is outweighed by the vague, general responses they are likely to elicit.

Checking references creates several legal risks. Even where an applicant has signed a release, an employer may be liable for invasion of privacy if specific questions intrude unreasonably on the applicant's private life in areas that are entitled to privacy. The more attenuated the question is about past job performance or dishonesty on the job, the greater the risk. Narrowly tailored questions regarding specific dishonest or illegal acts, such as cheating on tax returns or engaging in street crime, are not likely to be entitled to privacy.

Defamation poses another risk. A prospective employer can be held liable for defamation if it republishes defamatory remarks made by another employer. Employers seeking references, like those providing them, can assert a qualified privilege in disseminating the remarks, but only if the dissemination is limited to people with a "need to know." Therefore, interviewers should discuss negative references only with the person who is deciding whether to hire the applicant involved. Under no circumstances should negative references be discussed with co-workers, supervisors, or company officials unless they are involved in the decision-making process.

CREDIT CHECKS

Some 25 percent of employers that responded in a May 1988 survey said they investigate job applicants' credit records, although only a few said they do so for all applicants.[29] Credit reports can provide a great deal of information about applicants' current financial situations. The reports may indicate whether applicants have engaged in such illegal activities as credit card fraud, and they may contain information about their previous employment or interviews with other people that reveal discrepancies in their job applications. These possible advantages must be weighed against the fact that employers must comply with federal and state fair credit reporting laws. The use of credit references as a screening technique also can be challenged on discrimination and privacy grounds.

Under the federal Fair Credit Reporting Act,[30] a "consumer report" is defined as any written or oral information bearing on a person's credit worthiness, credit standing, character, general reputation, personal characteristics, or mode of living prepared by any consumer reporting agency. Any employer that denies a job to an applicant, either wholly or in part on the basis of information contained in a consumer report, must advise the applicant of this fact and must provide the name and address of the consumer reporting agency that provided the report.[31] When an employer intends to obtain or causes to be prepared an investigative consumer report based on interviews with friends, neighbors, associates, or past employers for use in hiring, promotion, reassignment, or retention of an employee, the employer first must notify the applicant or employee, in writing, that such a report will be prepared. The act allows employers not to notify people who are being considered for jobs or promotions for which they did not apply.[32] If a consumer reporting agency compiles information for employment purposes from public records (including arrest, indictment, and conviction records), the agency must inform the applicant ("consumer") that the public record information is being reported, and must give the applicant the name of the employer that requested it, unless the agency has strict procedures to assure the timeliness and accuracy of its information. No criminal records of any kind or any other adverse information can be included in any credit report if the information is more than seven years old, unless the report is used in connection with the employment of someone who will earn more than $20,000 a year.[33] Several states also have some form of consumer credit or investigation reporting laws. Many of these laws are similar to the federal law, but they vary in the ways in which such reports can be used for employment purposes, the notice that must be given to applicants or employees, the information available to applicants, and applicants' right to sue.

The use of credit reports also can be challenged under Title VII. The EEOC "Guide to Pre-Employment Inquiries" states that rejection of applicants because of poor credit ratings has a disparate impact on minority groups and hence has been found unlawful by the commission unless business necessity can be shown. Other inquiries into applicants' financial status, such as bankruptcy, car ownership, or length of residence at an address, also may violate Title VII.[34] Proving a business justification for these types of checks may be difficult in light of research showing that economic pressures on applicants does not, contrary to widespread belief, show a correlation to most types of employee theft other than embezzlement, a finding which indicates that "need" explains only a portion of workplace crime.[35]

To minimize the risk of successful Title VII challenges, employers can limit the use of the credit check to verifying other information on employment applications, or use them only for jobs that involve company finances or provide access to large sums of money. One court has upheld, under the business necessity test, a bank's requirement of favorable credit investigations as a condition of hiring, finding that such tests serve a legitimate, job-related purpose when they are used for bank teller positions.[36] Employers should not have credit reports and the remainder of background checks prepared until just before or just after they offer applicants a job. Credit checks and other background investigations are subject to challenge under privacy theories as unwarranted intrusions into the private affairs of applicants. Employers usually can avoid such claims if they obtain releases and inform applicants that credit checks will be conducted.

CRIMINAL RECORD CHECKS

Most screening procedures are designed to determine whether applicants have committed larceny or other illegal acts. The most accurate and objective evidence of such behavior, aside from applicants' admissions of illegal conduct, is an applicant's conviction record. A complete check of all state records of interest to employers is the best way to obtain this information. These include criminal records, driving records, and vital statistics. All of these records provide clues to the characteristics of applicants. Checks of this magnitude take time and usually are expensive. An in-depth check of state records by a private investigator costs from $30 to $200 for each applicant, depending on the thoroughness of the check. Employers also can obtain the information themselves. Most state criminal, driving, and other records on individuals are available free to prospective employers or for a nominal fee. Requests for information such as all misdemeanor or felony records or any civil fraud actions on applicants usually can be made by mail or telephone, provided the employer can supply the appropriate information (including the applicant's name, Social Security number, and date of birth). Some jurisdictions require written releases from the applicant.

Some states prohibit access to criminal records and others restrict their use. Most states are more restrictive with arrest records than with conviction records. Among the most restrictive in releasing criminal records are Delaware, Georgia,

Hawaii, Illinois, Kansas, New Hampshire, North Carolina, Ohio, Rhode Island, South Dakota, and Tennessee. Individual counties within a state may have more-restrictive provisions on access to court or criminal records.

Where employers need to screen a few employees annually, arrest and conviction information usually is available, even in states that forbid employers access to centralized or regional record repositories. In many states, criminal records are available at county locations, so employers should check all of the counties with which applicants have had significant contact.

ENDNOTES

[1] *Recruiting and Selection Procedures*, Personnel Policy Forum Survey No. 146 (BNA May 1988).

[2] *Pittard v. Four Seasons Motor Inn, Inc.*, 101 N.M. 723, 688 P.2d 333 (N.M. Ct. App. 1984).

[3] *Ponticas v. K.M.S. Investments*, 331 N.W.2d 907 (Minn. 1983). *See also Henley v. Prince George's County*, 305 Md. 320, 503 A.2d 1333 (1986)(parents of a child murdered by prison inmate employed by a county work-release program could take their claim against the county for negligent hiring before a jury).

[4] 42 USC 2000e, *et seq.*

[5] 29 USC 621, *et seq.*

[6] 401 U.S. 424, 91 S. Ct. 849, 3 FEP Cases 175 (1971).

[7] *Reynolds v. Sheet Metal Workers, Local 102*, 498 F. Supp. 952, 973, 24 FEP Cases 648 (D.D.C. 1980), *aff'd*, 702 F.2d 221, 25 FEP Cases 837 (D.C. Cir. 1981).

[8] 29 CFR 1607.

[9] *See Connecticut v. Teal*, 457 U.S. 440, 102 S. Ct. 2525, 29 FEP Cases 1 (1982); B. Schlei & P. Grossman, *Employment Discrimination Law* at 101 (2d ed. 1983).

[10] 798 F.2d 791, 41 FEP Cases 1179 (5th Cir. 1986), *vacated*, 108 S. Ct. 2777, 47 FEP Cases 102 (1988).

[11] 107 DLR D-1 (BNA) (June 6, 1989).

[12] 1 IER Cases 574 (E.D. Pa. 1986), *vacated*, 812 F.2d 105, 1 IER 1496 (3d Cir. 1987).

[13] *See Barry v. City of New York*, 712 F.2d 1554, 1559 (2d Cir.), *cert. denied*, 464 U.S. 1017, 104 S. Ct. 548 (1983), *Cf. Plante v. Gonzalez*, 575 F.2d 1119, 1132-33 (5th Cir. 1978), *cert. denied*, 439 U.S. 1129 (1979).

[14] 812 F.2d 120.

[15] *Cort v. Bristol-Myers Co.*, 385 Mass. 300, 431 N.E.2d 908, 115 LRRM 5127 (1982).

[16] *Reynolds v. Sheet Metal Workers Local 102*, 498 F. Supp. 952, 24 FEP Cases 648 (DDC 1980), *aff'd*, 702 F.2d 221, 25 FEP Cases 837 (D.C. Cir. 1981).

[17] *Reprinted in Fair Employment Practice Manual* (BNA) at 443:65.

[18] *See, e.g., Interviewing Skills: More Effective Interviewing Techniques for Better Personnel Selection*, Dun & Bradstreet Business Education Services, 1976 at 53.

[19] 316 F. Supp. 401, 2 FEP Cases 842 (C.D. Cal. 1970), *modified*, 472 F.2d 631, 5 FEP Cases 267 (9th Cir. 1972).

[20] Illinois Human Rights Act, ILL. ANN. STAT. ch. 68, para. 2-103.

[21] *See* Larson, *Employment Discrimination* § 73.21, Matthew Bender, 1983 at 14-18.

[22] *See, e.g., Battig v. Hartford Accident & Indemnity Co.*, 482 F. Supp. 338, 343 (W.D. La. 1987), *aff'd*, 608 F.2d 119 (5th Cir. 1979).

[23] *See generally* 66 Am. Jur. 2d, *Release*, 32 (1973).

[24] *Recruiting and Selection Procedures*, Personnel Policy Forum Survey No. 146 (BNA May 1988) at 22.

[25] "Employers Face Upsurge In Suits Over Defamation," *National Law Journal*, Vol. 9, No. 34, May 4, 1987 at 1.

[26] *Wall Street Journal*, Sept. 6, 1985 at 1.

[27] *The Guide To Background Investigations*, National Employment Screening Services: Tulsa, Oklahoma, 1988 at 379. The 1988 guide lists the names, addresses, telephone numbers, and procedures and fees for obtaining verification information from over 3,500 higher education institutions.

[28] Ward Howell, *Resume Inflation*.

[29] *Recruiting and Selection Procedures*, Personnel Policy Forum Survey No. 146 (BNA May 1988) at 23.

[30] 15 USC 1681, *et seq.*

[31] 15 USC 1681m.

[32] 15 USC 1681d.

[33] 15 USC 1681(c), 1681(k).

[34] *Johnson v. Pike Corp.*, 332 F. Supp. 490, 3 FEP Cases 1025 (C.D. Cal. 1971).

[35] Clark & Hollinger, *Theft by Employees* (Lexington Books, 1983) at 53-61.

[36] *EEOC v. American National Bank*, 420 F. Supp. 181, 21 FEP 1532 (E.D. Va. 1976), *aff'd in part and rev'd in part on other grounds*, 652 F.2d 1176, 26 FEP Cases 472 (4th Cir. 1981).

* * *

Psychological, Honesty Tests

Federal and state restrictions on employers' use of polygraphs have led many employers to try alternative forms of testing in their employee selection procedures. In particular, the use of various types of psychological tests has been increasing, including written honesty tests.

TYPES OF PSYCHOLOGICAL TESTS

Widespread psychological testing began during World War I to classify large numbers of recruits quickly and inexpensively so they could be assigned to appropriate positions. The test comprised "yes-no" questions regarding recruits' fears, obsessions, compulsions, tics, nightmares, and other feelings and was designed to determine whether a person was submissive or dominant in social relationships.[1] The types of psychological tests potentially useful in the employment context have increased rapidly, and they are used widely. Eighteen percent of the companies responding to a 1988 survey used "personality tests" and 31 percent administered some type of mental ability test.[2] Another 1988 survey indicated that 20 percent of employers use personality or psychological tests.[3]

Psychological tests used by employers range from aptitude tests involving simulated "work-sample" problems to complex exams designed to determine a job applicant's primary character and personality traits. The most commonly used tests in the employment context are personality inventories, integrated assessment programs, and honesty tests.[4] Employers use psychological testing in pre-employment screening to eliminate applicants who exhibit anti-social tendencies or lack traits deemed essential to successful job performance. One testing service advertises that because its test "measures the likelihood of an individual learning how to successfully perform any job, applicants can be selected and placed in positions that will neither bore nor frustrate them."[5]

Personality inventories are designed to determine an individual's personal characteristics and behavior by eliciting respondents' evaluations of traits that they think describe themselves. Most personality inventories measure several variables or traits. The California Test of Personality (CTP), a popular personality inventory, asks 180 "yes-no" questions designed to determine such traits as self-reliance, sense of personal worth, feeling of belonging, freedom from withdrawing tendencies, freedom from nervous symptoms, occupational relations, and overall social adjustment.[6] One problem with these tests is the common tendency for people to give answers they believe will make them appear in a better light, rather than answering truthfully. Special questions sometimes are added to detect untruthful or affected answers.[7]

One of the best-known traditional psychological tests is the Rorschach Inkblot Test. The testing procedure involves studying the response of the subject to inkblots of various sizes, shapes, and colors. People who see a lot of human movement in the blots and do not respond to the colors may be said to be thought-oriented rather than action-oriented. Color responses are said to indicate emotionalism, and delays in responding may indicate anxiety. Studies of the Rorschach test have not shown high reliability or validity, especially in the employment context.[8] The test is difficult to use on large groups of applicants, because responses must be interpreted by a qualified expert, and methods of interpretation vary widely.

The intelligence quotient (IQ) test is another well-known psychological test. Although these tests have proven to be reliable and useful tools in predicting academic success, some human resource experts think they are unsuited for most occupational selection because they measure only "intelligence" and do not measure other important traits such as motivation, creativity, or social or mechanical skills that may be important to job success.[9]

The Minnesota Multiphasic Personality Inventory (MMPI), another psychological test sometimes used by employers, tests for psychopathology or deviance. Applicants' test scores are measured against the response patterns of "normal" people as well as people suffering from such maladies as depression, hysteria, and paranoia.[10] Although the test may be useful in diagnosing psychological problems, the absence of psychopathology does not imply competence, good social skills, or other traits of interest to employers. The publisher of the MMPI does not encourage its use as an employment screening device.[11]

Some tests claim to measure vocational interests. Such tests are used most often to counsel high school and college students regarding their vocational plans, but they are sometimes used by employers to develop and assign employees. Applicants who score low probably have interests dissimilar to people in the vocational area and therefore are less likely to succeed on the job. Many vocational-interest tests have proven to be quite reliable and valid.[12]

Testing options may expand in the future. Researchers are trying to develop a system for analyzing "brain waves" in the hope that psychological traits can be discovered based on measurements recorded from the surface of the head and body in the form of magnetic signals. Brain waves are not well understood, despite decades of research. A recent government report states that brain wave analysis potentially could be used to gather extensive information about a subject's psychological state, genetic propensities, or honesty, but cautions that "the implications for privacy would be tremendous ... such technology might actually give the ability to 'read the mind,' removing all possibility of a person's keeping information private."[13]

LEGAL ISSUES

The Equal Employment Opportunity Commission's (EEOC) Uniform Guidelines on Employee Selection Proce-

dure cover any employment procedure that has a disproportionate impact on women or minorities. If a test is shown to
have an adverse impact, the employer must produce "empirical
data demonstrating that the selection procedure is predictive
of or significantly correlated with important elements of job
performance."[14] Under the guidelines, employers may be required to compile complex data showing "content validity,"
"construct validity," "criterion-related validity," or "job-
relatedness" to prove that the test does not disproportionately
screen out minorities and women. Some observers have suggested that the U.S. Supreme Court's decision in *Wards Cove
Packing Co. v. Atonio*[15] renders the EEOC guidelines inapplicable, even though the court did not specifically reject
them.[16] This conclusion is highly controversial and far from
universally accepted. Moreover, disparate impact claims may
still be made under state law, and federal contractors may be
required to submit validation studies under Executive Order
11246, which imposes affirmative action requirements on most
companies that receive federal contracts. Therefore, employers
should avoid using tests that, although facially neutral,
may have a disparate impact on minorities or women.
Critics of psychological testing contend that many tests are cul-
turally biased and reflect only white middle-class values and
experiences.[17]

Some courts have held that psychological testing is justified
where public safety outweighs the individual's right to privacy.
Psychological testing used to screen out unstable or disturbed
applicants from jobs in which they would pose a significant
threat to public safety is reasonable and justifiable, these
courts have concluded. For example, the Nuclear Regulatory
Commission requires certain employees at nuclear power
plants to take psychological tests. In a recent legal challenge to
a psychological testing program at a nuclear power plant, the
U.S. Court of Appeals for the Eighth Circuit recognized the
need for psychological testing to promote public safety and to
exclude potentially dangerous employees from the workplace.

However, the court upheld an arbitrator's determination that the test used was invalid, negative results on it did not constitute good reason for terminating employees, and the employer was unreasonable in not providing for clinical reviews of employees who failed it.[18]

Similarly, in *Redmond v. City of Overland Park*,[19] the court held that a clinical evaluation of a police department employee by trained psychologists was not an invasion of privacy. The department requested that the employee undergo a psychiatric evaluation because she exhibited what department officials considered to be bizarre and paranoid behavior on the job. The court concluded that the employer's interest in insuring that the employee was able to perform her duties outweighed the employee's privacy interest. According to the court:

> ... the local police officials had a substantial, valid interest in disclosing and obtaining this personal information about the plaintiff. The Department was entitled to use reasonable means to determine the plaintiff's ability and fitness to perform the duties of her position before placing her on the streets as an armed police officer.[20]

Employers also need to be concerned about the availability of psychological testing on potential liability for negligent hiring. To date, legal liability has not been found for failing to administer a psychological test to screen disturbed, violent, or dangerous individuals from sensitive occupations. Moreover, the U.S. Court of Appeals for the Fifth Circuit recently did not hold a police department liable for negligently hiring an officer who later raped a fellow officer.[21] The victim sued the police department for negligently failing to have the officer who raped her undergo a more extensive psychological/psychiatric examination. The court held that the police department was not negligent because it had arranged for psychological examination of the officer in compliance with applicable recommended guidelines. The court concluded that "failure to obtain a more complete examination certainly does not constitute gross negligence." However, if tests are developed in the future that screen out dangerous individuals, courts may require employers to use them in selecting employees for sensitive positions involving public safety.

HONESTY TESTS

Written honesty tests are psychological tests designed to determine the integrity of people who take them. Most honesty tests are designed to measure attitudes toward theft. Some researchers maintain that discovering which job applicants have favorable attitudes toward theft is the best way to predict which applicants will steal from the company if they are hired. They believe that people who tolerate stealing by others and who would punish thieves lightly are more likely to be thieves or potential thieves than people who are less tolerant of dishonest acts.[22]

Many honesty tests are being marketed to employers. The oldest is produced by Reid Psychological Systems of Chicago, whose Reid Report was the first written integrity test. The Stanton Corp. of Charlotte, N.C., produces the Stanton Survey, and London House Management Consultants Inc. markets the Personnel Selection Inventory. These three companies lead a growing $15 million-a-year honesty test industry.

Approximately 2 million honesty tests are given each year, according to Reid Psychological Systems. A 1988 survey by BNA revealed that 7 percent of responding organizations used written honesty tests.[23] The testing companies claim that written tests are used by between 5 percent and 10 percent of U.S. businesses.

Honesty tests usually comprise true-false, yes-no, or multiple choice questions, and they take about one hour to complete. The tests contain questions designed to measure applicants' willingness to steal and whether they condone or rationalize dishonest behavior. Other questions are designed to determine whether applicants are lying in an attempt to "outsmart" the test. Still others are merely filler questions that are not scored. Only the test manufacturers know which questions are which and how they are weighted. The tests usually are scored by computer, and some companies can score tests before the job applicant leaves. Applicants are categorized as high-risk, medium-risk, or low-risk, depending on their scores.

To demonstrate the validity of their tests, leading test manufacturers:

- Compare their test's scores to those of polygraph tests given later to the same people;
- Compare their test's results to the dollar value of previous thefts that test takers admit;
- Cite reductions in retail shrinkage at companies that use the tests; and
- Compare the subsequent job performances of applicants who take the tests and are hired with the performances of employees who have not taken the tests.

Stanton Corp. says the results of the Stanton Survey will agree with the results of a polygraph test 90 percent of the time, and another Stanton Corp. study shows that the test-retest reliability of its survey is approximately 90 percent.[24]

An independent literature review by Dr. Paul Sackett and Dr. M.M. Harris questioned the honesty test validity studies in a 1984 article. The authors concluded that comparisons with the polygraph should be dismissed because the polygraph itself is of questionable validity and as a result its findings are often disregarded in the scientific community. They also stressed that studies which rely on admissions of illegal behavior are flawed because applicants may not acknowledge that they have engaged in socially unacceptable behavior such as stealing. Also, Sackett and Harris argued that, while past behavior may be a valid basis for predicting future behavior, it is not always accurate and therefore it alone should not be used to determine the test's accuracy.[25]

In a 1989 update of the article, Sackett said studies that used the incidence of detected theft to determine a test's validity found that 75 of 91 employees found to be thieves had failed the London House PSI honesty test, and 49 of 66 of employees fired for gross misconduct, including theft, had failed the PDI Employment Inventory. However, the author noted that these studies also found that 58 percent of the employees not fired for misconduct failed the London House test, and 29 percent of those not fired for misconduct failed the PDI test. Sackett also noted in the original article and his update that in most studies high correlations usually were found between the attitude sections of various honesty tests and the self-admissions of dishonest or criminal behavior by the people who took the tests.[26]

Sackett concluded in 1989 that "a more compelling case that integrity tests predict a number of outcomes of interest to organizations can be made today than at the time of earlier review." He noted that many more criteria-related validity studies using external criteria are now available, and that they are more accurate than studies that rely on admissions of illegal behavior.[27] However, Sackett pointed out that these more favorable conclusions are tainted by the fact that the vast majority of the research on this topic reviewed by him and other authorities was conducted by affiliates of the test manufacturers. Sackett also observed that "the proprietary nature of scoring keys for many tests makes independent research difficult."[28]

Critics have expressed concern about the possibility of high false-positive rates with honesty tests. State and federal regulation of polygraphs was prompted primarily by false-positive rates as low as 5 percent. It is relatively easy to study false-positive polygraph results by using external evidence that a person did or did not lie or commit a crime in the past. However, honesty tests claim to be able to predict future behavior more than they reveal past behavior. False-positive results can be detected only by tracking rejected applicants to see if they later engage in dishonest behavior. Due largely to the logistical problems involved, few tracking studies have been conducted. Stanton Corp. offers experimental data showing that the number of false-positives generated by its honesty test is approximately equal to the number of false negatives.[29]

All of the major honesty test manufacturers claim their products comply with the EEOC guidelines and that their studies show no adverse impact on protected classes. James Walls, senior vice president of marketing for Stanton Corp., says "some minorities actually fare better on the tests." Reid Psychological Systems claims that "no cases in which a decision of adverse impact was rendered either against a client or Reid" have occurred. Nevertheless, the tests are open to legal challenges. Some sections, which inquire into possible past and present illegal conduct, drug and alcohol use, and personal background, resemble a series of interview questions. The answers to these questions, including admissions of past illegal behavior, sometimes are made available to employers.

An argument can be made that each interview-type question on these tests is subject to challenge for its disparate impact on minorities and on the basis that it is not job-related. Individual questions also could be challenged on privacy grounds by job applicants, especially those seeking public-sector jobs. However, applicants or employees who challenge the use of individual questions may have to prove that the particular question resulted in disparate impact or disparate treatment. This would be difficult, and perhaps impossible, if the employer received only the overall test result (for example, "high-risk") and not answers to individual questions. It is also unclear, as a result of *Wards Cove Packing*, whether an employer sued for disparate impact would have to provide a business justification for each question being challenged or only for the test as a whole.

Honesty tests are largely unregulated by the states, and no successful legal challenges to their use have been reported. Some states prohibit employers from probing some areas that are included on honesty tests, and a few states limit the use of written psychological tests. Massachusetts prohibits prospective employers from inquiring into applicants' criminal pasts and their drug and alcohol abuse tendencies. Under Rhode Island law, honesty tests cannot be used if the results form the primary basis for an employment decision. Some honesty-test manufacturers have devised separate tests for use in these states.

In Alaska, California, Delaware, Maryland, Wisconsin, and Washington plaintiffs could argue that state laws banning or limiting polygraph tests extend to written honesty tests. Laws in these states ban or limit polygraphs "and any test purporting to test the honesty of an employee or potential employee" or "other similar tests." No reported case has involved interpretation of the word "similar" in these laws, and written honesty tests are not expressly included in the language of any of these laws. Such a challenge was rejected in Minnesota. Although the Minnesota polygraph law regulates "any test purporting to test the honesty of any employee," the Minnesota Supreme Court ruled in *State v. Century Camera Inc.*[30] that this language is limited to tests that measure physiological changes, and excludes written psychological questionnaires.

Honesty tests have attracted significant attention since the federal Polygraph Protection Act was passed in 1988. The Office of Technology Assessment in mid-1989 was studying honesty tests at the request of several members of Congress. The American Psychological Association (APA) has requested 21 publishers of written honesty tests to provide information on the scientific basis of their tests, how they are scored, and how the test results are used. The APA also has asked test manufacturers to release their scoring keys to enable independent researchers to conduct validation studies.[31]

GUIDELINES FOR TESTING

Most psychological tests rely on statistical probability and correlation data to determine how well a score on a particular test predicts actual behavior or job performance. For example, manufacturers of personality inventory tests claim such tests detect personal traits that indicate how much applicants will like the jobs for which they are applying. Such traits are selected by analyzing the dominant traits of people who have such jobs and perform them well and like them, and by devising tests that detect these traits in the people who take them. Employers that are considering using such tests should consider the skills or traits that a particular test purports to measure and compare those traits with a job analysis of the tasks applicants would be required to perform on the job for which they are being tested.

Even if psychological tests are properly designed and administered, they usually should not be used as the only criterion for accepting or rejecting job applicants. Psychological test scores should be considered with other criteria such as interviews, references, and other qualifications. One psychological textbook says employers can use psychological screening programs more effectively if they:

- Know what skills and type of behavior are required by the jobs for which the tests are being used;

- Determine how close a particular set of scores is to these requirements; and

- Make decisions on the basis of statistical data in addition to personal data.[32]

Before employers decide to use psychological tests, they should determine whether they are practical, reliable, and valid. Such tests should be easy to administer and employers should be able to use test scores and ratings properly without difficulty. Tests are reliable if people score in the same ranges when they retake them. Tests are not reliable if people who take them receive significantly different scores each time they take them. Validity is the most important criterion for such tests. A valid test measures what it purports to measure, such as intelligence, honesty, or personality traits, and its results can be applied to a particular situation. For example, an intelligence test could be valid for measuring reasoning skills, but not for job success. Tests probably are efficient and effective if independent researchers have determined that they are reliable and valid, and that they can be administered easily and their results can be used easily. However, tests that meet these criteria do not necessarily comply with the EEOC guidelines and laws that may apply if they are used as employment screening devices.

Employers also should be particularly concerned with maintaining strict confidentiality of employee and job applicant psychological assessments. Some tests ask questions regarding such personal matters as sexual fantasies and body functions, forcing test subjects to reveal information about themselves that most would prefer to keep private. In using tests designed to detect mental deficiencies or psychopathology, confidentiality is extremely important because of the stigma attached to negative results. Publication or release of such information may give rise to liability for defamation. All applicants and employees who are tested should be informed of the purpose of the test in a forthright manner. Such disclosure will reduce the chance that subjects will think that their privacy is being invaded. Subjects also should be assured that the results will be kept confidential and that they will have access to the results.

ENDNOTES

[1] L. Aiken, *Psychological Testing And Assessment* (1976) at 258-59.

[2] *Recruiting and Selection Procedures*, Personnel Policies Forum (BNA), May 1988 at 19.

[3] P. Blocklyn, "Preemployment Testing," *Personnel*, February 1988 at 66.

[4] "True Or False?," *Industry Week*, Jan. 20, 1986, at 44.

[5] Wonderlic, 1989 Catalog, *Employment Tests And Procedures*.

[6] L. Aiken, *supra*, at 259-60.

[7] "Tests To Target Dependability," *Nation's Business*, March 1989 at 25.

[8] L. Aiken, *supra* at 276.

[9] *Id.* at 66-69.

[10] "Can You Pass The Job Test?" *Newsweek*, May 5, 1986 at 48.

[11] *Money*, June 1974 at 41.

[12] F. Brown, *Principles of Educational And Psychological Testing*, 3d ed. (1983) at 384, *et seq.*

[13] *The Electronic Supervisor: New Technology, New Tensions*, U.S. Congress, Office of Technology Assessment, OTA-CIT-333 (Washington, D.C.: U.S. Gov't Printing Office, Sept. 1987) at 138.

[14] 29 CFR 1607.5(B).

[15] 109 S. Ct. 2115, 49 FEP 1519 (1989).

[16] Craver, "Civil Rights in Employment: A Look at 3 Recent Supreme Court Rulings," *Employment Practices* (CCH) Rep. 364, July 17, 1989.

[17] G. Groth-Marnat, *Handbook of Psychological Assessment* (1984) at 31-32.

[18] *Daniel Construction Co. v. IBEW Local 257*, 856 F.2d 1174, 129 LRRM 2429 (1988).

[19] 672 F. Supp. 473, 45 FEP 591, 2 IER Cases 1439 (D. Kan. 1987).

[20] 2 IER Cases 1446.

[21] *Wassum v. City of Bellaire*, 861 F.2d 453, 3 IER 1772 (5th Cir. 1988).

[22] T.L. Baumer & D.P. Rosenbaum, *Combating Retail Theft: Programs and Strategies*, Butterworth, Boston, Mass., 1984.

[23] *Recruiting and Selection Procedures*, Personnel Policies Forum (BNA), May 1988 at 17.

[24] Douglas L. Grimsley, "Test-Retest Reliability of the Stanton Survey Integrity Measure," published by Stanton Corp.

[25] P.R. Sackett & M.M. Harris, "Honesty Testing for Personnel Selection: A Review and Critique," *Personnel Psychology*, Vol. 37, 1984 at 221.

[26] Sackett, Paul, "Integrity Testing for Personnel Selection: An Update," *Personnel Psychology* 1989, at 507-08.

[27] Sackett, et al., (1989) at 520.

[28] *Id.* at 521.

[29] Homer Reed, "A Survey of Employment Related Behavioral Traits," published by Stanton Corp.

[30] 309 N.W.2d 735 (1981).

[31] 255 DLR A-3, (BNA) Nov. 28, 1988.

[32] *Functional Psychological Testing: Principles and Instruments* (R. Cattell & R. Johnson, eds., 1986) at 443.

* * *

AIDS

No medical issue in recent history has caused more concern in the workplace than acquired immune deficiency syndrome (AIDS). Ten percent of the companies responding to a recent nationwide survey had experienced at least one employee with AIDS.[1] Another survey indicated that 98 percent of firms with 700 or more employees have had an employee or dependent of an employee diagnosed with AIDS.[2] Public health officials and other experts predict that the number of new AIDS cases will grow by more than 60 percent between 1989 and 1992.[3] A recent U.S. General Accounting Office (GAO) report suggests that because of bias in the way AIDS cases are identified and reported, such studies may be underestimating the number of future AIDS cases by as much as 50 percent.[4] The GAO concluded that between 300,000 and 480,000 people in the United States will contract AIDS by 1991. U.S. Public Health Service (PHS) estimates that between 1.2 million and 1.5 million individuals currently are infected with the human immunodeficiency virus (HIV).[5] Economists have forecast that the total annual cost of AIDS may reach $64 billion in 1991, including $55 billion in lost productivity.[6] The PHS has estimated that "cumulative lifetime medical costs for treating AIDS patients diagnosed in the five years beginning in 1988 are estimated at $24.3 billion."[7] Despite the increasing prevalence of the disease in the workplace and its significant impact, only 24 percent of the responding companies in one survey reported that they have an established AIDS policy.[8]

MEDICAL BACKGROUND

To evaluate the issue of AIDS in the workplace accurately, it is necessary to understand the disease. AIDS is the final stage of a progressive disease that destroys the body's immune system—its ability to prevent disease. AIDS is a disease caused by a virus called HIV (human immunodeficiency virus). The virus attacks white cells in human blood. When a person's immune system becomes sufficiently impaired, that person becomes susceptible to a wide range of bacteria, viruses, and other organisms that can cause life-threatening illnesses.

HIV disease comprises three recognized stages. The first stage is exposure to the virus. A positive test for the AIDS antibody in a subject's blood system indicates the person has been exposed to HIV. People who test positive are said to be "seropositive."

The second stage, AIDS-related complex (ARC), is characterized by exposure to the virus and the existence, for at least three months, of one or more symptoms such as fever, night sweats, sudden weight loss, fatigue, or swollen glands, with no other medical explanation for the symptoms.

The third stage, diagnosis of AIDS, results when a person tests positive for the AIDS antibody, has an otherwise unexplained weakened immune system, and has contracted infections or cancers that would not normally pose a threat to a person with a healthy, functioning immune system. One example of such an "opportunistic infection" is Kaposi's sarcoma, a malignancy usually seen only in elderly men.[9] Another common example is pneumocystis carinii pneumonia, a rare type of pneumonia. These and other infections that attack people with weakened immune systems are frequently disabling. Some therapeutic drugs have been used, with limited success, to slow the progress of HIV infection or to help combat certain infections. AZT is the best known of these drugs, and many others are being tested.[10] But no known cure exists for HIV disease, and no vaccine exists to prevent it.

AIDS has a long latency period; it can take up to nine years for symptoms to appear. According to current medical estimates, anywhere from 20 percent to 30 percent of those infected with the AIDS virus may develop AIDS within five years.[11] It can take up to six months after exposure to the

AIDS virus before the AIDS antibodies appear in a blood test. Current research indicates that it may be nine years or more before an infected person shows the symptoms of ARC or AIDS. The U.S. Surgeon General estimates that by the end of 1991, 270,000 cases of AIDS will have occurred in the United States and almost two-thirds of the people with AIDS will have died. These figures do not include people who show the symptoms of ARC. People with ARC may be severely incapacitated at times and may have those symptoms for many years, but they will not be diagnosed as having AIDS until they develop one of the infections that are part of the definition of the AIDS disease.[12] Moreover, many experts believe that the number of infected individuals in the United States may far exceed the number so far reported.[13]

No test that determines whether someone has AIDS or will get AIDS is commercially available. Several recognized tests licensed by the Food and Drug Administration (FDA) to screen blood for the AIDS virus can determine only whether subjects have the AIDS antibody in their blood system. A determination that someone is seropositive means that the person's body produced antibodies to combat the AIDS virus at some point in the past. These tests cannot measure whether a person has or will develop ARC or AIDS. The tests, however, are accurate about 97.5 percent of the time, and the use of a confirmation test usually can detect initial false-positive test results.[14]

Employers' interest and involvement in AIDS stems from many factors. Because AIDS is a disabling and often-fatal disease, financial issues involving the coverage of workers under employer-sponsored medical plans have arisen. In addition, practical and legal concerns exist about the extent to which employers must accommodate people with AIDS-related illnesses. Aside from these financial issues, most of the discussion and concern surrounding AIDS in the workplace has arisen because of co-workers' fears that they will contract the disease, fears of employers about the possible spread of AIDS to workers or customers, and fears of the general public. The evidence is now strong that these fears are largely unfounded.

The overwhelming weight of medical evidence available to date is that AIDS is not transmitted by casual contact, such as that which occurs between employees in most workplaces. Over 93 percent of all reported AIDS cases have been transmitted by sexual contact (especially among homosexuals) or by sharing contaminated intravenous drug equipment with an infected individual, according to the Centers for Disease Control (CDC). Hemophiliacs and other recipients of transfused blood or blood components account for less than 4 percent of all cases.[15] The CDC estimates that the risk of HIV transmission for health care workers following a needle-stick injury is less than 1 percent--or three to five infections per 1,000 people stuck by contaminated needles.[16]

Citing current medical evidence, the CDC has said no known risk of transmission of AIDS to co-workers, clients, or consumers exists in most employment settings. Recent research shows that the AIDS virus is extremely fragile, and breaks down when it comes in contact with the air or most surfaces. The virus needs a warm, moist environment to be transmitted. Blood and genital fluids provide such an environment. While experiments show that saliva and tears can contain traces of HIV,[17] they do not transmit the virus.[18]

The CDC also has found no evidence that AIDS is transmitted from clients to personal service workers, such as hairdressers, barbers, or cosmetologists, or from those workers to clients, and that the only known risk would be where one of the individuals suffered a needle-stick injury, and blood or other fluids passed from the infected person to the open tissue of the other. For example, CDC recommends that if food service workers injure their hands while preparing food, any food contaminated with blood should be discarded. But even if the food is not thrown away and the injured worker has AIDS, transmission of the disease is extremely unlikely.[19]

CDC has been concerned primarily with the transmission of AIDS between patients and health care workers. The risk of AIDS transmission in this context appears to be very low, especially compared with transmissions of the hepatitis B virus, which results in the death of hundreds of health care workers each year.[20] The CDC has published detailed guidelines regarding the care of AIDS patients and precautions to prevent the transmission of AIDS from patients to health care workers. The guidelines consider all patients and all bodily fluids to be potentially infected with HIV. They focus on the use of protective barriers such as gloves, masks, gowns, and eye wear, coupled with routine infection-control techniques such as hand-washing.[21]

The CDC also has stated that routine testing for evidence of AIDS infection is not necessary for health care workers who perform or assist in invasive procedures or for patients undergoing invasive procedures. CDC says the risk of transmission in these settings is so low that routine tests would do little or nothing additional to stop the spread of the disease if they were conducted in addition to the precautions the agency recommends.[22] The Occupational Safety and Health Administration (OSHA), prompted by several unions, on May 30, 1989, proposed a standard that would require all U.S. employers with workers who are exposed to blood or potentially infectious materials on the job to use training programs, protective clothing, and other measures to safeguard such employees.[23] The proposal also would incorporate CDC's universal precautions. Public hearings on the proposed rule were scheduled for late 1989.

Based on the medical evidence, a wide variety of organizations, including the American Hospital Association (AHA), the American Medical Association (AMA), and the National Education Association (NEA), have strongly recommended against mandatory or routine testing of employees for AIDS.[24] These organizations encourage employers to consider AIDS as a disease, and to treat people with AIDS in a fair and humane manner. Because the medical evidence shows that AIDS cannot be transmitted through casual workplace contact, most authorities agree employees with AIDS should not be removed from their jobs unless they become incapable of performing the duties of the position. This approach probably is necessary to comply with federal and state laws prohibiting discrimination against the handicapped for employers covered by those laws.

HANDICAP AND DISCRIMINATION LAWS

Nineteen states had passed AIDS-related anti-discrimination laws by 1988. These laws have addressed denial of public services (Nebraska, Florida, and Rhode Island) and medical care (Maine, Iowa, and Kentucky), release and use of information (California, Delaware, and Hawaii), and testing and counseling (Nebraska, Florida, and New York).[25] In addition, several states, including California, Florida, Texas, Massachusetts, and Wisconsin, have passed laws that prohibit employers from giving blood tests to detect the presence of AIDS or from using the results of any blood test in making employment decisions.[26] A New York Department of Health position statement says no scientific or medical justification exists for testing current or prospective employees for the AIDS antibody to assess job applicants' employability.[27]

In addition to these state laws prohibiting AIDS testing, employers must consider their obligations under more general state and federal laws that prohibit discrimination against the handicapped. These laws generally prohibit job actions against employees because of handicap or disability if they are qualified for and can perform the job. Fair employment agencies in 33 states and the District of Columbia have stated that they will accept AIDS-related discrimination complaints, and 21 of these have made formal declarations that AIDS-related discrimination is prohibited under state anti-discrimination laws.[28]

At the federal level, the question of whether AIDS is a protected handicap under the Rehabilitation Act of 1973 has not been addressed by the U.S. Supreme Court, but most authorities and courts agree that AIDS is a protected handicap. The Rehabilitation Act covers all federal employees, all private employers who receive federal government contracts in excess of $2,500,[29] and all recipients of federal financial assistance, including any grant, loan, or contract.[30]

In June 1986, the Department of Justice (DOJ) issued a legal memorandum interpreting the coverage of AIDS under the Rehabilitation Act. DOJ said although the disabling effects of AIDS may be considered a handicap under Section 504, the definition of handicapped does not include "the ability to transmit a disease." DOJ therefore concluded that employers could take adverse employment actions against employees with AIDS based on an individual's ability to transmit the disease, or merely the fear of contagion, if the basis for the action was not the actual disability caused by AIDS.[31]

DOJ's view that fear of contagion was not covered under the Rehabilitation Act was rejected by the U.S. Supreme Court in *School Board of Nassau County, Fla. v. Arline*.[32] The plaintiff was an elementary school teacher. After suffering a third relapse of tuberculosis within two years, she was discharged even though the medical evidence did not indicate that she posed a threat to the health of her students. Arline sued the school board under Section 504 of the Rehabilitation Act. The Supreme Court held that in defining a "handicapped individual" the contagious effects of a disease cannot be meaningfully distinguished from the disease's physical effects. Where the contagiousness and the plaintiff's physical impairment each resulted from the same underlying condition, the court said it would be unfair to allow an employer to seize on the distinction between effects of a disease on others and the effects of a disease on the person who has it, and to use that distinction to justify discriminatory treatment. The Rehabilitation Act reaches both those who are impaired and those who are regarded or perceived by others as being impaired; it does not exclude individuals from whom other people fear they will catch the disease.[33]

Having determined that contagious diseases such as tuberculosis are covered by the act, the court directed lower courts to determine on a case-by-case basis whether or not a handicapped individual with a contagious disease is "otherwise qualified" for a particular job. Based on reasonable medical judgments and given the state of medical knowledge about how the disease is transmitted, how long the carrier is infectious, the potential harm to third parties, and the probability that the disease will be transmitted and will cause various degrees of harm, the lower court in each case must determine whether the employee is fit for a particular job and, if not, whether the employer can reasonably accommodate the employee by a transfer to another job.[34]

Although the Supreme Court was careful to state in a footnote to *Arline* that it had not considered the question of whether an HIV-infected person who has not developed AIDS is a handicapped person within the meaning of the Rehabilitation Act, the court did reject the principal arguments made by DOJ in its 1986 AIDS memorandum. DOJ reversed its position a year after the *Arline* decision, following the passage of the Civil Rights Restoration Act (CRRA) and the surgeon general's rejection of DOJ's stance that the three stages of AIDS are medically "discrete."[35] CRRA amended sections 503 and 504 of the Rehabilitation Act and provided that as "such sections relate to employment, such terms do not include an individual who has a currently contagious disease or infection and who, by reason of such disease or infection, would constitute a direct threat to the health or safety of other individuals, or who, by reason of the currently contagious disease or infection, is unable to perform the duties of the job."[36]

Several lower federal courts since have held that AIDS is a protected handicap under Section 504,[37] and many authorities agree that *Arline* can be extended to cover people with AIDS.

In *Chalk v. U.S. District Court*,[38] a U.S. district ordered the Orange County Department of Education to reinstate the plaintiff, a school teacher diagnosed with the HIV virus, to his teaching position. The U.S. Court of Appeals for the Ninth Circuit upheld the order, and agreed with the lower court that *Arline* was fully applicable to people with contagious diseases. The appeal focused on the application of the four factors outlined in *Arline* — nature of risk, duration of risk, severity of risk, and probability the disease would be transmitted — to the facts of the case. The court held that the mere presence of the HIV virus was not a risk but that some of the opportunistic infections that may accompany AIDS could prove a risk in the future. The plaintiff was reinstated until such time as the risk proved more than speculative.

Given the emphasis the Supreme Court *Arline* decision placed on the state of the medical evidence, and the court's comments that public health officials should be relied on for this information, it is likely that most courts considering the question of workplace discrimination against people with HIV will look to the CDC guidelines to determine the risk that AIDS will be transmitted. Because CDC has determined that it is highly unlikely AIDS will be transmitted through casual workplace contact, and that only certain health care workers are at any substantial risk, most employees would be considered "qualified" under the Rehabilitation Act to continue to hold their jobs until AIDS makes them physically unable to do their job.

Legislation proposed in the 100th Congress would have prohibited discrimination against handicapped people by most employers. The bill, entitled the Americans with Disabilities Act, would have extended the Rehabilitation Act to all private employers. The same bill has been re-introduced as S 933, and hearings were held in 1989. The Bush Administration supports most of the bill.[39] As of August 1989, the bill had a good chance of being enacted. If passed, the bill would likely cover employees with AIDS.

CHALLENGE TO AIDS TESTING

Some companies screen current and prospective employees for exposure to HIV.[40] AIDS testing, like other forms of medical testing, raises claims of invasion of privacy. A blood test is an invasive procedure, involving the taking of bodily fluids. The test is designed to expose an employee's medical condition, which is an area where people have been held to have an expectation of privacy when the test is conducted by a government agency. Although AIDS is not confined to any definable group of people, those who test positive for AIDS are often subjected to scrutiny concerning their sexual preference. Because of this, proposals for mandatory AIDS testing by private employers may be subjected to stricter scrutiny than drug tests. Given the absence of significant medical evidence that any risk exists that AIDS will be transmitted in most workplaces, it would be difficult for most employers to provide a business justification for instituting AIDS testing or for discharging or taking other job actions against employees who have AIDS.

Very little litigation has occurred concerning employer attempts to test employees for AIDS. For several years the U.S. Army has been testing recruits and uniformed services personnel for AIDS, and rejecting everyone who tests seropositive. The Army bases this policy on the rationale that the military sometimes operates its own blood bank in wartime, and because soldiers may be exposed to a wide variety of viruses, to which AIDS victims would be especially susceptible.[41]

A similar testing program was instituted by the Department of State to test U.S. Foreign Service applicants for AIDS as part of a comprehensive medical examination prior to appointment or assignment to a new duty station. Under the policy, applicants who test positive for the AIDS infection are barred from employment with the Foreign Service, and current Foreign Service employees who test positive are given a limited medical clearance that allows them to work in the United States and 19 other countries. The State Department says it adopted the policy because employees who test positive would be at a significant risk if they were assigned to countries with levels of infectious disease substantially higher than the level in the United States.

The State Department AIDS policy was challenged by a union representing Foreign Service personnel. In what is currently the leading decision on AIDS testing, the union's request for a preliminary injunction was denied on April 22, 1987. The U.S. District Court for the District of Columbia held that because the State Department's asserted rationale was to determine fitness for worldwide duty, and no evidence of any intent to discriminate existed, the department's testing program could continue.[42] According to State Department officials, the policy was still in effect in July 1989. It is far from clear whether the department's program would survive a challenge under the Rehabilitation Act under the Supreme Court's analysis in *Arline*. If it did, it might be because the department cannot make a reasonable accommodation for AIDS victims by limiting the number of countries to which they can be assigned.

In the case of public employees, requiring an AIDS test would constitute a search and seizure invoking Fourth Amendment analysis. In *Glover v. Eastern Nebraska Community Office of Retardation*, a Nebraska state agency serving the mentally retarded sought to institute mandatory AIDS testing of all employees. The court rejected the agency's argument that the plaintiffs had a diminished expectation of privacy when working in a highly regulated state agency. The court held that given the small chance that a client would contract AIDS from a staff employee in a normal work situation, the use of mandatory testing was unreasonable. A petition for certiorari was filed in May 1989. The U.S. Supreme Court has not decided, at the end of its term, to grant the petition and hear an appeal. However, on July 3, 1989, the Court asked the U.S. Government to present its views on whether the case was properly decided.[43]

In *Leckelt v. Board of Commissioners of Hospital District No. 1*, the court upheld the dismissal of a homosexual hospital employee who refused to be tested after his roommate died of AIDS.[44] The employee, a nurse, had daily responsibility for giving patients intravenous injections and applying and removing dressings from patients. The court concluded that the plaintiff was not discharged because of a fear on the part of the hospital that he had AIDS, but because he was insubordinate in refusing to cooperate with the hospital's legitimate need to control the transmittal of infectious diseases. The court distinguished the case from *Glover* on two points: 1) the risk of spreading infection, and 2) the scope of the testing program. In *Glover*, all staff members had to be tested despite the fact that no risk existed that they would infect anyone. In *Leckelt*, testimony indicated that risk of infection was present and that the testing was narrowly focused.

In July 1987, Georgia became the first state to require AIDS testing for teachers and students in the state's secondary schools. The state board of education approved mandatory AIDS tests for any student, employee, or superintendent who, on reasonable cause, is suspected of having the disease. Teachers who refuse to take the test may be fired for insubordination.[45] The Illinois legislature also passed a controversial law that includes testing of prisoners convicted of sex and drug offenses, marriage license applicants, and some hospital patients. In addition, the law provides for tracking sexual partners of people who test positive for AIDS. The law also requires health care workers with AIDS to notify their employers in writing.[46] By July 1989, some provisions of the law remained unfunded and the legislature had submitted to the governor additional legislation that would repeal the 1987 law, but expand certain testing requirements.

ERISA AND AIDS

Section 510 of the Employee Retirement Income Security Act (ERISA) provides that employers cannot discriminate against participants and beneficiaries of employee benefit plans for exercising their rights under the plans or ERISA, and cannot discriminate for the purpose of depriving them of benefits to which they are or may become entitled.[47] The purpose of this section originally was to protect employees from employers that tried to deprive workers of their minimum pension eligibility, without any legitimate business reasons for doing so.[48] Despite its limited origins, however, Section 510 applies to all employee benefit plans,[49] including such welfare benefits as medical or health insurance. Consequently, Section 510 has been used as a vehicle to counter adverse actions against employees with disabling diseases, including AIDS.[50]

Section 510 of ERISA provides in part that:

> It shall be unlawful for any person to discharge, fine, suspend, expel, discipline, or discriminate against a participant or beneficiary for exercising any right to which he is entitled under the provisions of an employee benefit plan ... or for the purpose of interfering with the attainment of any right to which such participant may become entitled under the plan.

To be successful on a Section 510 claim, employees must establish that the purpose of the adverse action taken against them was to prevent them from attaining benefits or exercising rights.[51] Actual interference with the attainment of a benefit right must occur.[52] While most ERISA actions can be brought only against fiduciaries, a Section 510 action can be brought against any individual, employer, or union.[53] The remedies available to plaintiffs include broad equitable powers to make them whole.[54] To that end, awards have included back pay, front pay, and reinstatement to benefit programs.[55]

Section 510 addresses two types of employer conduct. The law is divided into an "exercise" clause covering present benefits and an "interference" clause covering future benefits or claims.[56] The interference provision has formed the basis for most employees' actions against employers that allegedly interfered with their welfare benefit rights because they were in poor health.

The leading Section 510 case relating to the denial of benefits due to a medical condition is *Folz v. Marriott Corp.*[57] The plaintiff, a general manager of a Marriott hotel, was discharged after he told Marriott management that he had been diagnosed as having multiple sclerosis. His 16-year employment history included numerous promotions, raises, and bonuses. The plaintiff sued Marriott, alleging that he was discharged to avoid liability under several Marriott benefit programs, including disability, sick leave, and a medical benefit plan.

The court found that depriving the plaintiff of benefits was part of the firm's motive for discharging him, and Marriott's claim that the discharge was "for cause" was entirely a pretext. The court based its finding primarily on three factors. First, it drew an inference of unlawful motivation from the timing of the discharge, which took place only a few months after the plaintiff notified management about his illness. Second, when discharging the plaintiff, Marriott did not follow its normal procedures with respect to the poor performance of general managers. The company normally would have put the general manager on probation or transferred him. Finally, the court noted that Marriott stood to gain financially from the discontinuance of benefits, which included a medical program funded 60 percent by Marriott.[58]

Similarly, in *Zipf v. American Telephone and Telegraph,*[59] the plaintiff was discharged for excessive absenteeism resulting from her rheumatoid arthritis. Under AT&T's disability plan, the plaintiff would have been entitled to benefits beginning on the eighth calendar day she was absent from work, and she would have been entitled to extended company benefits on the eighth day. She was discharged on the seventh day.

A U.S. district court dismissed the plaintiff's claim on the theory that she had failed to exhaust her remedies under the plan. The U.S. Court of Appeals for the Third Circuit reversed the decision and remanded the case for trial, noting that the plaintiff's immediate supervisor had said she was discharged to prevent her from qualifying for disability benefits.[60]

As these cases illustrate, any termination of an AIDS patient whom management knows has the disease may trigger a Section 510 claim that the plaintiff was discharged to avoid paying the large medical costs incurred by AIDS patients. An employee who was terminated two weeks after he revealed that he had AIDS filed such a suit in *Doe v. Cooper Investments*.[61] The plaintiff claimed that the company sought to avoid additional costs in health care premiums that would result from his use of health care benefits. The case was settled.[62]

Whether such claims succeed depends on the facts and circumstances of each and whether the plaintiff establishes an improper motive. If employer actions are based on an intent to deprive an AIDS patient of benefits, a Section 510 action usually will succeed. This is true regardless of whether the employer is justifiably concerned about the effect that the high cost of medical premiums may have on its business.[63] The fact that the termination of an AIDS patient will save an employer money is not sufficient to prevail.[64]

It is well recognized by courts that employers may act in their own interests when they make decisions as employers and not as administrators of a benefits plan.[65] A business action that incidentally affects an employee's rights to benefits does not violate Section 510.[66] Therefore, if independent grounds for discharging a worker are evident, such as economic circumstances, an employer may be able to defeat the creation of an inference of improper motive necessary for a Section 510 claim.[67]

ESTABLISHING AIDS POLICIES

Case law and statutory law provide some guidance to employers for their conduct in the workplace. Employers in most states and almost all employers that are federal contractors generally cannot discriminate against employees infected with HIV or who have been diagnosed with ARC or AIDS, if the employee is not a health risk and can perform the job. Because the Rehabilitation Act and most state anti-discrimination laws protect people with HIV, employers covered by these laws also may not reject job applicants solely because they have AIDS. Applicants and employees also can argue that mandatory testing for HIV by employers covered by these laws is not allowed, because no justification exists for most employers to know whether employees have the virus. An employer that tests for AIDS also is vulnerable to invasion of privacy claims.

In addition, if an employee has AIDS or develops it and the employer is covered by the Rehabilitation Act or similar laws, the employer must make reasonable accommodations so the employee can continue in the position. The federal government and some states have addressed the requirements for reasonable accommodation.[68] It can include modification of duties, adjustments to schedules to facilitate additional breaks or medical appointments, part-time employment, or personal assistance. Criteria to determine whether employers are making reasonable accommodations for employees with AIDS are the same as those used to determine whether they are making reasonable accommodations for workers with physical handicaps. These include the size of the business, composition of the workforce, nature of the work, and cost.

In some circumstances, the presence of an AIDS carrier may lead to difficulties in the workplace. The knowledge that a co-worker has AIDS or the fear that one might have the disease could result in demands for testing, the release of confidential information, or work stoppages. In such situations, the legal obligations of the employer are clear: Employers rarely can mandate testing, cannot give into demands that a person with AIDS be removed from the workforce, and cannot release confidential medical information except to those with a need to know.

Circumstances may arise where an employee refuses to work with an individual who has or is suspected of having AIDS. Federal labor laws protect employees from being disciplined when they withhold their services based upon a reasonable, good faith belief that working conditions are unsafe. OSHA regulations confirm the right of employees to "decline to perform their assigned tasks because of reasonable beliefs that working poses an imminent risk of death or serious bodily harm coupled with a reasonable belief that there is insufficient time to seek effective redress" through normal procedures.[69]

Under Section 7(b) of the National Labor Relations Act, employees who walk off the job because of a reasonable belief that working conditions are unsafe can assert that they are engaging in protected, concerted activity.[70] The reasonableness of these responses, and an employer's ability to react to these acts, may depend on how the employer has prepared its workforce to deal with AIDS. If the employees have been educated that AIDS cannot be transmitted through casual contact, they may have difficulty proving that their refusal to work is based upon a "reasonable" fear. The NLRB has not considered this precise issue, but it is likely to consider whether the employer acted to educate the employees about AIDS, and whether the employer's response contributed to the employees' fears. This issue has been raised in one arbitration case. In *Minnesota Department of Corrections,* a prison security guard was discharged for refusing to work with inmates suspected of carrying the AIDS virus.[71] The arbitrator held that an inaccurate memorandum prepared by the employer dealing with the threat of AIDS contributed to the employee's exaggerated fear of the disease and thus justified a lesser penalty.

With advance preparation and education, many of these problems can be avoided. An educational program instituted before any worker gets AIDS probably will be received by employees better than one instituted after an employee contracts the disease and concern and emotions are running high.[72] Educational programs convey management's concern regarding the health of company employees, information on workplace risks and how AIDS is transmitted, and, most importantly, how management expects employees to behave if any of them gets AIDS. To be effective, such programs should comprise more than distributing pamphlets. One recent study indicated that the more comprehensive the educational program, the more likely employee attitudes are to change.[73] Comprehensive education programs also give employers another way to deal with threatened work stoppages. If a group of employees that has been taught the risks associated with AIDS refuses to work with an AIDS victim, the refusal probably would be found to be unreasonable and members of the group could be discharged.[74]

The surgeon general has recommended that employers adopt responses to AIDS that:[75]

- Consider AIDS the same way other illnesses and disabilities are considered under existing health and disability plans and policies;
- Offer AIDS victims the right to continue working as long as they are able to perform their jobs satisfactorily and as long as the best available medical evidence indicates that continued employment does not present a health or safety threat to them, other employees, or customers;
- Make reasonable efforts to accommodate seriously ill workers by providing them, where possible, flexible work areas, assignments, and hours;
- Make satisfactory performance by AIDS victims a condition for continued employment;
- Ask employees to be sensitive to the needs of critically ill colleagues;

- Do not grant employees the right to transfer to avoid working with people with AIDS or those who are HIV positive;
- Maintain confidentiality of employees' medical records, consistent with accepted legal, medical, and management practices;
- Stress in all cases respect for the individual by management and co-workers, consistent with the company's existing practices; and
- Include an educational program based on the best currently available medical knowledge to help employees understand AIDS, and to understand the policies the company has for employees with all disabilities, including AIDS.

Several employer organizations have conducted programs to educate the business community on AIDS and to help develop educational programs. Employers need not implement totally new efforts in this area. Organizations available to assist employers and to educate employee groups include the American Red Cross, the National Leadership Coalition on AIDS in Washington, D.C., and the New York-based American Foundation for AIDS Research. The U.S. Public Health Service publishes many materials that identify workplace resources and information contacts.

In its recommendations to business, the President's Commission on the HIV Epidemic urged employers "to respond to HIV-infected individuals just as employers would to an individual with any other disease or disability, that is, in a compassionate, humane, and fair manner."[76]

ENDNOTES

[1] Leonard, "AIDS, Employment and Unemployment" *Ohio St. L.J.*, v. 49, No. 4, at 929 (1989).

[2] 21 DLR A-3 (BNA) (Feb. 2, 1989).

[3] "Report of the Second Public Health Service AIDS Prevention and Control Conference" *AIDS In the Workplace: Resource Material*, 3rd ed. (BNA 1989).

[4] United States General Accounting Office, *AIDS Forecasting: Undercount of Cases and Lack of Key Data Weaken Existing Estimates*, June 1, 1989, at 2-3.

[5] *AIDS Education: A Business Guide* (American Foundation for AIDS Research, American Council of Life Insurance, Health Insurance Association of America) (1987).

[6] "AIDS Education: A Business Guide" 1987.

[7] 46 DLR A-8 (BNA) (March 10, 1989).

[8] 69 DLR A-10 (BNA) (April 12, 1989).

[9] Report of the Surgeon General on AIDS (U.S. Public Health Service 1986); Centers for Disease Control, "Revision of the Case Definition of Acquired Immune Deficiency Syndrome for National Reporting," *Morbidity and Mortality Weekly Report* (1975).

[10] "Report of the Second Public Health Service AIDS Prevention and Control Conference" *AIDS In the Workplace: Resource Material*, 3rd ed. (BNA 1989).

[11] "Surgeon General's Report on Acquired Immune Deficiency Syndrome" *AIDS in the Workplace: Resource Material*, 3rd ed. (BNA 1989).

[12] "Surgeon General's Report on Acquired Immune Deficiency Syndrome" *AIDS in the Workplace: Resource Material*, 3rd ed. (BNA 1989).

[13] "Is AIDS Underreported?", *Newsweek*, June 19, 1989, at 71.

[14] Barry, "Screening for HIV Infection: Risks, Benefits, & the Burden of Proof," *Law, Med. & Health Care*, v. 14, No. 5-6, at 260-262 (Dec. 1986).

[15] Centers for Disease Control, *HIV/AIDS Surveillance*, July 1989; "Human Immunodeficiency Virus Infection in the United States: A Review of Current Knowledge" *Morbidity & Mortality Weekly Report*, v. 36, No. S-6 at 40 (Dec. 18, 1987).

[16] "Occupational Safety and Health: 7 Critical Issues for the 1990s," (BNA 1989).

[17] Turk, "AIDS: The First Decade" *Employee Relations L.J.* v. 14, No. 4 at 531 (1989).

[18] "Surgeon General's Report on Acquired Immune Deficiency Syndrome" *AIDS in the Workplace: Resource Material*, 3rd ed. (BNA 1989).

[19] Centers for Disease Control, "Summary: Recommendations for Preventing Transmission of Infection with Human T-lymphotropic Virus Type III/lymphadenopathy-associated Virus in the Workplace," *Morbidity and Mortality Weekly Report*, v. 34 at 681, (Nov. 15, 1985).

[20] 12 DLR A-4 (BNA) (Jan. 19, 1989). 3 LRW 675 (BNA) (July 19, 1989).

[21] "Update: Universal Precautions for Prevention of HIV, Hepatitis B-Virus, and other Bloodborne Pathogens in Health Care Settings," *Aids in the Workplace: Resource Material*, 3rd ed. (BNA 1989).

[22] Centers for Disease Control, "Recommendations for Preventing Transmission of Infection With Human Lymphotropic Virus Type III/Lymphadenopathy-Associated Virus During Invasive Procedures," *Morbidity and Mortality Weekly Report*, v. 35 at 221 (April 11, 1986).

[23] 99 DLR A-10 (BNA) (May 24, 1989).

[24] *AIDS In the Workplace: Resource Material*, 3rd ed. (BNA 1989); *Washington Post*, June 21, 1987, at A-1.

[25] State AIDS Policy Center, Intergovernmental Health Policy Project, The George Washington University (1988).

[26] Cal. Health & Safety Code, § 199.21(f)(West Supp. 1987); Fla. Stat. Ann. § 381.606; Tex. Rev. Civ. Stat. Ann. art. 44196-1 (Vernon Supp. 1988); Mass. Gen. Laws Ann. ch. 111, § 70F (West Supp. 1987); Wis. Stat. § 103.15 (West Supp. 1986).

[27] "Employment of people with AIDS, ARC or HTCU-III Antibody," New York Department of Health Policy Statement (Nov. 2, 1985).

[28] V. Schachter, "Legal AIDS: An Enlightened Corporate Policy," *Across the Board*, September 1987 at 12.

[29] 503; 29 USC 793.

[30] 504; 29 USC 794.

[31] U.S. Department of Justice, Memorandum for Ronald Robertson, General Counsel, Department of Health & Human Services, "Application of Section 504 of the Rehabilitation Act to People with AIDS, AIDS Related Complex, or Infection with the AIDS Virus," June 20, 1986.

[32] 480 U.S. 273, 107 S.Ct. 1123, 43 FEP Cases 81 (1987), *aff'g Arline v. School Board of Nassau County, Fla.*, 772 F.2d 759 (11th Cir. 1985)).

[33] *Arline*, 107 S. Ct. 1130.

[34] *Id.* at 1131.

[35] U.S. Department of Justice, Memorandum for Arthur B. Culvahouse, Jr., Counsel to the President, "Application of Section 504 of the Rehabilitation Act to HIV Infected Persons," Sept. 27, 1988.

[36] PL 100-259 (1988).

[37] *Thomas v. Atascadero Unified School District*, 662 F. Supp. 376 (C.D. Cal. 1986).

[38] 840 F.2d 701, 46 FEP Cases 279 (9th Cir. 1988).

[39] 120 DLR A-8 (BNA) (June 23, 1989).

[40] *Fortune* Magazine and Allstate Insurance, Co., *Business Response to AIDS: A National Survey of U.S. Companies* (1988).

[41] "Report of the Surgeon General on AIDS, U.S. Public Health Service," 1986; *N.Y. Times*, Feb. 2, 1986, at 14, col. 2.

[42] *Local 1812, American Federation of Government Employees v. United States Dept. of State*, 662 F. Supp. 50, 43 FEP Cases 955, 2 IER Cases 47 (D.D.C. 1987).

[43] 867 F.2d 461, 4 IER Cases 65 (8th Cir. 1989); *aff'g* 686 F. Supp. 243, 3 IER 135 (D. Neb. 1988), *pet. for cert. filed* May 1989. *See also* 7 ERW 869 (BNA) (July 10, 1989).

[44] F. Supp., 49 FEP Cases 541, 4 IER Cases 383 (E. D. La. 1989).

[45] 144 DLR A-1 (BNA) (June 16, 1987).

[46] "AIDS Tracing Wins Final OK," *Chicago Tribune*, June 30, 1987, p. 3.

[47] 29 USC 1140 (1982).

[48] *See* SRep 127, 93rd Cong. 2d Sess., reprinted at 1974 *U.S. Code Cong. & Admin. News* 4838, 4872.

[49] Employee benefit plans are defined in ERISA § 3 as including both employee welfare benefit plans and employee pension plans.

[50] *See, e.g.,* Leonard, "AIDS, Employment and Unemployment," 49 *Ohio L.J.* 929, 949 (1989).

[51] *Watkinson v. Great Atlantic & Pacific Tea Co.*, 585 F. Supp. 879, 36 FEP Cases 224 (E.D. Pa. 1984); *McKay v. Capital Cities Communications, Inc.*, 605 F. Supp. 1489 (S.D.N.Y. 1985).

[52] *See West v. Butler*, 621 F.2d 240 (6th Cir. 1980); *Zipf v. American Telephone and Telegraph Co.*, 799 F.2d 889 (3d Cir. 1986).

[53] *See Boesl v. Suburban Trust and Savings Bank*, 642 F. Supp. 1503, 1513-14 (N.D. Ill. 1986).

[54] *See Anthony v. Texaco, Inc.*, 803 F.2d 593, 597 (10th Cir. 1988); *See generally* 29 USC 1132.

[55] *See, e.g., Folz v. Marriott Corp.*, 594 F. Supp. 1007, 1016 (W.D. Mo. 1984).

[56] 29 USC 1140.

[57] 594 F. Supp. 1007 (W.D. Mo. 1984).

[58] 594 F. Supp. 1014-15.

[59] 799 F.2d 889 (3d Cir. 1986).

[60] 799 F.2d 894-95. *See also Bradley v. Capital Engineering & Manufacturing Co.*, 678 F. Supp. 1330 (N.D. Ill. 1988).

[61] *Doe v. Cooper Investments*, Civ. No. 89-B-597 (D. Col. April 18, 1989).

[62] "AIDS Discharge, Benefits Suit Resolved in $50,000 Settlement," 16 BPR 955 (BNA) (June 5, 1989).

[63] *See, e.g., Folz*, 594 F. Supp. 1014-15.

[64] In *Donohue*, the court noted that a Section 510 violation required more than showing that the employee's termination would save the employer money because under those circumstances ERISA violations would always occur when an employee entitled to benefits was terminated. 634 F. Supp. 1197.

[65] *See Phillips v. Amoco Oil Co.*, 799 F.2d 1464 (11th Cir. 1986), *cert denied*, 481 U.S. 1016 (1987); *Sutton v. Weirton Steel Division of Nation Steel Corp.*, 724 F.2d 406 (4th Cir. 1983), *cert. denied*, 467 U.S. 1205 (1984).

[66] *See Baker v. Kaiser Aluminum and Chemical Corp.*, 608 F. Supp. 1315 (N.D. Cal. 1984).

[67] *See, e.g., Donohue v. Custom Management Corp.*, 634 F. Supp. 1190, 1197-98 (W.D. Pa. 1986) (employer did not violate Section 510 where increasing economic losses forced elimination of plaintiffs' jobs and transfer of duties to another corporation).

[68] 34 CFR 104.12; 29 CFR 32.13; California Fair Employment and Housing Commission rules section 7293.9; New Jersey Civil Rights Division rules of practice section 13:13-2.5; Pennsylvania Human Relations Commission rules section 44.131.

[69] 29 CFR 1960.46.

[70] C. Morris, *The Developing Labor Law*, 2d. ed. (BNA 1983) at 156.

[71] Minnesota Dept. of Corrections 85 LA 1185 (1985).

[72] Printed material for use in an educational program is available from the National AIDS Information Clearinghouse, P.O. Box 6003, Rockville, Md. 20850 (1-800-458-5231).

[73] 7 ERW 6 (BNA) (Feb. 6, 1989).

[74] Turner and Ritter, "AIDS and Employment," *The Lab. Lawyer* v. 5, No. 1, at 104 (1989).

[75] C. E. Koop, Remarks to AMFAR Meeting of Chairmen and Chief Executive Officers of Major U.S. Corporations (Oct. 22, 1987).

[76] "Report of the Presidential Commission on the Human Immunodeficiency Virus Epidemic," *AIDS In the Workplace: Resource Material*, 3rd ed. (BNA, 1989).

* * *

Medical Screening

The collection of medical information on employees is a widespread practice. Pre-employment or periodic physicals, medical questionnaires, and other types of medical screening and monitoring are routine for many employers. Fifty percent of the employers in one recent survey indicated that they collect medical information and use it in making employment-related decisions.[1] Many legitimate reasons exist for obtaining and using medical information, but many legal restraints have been placed on the types of medical screening that are permissible, and on the uses of medical information.[2]

TYPES, USES OF MEDICAL SCREENING

Employers sometimes use medical screening to identify applicants who are especially vulnerable to workplace hazards or toxic substances, or to disqualify applicants who are not physically able to perform particular tasks. Some employers try to limit the costs of health insurance benefits and worker's compensation costs by screening employees who are more likely than others to suffer work-related illness or injury. Periodic monitoring of current employees is used to prevent workers from harmful exposure to workplace hazards when they show signs of increased vulnerability and to learn more about the effects of known or suspected environmental hazards. Employers also conduct medical screening of workers to design wellness programs tailored to the health needs, problems, and risks of their particular workforce.

Some employers are required by law to monitor employees periodically to reduce injuries. For example, Occupational Safety and Health Administration (OSHA) regulations mandate that asbestos workers be monitored to determine whether they have been exposed to harmful levels of asbestos.[3] OSHA's

Hazard Communication Standard requires chemical manufacturers to inform workers of environmental work-site hazards.[4] Under coke oven emission standards, employers must explain all risks to workers who refuse to undergo medical examinations.[5] Under OSHA's medical removal protection rules, employers must transfer workers from a hazardous area if a medical examination reveals they are susceptible to the hazard.[6] OSHA has established similar mandatory medical procedures for workers involved with one or more of a variety of hazardous substances. The Occupational Safety and Health Act of 1970 (OSH Act) and several other federal laws mandate the medical screening of employees, such as truckers[7] and airline pilots[8] to protect the public.

The National Institute for Occupational Safety and Health (NIOSH) reported that in 1988, 49 percent of U.S. companies required job applicants to pass medical screening tests, 30.1 percent required periodic medical exams, and about 33 percent of all collective bargaining agreements included provisions for employee medical examinations and testing.[9] The standard pre-employment physical examination with medical questionnaire is the most common type of medical screening. Many pre-employment questionnaires ask detailed questions regarding applicants' health and medical histories, and completion of this process is made a condition of employment. One large company's questionnaire asks:

> Detailed questions about hearing and vision; military service; allergies; prescription and non-prescription medications taken; exercise program; sports participation; sleeping habits; alcohol, beer, and wine consumption; coffee, tea, and soft drink consumption (including whether soft drinks were dietetic and coffee decaffeinated); recent weight changes; cigarette, cigar, pipe, snuff, and chewing tobacco usage; diet description; place of birth and travel to foreign countries; surgery (including urogenital); diseases of parents, grandparents, and siblings; prior workplace exposures; and prior accidents or injuries.[10]

Other pre-employment inquiries ignore broader lifestyle questions. Only 2 percent of the companies in one recent survey said their employee medical records contained information on whether the employee is a smoker or non-smoker.[11]

Some employers also conduct medical testing as part of their employee wellness programs. Such programs use information from predictive tests, medical exams, and questionnaires to help employees improve their health and reduce the risk of illness and injury.

LEGAL RESTRICTIONS

The most significant legal restrictions on medical screening of workers are the Rehabilitation Act of 1973[12] and similar state laws prohibiting discrimination on the basis of handicap or disability. Section 503 of the act requires federal contractors to "take affirmative action to employ and advance in employment qualified individuals."[13] Section 504 prohibits exclusion "solely by reason of their handicap" of "otherwise qualified individuals" by government agencies and employers that receive federal funds,[14] including those with federal contracts over $2,500. A handicapped individual is defined under the act as "any person who (i) has a physical or mental impairment which substantially limits one or more of such person's major life activities, (ii) has a record of such impairment, or (iii) is regarded as having such an impairment."[15] Employers must take special care to ensure that no individual is discriminated against "who is able to meet all of a program's requirements in spite of his handicap."[16] Before rejecting any job applicant, "both the legitimacy of the physical requirements and the possibility of reasonable accommodation must be considered."[17]

Case law interpreting the act has defined "handicap" broadly. For example, individuals with tuberculosis,[18] back injuries,[19] diabetes,[20] an inability to handle stress,[21] a surgically repaired dislocated shoulder,[22] a history of back injury,[23] sensitivity to tobacco smoke,[24] cancer,[25] or stiff joints[26] are all protected from discrimination under the act. However, individuals with acrophobia,[27] knee injuries,[28] left-handed individuals,[29] and overweight body builders[30] have been found not to be "hand-icapped."

Covered employers usually may refuse to hire handicapped individuals who are demonstrably unable to perform the essential functions of the job. Employers can "establish job qualifications and conduct pre-employment medical examinations, but to the extent the criteria tend to exclude handicapped individuals, they are to be related to the performance of the job and be consistent with business necessity and safe performance."[31]

Risk of possible future injury can be a justifiable basis under the Rehabilitation Act for excluding handicapped individuals from a job if the possible future injury would endanger the safety of the individual or others. Some federal courts have held that employers may consider potential safety risks to applicants, co-workers, and others in making decisions about employment criteria.[32] The burden in such cases, once a plaintiff has made out a prima facie case, is on the employer to prove that the employment qualifications are job-related and based on business necessity or safety concerns.[33] The employer's first burden is to establish the risk of future injury. Medical diagnoses often are contested when a worker claims a present injury in a worker's compensation case. The process of predicting future risk of injury is even more difficult, and experts strongly disagree about the reliability of such predictions. The U.S. Court of Appeals for the Ninth Circuit has held that employers must show a reasonable probability of substantial harm because "a mere elevated risk standard is not sufficient to insure handicapped people's right to employment."[34]

The Office of Federal Contract Compliance (OFCCP) of the Department of Labor (DOL) enforces the Rehabilitation Act's requirements for federal contractors. OFCCP regulations state that contractors are not prohibited from conducting comprehensive physical, mental, or other medical examinations prior to employment or any change in employee status, if the results are not used to discriminate in violation of the act and they are kept confidential. The only exceptions to the requirement of confidentiality are that:

- Supervisors and managers may be informed about restrictions on the work or duties of handicapped individuals and physical accommodations for them;

- First aid and safety personnel may be informed, to the extent necessary, if the handicapped employee's condition might require emergency treatment; and

- Government officials investigating compliance with the act shall be informed.[35]

Bills were pending in Congress in mid-1989 that would prohibit discrimination against disabled people in private employment. (See Chapter VII.) The Americans With Disabilities Act (HR 2273) and its Senate counterpart (S 933) would require private employers to make reasonable accommodation for disabled people who are otherwise qualified to work, unless the accommodation would cause "undue hardship" to the employer. A substitute version of the bill, limiting remedies to those available under Title VII of the Civil Rights Act of 1964, was approved by the Senate Labor and Human Resources Committee August 2, 1989. If passed, job applicants and employees would have a private right of action and could seek injunctive relief and lost wages after filing a charge with the Equal Employment Opportunity Commission (EEOC). The White House endorsed that version of the bill and stated that President Bush was committed to producing a civil rights bill for the disabled that could be passed and signed in 1989.[36]

Forty-four states and the District of Columbia have laws protecting people with handicaps or disabilities from employment discrimination.[37] Employers that want to conduct medical screening should determine whether the state where the screening will be conducted has such a law, what handicaps or disabilities are covered, the extent to which the medical condition can be a legitimate criterion for employment, and whether a duty of reasonable accommodation exists. Employers also should determine whether the law, administrative guidelines, or interpretive decisions limit the types of permissible inquiries.

For example, the Massachusetts Commission Against Discrimination has issued guidelines interpreting that state's handicap discrimination law.[38] Under the Massachusetts law, employers are not allowed to ask whether applicants are handicapped. The guidelines state that prohibited inquiries include questions relating to handicap or disability, medical conditions, receipt of worker's compensation, and limitations on ability to perform the work. The law allows employers to condition offers of employment on the results of a medical examination conducted solely to determine whether the employee, with reasonable accommodation, can perform the essential functions of the job. The only information that can be conveyed to the employer is the examining physician's conclusion; any other medical history must be kept confidential by the physician.

Employers also need to be concerned about the possible impact of medical criteria on other protected groups. Some facially neutral medical criteria may disproportionately screen out minorities or women, making the criteria subject to challenge under anti-discrimination laws. For example, the EEOC has held that the rejection of a black female's application for employment as a telephone operator because she suffered from sickle cell anemia was a prima facie violation of Title VII because the disease is especially prevalent among blacks and is virtually non-existent among other racial groups in the United States.[39]

When a medical testing program is challenged because it has a disparate impact on a protected group, an employer may defend the testing on safety grounds. One court expressed the courts' basic attitude that "The greater the safety factor, measured by the likelihood of harm and the probable severity of that harm in case of an accident, the more stringent may be the job qualifications...."[40] Such safety considerations may include the danger to the handicapped employee, the danger to the public of an employee who is likely to experience illness on the job, or the danger to other employees.

Employers that ask for personal medical information or conduct medical testing also may face claims of invasion of privacy. Tort liability can be minimized if the medical testing is conducted with the employee's written consent, the employee is given advance notice, disclosure of results is limited to those who need to know them, and testing procedures are the least-intrusive possible.[41]

To protect themselves from potential claims, employers that use medical questionnaires and employment physicals should be able to answer the following questions:

- What is the business justification for requiring a particular applicant or employee to complete a questionnaire or take an examination? Is it to have a medical record in case of emergencies? Are they required for insurance purposes? Does the job have physical requirements?

- What is the business justification for each medical inquiry; each question asked or procedure performed? Does that justification apply to all jobs, or only to certain positions?

- Who will have access to the results? Does a copy go in the employee's personnel file, or are all copies put in a secure set of medical records?

- What is done with the results? Under what circumstances will the employer refuse to hire or transfer an applicant based on test results?

Employers should answer these questions to help determine whether their medical screening program complies with applicable federal and state laws.

GENETIC TESTING

Identification and regulation of exposure to harmful chemicals and toxic substances in the workplace is a major priority of OSHA. The federal government and many state governments have adopted right-to-know laws designed to make employers identify hazardous chemicals in the workplace and communicate their dangers to employees.[42] As information about workplace diseases has increased, scientists have been better able to identify factors that may contribute to various occupational diseases. Advances in genetics research have led some scientists to conclude that certain genetic traits can make workers more susceptible to diseases caused by exposure to certain chemicals or toxins. As a result, a few companies, especially in the chemical industry, are conducting genetic screening as part of applicants' pre-employment physicals. A 1982 survey by the Office of Technology Assessment (OTA) identified six companies that were using genetic screening, and 55 firms were considering it. Seventeen companies had used genetic testing in the past and several reported that they had transferred "hypersusceptible" employees or had recommended that they seek other jobs.[43] In a 1987-88 survey of 245 personnel and industrial relations executives, only three companies said they used genetic screening.[44] OTA was updating its study on the use of genetic testing in mid-1989. The results are expected to be available in the fall of 1990.

Two types of genetic testing have been used in the workplace. Cytogenetic testing, also known as genetic monitoring, involves testing for chromosome breakage after an employee has been exposed to toxins or other chemicals. The principal purpose for monitoring is to determine whether and to what extent an employee has been harmed by on-the-job exposure. The other, more controversial, type of testing is genetic screening, in which healthy job applicants or employees are tested to determine their susceptibility to toxins.[45] The "purpose of genetic screening is to prevent hypersusceptible workers from entering certain jobs in the first place," whereas genetic monitoring "indicates excessive exposure levels."[46]

OTA concluded in its final report in April 1983 that while "none of the genetic tests evaluated by OTA meets established scientific criteria for routine use in an occupational setting ... there is enough suggestive evidence to merit further research."[47]

In a 1986 survey of biotechnology companies, OTA identified 20 firms that were developing genetic tests based on recombinant DNA methods. Several thought it was likely that employers could be using such tests by the year 2000 to exclude susceptible workers from hazardous jobs.[48]

Many scientists agree that genetic screening has great potential for protecting workers' health but consider genetic screening results to be of uncertain validity now. "Genetic tests have to be reliable, repeatable, and reasonably economical for them to be applied in an industrial setting. That hasn't been the case in our opinion," explained a chief medical officer of Dow Chemical, which began experimenting with genetic screening in 1972.[49] The U.S. Air Force had a screening program to detect carriers of sickle cell anemia, who were thought to be at increased risk to the lack of oxygen at high altitudes and to certain chemicals. The program was discontinued because of the lack of evidence of a link between such gene traits and risks.[50] Researchers concluded from a review of the scientific literature that the results of studies of the connection between certain genetic deficiencies and increased susceptibility to cancer and lung problems have not been statistically significant. These researchers recommended that three requirements be met before any genetic screening program is implemented:

> [C]linical reports must demonstrate that workers with the genetic condition are becoming sick at greater rates than "normal workers"; epidemiological evidence must show the link between populations of workers, exposure to workplace conditions and ill-

ness; and feasibility studies must be carried out to see whether screening workers actually reduces illness in the worker population.[51]

Employers have a general common-law duty to provide a safe workplace, and the general duty clause of the OSH Act requires every employer to maintain a place of employment "free from recognized hazards that are causing or are likely to cause death or serious physical harm."[52] OSHA has not promulgated any regulations that specifically cover the use of genetic screening. However, OSHA regulations covering numerous toxins require that employers provide workers with physical examinations by a physician before they are assigned to work in regulated areas. The examinations must include a "personal history of the employee, family and occupational background, including genetic and environmental factors.... The examining physician shall consider whether there exist conditions of increased risks, including reduced immunological competence...."[53]

One labor relations attorney has argued that this regulation requires genetic testing,[54] but a former OSHA director has stated that OSHA's intent is to enable the physicians to counsel workers rather than allow management to exclude workers from employment, adding that OSHA strongly condemns genetic screening because "exclusion of workers as a result of genetic testing runs contrary to the spirit and intent of the Occupational Safety and Health Act of 1970."[55]

Employees and unions are concerned about the privacy implications of genetic screening and the confidentiality of test results. Only 11 percent of 1,254 adults responding to a 1985 poll agreed that an employer should have the right to force a job applicant to undergo testing for a genetic disorder that would not become symptomatic for 20 years. Fifteen percent of the respondents were willing to undergo genetic testing for diagnostic and curative purposes, but not for employment or insurance purposes.[56]

Legal challenges to genetic screening or to the use of discoveries of worker hypersusceptibility as a basis for transferring employees or refusing them employment are more likely to occur under Title VII than under the OSH Act. Because many of the genetic traits identified so far are concentrated in ethnic or racial groups, genetic screening is subject to challenge under Title VII. For example, the sickle cell trait—found in people of African, Mediterranean, or Middle Eastern descent and in approximately 8 percent of American blacks—and another trait known as G-6-PD deficiency—found in Mediterranean Jews and American blacks—have been linked to diseases caused by benzene and other nitro-amino compounds. A deficiency involving serum antitrypsin, which occurs among people of Northern and Central European heritage, has been linked to hypersusceptibility to respiratory illnesses.[57]

Genetic screening also could be challenged under the Rehabilitation Act and state handicap laws. Employees could argue that they are perceived as being handicapped on the basis of a physical (genetic) trait, but the potential of a future injury from exposure is not a sufficient basis to disqualify them from a job. Florida, North Carolina, and Louisiana prohibit discrimination based on the sickle cell trait.[58] A Florida law directed at AIDS discrimination prohibits discrimination based on the results of blood tests and a New Jersey law prohibits discrimination based on sickle cell, the Tay-Sachs syndrome trait, and other genetic traits.[59]

PREGNANCY, REPRODUCTIVE, AND FETAL HAZARDS

Pregnancy screening or fertility screening is another form of screening sometimes used by employers because of the possibly increased susceptibility of pregnant women or their fetuses to toxic substances.[60] The Pregnancy Discrimination Act (PDA), a 1978 amendment to Title VII, prohibits employers from discriminating on the basis of pregnancy, childbirth, or "related medical conditions."[61] For all job-related purposes, disabilities from pregnancy, childbirth, or related medical conditions must be treated the same as all other disabilities under any health, disability, or sick-leave plan.[62]

Pregnancy has not been scientifically shown to cause an increase in women's susceptibility to environmental and workplace hazards.[63] EEOC has said that an employee who is unable to perform certain tasks such as heavy lifting due to pregnancy must be transferred or reassigned or given alternative assignments if all other temporarily disabled workers are given such opportunities.[64] In *Schneider v. Jax Shack, Inc.*, the court rejected the employer's argument that it was justified in switching a full-time bartender to a part-time waitress position after she became pregnant, to protect her from hazards such as heavy lifting and walking on wet floors. The court held that the employer's action violated the PDA, and no business necessity existed for the transfer.[65]

More complex problems arise in the context of fetal and reproductive protection policies. The incentives for employers to screen workers to protect them from reproductive and fetal hazards are greatly increased by the enormous potential liability an employer may risk in a lawsuit by a child with birth defects. Employers sometimes seek to require that employees sign a waiver by which the employees agree that they will not sue for workplace injuries to themselves or their fetuses. Such waivers are of questionable legal validity. Many state worker's compensation laws may not recognize such waivers, and it is unclear whether employees can waive the legal rights of their unborn children to sue for personal harm resulting from the parent's exposure to hazardous substances in the workplace.[66]

In late 1988, EEOC issued policy guidance on reproductive and fetal hazards[67] that establish an analytical framework for examining employers' exclusionary policies. Three federal appeals courts in separate cases have ruled that exclusion of fertile or pregnant women because of potential reproductive hazards constitutes illegal sex discrimination unless it is scientifically justifiable or no less-discriminatory alternatives exist.[68] Agreeing with the courts, EEOC said a policy that results in discrimination against fertile women to avoid risk to fetuses is a prima facie violation of Title VII. Such policies may be justified only if the risk is verified by independent, objective scientific evidence, and no less-discriminatory alternative is available for protecting fetuses.

To withstand legal scrutiny, an employer's reproductive or fetal protection program must be:

> ... neutrally designed to protect all employees' offspring from hazards existing in the workplace. Where substantial evidence exists that the risk of harm to employees' offspring takes place only through the exposure of one sex to a hazard existing in the workplace, an employer may exclude from the workplace employees of that sex, but only to the extent necessary to protect employees' offspring from reproductive fetal hazards.[69]

The proven risk must apply only to the excluded class and not be under-inclusive. For example, a hiring practice that rejects all women of childbearing years to protect them from pre-conception hazards also must reject men if the same toxins pose a similar risk to male reproductive capacity.[70] An exclusionary screening practice also must not be over-inclusive. Excluding all women of childbearing capacity, regardless of their age, marital status, use of contraception, and the fertility of their partner may be over-inclusive and discriminatory insofar as it operates as a conclusive presumption that all women capable of becoming pregnant will become pregnant.[71]

In assessing a reproductive health program, a court must contend with complex scientific information regarding the health risks and whether alternatives exist that are less restrictive. In *International Union, U.A.W. v. Johnson Controls, Inc.*,[72] the union challenged the employer's policy of excluding women of childbearing age who were capable of having children from working in areas where their blood lead levels probably would rise above 30 micrograms. The court focused on how to evaluate a risk when the scientific information does not clearly indicate whether the risk is greater to women or men or whether the fetus requires additional protection. The court held that the defendant's burden is not to resolve the scientific uncertainty but to:

> ... show that within (the scientific) community there is so considerable a body of opinion that significant risk exists, and that it is substantially confined to women workers, that an informed employee could not responsibly fail to act on the assumption that this opinion might be the accurate one.[73]

Because the evidence of potential harm was present and the plaintiffs failed to show that an acceptable alternative existed, the exclusionary policy was upheld.

EEOC's policy guidance lists these factors to consider in determining whether a policy is discriminatory:

- Consistent application: Can the employer show through scientific evidence that the hazard applies only to women or women of childbearing age and that it does not affect men or other employees?

- Awareness of all hazards: Does objective scientific evidence exist showing that the hazard causes harm at the level, duration, and manner of exposure that exists at the particular worksite?

- Balanced research: Has research been undertaken to determine the danger or risk to non-excluded classes of employees?

- OSHA and Environmental Protection Agency (EPA) standards: Has EPA or OSHA established any mandatory standards regarding the particular toxin or hazard involved?

- History or Equal Employment Opportunities: Prior to the institution of the exclusionary policy, were members of the excluded class given equal opportunities?

- Tailoring: Is the exclusionary policy limited in its effect to those people affected by the hazard, or is it over-inclusive?

- Harm to other body systems: Does the hazard affect any other non-fetal or non-reproductive body systems? Why is the policy concerned only with the possibility of ovarian cancer, for example, and not cancer of the liver?

- Alternatives: Has the employer considered any non-exclusionary practices or policies such as reducing exposure levels, improved ventilation, isolation of machinery, use of respirators, or the transfer of employees during pregnancy?

- Monitoring: Has the employer monitored scientific research and technological developments regarding the hazard in its workplace to find new alternatives to the exclusionary policy or to discover if the hazard causes harm to any members of any non-excluded class?[74]

ILLUSTRATIONS

Employer Can't Mandate Blood Test As Part Of Wellness Program Without Proper Justification

In an effort to help employees reduce their coronary risk and blood-sugar levels, the company in 1985 required all employees to participate in a YMCA health risk approval workshop. Each employee was required to give a blood sample to test for blood-sugar and cholesterol levels. In 1988 the company required mandatory retesting of all employees to determine whether its wellness program was working. The union filed a grievance alleging that employees cannot be subjected to mandatory physical exams without a compelling employment-related reason.

In a case of first impression, an arbitrator determined that
no employment reason existed to require all employees to submit to the blood test. Finding that the program unreasonably
invaded the privacy of the employees without proper justification, the arbitrator ruled that any future blood tests be voluntary unless bargained for with the union. [*Southern Champion
Tray Co.*, 92 LA 677 (1988).]

Removal Of Pregnant Flight Attendants Is Business Necessity

A flight attendant challenged her employer's policy of
removing all pregnant flight attendants from flight duty. The
court found that although the policy was a prima facie violation
of the PDA, the airline had established a business necessity for
the policy by showing that pregnant flight attendants pose a
threat to the safe operation of its flights, particularly in emergency situations, due to their susceptibility to pregnancy-re-
lated ailments such as spontaneous abortions, morning sick-
ness, and fatigue. The court cautioned that any justification for
a discriminatory policy must be addressed to the "essence" of
an employer's business operation. The court judged the danger
posed by pregnant flight attendants to be substantial, stating
that "the greater the safety factor, measured by the likelihood
of harm and the probable severity of that harm in case of an
accident, the more stringent may be the job qualifications."
[*Levin v. Delta Air Lines*, 730 F.2d 994, 34 FEP 1192 (5th Cir.
1984).]

Employer Violated Title VII By Refusing To Limit Pregnant Employee's Exposure To Chemicals

Stricklin was employed as a shop foreman and assistant
manager by Protek, which was in the business of automotive
"detailing" (cosmetic repair and cleaning of used cars) and
"make-ready" of new cars after they arrived at local dealer-
ships from the manufacturers. Stricklin's duties included supervision of all automotive detailing work and quality control, in-

ventory control, and ordering supplies. Shortly after she announced she was pregnant, the general manager moved the
detailing activity and Stricklin's work area from the main level
of the building to the lower level, where chemical protection of
vehicles took place and where caustic chemical fumes accumu-
lated. Stricklin each day asked the general manager to move
her back to the main level because she feared the chemicals
and fumes would harm her fetus. The general manager told
her she should buy a mask.

The court ruled that the general manager's refusal to accommodate Stricklin's request to limit her exposure to chemicals during her pregnancy violated Title VII. The court noted
that the general manager previously had granted a male
employee leave with pay for several weeks when he was unable
to perform his duties because of chemicals in his blood stream.
Therefore, the refusal to accommodate Stricklin constituted
disparate treatment due to pregnancy. [*EEOC v. Protek of Al-
buquerque, Inc.*, 49 FEP 1110 (D.N.M. 1988).]

ENDNOTES

[1] D. Linowes, *Privacy in America* (Univ. Ill. 1989) at 42.

[2] For a comprehensive analysis of medical testing, see Mark A.
Rothstein, *Medical Screening and the Employee Health Cost Crisis* (BNA
1989), and *Medical Screening of Workers* (BNA 1984).

[3] 29 CFR 1910.1001(d).

[4] 29 CFR 1910.1200(a).

[5] 29 CFR 1910.1029(e)(3).

[6] *See* M. Rothstein, *Medical Screening of Workers* (1984) at 100.

[7] 49 CFR 391.41-49.

[8] 14 CFR 671-31.

[9] Rothstein, "Medical Screening: A Tool With Broadening Use," *Bus. &
Hlth.* 3(10):7-9 (1986).

[10] Rothstein, *supra* at 15-16.

[11] Linowes, *supra* at 51.

[12] 29 USC 701-796.

[13] 29 USC 793.

[14] 29 USC 794.

[15] 29 USC 706(8)(B).

[16] *Southeastern Community College. v. Davis*, 442 U.S. 397, 406, 99 S. Ct. 236 (1979).

[17] *Wallace v. Veterans Admin.*, 683 F. Supp. 758, 762, 46 FEP 1012 (D. Kan. 1988).

[18] *School Bd. of Nassau County, Fla. v. Arline*, 480 U.S. 273, 107 S. Ct. 1123, 43 FEP 81 (1987).

[19] *Perez v. Philadelphia Housing Auth.*, 677 F. Supp. 357, 46 FEP 1385 (E.D. Pa. 1987), *aff'd*, 841 F.2d 1120 (3d Cir. 1988).

[20] *Serrapica v. City of New York*, 708 F. Supp. 64 (S.D. N.Y. 1989).

[21] *Doe v. New York Univ.*, 666 F.2d 761 (2d Cir. 1981).

[22] *Mahoney v. Ortiz*, 645 F. Supp. 22, 42 FEP 10 (S.D.N.Y. 1986).

[23] *E.E. Black v. Marshall*, 497 F. Supp. 1088, 23 FEP 1253 (D. Haw. 1980).

[24] *Vickers v. Veterans Admin.*, 549 F. Supp. 85, 29 FEP 1197 (W.D. Wash. 1982).

[25] *Harrison v. Marsh*, 691 F. Supp. 1223 (W.D. Mo. 1988).

[26] *Sisson v. Helms*, 751 F.2d 991, 36 FEP 1173 (9th Cir.), *cert. denied*, 474 U.S. 846 (1985).

[27] *Forrisi v. Bowen*, 794 F.2d 931, 41 FEP 190 (4th Cir. 1986).

[28] *Elstner v. S.W. Bell Telephone Co.*, 659 F. Supp. 1328, 43 FEP 1437, 125 LRRM 2551, (S.D. Tex. 1987), *aff'd*, 863 F.2d 881, 49 FEP 656 (5th Cir. 1988).

[29] *De La Torres v. Bolger*, 610 F. Supp. 593, 38 FEP 191 (N.D. Tex. 1985), *aff'd*, 781 F.2d 1134, 39 FEP 1795 (5th Cir. 1986).

[30] *Tudyman v. United Airlines*, 608 F. Supp. 739, 38 FEP 732 (C.D. Cal. 1984).

[31] 41 CFR 60-741.5(c); *Bentivegna v. U.S. Dept. of Labor*, 694 F.2d 619, 30 FEP 875 (9th Cir. 1982).

[32] *Serrapica v. City of New York*, 708 F. Supp. 64 (S.D. N.Y. 1989).

[33] *E.E. Black v. Marshall*, 497 F. Supp. 1088, 1104 (D. Haw. 1980).

[34] *Mantolete v. Bolger*, 767 F.2d 1416, 1422, 38 FEP 1081, 1517 (9th Cir. 1985).

[35] 41 CFR 60-741.5(c)(3).

[36] "Senate Panel Unanimously Clears Civil Rights Bill for the Disabled," 148 DLR (BNA), August 3, 1989, at A-6; "Hearing on Civil Rights for Disabled," 131 LRR 411 (BNA), July 24, 1989.

[37] For a complete listing, see *Fair Employment Practice Manual* (BNA) 499:511.

[38] *Fair Employment Practice Manual* (BNA) 445:957.

[39] EEOC Decision No. 81-8, 27 FEP 1781 (1980).

[40] *Usery v. Tamiami Trail Tours, Inc.*, 531 F.2d 224, 236, 12 FEP 1233 (5th Cir. 1976).

[41] U.S. Congress, Office of Technology Assessment, *Medical Testing and Health Insurance*, OTA-H-384 (Washington, D.C.: U.S. Government Printing Office) August, 1988 at 101.

[42] *See, e.g., Occupational Safety and Health Act of 1970, 2-33, 29 USC 651-678 (West 1985 and Supp. 1987); 29 CFR 1910, 1200 (1982); Pa. Stat. Ann. tit. 35, § 7301-7320 (Purden Supp. 1986); C. Harris and D. Berger, Sara Title III: A Guide to Emergency Preparedness and Community Right to Know*, Executive Enterprises Publications Co., Inc., (New York, 1988).

[43] *Recruiting and Selection Procedures* (BNA), at 17 (1988).

[44] E. Pierce, "The Regulation of Genetic Testing in the Workplace – A Legislative Proposal," 46 *Ohio St. L.J.* 771, 776-77 (1985).

[45] A. Diamond, "Genetic Testing in Employment Situations: A Question of Worker Rights," 4 *J. Legal Med.* 231 (1983).

[46] Note, "Genetic Testing in the Workplace," 4 *J. Contemp. Health L. & Pol'y* 375, 381.

[47] *The Role of Genetic Testing in the Prevention of Occupational Disease*, Office of Technology Assessment, 98th Cong., 1st Sess.

[48] *Medical Testing and Health Insurance, supra,* at 102-103.

[49] Paterson, "Genetic Screening: How Much Should We Test Employees?" 233 *Industry Week* 31, 45 (1987).

[50] *See* Tierney & Messing, "New Tricks For Old Dogs: Genetic Screening Makes Victim-Blaming Scientific," 14 *Alternatives* 31 (1987).

[51] *Id.* at 35-36.

[52] 29 USC 654(a)(1).

[53] 29 CFR 1910.1003(g)(1).

[54] McConnell, "Genetic Testing Conflicts with Discrimination Laws," *National Law Journal* v. 9, at 14 (Feb. 9, 1987).

[55] "Genetic Testing Not Required, OSHA Reiterates," 1980 OSHR 35 (BNA); "Opposition to Genetic Testing Pressed by OSHA, NIOSH Study of Programs," 1980 OSHR 90 (BNA).

[56] *Medical Testing and Health Insurance*, at 103.

[57] Pierce, *supra* at 778, citing Reinhardt, "Chemical Hypersusceptibility," *Journal of Occupational Medicine*, v. 20 at 319 (1979).

[58] FLA. STAT. ANN. § 228.201, 448.075-76 (West 1981 and Supp. 1986); N.C. GEN. STAT. § 95-28.1 (1975); LA. REV. STAT. ANN. 23.1001-1004 (West Supp. 1985).

[59] FLA. STAT. § 381.606(5) (West Supp. 1986); N.J.S.A. 10:5-5.

[60] *See* Paskal, "Dilemma: Save the Fetus or Sue the Employer," *Lab. L. J.*, no. 6 (1988).

[61] "Other related conditions" protected under the act include abortion. *See, e.g., Doe v. First National Bank of Chicago*, 668 F. Supp. 1110, 45 FEP 711 (1987), *aff'd*, 865 F.2d 864 (7th Cir. 1989).

[62] *EEOC Compliance Manual* (BNA) No. 92 § 626.2(a). *See also Ensor v. Painter*, 661 F. Supp. 21 (E.D. Tenn. 1987).

[63] M. Rothstein, *supra* note 6, at 64.

[64] *EEOC Compliance Manual* (BNA) No. 92 626.4 (1986).

[65] 794 F.2d 383, 41 FEP 266 (8th Cir. 1986).

[66] *See EEOC Compliance Manual.*

[67] "EEOC's Policy Guidance On Reproductive And Fetal Hazards," *Daily Labor Report* (BNA) No. 193 (Oct. 5, 1988) at D-1.

[68] *Hayes v. Shelby Memorial Hospital*, 726 F.2d 1543, 34 FEP 444 (11th Cir. 1984); *Zuniga v. Kleberg County Hosp.*, 692 F.2d 986, 30 FEP 650 (5th Cir. 1982); and *Wright v. Olin*, 697 F.2d 1172, 30 FEP 889 (4th Cir. 1982).

[69] "EEOC Policy Guidance," *supra.*

[70] Many of the same substances that pose a risk to female reproductive capacity or pose threats to a female's future offspring pose an even greater threat to male reproductive systems and their future offspring. Rothstein, *supra*, at 78.

[71] *EEOC Compliance Manual* (BNA) No. 92 § 626.4 (1986).

[72] 680 F. Supp. 309, 46 FEP 110 (E.D. Wisc. 1988).

[73] *Id.* at 315.

[74] *EEOC Compliance Manual* (BNA) 626.4 (1986).

* * *

Employee Investigations

Employers have many legitimate reasons to investigate their employees where problems with theft, misconduct, or poor performance exist, or to determine whether an employee is breaking company rules or is working for a competitor. Employers have a right to conduct such investigations if the reason for them is directly related to the job and the investigative techniques do not unreasonably intrude on the privacy of the employees. However, when an employer investigates an employee's private life, privacy concerns are raised and courts are less deferential to the employer's right to manage and control the company or operation. Significant limitations have been placed on employers' power to conduct investigations in some areas.

CONDUCTING INVESTIGATIONS

Employers should know which areas of questioning can lead to liability when they conduct investigatory interviews with employees. Employees have asserted claims under federal labor law and have sued employers for acts occurring during investigations under many common law theories including false imprisonment, assault and battery, intentional infliction of emotional distress, defamation, and invasion of privacy.

Employers should consider many factors when they plan and conduct investigations, including counsel's role of coordinating the investigation to preserve privileges, coordination with law enforcement agencies to prevent malicious prosecution actions, and the use of private investigators. Most of these matters are outside the scope of this report.[1] However, employers should always follow these basic guidelines to reduce the risk of liability:

- Do not erect physical barriers to prevent employees from leaving the premises, lock an employee in an office, or indicate in any way that employees are not free to leave. Such actions could lead to claims of false imprisonment.

- Limit inquiries to the relevant facts, always asking employees for their explanation or version of events. Investigators should avoid making direct accusations or expressing opinions on the issues.

- Information obtained during investigations, the identity of the person being investigated, and the issue being investigated should be discussed only among those who need to know.

- Investigate conduct outside the workplace only where such conduct is clearly work-related.

- Under no circumstances should investigators, security personnel, or other employees threaten the person being investigated. Bodily contact should be avoided unless the employee becomes violent and is a danger to others.

- Interviewers should not use loud, profane, or abusive language, or other techniques that could be viewed by a court as coercion.

- Respect, to the extent possible, the confidentiality of the people involved in the investigation.

SEARCHES OF OFFICES, PERSONAL BELONGINGS

The legality of searches of employer-provided lockers, desks, or offices, or personal items employees bring to the workplace depends largely on whether the employer is public or private and, among private employers, whether they act alone or with the help of the police or other government agencies. Private-sector employers usually have the right to search property they provide to employees for daily use, such as desks and lockers. In addition, private employers may require employees to submit to searches of packages they bring into or take out of the workplace. The U.S. Constitution does not protect employees from searches by non-governmental employers. Nevertheless, an increasing number of courts are sustaining claims in the private sector under the tort of intrusion. In a private-sector case where a jury awarded $100,000 in exemplary damages for a search of an employee's purse in a company locker without the worker's consent, the Texas Court of Appeals found that the employer had created a "legitimate expectation of privacy" in the locker assigned to the employee.[2]

Constitutional Rights of Public Employees

Where the employer is a government entity, searches are subject to challenges under the Due Process Clause and the Fourth Amendment prohibition of unreasonable searches and seizures. In this context, the primary issue is whether the employee has a legitimate expectation of privacy. Prior to March 1987, the U.S. Supreme Court recognized that employees might have a reasonable expectation of privacy against intrusions by the policy. In *Mancusi v. DeForte*,[3] a convicted union official sued on the ground that evidence used against him in a state prosecution had been seized from his office at union headquarters in violation of his Fourth Amendment rights. The court held that the official, who shared his office with other union employees, had a protectable privacy interest in the office:

> It has long been settled that one has standing to object to a search of his office, as well as his home .... [The employee was] entitled to expect that he would not be disturbed except by personal or business invitees, and that records would not be taken except with his permission or that of his union superiors.[4]

The Supreme Court applied *Mancusi* to a search of an office, desk, and files of a public hospital employee by his supervisor in *O'Connor v. Ortega.*[5] The court clearly recognized that public employees can have an expectation of privacy in their place of work, and that they do not lose their Fourth Amendment rights because they work for the government instead of for a private employer. Consequently, the court held that an employer's search of a desk or file is permissible only if it is reasonable under all of the circumstances. (See Chapter I.)

In *Ortega*, the court noted that an employee's expectation of privacy often could be limited by the nature of the employment relationship, such as how the office is used and how many people have access to it. But the court was careful to limit its decision to what Justice Sandra Day O'Connor called the "workplace context." The court defined the workplace context as the areas and items that are related to work and are generally under the employers' control. In the hospital, this included the halls, walkways, cafeterias, files, desks, and cabinets. The court said not everything that passes through the confines of the "workplace context" can be considered part of the workplace and thus subject to the reasonableness standard. The court gave as examples a piece of luggage that an employee brings to the office before going on a trip or a handbag or briefcase that a worker brings to the office each day. Employees who bring these items to work have no expectation that the items' presence is private. However, those employees have a high expectation of privacy in the contents of their briefcases or purses. Because these items are not part of the "workplace," the standard of reasonableness developed in *Ortega* as appropriate to the workplace does not necessarily apply to a closed suitcase, handbag, or briefcase.[6]

Prior to *Ortega*, several lower courts had upheld as reasonable searches of lockers, tool boxes, and other personal effects, especially when the employer had retained some type of control, such as retaining the locker keys, supplying locks, or reserving the right to search.[7] While many of these decisions may still be valid, those based on a finding that public employees can never have a reasonable expectation of privacy must be reconsidered in light of the standard set in *Ortega*.

Ortega left unresolved several issues, notably the appropriate standard to be used when a public employee is being investigated for criminal misconduct or breaches of other non-work-related statutory or regulatory standards. The U.S. Court of Appeals for the District of Columbia Circuit has indicated that the government cannot use the arguably relaxed "employer" standard for warrantless searches when its true purpose is to obtain evidence of criminal activity. Instead, the more stringent standards that protect citizens from unreasonably intrusive evidence gathering apply.[8] Subsequent cases have applied *Ortega* to uphold the premise that an employer's search of an employee's desk or file is permissible only if it is reasonable under all the circumstances.[9]

Private-Sector Employees

Most challenges to searches by private-sector employees have occurred in unionized settings, where arbitrators interpret the reasonableness of the search in the context of an employee discharge. In *Daniel International Corp. and International Union of Operating Engineers*,[10] the company had a search policy that included daily inspections of workers' lunch boxes to prevent employees from bringing items such as drugs, alcohol, or weapons to the job site. The policy was formulated under a labor contract that gave management extensive rights. An employee was fired after he refused to allow a search. The arbitrator held that the punishment of discharge was too severe, although he added that it would have been better for the grievant to have cooperated fully with the guard assigned to conduct the search and thereafter to have filed a grievance if he felt he had been wronged.

Arbitrators draw from many sources in evaluating the reasonableness of a search, including the U.S. Constitution. In *Congoleum-Nairn*,[11] government agents conducted an illegal search and seizure of gambling forms and materials. The arbitrator rejected the use of the evidence seized to support the discharge of the accused employee, noting that:

> [p]rinciples embodied in the fundamental law of the land are not to be regarded lightly. Although the Fourth Amendment applies to government action, and not to the unlawful seizure of private papers by private persons, we are not confronted in the instant case with a private seizure ... but a situation where a private employer seeks to justify its disciplinary action almost entirely upon a tainted transaction, in the form of an adjudicated unlawful search and seizure by government action.

In many other cases, arbitrators have sustained an employer's right to make reasonable searches of employee lockers, briefcases, or purses, where employers were plagued by theft or they had another reasonable cause for the search.[12] In one case, an arbitrator found that an employer had probable cause to conduct a search for drugs in a mine after an employee was found to be at work while under the influence of drugs. The arbitrator concluded that where any employee reports to work while under the influence of a controlled substance, an employer would be remiss if it did not become suspicious of the entire workforce and take necessary steps to correct the problem.[13] Employers also have successfully argued that invasion of privacy claims arising from the search of an employee's purse and work area for firearms are pre-empted by federal labor law, because searches are regulated by the terms of labor contracts.[14]

Common law tort suits against private employers usually have focused on the intrusion type of invasion of privacy. In *K-Mart Corp. Store No. 7441 v. Trotti*,[15] the Texas Court of Appeals noted that an employee who used his own lock on a locker had a reasonable expectation of privacy in a locker his employer provided for the storage of personal effects during non-working hours. While the employees could, on request, receive locks from the employer, who kept either a copy of the locks' combination or a master key, employees were allowed to purchase and use their own locks on the lockers.

The store manager testified that he searched the employee's locker because he suspected that an employee had stolen a watch. The manager said that during initial hiring interviews, all employees were told that company policy allowed the firm to conduct unannounced searches of lockers, and thus no expectation of privacy existed. In rejecting the employer's argument, the court set forth the common law definition of an invasion of privacy as "an unjustified intrusion of the plaintiff's solitude or seclusion of such magnitude as to cause an ordinary individual to feel severely offended, humiliated, or outraged." The court concluded that by having placed a lock on the locker at her own expense, the employee demonstrated a legitimate expectation of a right to privacy. Accordingly, a search by the employer that was not based on any reasonable grounds violated the employee's common law right to privacy.

Challenges to searches based on the tort of intrusion can fail unless all of the elements of the tort are established. One auto industry employee sued to enjoin his employer's policy of randomly searching vehicles leaving company property. A court found that because he refused to allow a search to be conducted, no intrusion occurred.[16]

Workplace Search Guidelines

Many employers that want to encourage their employees to feel comfortable in their work environments provide lockers, desks, or offices knowing that employees probably will have personal correspondence, photographs, and other items there with work-related materials. Employees contend that over time such an attitude leads them to expect that their lockers and desks will not be subjected to random searches by supervisors. Employers can take the following steps to retain the power to conduct random searches and searches connected to investigations while avoiding giving employees any legally binding expectation of privacy:

- When lockers, desks, or offices are assigned, make it clear to their users that the facility or equipment being assigned may be searched.

- Where offices or lockers have locks, keep duplicate keys to them. If employees are allowed to provide their own locks, require them to provide the employer with duplicate keys or combinations to the locks.

- Establish written policies outlining the circumstances under which searches will be conducted, and publicize these policies to all employees.

- To preserve the right to search at random, conduct random searches several times a year. A written policy that is never used is subject to challenge.

- Have employees confine their personal papers and files to one part of their offices or desks.

- Prohibit or place limits on the number or type of containers, such as luggage and gym bags, that employees can bring on employer property, or arrange for storage outside the entrance where employees will be checked to see they do not bring in such containers. For example, have employees park their cars in a central lot from which they must walk past the guard who conducts the checks.

OPENING EMPLOYEES' MAIL

Although the issue is seldom litigated, federal law prohibits any person from taking mail addressed to another person before it has been delivered, with the intent "to obstruct the correspondence, or pry into the business or secrets of another."[17] Violations carry a penalty of up to five years in prison and a fine of $2,000. Courts have said this law applies until mail "is physically delivered to the person to whom it is directed, or to his authorized agent."[18] No case has discussed the circumstances in which employers become "authorized agents" to receive the mail of their employees, or whether mail received in an employee's official capacity differs from mail marked "personal." However, one court recently found no violation of this law when an employer seized letters from an employee's office, because the letters were unmailed or had been received.[19]

The federal mail law does not allow a private action for damages.[20] At least one court has held that an employee who opened a fellow employee's mail that was delivered to the employer's office but was marked "personal" was liable for an intrusion on the co-worker's right of privacy.[21] To avoid possible civil or criminal liability, employers should not open employees' mail until it has been delivered to the employee, regardless of what evidence of criminal activity it may contain.

PROBES OF NON-WORK ACTIVITIES

Concerns about possible adverse publicity that may arise out of employee conduct during non-working hours, or evidence that employees may be defrauding their employer, violating non-competition agreements, or otherwise breaking company rules, have motivated some employers to investigate their employees' off-duty conduct away from the workplace. In doing so, public and private employers risk claims of invasion of the employee's right to privacy.

Surveillance or investigation by the employer outside the workplace, whether conducted in the public or private sector, may withstand legal challenge if it is initiated for business-related purposes and conducted in a reasonable and unobtrusive manner. Privacy challenges almost always succeed when employers engage in covert investigations in an obviously intrusive manner for reasons unrelated to the job.

Public employees have successfully claimed that their off-duty activities fall within a protected zone of privacy and therefore any investigation into those activities is improper. A good example is *Shuman v. City of Philadelphia*,[22] where an investigation was conducted into a police officer's allegedly adulterous conduct with a woman. The couple was followed, and the employee was told he had to answer questions about his relationship as part of the investigation. He refused and was fired.

A U.S. district court found that the police department's policy of investigating employees' activities that are unrelated to the performance of their official duties was unconstitutional. Citing *Whalen v. Roe*,[23] the court recognized the strong individual interest in avoiding disclosure of personal matters protected by the U.S. Constitution. Finding that a person's private sexual activities are within the protected "zone of privacy," the court held that unless those activities adversely affected his on-the-job performance, inquiry into them was unconstitutional. The court found that the city's policy requiring employees to answer all questions in protected areas on penalty of losing their jobs was unconstitutional. Similar cases frequently have involved investigations into political beliefs or personal associations of employees in non-sensitive jobs.[24] In these cases the government must show a paramount or vital governmental interest and choose the least-restrictive means to conduct the investigation.

While private employees cannot use the Constitution to protect their "zone of privacy" in their non-working activities, the tort of intrusion is applicable. To be actionable, the non-work activity must be private, interference with the employee's seclusion must occur, and the interference must be highly offensive. One court held that the surveillance of cars outside a union meeting in a public place was not an intrusion on seclusion because no person has a legitimate expectation of privacy in being free from inferences drawn from observations made in public.[25] Some legal experts contend that no right to privacy exists on a public street, and several courts have adopted this approach in finding that employers' surveillance of their employees in public was not intrusive.

In *Pemberton v. Bethlehem Steel Corp.*,[26] a Maryland court
considered the permissibility of an employer's surveillance of
an employee as well as dissemination of the results of the surveillance. The employer observed the employee's extramarital
affair and told union officials and the employee's wife. In its
analysis of the employee's invasion of privacy challenge, the
court noted that Maryland in proper circumstances would
recognize an action for unwarranted invasion of privacy,[27] but
no liability exists for observing an employee in public places.
Liability arises only when an employer uses methods of more
extensive intrusion, such as placing a detection device on the
employee's door at his house.[28]

In *Pemberton*, the surveillance was conducted to determine
whether the employee was responsible for sabotaging certain
equipment at Bethlehem's shipyard. The court concluded that
the surveillance and the circulation of information from detective reports to the employee's wife and union officials were not
actionable invasions of privacy. The surveillance comprised observing the plaintiff from outside his residence, outside what
appeared to be his girlfriend's home, and in public places. That
evidence, coupled with the plaintiff's testimony that he was not
aware of the surveillance while it was being conducted, aided
the court in determining that the employer did not invade the
plaintiff's privacy.

ILLUSTRATIONS

*U.S. Postal Service Did Not Violate Fourth Amendment By
Searching Employees' Lockers*

Postal inspectors, accompanied by union stewards, conducted unannounced searches of more than 1,600 employee
lockers at the Columbus, Ohio, post office. The searches were
conducted after postal officials were told of possible illicit drug
traffic and drug use at the facility, possible concealed weapons
on employees during working hours, and possible intoxication

of some employees at work. During the searches the inspectors found 582 pieces of mail illegally stored in one locker; intoxicants in three lockers; a file box with gambling records; and postal property in another locker. The American Postal Workers Union and six employees representing the class of postal workers whose lockers were searched sued the U.S. Postal Service and its agents, alleging a violation of the employees' Fourth Amendment rights.

The U.S. Court of Appeals for the Sixth Circuit ruled that the employees had no reasonable expectation of privacy in their respective lockers that was protected by the Fourth Amendment because of "clearly expressed provisions permitting random and unannounced locker inspections." The court noted that employees were required to sign a waiver that made the lockers subject to random inspection by authorized postal authorities. In addition, the collective bargaining agreement provided for random inspection of the lockers when reasonable cause existed to suspect criminal activity and a steward was allowed to monitor the search. Both conditions were satisfied in this case, providing further grounds for upholding the search. [*American Postal Workers Union v. United States Postal Service*, 871 F.2d 556, 4 IER 368 (6th Cir. 1989).]

Search Upheld Where Employer Had Policy Limiting Employees' Privacy Expectations

Kawneer Company, Inc. tried to search an employee's personal tool box during business hours after learning that a supervisor had observed the employee in what appeared to be a gambling transaction. The employer and the employee had keys to the tool box. The employee allowed the employer to search the tool box after he was threatened with termination for insubordination. Only empty envelopes and some brochures were found. The arbitrator ruled that the employer's dual-key policy "in effect, endowed the tool boxes with a half-private and half-company property characterization," and concluded that the employer had a right to search the boxes because it had reason to believe that properly promulgated and published rules had been violated. [*Kawneer Company, Inc.*, 86 LA 297 (1985).]

Surveillance Of Employee's Off-Duty Activities Upheld Where It Is Conducted In A Reasonable And Unobtrusive Manner

After a period of treatment for injury on the job, the Boise Cascade Corp.'s medical experts concluded McLain could safely return to work. Although McLain was given only "light" duties under which he was not required to lift more than 50 pounds, he complained that the work aggravated his alleged back injury. The company, through private investigations, took movies of the employee performing various physical tasks at his home, such as mowing his lawn and rototilling his garden. The Oregon Supreme Court held that because the investigators did not question any of the employee's neighbors or friends and limited their activities to filming while the employee was engaged in various activities outside his home, which could have been viewed by any member of the public, no intrusion had occurred. [*McLain v. Boise Cascade Corporation*, 271 Or. 549, 533 P.2d 343 (1975).]

ENDNOTES

[1] For a complete discussion of conducting interviews and investigations of employees, see *Thieves at Work* (BNA) 1988.

[2] *K-Mart Corp. Store No. 7441 v. Trotti*, 677 S.W.2d 632 (Tex. Ct. App. 1984), *writ refused*, 686 S.W.2d 593 (1985).

[3] 392 U.S. 364 (1968).

[4] *Id.* at 369.

[5] *Ortega*, 107 S. Ct. 1492.

[6] *Id.* at 1497.

[7] *See, e.g., Los Angeles Police Protective League v. Gates*, 579 F. Supp. 36, 44 (C.D. Cal. 1984) (police regulations establishing the right to search officer's locker eliminated any expectations of privacy); *Williams v. Collins*, 728 F.2d 721, 728 (5th Cir. 1984) (federal employee had no reasonable ex-

pectation of privacy in the locked drawer of his government-furnished desk); *United States v. Bunkers*, 521 F.2d 1217 (9th Cir. 1975), *cert. denied*, 423 U.S. 989 (1975) (search of the employee's locker furnished by the employer was found reasonable where the locker was subject to search by supervisors and postal inspectors as provided in the collective bargaining agreement). *United States v. Donato*, 269 F. Supp. 921, *aff'd* 379 F.2d 288 (3d Cir. 1967) (search of U.S. Mint employee's locker upheld where mint regulations provided that lockers were not private and security guards kept master key for regular sanitation inspections).

[8] *National Federation of Federal Employees v. Weinberger*, 818 F.2d 935, n.12 (D.C. Cir. 1987). *Accord U.S. v. Kahan*, 350 F. Supp. 784 (S.D.N.Y. 1972); *U.S. v. Hagarty*, 388 F.2d 713 (7th Cir. 1968); *Cf., U.S. v. Nasser*, 476 F.2d 1111 (7th Cir. 1972); *Allen v. Marietta*, 601 F. Supp. 482 (N.D. Ga. 1985).

[9] *See Schowengerdt v. General Dynamics Corp.*, 823 F. 2d. 1328 (9th Cir. 1987); *Bateman v. Florida*, 2 IER Cases 1075 (Fla. Dist. Ct. App. 1987).

[10] 83 LA 1096 (1984).

[11] 63-2 ARB 8843.

[12] Elkouri & Elkouri, *How Arbitration Works*, 790-91 (4th ed. 1985). *See, e.g., Lake Park of Oakland California & Hospital Employees, Local 250*, 83 LA 27 (1984).

[13] *Boone Energy and United Mine Workers of America, District 17, Local 1696*, 85 LA 233 (1985).

[14] *Hamrick v. Goodyear Aerospace Corp.*, 3 IER Cases 1246 (Ohio Ct. App. 1987).

[15] 677 S.W.2d 632 (Tex. Ct. App. 1984), writ refused, 686 S.W.2d 593 (1985).

[16] *Gretencord v. Ford Motor Co.*, 538 F. Supp. 331 (D. Kan. 1982).

[17] 18 USC 1702.

[18] *U.S. v. Ashford*, 530 F.2d 792, 795 (8th Cir. 1976).

[19] *Schowengerdt v. General Dynamics Corp.*, 823 F.2d 1328, 1340 (9th Cir. 1987).

[20] *Hill v. Sands*, 403 F. Supp. 1368, 1371 (N.D. Ill. 1975); *Schowengerdt*, 823 F.2d at 1340, n. 20.

[21] *Vernars v. Young*, 539 F.2d 966 (3d Cir. 1976).

[22] 470 F. Supp. 449 (E.D. Pa. 1979).

[23] 429 U.S. 589 (1977).

[24] *See, e.g., Clark v. Library of Congress*, 750 F.2d 89 (D.C. Cir. 1984).

[25] *International Union v. Garner*, 601 F. Supp. 187, 191 (M.D. Tenn. 1985).

[26] 66 Md. App. 133, 502 A.2d 1101, *cert. denied,* 306 Md. 289, 508 A.2d 488, *cert. denied,* 479 U.S. 984, 107 S.Ct. 571, 123 LRRM 3128 (1986).

[27] *See Carr v. Watkins,* 227 Md. 578, 177 A.2d 841 (1962).

[28] *See, e.g., Hamberger v. Eastman,* 106 N.H. 107, 206 A.2d 239 (1964); *McDaniel v. Atlanta Coca-Cola Bottling Co.,* 60 Ga. App. 92, 2 S.E.2d 810 (1939); *Roach v. Harper,* 143 W. Va. 869, 105 S.E.2d 564 (1958).

* * *

Workplace Surveillance

Monitoring and surveillance of employees in the workplace to combat crime and improve productivity has become increasingly common in recent years.[1] Employers have legitimate interests in observing employees to determine their productivity, efficiency, and compatibility with the organization. Employee advocates argue, however, that a critical distinction exists between overt observation of employees' work activities and secret surveillance of their actions or activities, which they claim is an invasion of privacy. While these practices may make employees dislike management, most on-the-job monitoring and surveillance cannot be successfully challenged under constitutional or common-law privacy theories. However, several federal and state laws regulate employee monitoring and surveillance.

TELEPHONE CONVERSATION MONITORING

About 200,000 telephone workers represented by the Communications Workers of America (CWA) are monitored, according to officials of that union. The union says 15 million Americans work in industries that monitor their employees. Workers who are subject to telephone monitoring include directory assistance and long-distance operators, health insurance company personnel, Internal Revenue Service employees, and airline and hotel reservations clerks. According to U.S. Rep. Don Edwards (D-Calif), in one year "14,000 employers regularly eavesdropped on the telephone conversations of close to 1.5 million employees."[2]

State Tort Claims

The tort of intrusion upon a person's solitude or seclusion extends to eavesdropping on private conversations by any means, including wiretapping telephones. In *Rhodes v. Graham*,[3] the plaintiff brought an action to recover damages for the tapping of telephone wires running into his home. The court recognized that an unwarranted invasion of the right to privacy occurred, stating that the "evil incident to the invasion of the privacy of the telephone is as great as that occasioned by an unwarranted publicity in newspapers and by other means of a man's private affairs for which courts have granted the injured persons redress."[4] Courts also have upheld invasion of privacy claims in cases involving a landlord eavesdropping on a tenant's bedroom with listening devices[5] and a telephone company that tapped a customer's line and listened to her conversations.[6]

Most jurisdictions recognize that improper interception of telephone conversations is tortious conduct.[7] The courts try to protect people's private conversations from unauthorized listeners. Thus, a basic element of this tort is the intentional overhearing of the contents of a private conversation by someone who is not intended to be a party to the communication.[8]

It is less obvious whether an employer's monitoring of an employee's telephone conversations during working time constitutes a similar invasion of the common-law right to privacy. The early wiretapping cases did not arise in the employment context, although the rationale for these cases might apply where the employees have permission to use their phones after hours, or to make private calls. In *Oliver v. Pacific Northwest Bell Telephone Co.*,[9] the plaintiff alleged that during his employment at North Pacific Lumber Co. and immediately thereafter, his telephone calls to and from the firm were monitored secretly. He claimed that this action constituted an invasion of privacy and a violation of the federal wiretap law.[10] The record in a previous suit brought by the employee indicated that on at least four occasions the employer monitored other employees' calls to spy on him and that once this was done to discover what the employees were doing.[11] The court dismissed Oliver's case, concluding that while the evidence indicated the employer had listened to conversations of other employees, no evidence existed to indicate any intrusion on the plaintiff's phone conversations.

Federal and State Wiretap Laws

The federal Omnibus Crime Control and Safe Streets Act of 1968 makes it a crime to "intentionally intercept ... any wire, oral or electronic communication."[12] The ban on intercepting "oral" communications is directed at "bugging," while the prohibition on intercepting wire or electronic communications is directed at "wiretapping." The law is intended as a comprehensive ban on wiretapping and electronic surveillance by people other than law enforcement agents, with certain limited exceptions.[13] Individual violators are subject to criminal penalties of up to five years in prison and a fine of up to $250,000, while organizations can be fined up to $500,000 for violations.[14] The law also authorizes civil damages. A person whose communication is unlawfully intercepted may recover actual damages, punitive damages, and attorney's fees from the interceptor.[15] Even if no actual damage is proven, the law provides for a minimum recovery of $100 for each day of the violation, or $10,000, whichever is greater.[16] Thus, a person may be entitled to minimum statutory damages and attorney's fees even if the intercepted communication is kept private and no harm results from the interception.[17]

The anti-wiretapping provisions of the act cover the interception of wire communications transmitted on any system capable of functioning in interstate commerce, such as the telephone system, even if the intercepted communication does not cross state lines.[18] Employees have used this provision to attack telephone monitoring by their employers. An employer can avoid liability if the monitoring of employee telephones comes within one of two exceptions to the general prohibition on intercepting wire communications.

The "telephone extension" exception[19] provides that the use of an extension telephone by an employer to monitor employee calls "in the ordinary course of business" is not a violation of the law. The "provider" exception states that it is not unlawful for a provider of wire communication service, such as the telephone company, to conduct service-observing or random monitoring for mechanical or service-quality control checks.[20] Cases brought under the federal wiretap law indicate that the legality of an employer's telephone monitoring depends on several factors, including how the monitoring is conducted, the purpose of the monitoring, and the nature of the call that was intercepted.

In *James v. Newspaper Agency Corp.*,[21] the U.S. Court of Appeals for the 10th Circuit concluded that the employer's monitoring fell within the "ordinary course of business" exception. The employer had the telephone company install a monitoring device on employee phones so supervisors could listen to business calls and thereafter instruct employees on how to deal with the public better, and to protect employees from abusive calls. The employer notified all affected personnel of the decision to install the device and no one objected. The court ruled that the plaintiff, whose main duties included collecting unpaid bills from advertisers, was not entitled to damages for the monitoring of her telephone.

Courts agree that routine monitoring of business calls to improve customer relations is a legitimate business purpose and falls within the "ordinary course of business" exception.[22] In *Watkins v. L.M. Berry Co.*,[23] however, the court held that a supervisor's interception on a monitoring system of an employee's personal call was not within the ordinary course of business. The employer used extension phones to allow supervisors to listen to sales calls. Employees were allowed to make personal calls on the system, and they were told that personal calls would be monitored only to the extent necessary to determine if they were personal. A supervisor listened to a phone call in which an employee discussed with her friend her hope that she would get a new job for which she had interviewed. The court rejected the employer's argument that monitoring was in the ordinary course of business because the employer had a business interest in whether it would lose an employee. The phrase "in the ordinary course of business," the court reasoned, "cannot be expanded to mean anything that interests a company," such as an employee's desire to quit or whether an employee has nice friends.[24]

The *Watkins* court laid down a general rule governing the interception of personal calls by monitoring systems. It held that a personal call may not be intercepted under the "ordinary-course" exception except to the extent necessary to guard against unauthorized use of the telephone or to determine whether the call is personal; that is, a personal call may be intercepted in the ordinary course of business to determine its nature but once the call is determined to be personal the monitoring must cease.

It is important to note that the general restrictions of the federal wiretap law — and the exceptions — apply to interception of calls between an employee and a third party. It is not unlawful under federal law for one agent of a corporate employer to listen to — or record — telephone conversations with another agent of the employer, if at least one party to the conversation has consented to the interception.[25] That is why, under federal law, an employer can tape-record telephone conversations to which it is a party as part of an investigation into employee misconduct.

Most states have enacted some type of restriction on wiretapping. Several of these laws are stricter than the federal law, and some prohibit the interception or recording of conversations without the consent of all parties.[26] Other states allow monitoring and electronic recording with the consent of one party.[27] Georgia's broad law has been interpreted to provide a private right of action when an employer places a wiretap on its employees' telephones.[28]

Through regulations promulgated in 1983 by its Public Utilities Commission, California has virtually banned telephone monitoring of employees.[29] The regulations require that no monitoring take place unless all parties consent to the monitoring or they are notified of the monitoring by:

- An audible "beep tone";
- Verbal announcement by the operator of the monitoring equipment; or
- A telephone instrument transmitter that is operationally connected to the communication circuit being monitored.

State telephone companies' use of "administrative monitoring" or "service observing" for training and quality control purposes is excluded from the ban. Violation of the regulations can result in discontinuation of service to a customer.

Proposed Legislation

Concerns about abuse of the exceptions to the wiretap laws and the broad use of monitoring by telephone companies has prompted a push for new federal and state legislation.

On April 6, 1987, Edwards introduced federal wiretap law amendments (HR 1950) that would have made it "unlawful for an employer to listen in on an employee's work phone unless a repeating audible tone is utilized to warn parties to the call."[30] Over 155 representatives co-sponsored the bill, but it failed to be voted out of the Judiciary Committee.

A substantially revised and expanded bill (HR 2168) has been introduced in the 101st Congress. The measure would require employers to provide:

- Notice to prospective employees of any existing forms of electronic monitoring, not just telephone monitoring;
- Written notice, if requested by a potential employee, regarding the types of monitoring used, the data collected, the frequency of monitoring, the use of the data, guidance on the interpretation of the information collected, existing production standards

and performance expectations, and methods for determining production standards and performance expectations based on the data collected;

- A system to warn the employee when monitoring is being conducted; and

- Notice to any affected customer of the employer that monitoring is being conducted.

In addition, the definition of "electronic monitoring" would be expanded to include "the collection, storage, analysis, and reporting of information concerning an employee's activities by means of a computer, electronic observation and supervision, remote telephone surveillance, telephone call accounting, or other form of visual, auditory, or computer-based surveillance conducted by any transfer of signs, signals, writing, images, sounds, data, or intelligence of any nature transmitted in whole or in part by a wire, radio, electromagnetic, photoelectronic, or photo-optical system."[31]

The bill could reach video surveillance and monitoring of security access systems in addition to telephone calls. The bill does not exempt employer investigations into employee misconduct. It would provide for civil fines of up to $10,000 for any violation, and affected employees could sue for compensatory and punitive damages and attorney's fees.

In addition to this federal effort, interested groups such as the CWA, the American Civil Liberties Union, the New York State AFL-CIO, and the National Organization for Women have pressed for legislation to limit monitoring of employees in many states, including New York, Minnesota, and Massachusetts. In 1983, West Virginia enacted a law requiring a beep tone when a supervisor is on the line monitoring a call, and requiring telephone companies to publish a notice to customers that their calls might be monitored. However, the law was repealed in 1986 after AT&T, which was planning to build a new credit management center in West Virginia, threatened to move the project to another state.[32] The CWA has launched a major drive in New York for a bill that, like the California regulations, would require employers to use a beep tone when they monitor an employee's phone conversation.[33] Currently, no state laws prohibit telephone monitoring under either the "telephone extension" or "ordinary course of business" exemptions.

ELECTRONIC SURVEILLANCE

While the types of electronic surveillance available to employers are constantly expanding as new technologies develop, most legal decisions address employer rights to use less-sophisticated technologies such as video cameras and eavesdropping equipment.

Different arbitrators who have ruled on cases where employers installed closed-circuit cameras have come to different conclusions about their appropriateness and legality. In one case, the arbitrator ruled that the use of an electronic eye in addition to the human eye is not an intrusion on the employee's privacy, and the only difference is that employees know they are being watched.[34] A contrary decision was reached where the arbitrator found that increased surveillance violated a labor contract provision requiring the employer to maintain the existing working conditions.[35] In a more recent case, another arbitrator ruled that the use and operation of a closed-circuit television monitoring system is an appropriate subject of bargaining and an employer cannot unilaterally impose such a system without first bargaining with the union.[36]

Visible television cameras, which the employees know will be operated at some time, usually concern employees less than secret monitoring or electronic eavesdropping. These types of surveillance are regulated by the federal wiretap law and several state laws. The anti-bugging provision of the Omnibus Crime Control and Safe Streets Act outlaws the use of a listening device to intercept a spoken communication "uttered by a person exhibiting an expectation that such communication is not subject to interception under circumstances justifying such expectation."[37] This definition is intended to incorporate the "expectation of privacy" requirement developed in Fourth Amendment cases.[38] Therefore, whether people have a reasonable expectation that their words will not be overheard depends on the circumstances.

In *United States v. McIntyre*,[39] the U.S. Court of Appeals for the Ninth Circuit concluded that an assistant chief of police had a reasonable expectation of privacy to a conversation in his office, even though the door to his office was open.[40] The court affirmed a criminal conviction of two fellow police officers who bugged the assistant chief's office for about 45 minutes with a briefcase containing a transmitter. The bug was authorized by police officials who suspected the assistant chief of drug trafficking and leaking damaging information to political enemies of the chief of police.[41]

The "bugging" provision requires a "federal nexus."[42] The bugging must violate the U.S. Constitution or affect commerce to be in violation of the federal wiretap act.[43] Because of this, the bugging prohibition may not be as broad as the ban on telephone wiretapping. Little litigation has occurred on the extent to which the law encompasses other forms of electronic surveillance in the workplace. The act also does not address video surveillance.[44]

Some states have prohibited certain forms of electronic surveillance and eavesdropping in the workplace and legislation has been proposed in several other states. Connecticut prohibits some types of electronic surveillance, including video surveillance of any area designed for the health and comfort of employees or for safeguarding their possessions, including rest rooms, locker rooms, and lounges.[45] A Massachusetts law struck down by the Massachusetts Supreme Court as unconstitutionally broad had provided that no employer could operate a monitoring device in a manufacturing establishment or factory for surveillance of a person's appearance, actions, and speech, without the consent of, and notice to, employees.[46] In 1987, California Gov. George Deukmejian (R) vetoed a bill to outlaw employers' use of computer software containing sub-liminal messages. In addition to such messages, the measure as introduced would have made it unlawful for an employer to engage in computer monitoring, electronic supervision, or other types of surveillance without notifying workers.[47] How-ever, all provisions except that on subliminal messages were deleted before the General Assembly passed the bill.

Although existing state wiretap laws could be applied in private arbitrations of union grievances over surveillance, they are not always used by arbitrators. One arbitrator has held that the installation of videotaping equipment for surveillance of a time clock did not violate a state law banning the use of any "eavesdropping device" to "hear or record oral con-versation."[48]

The number of employees being monitored probably will in-crease as monitoring technology becomes more sophisticated. New technologies already are being applied beyond the office. Tripmaster™, an "on-board computer" installed in truck cabs, is designed to reduce maintenance and improve efficiency for truck fleet operators. It monitors speed, shifting, idling, the length and frequency of drivers' work breaks, and the number of times the rear door of the trailer is opened. Similar com-puter systems are in operation in taxicabs, monitoring informa-tion such as the number of trips, the location of the vehicle, and the amount of the fares charged.[49]

COMPUTER-BASED MONITORING

Video display terminal (VDT) and other computer-based monitoring is the latest contested area of employer surveil-lance. Many workplaces are undergoing major technological changes. Automated information processing—comprising mainly computers and VDTs—is rapidly replacing typewriters, card indexing systems, and file cabinets. While VDTs benefit employees, they also are generating problems that probably will increase as their use increases. Much attention has been focused on the health hazards of VDTs, but employee groups also are advocating a right to know about VDT monitoring by their employers.

VDT monitoring can be used to develop data to set production quotas. Where systems are properly networked, monitoring could be used to determine what employees are typing on word processors in their offices. VDT monitoring advocates believe that it can increase productivity. Opponents argue that secret monitoring and monitoring to set production quotas are unfair and an invasion of privacy.

The Office of Technology Assessment of the U.S. Congress issued a comprehensive report in September 1987 on the uses of computer-based technologies to measure how fast or accurately employees work. The report found that such monitoring is useful to managers in managing resources, planning workloads, and reducing costs. The report found that the intensity and continuousness of computer-based monitoring raises questions about privacy, fairness, and quality of worklife, but that most of the workplace privacy issues have not been resolved. The report noted that existing concepts of privacy do not address many concerns over employee monitoring, because "the performance of tasks at work is, for the most part, an inherently public activity, which is done on behalf of the employer at the place of employment." Thus, unless an employee has an expectation in the activity itself or the location while at work, employers are generally free to collect as much information about employees' performance as they see fit.[50]

While proposed state legislation has been aimed primarily at health hazards, the California bill as introduced would have restricted some forms of VDT monitoring. Little legislative activity directed at VDT monitoring has occurred in Congress. However, a recent amendment to the Omnibus Crime Control Act could potentially apply to some forms of VDT monitoring. As enacted in 1968, the law applied only to interceptions of wire communications sent by common carrier, and only where the communication could be overheard and understood by the human ear.[51] In *U.S. v. Gregg*,[52] a U.S. district court concluded in 1986 that the law did not apply to a telex communication because a telex transmission could not be overheard in the sense of hearing its content.

Subsequently, Congress amended the law through the Electronic Communications Privacy Act of 1986 to make it reflect technological developments and changes in the telecommunications industry.[53] Congress extended the law's coverage to private communications systems that affect interstate commerce, including intra-company networks, and broadened the definition of "wire communication" to include digitized voice transmissions and voice transmissions by radio or fiber optic cable.[54] As a result, it is now illegal to intercept the non-voice data or digitized portion of a voice transmission. Finally, Congress added "electronic communication" to the activities protected by the law. The amendments define "electronic communication" as "any transfer of signs, signals, writing, images, sounds, data, or intelligence of any nature transmitted in whole or in part by a wire, radio, electromagnetic, photoelectronic or photo-optical system ...." This includes electronic mail, digitized transmissions, and video teleconferences.[55] The law as amended retains the "telephone extension" and "provider" exceptions.[56] Through mid-1989, no cases had been brought challenging an employer's monitoring of employee use of communication systems other than telephones.

The federal law is intended to cover the content of communications. It does not prohibit monitoring to record the existence of the communication.[57] For example, the U.S. Supreme Court has held that the use of a pen register, a device that records numbers dialed on a telephone, is not covered by the law.[58] By analogy, it can be argued that employer monitoring of employee speed or efficiency on a VDT also is not covered by the law. Whether and under what circumstances such monitoring violates the federal law or other laws protecting privacy has not been determined.

GUIDELINES FOR EMPLOYEE MONITORING

As workplace technology becomes more sophisticated, electronic monitoring will increase. Authorities in the field offer these suggestions for employers that want to monitor with a minimum risk of being sued for invasion of privacy:

- Employees whose performance is being monitored should be told when and why they will be monitored.

- Management should create reasonable work standards that account for different types of tasks and for short-term variations in employee performance.

- The interval between measurements should be no more frequent than it takes to make accurate calculations.

- Monitoring systems should give employees complete access to their records.[59]

ILLUSTRATIONS

Hearsay Testimony Cannot Be Used In Proving Violations Of The Federal Wiretap Law

Holles, a letter carrier at the Florence, Ala., post office, told Walker, another letter carrier, that his work station was bugged. Holles said he learned of the bugging during a conversation with one of his supervisors, Day, who said Walker's supervisors could stand in their offices and "hear everything that [Walker] says." Walker sued three of his supervisors, alleging that they had violated federal wiretapping law by eavesdropping on his private work site conversations with third parties. He also claimed an invasion of privacy under Alabama law.

In ordering summary judgment for the supervisors, the U.S. district court ruled that to prevail under the federal wiretap

law Walker must show that "the oral communications were in
fact interpreted, disclosed or used by the defendants and that
this cannot be established by hearsay testimony, either double
or single." Walker had failed to show the nature of his oral
communications allegedly intercepted by his supervisors; which
supervisor intercepted his communication; how, when, or in
what manner his oral communications were intercepted; or
what evidence proved that his work site conversations were intercepted. [*Walker v. Darby*, 706 F. Supp. 1467 (N.D. Ala.
1989).]

Monitoring And Disclosure Of An Employee's Personal Calls From A "Testdesk" Are Lawful Under The Federal Wiretap Law

A telephone company had all customer-trouble reports
received and handled at a testdesk. Supervisors monitored the
testdesk phones for service quality and to expedite work in
progress. A written company policy prohibited personal calls
from the testdesk, and other telephones were provided for this
purpose.

The employee had been warned repeatedly about his excessive use of the testdesk for personal calls. The court concluded
that the telephone company had a legitimate interest in maintaining quality control and in preventing the plaintiff's persistent use of the testdesk for personal calls, because keeping the
lines free for customers was of paramount importance. The
monitoring was lawful because it fell within the "provider" exception to the federal wiretap law. [*Simmons v. Southwestern
Bell Telephone Co.*, 452 F. Supp, 392 (W.D. Okla. 1978), *aff'd,*
611 F.2d 342 (10th Cir. 1979).]

Telephone Monitoring To Investigate Possible Leaks Did Not Violate Law

The employer suspected an employee of leaking confidential business information to his close friend, the owner of a
competing company. The employer used an extension phone to

listen secretly to a conversation between the employee and his friend, and to record it secretly. The employee admitted that the call concerned business. The court concluded that the employer's eavesdropping fell within the "ordinary course of business" exception of the federal wiretap law because it was closely tied to a legitimate business purpose — protection of confidential information — and the employer listened only long enough to confirm that business secrets were being disclosed. Had the employer's business reason been less compelling, the court added, the absence of a prior warning or policy might have been significant. [*Briggs v. American Filter Co.*, 630 F.2d 414 (5th Cir. 1980).]

ENDNOTES

[1] Craver, "The Inquisitorial Process In Private Employment," 63 *Cornell L. Rev.* 54-55 (1977).

[2] 17 IER 1 (BNA) (Apr. 14, 1987).

[3] 238 Ky. 225, 37 S.W.2d 46 (1931).

[4] *Id.* at 47.

[5] *Hamberger v. Eastman*, 106 N.H. 107, 206 A.2d 239 (1964).

[6] *LaCrone v. Ohio Bell Telephone Co.*, 114 Ohio App. 299, 182 N.E.2d 15 (1961).

[7] *See, e.g., Fowler v. Southern Bell Tel. & Tel. Co.*, 343 F.2d 150 (5th Cir. 1965); *Nader v. General Motors Corp.*, 25 N.Y.2d 560, 307 N.Y.S.2d 647, 255 N.E.2d 767 (1970); *Billings v. Atkinson*, 489 S.W.2d 858 (Tex. 1973); *Roach v. Harper*, 143 W. Va. 869, 105 S.E.2d 564 (1958).

[8] *See Marks v. Bell Tel. Co. of Pennsylvania*, 460 Pa. 73, 331 A.2d 424 (1975).

[9] 53 Or. App. 604, 632 P.2d 1295, *rev. denied*, 292 Or. 108, 642 P.2d 310 (1981).

[10] 18 USC 2510 *et seq.*

[11] *North Pacific Lumber Co. v. Oliver*, 286 Or. 639, 596 P.2d 931 (1979).

[12] 18 USC 2511 (1)(a).

[13] *1968 U.S. Code, Cong. & Ad. News* 2113, 2153, 2156.

[14] 18 USC 2511(1) and 4(a); *1986 U.S. Code, Cong. & Ad. News* 3575.

[15] 18 USC 2520; *1986 U.S. Code, Cong. & Ad. News* 3581.

[16] *Id.*

[17] *See Watkins v. L.M. Berry Co.*, 704 F.2d 577, 584 (11th Cir. 1983).

[18] *1968 U.S. Code, Cong. & Ad. News* 2180. *See, e.g., Epps v. St. Mary's Hospital of Athens, Inc.*, 802 F.2d 412, 414-415 (11th Cir. 1986) (call between employer's ambulance stations).

[19] 18 USC 2510 (5)(a).

[20] 18 USC 2511 (2)(a)(i).

[21] 591 F.2d 579, 18 FEP Cases 1547 (10th Cir. 1979).

[22] *See, e.g., Watkins v. L.M. Berry Co.*, 704 F.2d at 582 (11th Cir. 1983); *James*, 591 F.2d 579; *Simmons v. Southwestern Bell Telephone*, 452 F. Supp. 392 (W.D. Okla. 1978), *aff'd*, 611 F.2d 342 (10th Cir. 1979).

[23] 704 F.2d 577 (11th Cir. 1983).

[24] *Id.* at 582-583.

[25] *See U.S. v. Boley*, 730 F.2d 1326 (8th Cir. 1984); *U.S. v. McNulty*, 729 F.2d 1243 (10th Cir. 1983).

[26] *See* MICH. COMP. LAWS ANN. § 28.807(3)(anyone who uses a device to eavesdrop on a conversation without the consent of all parties is guilty of a felony); *Ribas v. Clark*, 696 P.2d 637 (Cal. 1985).

[27] Ga. Code Ann. § 16-11-62; *State v. Birge*, 240 Ga. 501, 241 S.E.2d 213, *cert. denied*, 436 U.S. 945 (1978).

[28] *Awbrey v. Great Atlantic & Pacific Tea Co.*, 505 F.Supp. 604 (N.D. Ga. 1980).

[29] Cal. Pub. Util. Comm., General Order 107-B, "Rules and Regulations Concerning the Privacy of Telephone Communications" (effective Oct. 19, 1983).

[30] HR 1950 (April 6, 1987). The Senate companion bill was S 1124.

[31] HR 2168 (May 2, 1989).

[32] *The Electronic Supervisor: New Technology, New Tensions*, US Congress, Office of Technology Assessment (Sept. 1977) at 47.

[33] S 1776/A 2640.

[34] *FMC Corp.*, 46 LA 335, 338 (1966).

[35] *EICO, Inc.*, 44 LA 563, 564 (1965).

[36] *Super Market Service Corp.*, 89 LA 539 (1987).

[37] 18 USC 2510 (2),(4); 18 USC 2511 (1)(a).

[38] *1968 U.S. Code, Cong. & Ad. News* 2178.

[39] 582 F.2d 1221 (9th Cir. 1978).

[40] *Id.* at 1224.

[41] 582 F.2d at 1223.

[42] *U.S. v. Burroughs*, 379 F. Supp. 736 (D.S.C. 1974), *aff'd*, 564 F.2d 1111 (4th Cir. 1977).

[43] 18 USC 2511(1)(a) and (b); *1968 U.S. Code, Cong. & Ad. News* 2180-2181.

[44] *1986 U.S. Code, Cong. & Ad. News* 3570; *People v. Teicher,* 439 N.Y.S. 2d 846, 52 N.Y.2d 638, 422 N.E.2d 506 (1980).

[45] CONN. GEN. STAT. ANN. § 31-48b(b)(West 1987).

[46] *Opinion of the Justices,* 356 Mass. 756, 250 N.E.2d 448 (1969).

[47] Assembly Bill 1279.

[48] *Casting Engineers,* 76 LA 939, 941 (1981).

[49] Gary T. Marx and Sanford Sherizen, "Monitoring on the Job: How to Protect Privacy as Well as Property," *Technology Review* (November/December 1986).

[50] *The Electronic Supervisor, supra,* note 32, at 7-120, 90, 113.

[51] *1986 U.S. Code, Cong. & Ad. News* 3556.

[52] 629 F. Supp. 958 (W.D.Mo. 1986).

[53] *1986 U.S. Code, Cong. & Ad. News* 3556-3557. *See also The Electronic Supervisor* at 108.

[54] 18 USC 2510(1); *1986 U.S. Code, Cong. & Ad. News* 3566.

[55] 18 USC 2510(4); and (12); (1986) *U.S. Code, Cong. & Ad. News* 3567-68.

[56] 18 USC 2510(5)(a), § 2511 2(a)(i); *1986 U.S. Code, Cong. & Ad. News* 3574.

[57] 18 USC 2510(4) and (8); *1986 U.S. Code, Cong & Ad. News* 3567-3568.

[58] *U.S. v. New York Telephone Co.,* 434 U.S. 159, 98 S.Ct. 364 (1977); 1986 *U.S. Code, Cong. & Ad. News* 3568-3569.

[59] 4 ERW 1074 (BNA) (Aug. 26, 1986).

* * *

Sexual Harassment

Some employers are finding that certain jokes are no laughing matter. If a male supervisor continually makes sexual jokes or comments to a female employee who finds them offensive and unwelcome, the supervisor's conduct might be considered sexual harassment for which the employer can be held liable.

TITLE VII

Title VII of the Civil Rights Act of 1964[1] makes it an unlawful employment practice for an employer to discriminate against "any individual with respect to his compensation, terms, conditions, or privileges of employment, because of such individual's ... sex ...." Title VII protects any victim of sexual harassment who is an employee of an employer in interstate commerce that has 15 or more employees, or of a city, state, or federal government employer (except the military).

Sexual harassment claims are not limited to female employees complaining about their male supervisors; a male employee also could bring a sexual harassment claim against an employer for the conduct of its female (or male) supervisor. In one case, a male employee of the Wisconsin Department of Health and Social Services received a probationary promotion to a supervisory position supervised by a female.[2] When the employee's relationship with his supervisor turned from romantic to platonic and he refused to comply with her sexual requests, she threatened to give him an unfavorable recommendation. The court held that he had no legal basis for bringing the claim—but only because his supervisor was not considered to be his "employer."[3] Because Title VII protects employees who are harassed because of their sex, regardless of the victim's sexual preferences, employers also may be liable for sexual harassment committed by a supervisor of the same

sex as the alleged victim. The court in one case held an
employer liable when a male employee was discharged because
he refused his manager's homosexual advances.[4]

Recent interpretations of Title VII recognize that sexual
harassment may violate the act in either or both of "quid pro
quo" situations and "hostile environment" situations. Conditioning employment benefits on an employee providing
sexual favors to a supervisor or another person who controls
the benefits may constitute quid pro quo sexual harassment.
Hostile environment Title VII violations occur when the sexual
harassment by any employee, including co-workers, creates a
hostile work environment.

The Equal Employment Opportunity Commission (EEOC)
has adopted the following definition of sexual harassment:

> Unwelcome sexual advances, requests for sexual favors, and other
> verbal or physical conduct of a sexual nature constitute sexual
> harassment when (1) submission to such conduct is made either
> explicitly or implicitly a term or condition of an individual's
> employment, (2) submission to or rejection of such conduct by an
> individual is used as the basis for employment decisions affecting
> such individual, or (3) such conduct has the purpose or effect of
> unreasonably interfering with an individual's work performance or
> creating an intimidating, hostile, or offensive working environment.

> [A]n employer ... is responsible for its acts and those of its agents
> and supervisory employees with respect to sexual harassment
> regardless of whether the specific acts complained of were
> authorized or even forbidden by the employers and regardless of
> whether the employer knew or should have known of their occur-
> rence.[5]

Courts have held employers liable for sexual harassment in
numerous situations. One court found liability because por-
nographic magazines were in the workplace, sexually oriented
pictures were shown at a company-sponsored presentation, and
a supervisor made offensive sexual comments concerning a
female employee who had been touched in an offensive manner by a co-worker.[6] Another employer was held liable for the
actions of its supervisor who had authority to recommend an
employee's discharge when that supervisor made sexual advan-

ces to the employee, even though the advances occurred off-premises and after work hours.[7]

EEOC adopted policy guidelines in October 1988 interpreting the application of Title VII to sexual harassment claims. Although not binding on courts, these guidelines may be given significant weight as interpretations of the law and as a summary of existing decisions.

Under both the quid pro quo and hostile environment theories, claimants must show that they were subjected to "unwelcome" sexual conduct, and that the harassment was based on their sex. In a quid pro quo sexual harassment claim an employee also must establish that submission to the unwelcome sexual advances or requests for sexual favors was an expressed or implied condition for receiving job benefits, or that refusal to accede to sexual demands resulted in a tangible job detriment.[8]

Unwelcome Conduct

Although the sexual conduct of a harasser is construed as "unwelcome" depends on the specific circumstances of the case, some general considerations usually are applied. It is no defense to a sexual harassment charge to claim that plaintiff submitted voluntarily to the sexual conduct of a supervisor.[9] Because the employee's acquiescence may be the result of fear of adverse repercussions, it cannot be assumed that an employee's voluntary behavior is the equivalent of "welcomed" sexual conduct. However, an employee's non-participation with the alleged harasser would indicate that the behavior was not welcomed.[10]

A fine line often exists between conduct that may be viewed as "welcome" or as "unwelcome." If an employee and her supervisor were engaged in a consensual social relationship but the employee decided she no longer wanted to be romantically involved with her supervisor, his continued overtures may be unwelcomed by her, but the supervisor may not be aware of the changed circumstances. The unwelcomed nature of the supervisor's conduct would be more readily apparent if that employee gave him some type of notice of her changed feelings. When EEOC is confronted with conflicting evidence as to welcomeness, it looks at the totality of the circumstances and evaluates each case separately.[11]

In a sexual harassment case a court probably will weigh the claimant's conduct against the existence of corroborating evidence and specific circumstances. Some courts have considered the dress or speech of an employee who has alleged sexual harassment to determine whether the sexual conduct was perceived as unwelcome.[12] If employees habitually wore sexually provocative clothing or spoke in a sexually suggestive manner, courts might find that their actions were inconsistent with their sexual harassment claims. One court rejected the harassment claims of an employee who regularly used vulgar language, asked male employees about their sex lives, and openly discussed her own sexual encounters. The court found that her sexual aggressiveness led to any propositions or sexual remarks directed to her by her co-workers.[13] EEOC has suggested that although a complaining employee's behavior toward the alleged harasser should be examined carefully, the employee's general character and past behavior toward others is of limited probative value.[14]

While some courts find that a complaining party's sexually oriented language should be considered, EEOC advised in its policy guidance that the occasional use of sexually explicit language will not automatically rebut an employee's claim that the sexual conduct was unwelcome. Moreover, consideration of the complaining employee's conduct will not contravene a finding of extreme or quid pro quo harassment.[15] In *Henson v. City of Dundee*,[16] the court defined "unwelcome conduct" as conduct that the employee did not solicit or incite, and of the type that the employee regarded as "undesirable or offensive."

A court assessing a sexual harassment claim probably will be influenced by a complaining employee's corroborating evidence, such as eyewitnesses, accounts of co-workers, and the results of similar harassment cases. The EEOC policy guidance states that employees' claims will be "considerably strengthened" where they have made a contemporaneous complaint or protest. Corroborating evidence is especially important when "the alleged harasser may have some reason (e.g., a prior consensual relationship) to believe that the advances will be welcomed." In those cases, it is particularly important for the employee to tell the supervisor that the conduct is unwelcome.[17]

The timing of the complaint or protest also is a factor. EEOC says that to be "contemporaneous" a complaint should be made during or shortly after the harassment. If the employee waits a long time before filing a complaint, it can be inferred that the sexual conduct was not as offensive as the employee claims.

Courts also will consider whether the employer has a procedure for filing complaints to determine whether it was possible to make a complaint and, if so, whether the complaint had to be filed with the same supervisor the complainant is charging with sexual harassment. Such circumstances may explain an employee's delay or failure in making a complaint or protest; it would be understandable for an employee to feel either apprehensive about confronting the accused supervisor or to feel that filing such a complaint would be futile.[18]

Liability for Quid Pro Quo Harassment

Neither supervisors nor employers may make an employee's submission to sexual demands a quid pro quo for job benefits. Any such actions resulting in a tangible or economic job consequence for the employee constitute quid pro quo sexual harassment for which an employer may be held liable.[19] Recent decisions indicate that generally an employer is strictly liable for all discriminatory actions of its supervisors that affect its employees' tangible job benefits, even if the employee did not complain and more-senior officials were unaware of the harassment.

For the employer to be held liable for quid pro quo sexual harassment by one of its supervisors, the supervisor must have actual or apparent authority to alter the employment status of the complaining employee. In *Meritor Savings Bank v. Vinson*,[20] the U.S. Supreme Court approved EEOC's position that sexual harassment by a supervisor is imputed to the employer when that supervisor acts with actual authority and threatens to make or makes employment-related decisions affecting subordinates. A supervisor who is authorized to recommend or direct the hiring, firing, or disciplining of an employee has the requisite authority to make the employer liable for the supervisor's sexual harassment. An employer will not be held liable for the sexual conduct of a supervisor who does not have authority to take adverse employment action against the employee.[21]

Liability for Hostile Environments

To establish Title VII violations resulting from employers' hostile work environments, claimants must show that they were the victim of sex-based harassment sufficiently severe to alter the conditions of employment and to create an abusive working environment.[22] In addition, claimants must demonstrate that the employer knew or should have known of the harassment but failed to take appropriate remedial measures.[23]

Stating that the language of Title VII is not limited to economic or tangible discrimination, the Supreme Court in *Meritor* followed the EEOC guidelines and held that a plaintiff "may establish a violation of Title VII by proving that discrimination based on sex has created a hostile or abusive work environment."[24] The court held that for sexual harassment to be actionable, it must be sufficiently severe or pervasive to alter the employee's employment conditions and create an abusive working environment.

In *Meritor*, Vinson, a female bank employee, alleged that she had been subjected to sexual harassment by her branch manager over the course of four years, but that she had failed to complain to any bank representative about the harassment. Vinson claimed her participation in a sexual relationship with her supervisor was out of fear that refusing his demands would cause him to discharge her. After the sexually oriented activities of her supervisor ceased, Vinson notified him that she was taking sick leave for an indefinite period; she was then discharged by the bank for excessive use of her sick leave.

According to EEOC guidelines, sexual conduct may be prohibited when it "has the purpose or effect of unreasonably interfering with an individual's work performance or creating an intimidating, hostile, or offensive working environment."[25] Whether the work environment is sufficiently pervasive, severe, and offensive is determined by the "reasonable-person" standard, rather than the complaining party's views.[26] That is, would the conduct of the supervisor or employer have interfered with a reasonable person's work performance, and would the conduct have seriously harmed the psychological well-being of a reasonable employee? If so, that workplace could be considered a hostile environment in violation of Title VII.

EEOC says that the more severe the harassment incident — especially if it was physical harassment — the less a need exists to show a series of incidents occurred. EEOC says courts should assume that "the unwelcome, intentional touching of a charging party's intimate body areas is sufficiently offensive to alter the conditions of her working environment and constitute a violation of Title VII."[27] Most courts, however, look at the totality of the circumstances and seldom find a hostile environment on the basis of a single isolated incident, no matter how severe it was.

In determining whether non-physical harassment is sufficiently offensive, the nature, frequency, context, and intended target of the remarks should be considered.[28] The U.S. Court of Appeals for the Sixth Circuit rejected an employee's sexual harassment claim, relying in part on the rationale that society condones and exploits erotica, coupled with the fact that the employee voluntarily entered her work environment and should have had "reasonable expectations."[29] EEOC takes the opposite position.[30]

Plaintiffs can establish hostile environment sexual harassment by presenting evidence that pervasive sexual conduct directed at other employees created an offensive work atmosphere for the plaintiff. The U.S. District Court for the District of Columbia in 1988 extended the *Meritor* ruling and found sexual harassment in a case where an attorney complained that the ongoing sexual conduct of others in her office created a hostile environment for her.[31] Although the court found the plaintiff to be sexually harassed, its holding rested primarily on its conclusion that the plaintiff was forced to work in an environment in which the managers harassed other female employees and her by bestowing preferential treatment on those who submitted to their sexual advances.

Another case that gave an expansive reading to *Meritor* was *Hall v. Gus Construction Co.*[32] In finding that offensive incidents and insults directed at three female employees by their male co-workers were sufficient to create an abusive working environment, the court considered conduct that was not sexual in nature. Because the employer's foreman had actual and constructive notice of the harassment complained of by the plaintiffs, the court held both the foreman and the employer liable for failing to take appropriate remedial measures to end the harassment.

Employers are not always liable in hostile environment situations. Where the harasser in a hostile environment case is a supervisory employee or a co-worker, courts will apply a knowledge standard: whether the employer knew or should have known of the harassment and failed to take immediate and appropriate remedial action.[33] In addition, the conduct must be sufficiently offensive to place the employer at risk.

The types of "knowledge" capable of imposing liability on employers includes actual knowledge, notice, or constructive knowledge. "Actual" knowledge may come from proof by appropriate observers. "Notice" may be provided by a victim who has used the grievance procedure. "Constructive" knowledge may result from proof that the employer should have known of the harassment because it was sufficiently pervasive.[34]

Although the court in *Meritor* declined to rule definitively on employers' liability in hostile environment cases, it noted that an employer is not always shielded from liability when it did not have notice of its agent's acts.[35] The court also said the fact that a place of employment has a grievance procedure and a policy against discrimination does not necessarily insulate the employer from liability when a complaining employee fails to use that grievance procedure.[36] In *Meritor*, the employer's policy against discrimination did not denounce sexual harassment, and the bank's grievance procedure required employees to complain first to their supervisor, who, in *Meritor*, was the alleged harasser. Although the Supreme Court found the existence of a non-discrimination policy and grievance procedure to be relevant to the issue of liability, it stated that the employer's argument would be "substantially stronger if its procedures were better calculated to encourage victims of harassment to come forward."[37]

Citing the *Restatement (Second) of Agency*, the law outlining the legal relation of principles and agents that are frequently applied in employment situations, the court in *Meritor* held that the appeals court had erred in concluding that employers are always liable for the sexual harassment of their supervisors.[38] Section 219 of the Restatement provides:

> A master is subject to liability for the torts of his servants committed while acting in the scope of their employment. A master is not subject to liability for the torts of his servants acting outside the scope of their employment, unless: (a) the master intended the conduct or the consequences, or (b) the master was negligent or reckless, or (c) the conduct violated a non-delegable duty of the master, or (d) the servant purported to act or to speak on behalf of the principal and there was reliance upon apparent authority, or he was aided in accomplishing the tort by the existence of the agency relation.

In hostile environment cases where a supervisor has committed the sexual harassment it is unclear under what circumstances the employer will be liable for its supervisor's acts. Some courts have applied principles of agency law and have focused on whether supervisors acted within the scope of their employment, and if not, whether the employer should be held liable because the employer's delegation of authority to the supervisor made it easy for the supervisor to harass employees.[39] Because no job description is likely to include "sexual harassment" as part of the job it describes, the "scope of employment" phrase may not always apply literally. EEOC maintains that a supervisor's behavior is within the scope of employment if it represents "the exercise of authority actually vested in him."[40]

Even if supervisors' actions fell outside the scope of their employment because they lacked authority, employers can be held liable if they "ratify" those acts. If the employer becomes aware of work-related sexual harassment and fails to stop it, the employer's acquiescence brings the supervisor's actions within the scope of employment for which the employer may be held liable.[41]

Some courts have applied an exception to the "within the scope of employment" requirement, relying on Section 219(2)(d) of the *Restatement (Second) of Agency*, and holding an employer liable — irrespective of the employers' knowledge — where (1) reliance on the supervisor's apparent authority existed or (2) the supervisor's relationship to the employer helped the supervisor accomplish the harassment.[42] If the supervisor's actions may reasonably be viewed as the exercise of authority condoned by the employer's conduct, the employer may be liable for the actions of a supervisor who has acted with apparent authority.[43] For example, if the employer has no policy against sexual harassment or no effective complaint procedure and a supervisor has harassed an employee, that employee could reasonably believe that the employer tolerates the supervisor's behavior. The more authority supervisors have, the more likely they are to have apparent authority to make the employee endure a hostile environment out of fear of retaliation.

To divest its supervisors of apparent authority, employers should implement policies against sexual harassment and maintain effective grievance procedures.[44] Under EEOC's policy guidance it is unreasonable for employees to believe that their supervisor had actual or apparent authority when a well-publicized policy against sexual harassment and an effective grievance procedure exist.[45] If the employee fails to file a complaint through the grievance procedure, and the employer did not have notice from some other source, the employer may be able to establish the lack of an agency relationship in that no apparent authority existed, thereby escaping liability for hostile environment sexual harassment. However, an employer usually will be liable for supervisory actions affecting employees' employment status, whether or not the employer had a policy against harassment.[46]

In a recent case where a plaintiff brought an action against a university for sexual harassment directed at her by male medical residents, the court applied a knowledge standard and found sufficient facts establishing that the university had actual or constructive knowledge of the residents' conduct.[47] The court held that the failure of the plaintiff's supervisors to investigate and end the sexual harassment constituted acquiescence in the residents' unlawful conduct and encouragement of it.

Other theories can make an employer liable for the acts of its supervisors. The EEOC policy guidance provides that under an agency-by-estoppel theory an employer is liable when it "intentionally or carelessly causes an employee to mistakenly believe the supervisor is acting for the employer, or knows of the misapprehension and fails to correct it." This situation would occur, for example, where the employer does not respond to past incidents of harassment and thereby leads employees to believe that future incidents will be accepted.

When an employer is negligent or reckless in its supervision of the harasser, liability may also be imputed.[48]

"Respondeat superior" is another doctrine that makes a principal liable for the acts of its agent, provided that the agent's failure to use care toward those whom the principal owes a duty is within the course of employment.[49] Respondeat superior requires the employee to show that the harassing employee had the ability to make decisions affecting the victim's employment.

Remedies and Damages Under Title VII

Remedies available under Title VII include restitution, declaratory and injunctive relief against further harassment, back pay, front pay under certain conditions where reinstatement is inappropriate, and attorney's fees and costs. Under Title VII a victim of sexual harassment is unable to recover compensatory damages (emotional distress) or punitive damages. However, plaintiffs may be awarded economic damages if they establish loss of tangible job benefits such as lost promotion, or constructive discharge.

STATE FAIR EMPLOYMENT PRACTICE LAWS

Sexually harassed employees may have other avenues of relief available to them in addition to Title VII. Some state and local laws relating to fair employment practice may prohibit sexual harassment and reach smaller employers. Some of these laws, unlike Title VII, may allow jury trials, and allow for emotional distress damages and punitive damages.

For example, California's Fair Employment and Housing Act makes sexual harassment unlawful and prohibits unwelcome sexual advances that condition an employment benefit on an exchange of sexual favors.[50] In one case, the California Fair Employment Housing Commission (FEHC) found the actions and comments of a supervisor had been ratified by the employer so as to constitute sexual harassment of an employee, causing her to suffer significant emotional injury. The FEHC ordered the employer to stop condoning the sexually harassing conduct of its supervisory employees and to pay the plaintiff $20,000 as compensatory damages for emotional injury and $50,000 in punitive damages.[51]

In Delaware, the state Department of Labor requires employers to post a notice that sexual harassment is prohibited. Employers are required to post the notice in a place that is well-lighted and easily accessible. The notice must address employees and must describe sexual harassment to include:

- Employees being forced to submit to sexual demands to keep their jobs, get a promotion, or obtain other favorable job-related decisions; and

- Sexual suggestions, jokes, or sexual language that make the working environment intolerable or otherwise interferes with employees' work performance.

In addition, the notice must explain that if the harassment is by a supervisor, the employer is responsible even if employees have not complained. If the harassment is by a co-worker or a non-employee, employers are responsible if employees have complained and the employer has not taken corrective action.[52]

State laws also may influence evidentiary matters. For example, California and several other states have "shield laws" limiting evidentiary searches into sexual harassment victims' personal lives by prohibiting inquiries about their sexual past, fantasies, and manner of dress.

Because the remedy for violations of state laws often includes monetary damages, employers must obey their state laws and comply with related requirements, such as posting required notices, to avoid financial liability.

STATE COMMON LAW REMEDIES

Employees and former employees have asserted a variety of claims under state common law based on the same facts as their sexual harassment claims under Title VII. State common law claims vary among the states, depending on each state's law. Federal courts also have entertained such claims under the doctrine of pendant jurisdiction, but such jurisdiction is discretionary.[53] One important reason employees bring state common law claims is that some of these claims allow punitive and compensatory damages, which are not allowed under Title VII.[54] State claims also enable employees to bring an action for sexual harassment after the Title VII statute of limitations has expired.[55] The nature of claim brought by employees will depend in part on the facts of each case. For example, a case involving physical actions also may prompt a complaint of assault and battery. The following are state common law causes of action in the areas of tort and wrongful discharge law that have been utilized in sexual harassment cases.

Intentional Infliction of Emotional Harm

To succeed under this cause of action, a plaintiff generally must establish that the harassment was extreme or outrageous, intentional or reckless, and caused severe emotional distress.[56] The nature of the harassing actions will determine whether the conduct complained of was sufficiently outrageous, and courts have denied plaintiffs recovery for intentional infliction of emotional harm where the conduct was otherwise actionable under Title VII but not sufficiently "outrageous."[57]

Assault and Battery

Actions for assault and battery often are brought in conjunction with sexual harassment claims when instances of unwelcome touching have occurred.[58] In *Pease v. Alford Photo Industries*, a court held for the plaintiff on sexual harassment, assault and battery, and a variety of other state law claims where the employer had touched intimate parts of the plaintiff's body.[59]

Invasion of Privacy

Such claims arise in conjunction with sexual harassment actions where the employee's right of privacy is unlawfully invaded by unreasonable intrusion by the employer or its agents.[60] The intrusion may take the form of physical actions, such as unwelcome touching, or through verbal communications such as loud or suggestive remarks. However, with regard to the latter, a plaintiff asserting an invasion of privacy claim in the context of sexual harassment may have to assert "publication" of the remarks to a large number of people or to the public in general.

Negligent Failure to Warn

The U.S. Court of Appeals for the Fourth Circuit in *Paroline v. Unisys Corp.* (discussed below) considered the question of whether an employer was liable to an employee asserting sexual harassment under a cause of action for negligent failure to warn where the offending supervisor had been warned several times previous to the employee's complaint to refrain from sexual harassment. The court remanded the issue to the U.S. district court for clarification by the plaintiff without deciding whether such a claim exists under Virginia law.

Employees also may use sexual harassment as a basis for a wrongful discharge claim. Such claims most likely would be brought under the public policy exception to at-will employment.[61] To succeed on such a claim, the plaintiff must show that the reasons for the discharge are so reprehensible they are against public policy.[62]

As a defense to state common law tort actions in sexual harassment cases, employers have been successful in asserting that such claims are precluded by the exclusivity provisions of the worker's compensation law in the state where the plaintiff was employed. These provisions usually prevent employees from suing employers for injuries sustained by a co-worker's actions.[63] This defense has been successful with regard to a cause of action based on sexual harassment for assault and battery[64] and intentional infliction of emotional harm.[65] However, some states do not recognize the exclusiveness provisions of a worker's compensation law as a defense where the actions that allegedly took place were intentional, which usually is the case in sexual harassment actions.[66]

MAINTAINING THE BALANCE OF PRIVACY

Employers that try to prevent sexual harassment liability must sometimes balance taking precautions and infringing on their employees' rights to privacy in personal matters. By restricting or prohibiting romances in the workplace, an employer may be guarding against charges of sexual harassment in situations where, for example, the relationship sours. However, these precautions may result in invasion of privacy claims. (See Chapter XII.)

EEOC policy guidance on sexual harassment does not address the issues that arise from voluntary consensual relationships in hostile environment, favoritism, or retaliation cases.

The difficult issues posed by voluntary relationships were addressed in *Keppler v. Hinsdale Township School Dist.*[67] Keppler held an administrative position that reported directly to the superintendent, but her office was in one of the district's two high schools. In late 1982, she began a relationship with the assistant principal, Miller. Miller became principal in 1984. The relationship continued until March 1986. Keppler alleged that on at least two occasions in March 1986, Keppler and Miller saw each other socially, but she rejected his sexual advances.

From August 1986 until February 1988, Miller made several negative comments to the superintendent about Keppler's performance. The superintendent recommended that Keppler resign her administrative position because of her poor relationship with the two high school principals. Shortly thereafter, the school board terminated Keppler. Keppler sued Miller and the school district for sexual harassment.

The court assumed that Miller was Keppler's "employer," not a co-worker, because he was responsible for reporting on her work. Nevertheless, the court granted the defendants' motion for summary judgment, relying on the decision of the U.S. Court of Appeals for the Seventh Circuit in *Huebschen v. Dept. of Health and Social Services.*[68] The court distinguished between conventional quid pro quo cases involving express or implied demands for sexual favors in return for job benefits, and "sexual retaliation" cases, where an employer makes sexual advances without any express or implied quid pro quo, the employee rejects the advances, and the employer fires, demotes, or takes other retaliatory actions against the employee. In normal situations, employees have a right to expect to be treated the same if they decline their employer's sexual advances. But where a prior consensual relationship existed, employers who retaliate because their former lover jilted them may be reacting not just to the refusal of sexual advances, but to the end of the intimate physical and emotional relationship. The court said:

> An employee who chooses to become involved in an intimate affair with her employer, however, removes an element of her employment relationship from the workplace, and in the realm of private affairs people do have the right to react to rejection, jealousy and other emotions, which Title VII says have no place in the employment setting.

> Such an employee, of course, always has the right to terminate the relationship and to again sever her private life from the workplace; when she does so, she has the right, like any other worker, to be free from a sexually abusive environment, and to reject her employer's sexual advances without threat of punishment. Yet, she cannot then expect that her employer will feel the same as he did about her before and during their private relationship. Feelings will be hurt, egos damaged or bruised. The consequences are the result not of sexual discrimination, but of responses to an individual because of her former intimate place in her employer's life.[69]

Although the approach taken in *Keppler* was well-reasoned, it will not necessarily be applied in all cases. Of particular concern to employers is the possibility that a court could find no sexual harassment by the supervisor or co-worker, but could find disparate treatment on the basis of sex by the employer where, for example, an employer transferred the woman instead of the man where a personal relationship became acrimonious and was damaging job performance or morale.

No simple guidelines exist in this area. It comprises problems that require careful handling by human relations and equal employment opportunity personnel on a case-by-case basis.

LIABILITY FOR WRONGFUL TERMINATION

Employers can escape or limit the extent of liability for hostile environment sexual harassment by taking prompt remedial action against the harassing employee. Employers are in the unenviable position of having to decide whether circumstances merit discharging the offending employee. An employer can be sued by the harassed employee for a supervisor's conduct and also be sued by the supervisor for wrongful discharge or demotion. The courts and EEOC provide no guidance on when the offending employee's discharge is necessary to constitute an appropriate response to sexual harassment complaints.

In several cases supervisors fired for alleged sexual harassment have filed claims of wrongful discharge, age discrimination, defamation, and other theories. Employers should consider the evidence of harassment, the business considerations involved in disciplining harassers, and the comparative risks of liability. In states that provide compensatory or punitive damages for wrongful discharge, but not for sexual harassment, it may be in the employer's interest to discipline the harasser with something less than firing, such as a transfer or demotion.

MINIMIZING THE RISK OF LIABILITY

Establishing Internal Policies and Procedures

To reduce their risk of liability, employers must:

- Establish highly visible written policies that explicitly condemn sexual harassment, and
- Inform all employees about the employer's internal complaint procedures that are available for employees who think they are the victims of sexual harassment.

To be effective, complaint procedures should: (1) provide for full investigation of issues raised; (2) provide corrective measures for any sexual harassment that is uncovered; and (3) provide safeguards against the recurrence of such conduct.

The EEOC policy guidance suggests that employers discuss the issue of sexual harassment with all employees, express strong disapproval, and explain the penalties for harassment. Employers also should establish a grievance procedure designed to encourage employees who are sexually harassed by their supervisor to tell the appropriate company officials about it without having to complain first to the supervisor.[70]

Take Prompt Action

Employers have a duty to investigate complaints of sexual harassment in the workplace promptly and thoroughly.[71] Employers also have a responsibility to take "immediate and appropriate" corrective action to compensate victims for lost employment benefits and opportunities and to take preventive measures to prevent such harassment in the future, including ensuring that victims do not suffer retaliation for lodging their complaint.[72]

"Appropriate" disciplinary action an employer may take against supervisors who sexually harass employees ranges from a reprimand to discharge, depending on the severity of the supervisor's misconduct. For example, where a victim had told her employer that a co-worker had spoken to her about sexual activities and touched her offensively, a court held that the employer's response was immediate and appropriate.[73] Within four days of receiving the information, the employer investigated the complaint, reprimanded the co-worker, put him on probation, and warned him that he would be fired for further misconduct. The employer also reprimanded another co-worker who had witnessed the harassment and had not intervened or reported the misconduct.[74]

Conducting Investigations

Investigating an employee's sexual harassment complaint is an essential employer response, and the investigation must be conducted properly to avoid adverse repercussions. In one recent case, a female employee's parents complained that Kestenbaum, head of guest operations at the ranch where their daughter worked, sexually harassed their daughter. The owner of the ranch, Pennzoil, investigated the complaint and interviewed other female employees.[75] Pennzoil officials spoke with Kestenbaum, allowed him to confront its investigators, and to comment on the people who were interviewed. Moreover, Kestenbaum was asked to name witnesses who would speak on his behalf. Following the investigation, he was fired.

The Supreme Court of New Mexico upheld a jury finding that Pennzoil had not acted reasonably in terminating Kestenbaum and the jury's compensatory damages award of $500,000 to him. The supreme court criticized Pennzoil's investigative report because the investigator failed to evaluate the credibility of the people who were interviewed, and failed to differentiate between first-hand knowledge and rumor.

Another jury recently awarded $1 million to a corporation general foreman whom they found to have been wrongfully discharged.[76] One of the company's female employees had brought sexual harassment charges against the foreman for unzipping his fly in front of female employees and saying, "If you want it, here it is." In response to the harassment complaint, the corporation fired the employee, who worked for the firm for 12 years, stating that he was an at-will employee.

Although the jury found the corporation's response to be unduly harsh, the U.S. Court of Appeals for the 10th Circuit said the appropriate issue was whether the firing was legal under the circumstances, and ruled against the foreman.

To guard against the possibility of other juries making similar findings, employers should ensure that their investigations of sexual harassment complaints are thorough, fair, prompt, and beyond reproach. Such investigation also should be as confidential as possible to prevent defamation and other claims against the employer.

Keeping the complaints confidential is an especially difficult problem for employers. Agreeing to a complainant's request that the complaint be kept confidential probably will inhibit the investigation. Employers can interview some personnel among the workforce involved with the complaint, but it will often be difficult to confront a supervisor and maintain confidentiality. Employers also face potential liability if the complainant or a co-worker subsequently files a formal complaint and alleges that the employer failed to take prompt action to solve the problem.

EEOC General Counsel Charles A. Shanor said in March 1988 that employers presented with a complaint and a request for confidentiality, should advise the employee that confidentiality cannot be maintained "to the extent that the employer would be prohibited from investigating and resolving the problem identified."[77] Several cases suggest that the employer's duty to investigate sexual harassment is strong.[78] Employers need to decide in each case whether to place the duty to investigate and to take prompt remedial action above requests for confidentiality when the two come into conflict, even though employers' refusals to keep complaints confidential may dissuade employees from filing complaints.[79] The courts have provided little guidance to employers on how to resolve these competing interests.

ILLUSTRATIONS

Employer Not Liable For Damages To Former Employee Arising From Sexual Assault By Co-Employee

An employee was found to have been sexually assaulted on at least one occasion by a co-worker at a fast-food restaurant. The court rejected the employee's claim under Title VII because she failed to establish that the employer knew or should have known of the harassment.

Faced with conflicting testimony, the court found that the employee's supervisors did not have actual notice of the harassment that occurred despite the plaintiff's testimony that she had lodged complaints of harassment against the co-worker. The court also found that the on-the-job sexual harassment was not pervasive enough to establish an inference of such notice. Consequently, because the court held that some knowledge by the employer must be present to establish the employer's liability for sexual harassment damages pursuant to Title VII, the plaintiff could not succeed on her claim. [*Valdez v. Church's Fried Chicken*, 683 F. Supp. 596, 47 FEP Cases 1155 (W.D. Tex. 1988).]

IRS Sexual Harassment Charges Against Employee's Supervisor Are Outside Agency's Mission And, Therefore, Unfounded

The Internal Revenue Service (IRS) demoted a supervisor for actions that allegedly occurred at an after-hours Halloween party. The agency brought a charge of sexual harassment for an episode occurring after the party where the supervisor allegedly kissed an employee, leaned against her, and was sexually aroused. The U.S. Court of Appeals for the Federal Circuit held that no basis existed for disciplining the supervisor because what happened at the party was a private matter. The court also reversed and remanded after holding that none of the charges against the supervisor was supported by substantial evidence. [*Grubka v. Dept. of Treasury*, 858 F.2d 1570, 48 FEP Cases 48 (Fed. Cir. 1988).]

Employer Held Not Liable Because It Took Prompt Remedial Action Against Hostile Work Environment

Two female employees brought an action against their former male supervisor and former employer on several theories, including invasion of privacy and sexual harassment under Title VII. The conduct about which they complained included sexual innuendoes and joking. The employees took detailed notes of the supervisor's comments and reported the supervisor to his superiors. However, they also engaged in sexually oriented joking with the supervisor. After receiving the employees' complaint, the employer issued a verbal reprimand to the supervisor and told him the behavior must stop. The employer's EEO officer told the employees that the supervisor would stop making offensive comments. The offensive behavior ceased after the supervisor was reprimanded. The employees quit less than two weeks later.

The U.S. Court of Appeals for the 11th Circuit upheld the U.S. district court's denial of the invasion of privacy charge because it was found that adequate publication had not occurred. The appeals court also upheld the district court's determination that quid pro quo sexual harassment had not occurred because no evidence existed of changes in the working conditions of the complaining employees, and it also upheld the lower court's finding that the sexual innuendoes and jokes had created a hostile work environment.

However, the appeals court held that the employer was not directly liable for the supervisor's actions because it did not know nor should it have known of the supervisor's actions. The court rejected strict liability of an employer in a hostile environment action as illogical. Rather, the court held that a respondeat superior standard must be applied and, because the employer had taken the necessary remedial action, no liability existed under such a standard. [*Steele v. Offshore Shipbuilding, Inc.*, 867 F.2d 1311, 49 FEP Cases 522 (11th Cir. 1989).]

Employee Was Constructively Discharged When She Was Told She Should Admit That An Incident Of Sexual Harassment Was Accidental

When the former employee of a family-operated business complained to her former supervisor, who was the employer's son, about sexual harassment by the employer, she was told by the employer's wife that the company would make trouble for her unless she said the incident was an accident. The employee was then escorted from the premises.

A court found that an employer was liable for quid pro quo sexual harassment when he touched one of his employees against her wishes. The court weighed the testimony of the employer, the former employee, and other former employees who had made similar complaints.

The court held that this amounted to constructive discharge. The former employee also was successful on state law claims of assault and battery, intentional infliction of emotional distress, invasion of privacy, and outrageous conduct based on the actions of the employer. [*Pease v. Alford Photo Industries*, 667 F. Supp. 1188, 49 FEP Cases 497 (W.D. Tenn. 1987).]

Employer Denied Summary Judgment On Employee's Claims Of Sexual Harassment And Constructive Discharge

An employee brought an action under Title VII and certain state law causes of action against her employer and her supervisor for sexual harassment and constructive discharge. The employee had allegedly been the object of the supervisor's sexual advances both on and off the job. The supervisor had a history of similar behavior involving other women employees and had been warned against such actions by the employer.

The U.S. Court of Appeals for the Fourth Circuit held that the trial court had erred in granting summary judgment to the employer on the sexual harassment and constructive discharge claims. The appeals court held that whether the supervisor's harassment was sufficiently severe or pervasive was a matter of fact that was in dispute. Based on the record, the court held that the supervisor's unwelcome touching and sexual innuendo could be found by a reasonable person to be harassment.

With regard to the liability of the employer, the appeals court held that a fact-finder could find that the warning given to the supervisor was insufficient in light of his past actions and that the reprimand of the supervisor, following the employee's complaint, did not have a deterrent effect. The appeals court concluded that the employer may not have taken a suitable remedial action by merely reprimanding the supervisor, in light of his history.

With respect to the state law claims, the court remanded the employee's failure-to-warn cause of action for clarification by the employee. The court also held that the conduct complained of was not so outrageous as to support a claim for intentional infliction of emotional harm. [*Paroline v. Unisys Corp.*, F.2d, 1989 WL 67915 (4th Cir. 1989).]

ENDNOTES

[1] 42 USC 2000e, *et seq.*

[2] *Huebschen v. Department of Health and Social Services*, 716 F.2d 1167, 32 FEP Cases 1582 (7th Cir. 1983).

[3] Although cases of sexual harassment where a female employee has complained of offensive conduct by her male supervisor outnumber cases of male employees complaining of sexual harassment by their female supervisors, this special report adheres to BNA's style of using non-sexist language, where feasible and appropriate, including the use of plural pronouns instead of singular pronouns that indicate the subject's sex.

[4] *Joyner v. AAA Cooper Transportation,* 597 F. Supp. 537, 542-44 (M.D. Ala. 1983), *aff'd,* 749 F.2d 732 (11th Cir. 1984).

[5] 29 CFR 1604.11 (a) & (c).

[6] *See Barbetta v. Chemlawn Services Corp.,* 669 F. Supp. 569, 44 FEP Cases 1563 (W.D.N.Y. 1987).

[7] *See Schroeder v. Schock,* 42 FEP Cases 1112 (D. Kan. 1986).

[8] *Henson v. City of Dundee,* 682 F.2d 897, 29 FEP Cases 787 (11th Cir. 1982).

[9] *Meritor Savings Bank FSB v. Vinson,* 477 U.S. 57, 106 S. Ct. 2399, 2406 (1986).

[10] *See, e.g., Lamb v. Drilco,* 32 FEP Cases 105 (S.D. Tex. 1983).

[11] *See EEOC Policy Guidance On Current Issues of Sexual Harassment* ("EEOC Policy Guidance") (1988) at 6.

[12] *EEOC Policy Guidance* at 9-11.

[13] *Gan v. Kepro Circuit Systems,* 27 EPD 32,379 (E.D.Mo. 1982).

[14] *EEOC Policy Guidance* at 10.

[15] *See EEOC Policy Guidance* at 9.

[16] 682 F.2d 897, 903 (11th Cir. 1982).

[17] *EEOC Policy Guidance* at 7.

[18] *EEOC Policy Guidance* at 7.

[19] *See, e.g.,* 29 CFR 1604.11(a)(2); *Schroeder v. Schock,* 42 FEP Cases 1112 (D. Kan. 1986).

[20] 477 U.S. 57, 106 S. Ct. 2399 (1986)

[21] *See Koster v. Chase Manhattan Bank,* 687 F. Supp. 848, 46 FEP Cases 1436 (S.D.N.Y. 1988)

[22] *Meritor,* 106 S. Ct. at 2406.

[23] *See, e.g., EEOC Policy Guidance* at 28.

[24] 106 S. Ct. at 2405-6.

[25] 29 CFR 1604.11(a)(3).

[26] *EEOC Policy Guidance* at 13.

[27] *See EEOC Policy Guidance* at 16.

[28] *EEOC Policy Guidance* at 13.

[29] *Rabidue v. Osceola Refining Co.,* 805 F.2d 611, 42 FEP Cases 631 (6th Cir. 1986), *cert. denied,* 481 U.S. 1041, 107 S.Ct. 1983 (1987).

[30] *EEOC Policy Guidance* at 17.

[31] *See Broderick v. Ruder,* 46 FEP Cases 1272 (D.D.C. 1988).

[32] 46 FEP Cases 573, 576-7 (S.D.Iowa 1988).

[33] *See, e.g., Hall v. Gus Construction Co., Inc.*, 842 F.2d 1010, 46 FEP Cases 573 (8th Cir. 1988); *Swentek v. U.S. Air, Inc.*, 830 F.2d 611, 44 FEP Cases 1808 (4th Cir. 1987).

[34] *See, e.g., Meritor Savings Bank v. Vinson*, 477 U.S. 57 (1986); *Hensen v. City of Dundee*, 682 F.2d 897 (11th Cir. 1982).

[35] *Meritor*, 106 S. Ct. at 2408.

[36] *Id.*

[37] 106 S. Ct. at 2409.

[38] 106 S. Ct. at 2408.

[39] *See, e.g., Yates v. Avco Corp.*, 819 F.2d 630, 43 FEP Cases 1595 (6th Cir. 1987).

[40] *EEOC Policy Guidance* at 24.

[41] *EEOC Policy Guidance* at 24.

[42] *See, e.g., Hicks v. Gates Rubber Co.*, 833 F.2d 1406, 45 FEP Cases 608 (10th Cir. 1987); *Huddleston v. Roger Dean Chevrolet, Inc.*, 845 F.2d 900, 46 FEP Cases 1361 (11th Cir. 1988).

[43] *EEOC Policy Guidance* at 24.

[44] *EEOC Policy Guidance* at 24-25.

[45] *EEOC Policy Guidance* at 20-23.

[46] *EEOC Policy Guidance* at 24, n.32.

[47] *Lipsett v. University of Puerto Rico*, 864 F.2d 881 (1st Cir. 1988).

[48] *EEOC Policy Guidance* at 26.

[49] *See Black's Law Dictionary* 1179 (5th ed. 1979).

[50] Cal. Admin. Code, tit. 2 §§ 7291.1f(1) and 7287.6(b)(1)(D) of FEHC Rules and Regulations, 453 FEPM 866b; 453 FEPM 871.

[51] *Department of Fair Employment and Housing v. Rockwell International Corporation*, Case No. FEP 83-84, B1-011178e, L-32630, 87-26 (California) (1985).

[52] 453 FEPM 1575.

[53] *Phillips v. Smalley Maintenance Services, Inc.*, 711 F.2d 1524, 1531 (11th Cir. 1983).

[54] *See, e.g., Clark v. World Airways*, 24 FEP Cases 305, 310 (D.D.C. 1980).

[55] *See, e.g., Lucas v. Brown & Root, Inc.*, 736 F.2d 1202, 116 LRRM 2744 (8th Cir. 1984).

[56] *Bowersox v. P.H. Glatfelter Co.*, 677 F. Supp. 307, 311-12, 45 FEP Cases 1443 (M.D. Pa. 1988).

[57] *See Studstill v. Borg Warner Leasing*, 806 F.2d 1005, 1008 (11th Cir. 1986).

[58] *See, e.g., Clark, supra*, 472 F. Supp. 478, 24 FEP Cases at 310 (D.D.C. 1980).

[59] 667 F. Supp. 1188, 49 FEP Cases 497, 509 (W.D. Tenn. 1987).

[60] See Restatement (Second) of Torts § 652A (1977); See, e.g., Pease, supra, 49 FEP Cases at 509.

[61] See, e.g., Lucas v. Brown & Root, Inc., 736 F.2d 1202 (8th Cir. 1984).

[62] Id. at 1203-05. The court in Lucas likened the employer's invitations to trade her job for sex to prostitution, which it found to be illegal by law. Thus, the employee's refusal to engage in an illegal act and her termination were against public policy.

[63] See, e.g., New York Work. Comp. Law §§ 11, 29(6).

[64] See, e.g., Studstill v. Borg Warner Leasing, 806 F.2d 1005, 1007 (11th Cir. 1986).

[65] See, e.g., Bailey v. Unocal Corp., 700 F. Supp. 396 (N.D. Ill. 1988).

[66] Cremen v. Harrah's Marina Hotel Casino, 680 F. Supp. 150 (D.N.J. 1988).

[67] 50 FEP Cases 295 (N.D. Ill. 1989).

[68] 716 F.2d 1167, 32 FEP Cases 1587 (7th Cir. 1983).

[69] 50 FEP Cases at 300.

[70] EEOC Policy Guidance at 27-28.

[71] EEOC Policy Guidance at 28.

[72] Id. at 28-29.

[73] See, Barrett v. Omaha National Bank, 726 F.2d 424, 35 FEP Cases 593 (8th Cir. 1984).

[74] Id.

[75] Kestenbaum v. Pennzoil, 766 P.2d 280, 4 IER Cases 67 (N.M. 1988), cert. denied, 109 S. Ct. 3163, 4 IER Cases 672 (1989).

[76] Williams v. Maremont Corp., 875 F.2d 1476, 49 FEP Cases 1576 (10th Cir. 1989).

[77] "React to Harassment, Shanor Advises," CUPA News (March 25, 1988).

[78] See Bundy v. Jackson 641 F.2d 934, 947, 24 FEP Cases 1155 (D.C. Cir. 1981).

[79] See, e.g., Waltman v. International Paper Co., 875 F.2d 468, 50 FEP Cases 179, 189 (5th Cir. 1989).

* * *

Personal Relationships

In many situations employers are compelled by economic necessity to become involved with their employees' family lives. These include day care, flex-time, maternity leave, and the "mommy track," which limits the career opportunities of working mothers. Issues like these arise when employees want employers to be aware of the impact of employees' decisions to marry and raise families and respond to it. These and many other work-and-family matters usually are not viewed by employees as privacy issues when employers are being asked to accommodate and pay for employees' freely made decisions regarding their off-duty family lives. Claims of invasion of privacy arise when employers try to limit employees' choices through no-spouse rules or rules against dating co-workers or competitors' employees, or when employees think their employers are making moral judgments about their behavior, such as firing an employee whose adultery or sexual preference is found offensive.

Many employees believe that no area is more private — and more irrelevant to the employment relationship — than their off-duty personal or romantic relationships. Challenges to employer policies or decisions affecting employees' relationships illustrate, in dramatic ways, the questions of what employers can do or should do concerning workplace policies and whether those policies should be applied to situations and conduct that occur outside of the workplace. Employers have legitimate interests in maintaining a reputable and credible work environment that is capable of meeting the organization's goals of productivity and efficiency. On the other hand, society recognizes and encourages the right of employees to associate freely and pursue personal relationships that do not harm job performance. Many employees cannot accept an employer's interference with their off-duty personal relationships or activities. Regardless of the law, their reaction is often, "That's none of your business."

The courts, caught in the middle of this tension, usually favor the employee's right to pursue personal relationships without interference unless the relationship creates a serious conflict with the employee's job performance, adversely affects co-workers' morale, or damages the employer's public image. As the employment-at-will doctrine continues to erode, employers can expect more challenges to employment decisions based in part on an employee's personal, off-duty relationships.

ANTI-NEPOTISM AND NO-SPOUSE RULES

Decisions relating to dating and marriage are extremely personal. Employers do not control these choices, but some employers create a conflict between employees' work and private lives through anti-nepotism and no-spouse rules.

"Nepotism" connotes favoritism, undeserved rewards, or undue consideration to relatives in granting employment or other advantages.[1] *Webster's Third New World International Dictionary* defines nepotism as "favoritism shown to relatives, especially in appointment to desirable positions."[2] Few people other than those who benefit directly from the practice disagree with anti-nepotism rules adopted by employers to prevent favoritism and the employment of clearly unqualified individuals. Many companies that favor anti-nepotism policies also contend that relatives, especially spouses, may compromise the business by talking about business matters outside the workplace. But these policies also can harm employers. The exclusion of talented individuals who are married or related to employees or managers may unnecessarily reduce the pool of skilled labor available to the enterprise. When the excluded worker is the spouse of an employee, the employer may lose the services of two qualified employees if the couple is able to locate other work with another employer, possibly a competitor, that does not bar hiring spouses.

Anti-nepotism policies range from bans on the employment of any relative of any employee to rules that only prohibit one relative from supervising another. In between are rules that bar employment of relatives at the same facility or allow relatives to work at the same site but not in the same department.[3] Some state governments have anti-nepotism laws that prohibit employers from refusing to hire an applicant merely because the applicant is a member of a current employee's immediate family. States have taken different approaches in defining "immediate family." Alaska courts have interpreted the term as used in that state's nepotism law to include (1) husband and wife; (2) father and son or daughter; (3) mother and son or daughter; and (4) brother or sister.[4] Texas has defined "immediate family" to include in-laws, aunts, uncles, nieces and nephews, grandparents, and stepchildren.[5]

Anti-nepotism and no-spouse policies have been challenged in the courts under the U.S. Constitution, anti-discrimination laws, and common law privacy theories.

Constitutional Challenges

Married couples affected by the anti-nepotism policies of public employers have challenged those policies on constitutional grounds. The Fifth and 14th Amendments to the Constitution prohibit states from denying citizens "equal protection" under the law; states must treat similarly situated people in a similar manner. To establish a violation of the Equal Protection Clause plaintiffs must prove that a public employer engaged in purposeful discrimination against individuals in a protected class. Thus, a public employer's no-spouse rule that applied only to women would be unlawful.

Governmental no-spouse rules also must not abridge the fundamental privacy interests protected by the Due Process Clause. Constitutional challenges arise when anti-nepotism rules threaten to deprive couples of their jobs when they contemplate marriage. In a long line of cases, the U.S. Supreme Court has stressed the fundamental nature of the constitutionally protected "right to marry."[6] In one case, the court ruled that a Wisconsin law violated the right to marry because it required all parents who did not have custody of their minor children and who were under court orders to support them to seek court permission before marrying. The Supreme Court explained that regulations which "directly and substantially" interfere with the right to marry would be subject to a standard of "strict scrutiny" while other policies would be judged under a "rational basis" standard.[7]

Federal courts have addressed the issue of whether no-spouse rules infringe on the right to marry in several cases. In *Keckeisen v. Independent School Dist. 612*,[8] the U.S. Court of Appeals for the Eighth Circuit decided that a school board rule prohibiting the employment of spouses in an administrator-teacher relationship did not substantially infringe on a school principal's constitutional rights of privacy or freedom to marry a teacher at that school. The rule did not deny employees the right to marry, but prohibited only the employment of married couples in a particular supervisor-subordinate relationship. The court held that this indirect interference with the right to marry was justified because the rule furthered the school district's legitimate interest in providing good education, preventing potential favoritism, and maintaining the morale of other teachers. Similarly, in *Cutts v. Fowler*[9] the U.S. Court of Appeals for the District of Columbia Circuit considered a rule that prohibited federal agencies from employing any person if an immediate relative would be in a position to supervise that person. The court concluded that where definite possibilities of conflicts of interest exist, government agencies do not have an obligation to wait until a conflict of interest becomes a problem before it can take action, such as transferring the lower-ranked spouse.[10]

These and similar cases have involved narrow rules involving supervisor-subordinate relationships, or employment situations where a potential conflict of interest raised public safety claims. It is unclear how the courts would respond to a claim by a public employee discharged under a broad no-spouse rule that prohibited spouses from working for the same public employer.

Title VII Challenges

Title VII of the Civil Rights Act of 1964 prohibits discrimination by employers on the basis of sex.[11] Most anti-nepotism rules are facially neutral, prohibiting the hiring of a spouse of any employee, male or female. In many situations the employer allows affected spouses who marry after they have started to work for the company to choose which spouse will resign. Although such policies have been challenged under Title VII, the courts have been reluctant to conclude that neutral no-spouse rules discriminate against people based on sex.

Plaintiffs have attacked no-spouse rules under both disparate treatment and disparate impact theories. Under the disparate treatment theory, the plaintiff must show that the employer has intentionally treated some applicants less favorably than others because of their sex.[12] While facially neutral rules cannot easily be attacked on this basis, a no-spouse rule that facially discriminates against one sex (such as refusing employment only to the wives of male employees) usually will be struck down under Title VII.[13] An unwritten policy under which the employer decides which spouse to discharge, where the employer consistently chooses to fire the wife, also could be attacked on this basis.

In a disparate impact case, the primary concern is the effect of the employer's policies rather than the underlying motivation for them. A prima facie case of unlawful discrimination may be established by demonstrating that a policy has a substantially adverse impact on the protected group, even though its terms are facially neutral. For example, an employee could try to show that a policy which requires the lesser-paid or less-senior spouse to resign affects a higher percentage of women than men. If the statistical evidence shows an adverse disparate impact on women, the employer may answer the adverse impact claim by showing that a non-discriminatory business justification existed for the policy. The Supreme Court's 1989 decision in *Wards Cove Packing Co. v. Atonio*[14] put the ultimate burden on the employee to prove the policy is discriminatory.

A claim of business necessity was used to defend a no-spouse rule in *Yuhas v. Libby-Owens-Ford Co.*[15] Only three male job applicants were refused employment under the rule, whereas 73 female applicants were turned down. The trial court felt that the statistical imbalance was evidence of a prima facie violation of Title VII. Libby-Owens-Ford argued that spouses who work together often are tardy or absent, that spouses working for the same firm create problems in scheduling vacations, and that the presence of spouses undermines employee efficiency and morale. The trial court concluded that the no-spouse rule was invalid under Title VII, but this holding was reversed by the U.S. Court of Appeals for the Seventh Circuit, which found that the employer's reasons were legitimate, job-related reasons for a no-spouse rule.[16]

A different problem arises in challenges to policies that prohibit the continued employment of spouses who marry after they are employed by the same company. The number of employees affected by such rules often may be too small to enable a plaintiff to demonstrate statistical significance in a disparate impact case.[17] The plaintiff in *Harper v. Trans World Airlines, Inc.*,[18] faced this problem when the airline terminated her after she married an employee in the same department. The airline's anti-nepotism policy prohibited spouses from working in the same department, and allowed the affected parties to decide which of them would resign. Because neither Harper nor her spouse was willing to resign, the company fired Harper. While in four of the five previous cases the wife voluntarily left the airline, the court held this evidence was insufficient to prove a violation of Title VII.

Nepotism and favoritism are not, per se, unlawful acts under Title VII. Employers have won several Title VII disparate treatment cases by showing that a supervisor's motivation was to favor one employee for personal reasons, not to discriminate against another worker on the basis of race, sex, or other prohibited reasons. For example, the U.S. Court of Appeals for the Fourth Circuit recently held that evidence that nepotism played a part in a city's decision to promote a white job applicant rather than a black candidate did not constitute proof of intentional race discrimination.[19] However, nepotism and favoritism may constitute unlawful discrimination if they result in a disparate impact on protected classes. Courts have found these practices unlawful under Title VII where they perpetuate past discrimination.[20]

State EEO Laws and Other Statutes

No-spouse rules of public and private employers have been challenged under state laws barring discrimination in employment on the basis of "marital status." Twenty-three states and the District of Columbia have enacted such laws.[21] For example, a state of Washington law makes it unlawful for an employer to refuse to hire any person because of marital status.[22] In *Washington Water Power Co. v. Washington State Human Rights Comm'n*,[23] the Human Rights Commission determined that employers' anti-nepotism policies constituted unfair discrimination on the basis of marital status under the state's anti-discrimination law. In upholding the commission's interpretation of the law, the court held that the law was intended to prohibit this type of classification, in addition to distinctions based solely on marital status.[24]

Oregon's law also makes broad no-spouse rules illegal. The law prohibits firing or hiring anyone because a member of the individual's family also works for the employer. However, the law allows employers to refuse to hire anyone who would exer-

cise "supervisory, appointment, or grievance adjustment
authority" over a relative.[25] Washington and California also
have promulgated regulations that limit the use of no-spouse
rules to situations involving compelling business interests or
supervisory relationships.[26]

Challenges to no-spouse rules under these state laws have
achieved mixed results due to the varied definitions and judicial interpretations given to the term "marital status." A no-
spouse rule is more likely to be invalidated under a law that
prohibits discrimination based on the identity or situation of an
individual's spouse than under one that merely prohibits an
employer from considering marital status, that is, whether the
person is married, single, divorced, or separated, in making
employment decisions. In *Kraft, Inc. v. State of Minn.*,[27] four
part-time employees were denied full-time positions because
Kraft prohibited the full-time employment of more than one
family member at any company office. The plaintiffs sued,
claiming that the policy constituted a discriminatory practice
based on marital status.[28] The Minnesota Supreme Court ruled
that discrimination based on "marital status" encompasses
more than just discrimination against married, single, or
divorced individuals; it also includes discrimination based on
the "identity or situation of one's spouse." The court rejected
a more narrow reading of the law, which would have allowed
the company to continue hiring all married individuals except
those married to full-time Kraft employees.

The opposite view was taken by the New York Court of Appeals in *Manhattan Pizza Hut, Inc. v. New York State Human
Rights Appeals Board,*[29] where the plaintiff was discharged
under a rule that prohibited employees from working under
the supervision of a relative. The court held that the protection
extended by the New York Human Rights Law is limited to
discrimination based on "marital status" and does not apply to
employment restrictions based on who the spouse of the
employee is or what that spouse does for a living.[30]

The courts have held uniformly that where employees are discharged for legitimate business reasons and not because of their job relationship with their spouse, the discharge is not unlawfully discriminatory on the basis of marital status. In *National Industries, Inc. v. Comm'n on Human Relations*,[31] the company had discharged a female employee to keep her spouse away from the company premises after he was fired by the company for misconduct and potential violence. The court concluded that the discharge of the female employee to keep her husband off company premises was a decision based on legitimate business concerns and not because of her marital status or the fact that she was the discharged employee's wife.

The National Labor Relations Act (NLRA) and collective bargaining agreements also may serve as the legal underpinning for challenges to anti-nepotism policies. The National Labor Relations Board (NLRB) case of *Spencer Foods, Inc.*[32] involved a plant closing in 1977 for economic reasons. Another company acquired ownership of the facility and began hiring under a rule that prohibited the employment of more than one member of an immediate family. When the plant re-opened, the new workforce included only about 33 percent of its former employees. The NLRB found that the new employer, when designing the rule, was aware that approximately 50 percent of the previous owner's unionized workforce were related to other employees. The NLRB also found that the rule had not been adopted or applied uniformly at the employer's other operations. Thus, the board held that the rule had been adopted as part of a pattern to inhibit the hiring of former unionized employees in violation of Sections 8(a)(1) and (3) of the NLRA.

Arbitration Decisions

Most arbitrators subject no-spouse rules to strict scrutiny, especially where they are applied to co-workers who marry. Company actions based on no-spouse rules have been overturned where they have been applied discriminatorily or arbitrarily, or where the rule had no rational justification. In *Distribution Center of Columbus, Inc.,*[33] two employees who had worked for the organization for five years and seven years, respectively, were married. The company discharged the spouse who had less seniority under its anti-nepotism policy. The arbitrator held that while the rule was reasonable on its face, no "just cause" existed to discharge either employee. The company had an ample opportunity to determine that these were capable, mature, loyal employees, and the theoretical future harm their marriage might cause was not a sufficient basis to discharge an employee. While not all arbitrators have reached similar conclusions in similar cases, many of the more recent decisions have sustained employee grievances against no-spouse rules.[34]

DATING CO-WORKERS OR COMPETITORS

Most employers acknowledge that intra-company romance can create a host of potential personnel problems, including actual or perceived favoritism, envy or jealousy by co-workers, and a decline in productivity by the couple or co-workers. Nevertheless, surveys show that few employers impose direct restrictions on intra-company dating. The most common approach is to ignore the issue, or to encourage the couple to confine their romantic relationship to non-work hours.[35]

Not all intra-company romances disrupt the workplace. If two co-workers who are having a romance handle it discreetly and properly, the employer need not become involved with their relationship. On the other hand, open affairs between supervisors and subordinates can lead to charges of favoritism and declines in morale. Employers need to address these intra-office romances because they damage the working environment.

Employers have a right to expect that employees' love lives will not affect their work performance, regardless of whether one or both members of a couple work for the firm. It is not an invasion of an employee's privacy to limit personal phone calls, to expect a certain level of performance regardless of the employee's social life, or to ask all employees to limit conversations about issues not related to work. Some employers have conducted group counseling sessions with trained psychologists to address the effect that romance in the workplace has on the entire workforce. Employers also can transfer or discharge employees engaged in intra-company dating if it affects an employee's job performance and other employees' productivity and morale.

Employers that establish policies to forbid employees from dating co-workers or employees of competitors usually do so for reasons other than preventing a decline in productivity. The most prevalent reason is to avoid potential conflicts of interest that may arise when people involved in a close personal relationship work together or in competition with each other. Bans on such relationships can result in claims that the employer is invading the employee's privacy.

Regardless of how employers deal with intra-company romance, bans or restrictions on dating between employees and their supervisors, co-workers, and employees at competing firms may give rise to lawsuits based on sexual harassment, invasion of privacy, and discrimination based on marital status.

The leading case involving a private employer's interference with its employees' personal relationships is *Rulon-Miller v. International Business Machines Corp.*[36] Rulon-Miller began dating a co-worker named Blum while both worked for IBM. The following year Blum left IBM to join a competitor. Several years later IBM management confronted Rulon-Miller about the relationship and informed her that because of the perceived conflict of interest, she would have to stop dating Blum. She refused and was summarily fired. Rulon-Miller successfully sought damages on claims of wrongful discharge and intentional infliction of emotional distress when she was fired. A jury awarded Rulon-Miller $100,000 compensatory damages and $200,000 punitive damages against IBM, and the verdict was upheld on appeal.

In analyzing the wrongful discharge claim, the appeals court noted that IBM's written personnel policies prohibited its employees from becoming involved in conflicts of interest, but did not specifically prohibit employees from socializing with employees of competitors or entering into romantic relationships with them. Moreover, IBM had an express policy, articulated by its president and distributed throughout the company, of not interfering in an employee's private life unless it "reduced his ability to perform regular job assignments, interfered with the job performance of other employees, or ... affected the reputation of the company in a major way." IBM argued that it had the right to inquire into managers' personal relationships even without evidence that those relationships interfered with their job performance, because the morale of the managers' subordinates might be lowered. The court found no evidence to support this argument. Moreover, the court noted that IBM had distributed to all employees a memorandum by a former company chairman stating that IBM's "first basic belief is respect for the individual and the essence of this belief is a strict regard for his right to personal privacy."[37]

The court ultimately based its decision in *Rulon-Miller* on a contractual privacy right granted by IBM's personnel policies, finding that those policies gave IBM employees a legitimate expectation of privacy in their personal relationships. In this sense, the case is primarily an implied-contract wrongful discharge case, and it emphasizes the need for employers to ensure that corporate policies and procedures are followed by individual managers. The court also found sufficient evidence that IBM's conduct caused Rulon-Miller emotional distress and was so extreme and outrageous as to go beyond all possible bounds of decency. The court relied on management's flagrant disregard of its own corporate policies, and on the supervisor's statements implying that Rulon-Miller could not act for herself, and therefore the company would decide for her that her relationship with Blum should be terminated. This portion of the appeals court's opinion reflects the underlying concern of the jury and the judge that the company had unreasonably interfered with the private life of an employee.

Some employees have sought to overturn rules prohibiting co-employee dating by filing claims under state laws that bar marital status discrimination. One federal court, analyzing such a claim under Michigan's Elliot-Larsen Act, concluded that no state had extended statutory protection to employee social relationships. The court refused to extend the scope of the Michigan law, noting that the strong policies protecting the marital relationship do not apply to dating.[38]

Employers may be justifiably concerned about the effect of intra-company dating on the morale of other employees, especially where a supervisor begins a relationship with a subordinate. The morale problems may be real, but claims of favoritism are unlikely to result in liability. Most of the Title VII favoritism cases noted above have involved lovers. The courts usually have ruled that supervisors who advance the careers of their lovers at work or give them other special treatment do not violate Title VII because they are discriminating equally against men and women—against everyone except their lover.[39] In May 1989, the Michigan Court of Appeals held in *Hickman v. W-S Equipment Co., Inc.*[40] that although a boss' favoritism toward his girlfriend may be unfair, it is not unlawful job discrimination, rejecting the claim of a female employee who lost her job to a woman who was romantically involved with the company president. However, if the same employee could show that promotional opportunities were denied because she spurned her employer's advances, and given to another employee who acquiesced, the result might be different. Moreover, a prospect of liability would exist if a supervisor picked her boyfriend for a promotion and a better-qualified employee who was passed over showed in a common-law implied contract claim that under the employer's personnel policies all career decisions were to be based on performance.

As these examples indicate, employers should be concerned about the fine line between voluntary romantic relationships and sexual harassment. An employee who at first responds favorably to a supervisor's advances and later tries to end the relationship can sue for sexual harassment if the supervisor refuses the request. The U.S. Supreme Court made it clear in *Meritor Savings Bank v. Vinson*[41] that the fact that a company has guidelines and training programs on sexual harassment is no defense if a supervisor coerces continued sexual favors from a subordinate. (See Chapter XI.) This problem, more than any other, should force employers to discuss the issue of intra-company dating as part of their equal employment opportunity (EEO) and sexual harassment training. Employers need not implement no-dating policies to protect themselves, and those policies cannot by themselves stop sexual harassment. However, employers that decide not to interfere with their employees' dating habits should regularly explain to their managers and to all other employees that voluntary, off-duty conduct differs from sexual harassment, and the company will not tolerate harassment.

OFF-DUTY SEXUAL BEHAVIOR

No-spouse and intra-company dating prohibitions often are adopted and upheld because of the legitimate concerns raised by employers concerning potential conflicts of interest. This rationale does not apply to many cases where an employee is discharged for off-duty sexual behavior that the employer views as inappropriate or immoral, such as cohabitation, adultery, or homosexuality. In these situations, if the fired employee sues the company the claim is almost sure to be that the discharge violated constitutional or common-law privacy protections, but the outcome of the case is not so certain.

Constitutional Rights of Public Employees

Justice William Brennan observed in 1983, in a dissent to the denial of review in *Whisenhunt v. Spradlin*,[42] that "although issues concerning the regulation of the private conduct of public employees arise frequently, the lower courts have divided sharply both in their results and in their analytic approach." The issues remain unsettled in 1989.

Several federal courts have declared that the U.S. Constitution embodies no "fundamental" privacy right for two people, one of whom is married, to live together. In one of these decisions, *Suddarth v. Slane*,[43] a state trooper was terminated for adultery pursuant to a state police department regulation that prohibited "criminal, infamous, dishonest, immoral, or other conduct prejudicial to the Department." In rejecting the trooper's claim that his First Amendment right to freedom of association and his general right to privacy had been violated, the court held that by engaging in adultery the trooper had pursued an activity not protected by the First Amendment and had violated state law in addition to department regulations.[44]

Other federal courts have taken the opposite position. In *Briggs v. Northern Muskegon Police Department*,[45] the U.S. Court of Appeals for the Sixth Circuit upheld a ruling that dismissal of a married, part-time police officer for cohabiting with a woman who was not his wife violated the officer's right to privacy. The trial court rejected the argument that regulation of a public employee's conduct could be justified by general community disapproval. The court held that although the police department had a legitimate interest in regulating the personal sexual activities and living arrangements of its employees when such activities affect job performance, it found no adverse impact on the officer's job performance. The court also rejected the argument that the officer's conduct violated a criminal law that makes unlawful the cohabitation of unmarried people in a "lewd and lascivious" manner.

Many of these cases involve the sexual activities of law enforcement officers, with employers asserting the need of officers to uphold the law. Even the U.S. Court of Appeals for the Ninth Circuit, which issued a decision similar to *Briggs*, has recognized that the right to privacy is not unlimited if it affects job performance. In *Fugate v. Phoenix Civil Service Board*,[46] the court found that the constitutional right to privacy does not protect police officers who engage in open, public, on-duty affairs with prostitutes. The court distinguished from its earlier decision because the affairs in *Fugate* occurred during working hours, created a conflict of interest with the officers' enforcement of the law, and exposed them to the possibility of blackmail. The court concluded that the legitimate interest of the city in prohibiting conduct unbecoming of an officer justified the intrusion into the officers' private lives.

The question of whether any form of sexual conduct outside the marital relationship is entitled to constitutional protection is highly divisive. Some courts have tried to take an intermediate approach, finding that private sexual conduct, although not entitled to the same protection as political expression, is covered by the constitutional right of privacy and is entitled to some protection. The cases have applied a balancing test and have held that the reasons given for infringing on the employees' privacy rights in discharge cases must have more than a minimum justification.[47]

The U.S. Supreme Court's workplace privacy decisions, which have been limited to various search and seizure cases, provide limited insight into how this controversy will be resolved. Under the analysis of *Ortega* and *Von Raab*, the court first must determine whether society recognizes a right of privacy in public employees' off-duty consensual sexual conduct, or whether the public employer has created such an expectation through its policies. Lower court decisions frequently have distinguished between conduct that is deemed immoral and conduct that is illegal under state law. As a result, the existence and scope of privacy rights of public employees may depend on where they live and what sexual conduct is against the law in that state, just as the scope of public employees' rights on termination sometimes depend on state law. If such a privacy right is acknowledged, the court must then balance the governmental interests involved against the extent of the government's interference in its employees' private lives. If the Supreme Court follows the analysis it has applied to state regulation of homosexual conduct,[48] it probably would uphold the employer's actions if the employee's conduct was illegal under state law and the employee was in a law-enforcement job. It is less clear whether a public employer's interest in upholding public morals would be a sufficient governmental interest.

Common Law and Public Policy Claims

The extent of common-law privacy protections in cases where an employee is discharged for off-duty sexual activity is no clearer. Some privacy claims have been successful, especially those focusing on how employers found out about their off-duty sexual behavior.[49] For example, the tort of intrusion is designed to prevent surveillance or invasion of people's homes, regardless of who may be inside or what they may be doing. Public disclosure of employees' private sexual activities also are actionable. If an employer fired an employee for adultery and publicized this fact widely, the employee could sue for invasion of privacy under the "public disclosure of private facts" doctrine, even if the allegation of adultery were true. If it were false, the employee could also sue for defamation.

Neither Congress nor the states are likely to enact legislation to protect employees in this area.[50] Many states have criminal prohibitions on fornication, adultery, sodomy, and other private, consensual conduct. As long as those laws are on the books and the U.S. Supreme Court has not clearly extended the constitutional right to privacy to private consensual conduct, courts in most states are not likely to find a clear, protectable privacy interest in such acts. However, labor arbitration decisions contain authority for the idea that the right to be let alone is fundamental, and that any off-duty behavior or activities that do not hinder an employee's job performance or injure the employer should not be the basis for discipline.[51] That is why many employees are using the theory of wrongful discharge in violation of public policy to challenge discharges based on their off-duty conduct.

In *McCluskey v. Clark Oil and Refining Corp.*,[52] a female employee was discharged because she married a co-worker. The issue presented was whether a sufficiently mandated public policy was expressed in the Illinois Marriage Act, and in the inherent right of individuals to marry the person of their choice, to provide an action for retaliatory discharge. The court concluded that the law was intended only to regulate marriage, not the conduct of employers, and that constitutional decisions upholding the right to marry did not require that all restrictions affecting marriage be eliminated. The success or failure of a public policy claim depends largely on how the state defines "public policy." Oregon recognizes wrongful discharge claims only when employees are fired for pursuing private statutory rights that relate directly to their status or role as an employee. As a result, Oregon courts have held that when employees choose to date a co-worker, they are engaging in purely private conduct and are exercising a right not related to their role as an employee. Therefore, they may not sue for wrongful discharge if they are fired for dating a co-worker.[53]

SEXUAL PREFERENCE

An employer's right to make employment decisions based on an employee's sexual preference has been an extremely volatile area of labor and employment law during the last several years. It is well-settled that Title VII offers no relief to employees for employment decisions based in part on their sexual preference. Courts have held uniformly that sexual orientation or preference is not a protected classification under

Title VII.[54] The judicial decisions involving constitutional claims by public employees have been less consistent.

Several courts ruled in the early 1970s that people cannot be dismissed from public employment solely because they are homosexual, unless homosexual activity impairs their efficiency or job performance.[55] However, in 1986 the U.S. Supreme Court, in *Bowers v. Hardwick*,[56] stated that the right of privacy does not protect all private sexual conduct. The court rejected a constitutional challenge to a Georgia law criminalizing sodomy. The law was challenged by an adult homosexual prosecuted for engaging in consensual sodomy in his home with another adult homosexual. In concluding that consensual homosexual sodomy is not entitled to constitutional protection, the court stressed that numerous state laws outlawing sodomy reflect general societal disapproval of such conduct. The court concluded that the constitutional right to privacy did not extend to homosexual sodomy committed in private, because sodomy is analogous to other crimes, such as possession of illegal drugs, firearms, or stolen goods, that do not escape the law merely because they are committed at home. Four justices vigorously dissented, arguing that the right of privacy extends to all private consensual sexual activity.

Relying in part on *Bowers*, the U.S. Court of Appeals for the District of Columbia held in *Padula v. Webster*[57] that the FBI did not violate the constitutional rights of an openly homosexual job applicant by refusing to hire her as an agent. The court emphasized that agents who engage in conduct deemed criminal in half of the states could undermine law enforcement credibility. Therefore, it would not be irrational for the bureau to conclude that the criminalization of homosexual conduct, coupled with general public opinion toward homosexuality, exposes many homosexuals to possible blackmail.[58]

Numerous challenges have been raised since 1986 to employers' decisions to discharge or discipline employees because of their sexual orientation. Many of these cases have involved the military. In 1989, the U.S. District Court for the Eastern District of Wisconsin held in *BenShalom v. Marsh*[59] that Army reserve regulations barring re-enlistment to members of the services who declared themselves to have a homosexual orientation, without regard to whether they engaged in homosexual conduct, violate the First Amendment and the Due Process Clause of the U.S. Constitution. The secretary of the Army defended the regulations on the grounds that "the presence in the military environment of people who engage in homosexual conduct, or who by their statements demonstrate a propensity to engage in homosexual conduct, seriously impairs the accomplishment of the military mission."[60] Although the court recognized that the government interests sought to be protected by regulation were compelling, it held that they were not rationally advanced by an Army rule that distinguished military personnel on the basis of their sexual orientation. The court pointed out that an individual's sexual orientation is a trait that bears no relationship to that individual's ability to perform in the military. The court did recognize that the military has a legitimate interest in the regulation of sexual conduct of its personnel. However, regulations covering sexual behavior must deal with the conduct itself and they cannot be based on stereotypes of people with certain orientations.[61]

Although private employers usually are not liable for employment decisions based on an individual's sexual preference, some states protect sexual preference through statutory and case law. For example, Wisconsin and the District of Columbia have anti-discrimination laws that include sexual orientation as a protected classification.[62] The general absence of federal and state protection of sexual orientation under anti-discrimination laws does not insulate employers from liability for discriminatory treatment of employees on the basis of their sexual preference. A few jurisdictions have allowed plaintiffs to state claims of defamation, invasion of privacy, and infliction of emotional distress for discriminatory treatment by employers based on their sexual orientation or preference.[63]

ILLUSTRATIONS

Two Employees Living In Open Adultery Have No Constitutional Right To Privacy

Hollenbaugh, a librarian, and Philburn, a janitor, were discharged by their employer for living together in "open adultery." Hollenbaugh, who was divorced, became pregnant by Philburn, who was married. Philburn left his wife and moved in with Hollenbaugh. The plaintiffs' living arrangement was not clandestine. The plaintiffs contested their terminations, contending a violation of the constitutional right to privacy.

The U.S. district court, citing the employer's concern that it not give tacit approval to the relationship, found no constitutional violation in the discharges. Noting that the right of privacy has been extended to several "immoral" areas, the court said that these decisions make it clear that "only personal rights that can be deemed 'fundamental' or 'implicit in the concept of ordered liberty' are included in this guarantee of personal privacy." Two people, one of whom is married, living together does not fit this definition. [*Hollenbaugh v. Carnegie Free Library*, 436 F. Supp. 1328 (W.D. Pa. 1977), *aff'd*, 578 F.2d 1374 (3rd Cir.), *cert. denied*, 439 U.S. 1052 (1978).]

Off-Duty Affair With Married Police Officer Was Not Grounds For Refusal To Hire Applicant for Police Officer Position

Thorne scored second highest in the written and oral tests when she applied for a job as a police officer in El Segundo. She then took a polygraph test and was asked numerous questions about her sexual activities, including questions about an affair with a married police officer that had resulted in a pregnancy and subsequent miscarriage. When her name was removed from the eligibility list, she sued, alleging that the city refused to hire her because those responsible for reviewing her application applied a different standard of moral integrity to her than was applied to similarly situated males; that is, they denied her the job because she had had a love affair.

The U.S. Court of Appeals for the Ninth Circuit found that Thorne's interests in the privacy of her sexual activities were within the zone protected by the U.S. Constitution. It also found that without any showing that private, off-duty, personal activities of the type protected by the constitutional guarantees of privacy and free association harm the applicant's job performance, and without specific policies with narrow implementing regulations, the police department could not rely on these activities to deny employment. [*Thorne v. City of El Segundo*, 726 F.2d 459, 1 IER Cases 299 (9th Cir. 1983), *cert. denied*, 469 U.S. 979 (1984).]

Consensual Sexual Relations That Comprised Statutory Rape Are Not Protected By Constitutional Right of Privacy

Fleisher, a 19-year-old Explorer Scout serving with the Signal Hill Police Department under a program for such scouts, had a consensual sexual relationship with a 15-year-old girl who also was in the program, after he became the leader of the Explorer group. Three years later Fleisher was hired as a probationary police officer. During the first five months of probation he received three reprimands for not performing his duties properly. Also during his probationary period, the girl filed a forcible rape charge against another officer and named Fleisher as one of three other officers with whom she had had sex. Fleisher was fired on the basis of the reprimands and his sexual relationship with the girl.

Fleisher sued the police department for violating his rights of privacy and freedom of association. A jury returned a verdict for Fleisher in the amount of $175,000 plus attorney's fees, but the U.S. Court of Appeals for the Ninth Circuit vacated the verdict. Relying on *Thorne* and *Fugate*, the court found that the right of privacy does not extend to "sexual conduct that is concededly illegal." The court emphasized that the illegality of the officer's behavior created a substantial barrier to his successfully asserting a privacy claim. The court found that acts that comprise statutory rape are not protected by an individual's constitutional right of privacy, even if they are not prosecuted. [*Fleisher v. City of Signal Hill*, 829 F.2d 1491 (9th Cir. 1987), *cert. denied*, __U.S.__, 108 S. Ct. 1225 (1988).]

Policy That Prohibited Spouses Of Law Enforcement Officers From Employment As Dispatchers Does Not Violate Equal Protection Or Due Process Clauses

The Kenosha City and County Joint Service Board issued a written policy directive in October 1982 providing that spouses of sheriff's deputies and police officers would not be hired as dispatchers but they would be offered jobs in the records department if they were qualified. The board issued the policy because it feared that being married to a deputy or officer could impair a dispatcher's judgment in emergencies. A conflict of interest could occur between dispatchers' ability to react quickly and their concern for the welfare of their spouse.

Heyden and Sebatic challenged the policy. Heyden, whose husband was a deputy, was about to be hired as a dispatcher, but when the policy was issued she was told she would not be offered the job. Sebatic, who was unmarried when she became a dispatcher, later married a deputy. She was told that she or her husband must resign. When they refused she was fired, but later was rehired as a records clerk. Both women alleged that the policy violated the 14th Amendment's Equal Protection Clause because it had a disparate impact on females, thus causing gender-based discrimination. They also contended the policy violated the Due Process Clause "by interfering with marital relations ...."

A U.S. district court rejected the equal protection claim, finding the policy was a rational means of serving the board's legitimate goal and was not a pretext for gender discrimination. It also rejected the due process claim, finding the policy did not interfere with the right to marry. "The policy is a reasonable public safety measure with minimal residual impact on the decision to marry; indeed, the policy did not deter the plaintiffs themselves from getting married." [*Sebatic v. Hagerty*, 640 F. Supp. 1274 (E.D. Wis. 1986), *aff'd*, 819 F.2d 1144 (7th Cir.), *cert. denied*, 108 S. Ct. 235 (1987).]

ENDNOTES

[1] *See* Wexler, "Husbands and Wives: The Uneasy Case for Antinepotism Rules," 62 *B.U.L.* 75 (1982).

[2] *Webster's New World Dictionary*, (2d College ed. 1976) 1510.

[3] *See* Bierman and Fisher, "Antinepotism Rules Applied to Spouses: Business and Legal Viewpoints," 35 *Lab. L. J.* (CCH) 634 (Oct. 1984).

[4] *Degnan v. Bering Strait School Dist.*, 753 P.2d 146 (Alaska 1988).

[5] *Collier v. Civil Service Comm'n of Wichita Falls*, 764 S.W.2d 364 (Tex. Ct. App. 1989).

[6] *See, e.g., Loving v. Virginia*, 388 U.S. 1, 87 S. Ct. 1817 (1967); *Skinner v. Oklahoma*, 316 U.S. 535, 62 S. Ct. 1110 (1942); *Meyer v. Nebraska*, 262 U.S. 390, 43 S. Ct. 625 (1923).

[7] *Zablocki v. Redhail*, 434 U.S. 374, 98 S. Ct. 673 (1978).

[8] 509 F.2d 1062 (8th Cir.), *cert. denied*, 423 U.S. 833, 96 S. Ct. 57 (1975). *See also, Cutts v. Fowler*, 692 F.2d 138, 34 FEP Cases 698 (D.C. Cir. 1982); *Parsons v. County of Del Norte*, 728 F.2d 1234, 34 FEP Cases 571, 115 LRRM 3591 (9th Cir.), *cert denied*, 469 U.S. 846, 105 S. Ct. 158 (1984).

[9] 462 F. Supp. 289 (S.D. W.Va. 1978).

[10] *See also Southwestern Community Action Counsel, Inc. v. Community Services Administration*, 462 F. Supp. 289 (S.D. W.Va. 1978).

[11] 42 USC 2000e, *et. seq.*.

[12] *See, e.g., International Brotherhood of Teamsters v. United States*, 431 U.S. 324, 335, 97 S. Ct. 1843, 14 FEP Cases 1514 (1977).

[13] *See McArthur v. Southern Airways, Inc.*, 404 F. Supp. 508 (N.D. Ga. 1975), *vacated on other grounds*, 556 F.2d 298 (5th Cir. 1977), *dismissed*, 569 F.2d 276 (5th Cir. 1978).

[14] 107 DLR D-1 (BNA) (June 6, 1989).

[15] 411 F. Supp. 77, 16 FEP Cases 815 (N.D. Ill. 1976), *rev'd*, 562 F.2d 496, 16 FEP Cases 891 (7th Cir.), *cert. denied*, 435 U.S. 934 (1977).

[16] 562 F.2d at 498-500.

[17] Wexler, *Supra* note 1, at 106.

[18] 525 F.2d 409, 11 FEP Cases 1074 (8th Cir. 1975).

[19] 867 F.2d 823, 49 FEP Cases 47 (4th Cir. 1989).

[20] *See* B. Schlei and P. Grossman, *Employment Discrimination* (2d Ed. 1983) at 773, and the cases cited.

[21] *See* 8A FEP Manual (BNA) 451:102-04. *See also*, Bierman at 641-42.

[22] WASH. REV. CODE § 49.60.180(1).

[23] 91 Wash. 2d 62, 586 P.2d 1149, 27 FEP Cases 1499 (1978).

[24] *See also, Kraft, Inc. v. State of Minn.*, 284 N.W.2d 386, 40 FEP Cases 31 (Minn. 1979); *Thompson v. Board of Trustees*, 627 P.2d 1229 (Mont. 1981).

[25] OR. REV. STAT. § 659-340 (1981).

[26] *See* WASH. ADMIN. CODE § 162-16-150 (1980); CAL. ADMIN. CODE tit. 2, R. 80 § 7292 (1980).

[27] 284 N.W.2d 386 (1979).

[28] MINN. STAT. § 363.03(1)(1976).

[29] 51 N.Y.2d 506, 415 N.E.2d 950, 434 N.Y.S.2d 961 (1980).

[30] *See also Miller v. C.A. Muer Corp.*, 420 Mich. 355, 362 N.W.2d 650, 43 FEP Cases 1195 (1984); *Whirlpool Corp. v. Civil Rights Comm'n*, 425 Mich. 527, 390 N.W.2d 625 (1986); *Johnson v. Bozeman School Dist. No. 7*, 734 P.2d 209 (Mont. 1987).

[31] 527 So. 2d 894 (Fla. Dist. Ct. App. 1988).

[32] 268 NLRB 1483 (1984).

[33] 83 LA 163 (1984)(Seidman).

[34] Elkouri and Elkouri, *How Arbitration Works* 782-83 (4th ed. 1985), and the cases cited therein.

[35] *Corporate Affairs: Nepotism, Office Romance, and Sexual Harassment*, 5-6, 41 (BNA Special Report 1988).

[36] 162 Cal. App. 3d 241, 208 Cal. Rptr. 524, 117 LRRM 3309 (1984).

[37] 208 Cal. Rptr. at 530.

[38] *Sears v. Ryder Truck Rental, Inc.*, 596 F. Supp. 1001, 41 FEP Cases 1347, 117 LRRM 3237 (E.D. Mich. 1984).

[39] *Autry v. North Carolina Dept. of Human Resources*, 820 F.2d 1384, 1386-87, 44 FEP Cases 169 (4th Cir. 1987); *DeCinto v. Westchester County Medical Center*, 807 F.2d 304, 42 FEP Cases 921 (2d Cir. 1986), *cert. denied*, 108 S. Ct. 89, 44 FEP Cases 1672 (1987); *Miller v. Aluminum Co. of America*, 679 F. Supp. 495, 501, 45 FEP Cases 1775 (W.D. Pa.), *aff'd*, 856 F.2d 184 (3d Cir. 1988).

[40] 176 Mich. App. 17, 438 N.W.2d 872 (1989). *See also, Freeman v. Continental Technical Serv.*, 710 F. Supp. 328, 48 FEP Cases 1398 (N.D. Ga. 1988).

[41] 477 U.S. 57, 106 S. Ct. 2399, 40 FEP Cases 1822 (1986).

[42] 464 U.S. 965, 104 S.Ct. 404, 1 IER Cases 164 (1983).

[43] 539 F. Supp. 612 (W.D. Va. 1982).

[44] *See also, Shawgo v. Spradlin*, 701 F.2d 470, 1 IER Cases 164 (5th Cir.), *cert. denied*, 464 U.S. 965, 104 S. Ct. 404 (1983) (police department did not infringe on rights of male police sergeant and patrol woman disciplined for cohabitation); *Baron v. Meloni*, 556 F. Supp. 796 (W.D.N.Y.) *rem.*, 742 F.2d 1439 (2d Cir. 1983); *aff'd*, 779 F.2d 36 (2d Cir. 1985) (adultery not protected).

[45] 563 F. Supp. 585, 1 IER Cases 195 (W.D. Mich. 1983), *aff'd*, 746 F.2d 1475, 1 IER Cases 1136 (6th Cir.), *cert. denied*, 473 U.S. 909 (1984).

[46] 791 F.2d 736, 1 IER Cases 603 (9th Cir. 1986).

[47] *Kukla v. Village of Antioch*, 647 F. Supp. 799 (N.D. Ill. 1986).

[48] *See Bowers v. Hardwick*, 478 U.S. 186, 106 S. Ct. 2841 (1986).

[49] *See, Slohoda v. United Parcel Service, Inc.*, 193 N.J. Super. 586, 475 A.2d 618 (App. Div. 1984).

[50] *See e.g.*, D.C. CODE ANN. § 1-2902, *et seq.* (1981 and Supp. 1985); WIS. STAT. ANN. § 111.321 (West Supp. 1986).

[51] *See* Elkouri at 782-83; Chapter III.

[52] 147 Ill. App. 2d 822, 498 N.E.2d 559 (1986).

[53] *Patton v. J.C. Penney Co.*, 301 Or. 117, 719 P.2d 854, 122 LRRM 2445 (1986); *Karren v. Far West Federal Savings*, 79 Or. App. 131, 717 P.2d 1271, *review denied*, 301 Or. 666, 725 P.2d 1293 (1986).

[54] *Williamson v. A.G. Edwards & Sons*, 50 FEP Cases 95 (8th Cir. 1989); *DeSantis v. Pacific Tel. & Tel. Co.*, 608 F.2d 327, 19 FEP Cases 1493 (9th Cir. 1979); *Smith v. Liberty Mutual Insurance Co.*, 569 F.2d 325, 17 FEP Cases 28 (5th Cir. 1978). Cf. *Carlucci v. Doe*, 109 S. Ct. 407, 48 FEP Cases 555 (1988).

[55] *Saal v. Middendorf*, 427 F. Supp. 192, 17 FEP Cases 254 (N.D. Cal. 1977), *rev'd*, 632 F.2d 788, 24 FEP Cases 289 (9th Cir. 1980); *Society for Individual Rights, Inc. v. Hampton*, 63 FRD 399, 11 FEP Cases 1243 (N.D. Cal. 1973), *aff'd on other grounds*, 528 F.2d 905, 12 FEP Cases 534 (9th Cir. 1975).

[56] 478 U.S. 186, 106 S. Ct. 2841, *reh. denied*, 478 U.S. 1039, 107 S. Ct. 29 (1986). The court did not address the constitutionality of the Georgia law as applied to other acts of sodomy. 106 S.Ct. at 2842 n.2. *See also, Woodward v. United States*, 871 F.2d 1068 (Fed. Cir. 1989).

[57] 822 F.2d 97, 44 FEP Cases 174 (D.C. Cir. 1987).

[58] *See also, Dronenburg v. Zech*, 741 F.2d 1388, 35 FEP Cases 898, *reh. denied*, 746 F.2d 1579, 36 FEP Cases 1419 (D.C. Cir. 1984) (Navy's policy of mandatory discharge for homosexual conduct does not violate the constitutional right to privacy).

[59] 703 F. Supp. 1372 (E.D. Wis. 1989).

[60] *Id.* at 1377.

[61] *Id.* at 1380.

[62] WIS. STAT. ANN. 111.31 *et seq.*; D.C. CODE § 1-2501 *et seq.*; *see also Gay Law Students Ass'n v. Pacific Tel. & Tel. Co.*, 24 Cal. 3d 458, 595 P.2d 592, 156 Cal. Rptr. 14, 19 FEP Cases 1419 (1979).

[63] *Madsen v. Erwin*, 395 Mass. 715, 481 N.E. 2d 1160, 38 FEP Cases 1466, 120 LRRM 2408 (1985).

* * *

Work Record Confidentiality

Co-workers and supervisors often are privy to a great deal of knowledge about employees' personal lives. The typical personnel file contains large amounts of sensitive information about an employee's background, family, and finances. Some employee records in personnel files, such as job applications, performance reviews, and attendance records relate directly to employment decisions. Those files also may contain credit information, letters of recommendation, reports on suspected misconduct on or off the job, and confidential medical information submitted to the employer to support worker's compensation claims, medical reimbursements, sick leave, disability claims, and medical treatment that may affect the way employees do their jobs and how well they do them.

Most employers allow employees access to their personnel files. A recent survey by the American Society for Personnel Administration (ASPA) found that 96 percent of the 520 responding companies let their employees see their own personnel files.[1] Fifty percent of these said state law required employers to allow workers to see their personnel files. The percentage of employers that allowed employees to see their files was about the same in states without such laws as it was in states with them, ASPA found.

The survey also found that:

- Seventy percent of the respondents maintain pre-employment records, including reference letters, test scores, and medical records, and 88 percent grant employees access to these files.

- Only 53 percent of the employers retain investigatory records, which include results of credit, background, and criminal checks. Nearly 80 percent of these

organizations allow employees access to this
information.

- Records most likely to be maintained separately from
  general personnel files include medical records (80
  percent) and investigatory records (65 percent).

- Many employers control access to records. In 98
  percent of responding companies, a member of the
  personnel department must be present while
  employees review their files. In 52 percent of the
  companies, copying records is limited or is not
  allowed.

Many employers do not have policies that are adequate to
protect sensitive confidential employee data from possible
abuse, according to a 1989 survey of 126 Fortune 500 companies employing 3.7 million people, conducted by David
Linowes, former chairman of the U.S. Privacy Protection Commission.

The survey found that:

- While 87 percent of companies allow employees to
  look at their personnel files, only 27 percent give
  employees access to their supervisors' files on them,
  which often contain more extensive information.

- Fifty-seven percent use private investigative agencies
  to collect or verify information about employees, and
  42 percent collect information without telling the
  employee.

- Thirty-eight percent have no policy covering release
  of data to the government; of the 78 that have a
  policy, 30 do not require a subpoena.

- Eighty percent of companies will give information to
  an employee's potential creditor without a subpoena,
  and 58 percent will give information to landlords.[2]

When a supervisor learns of confidential information from
an employee or keeps confidential personnel records, that supervisor and the employer should keep the information con-

fidential. Employers that disclose inaccurate, potentially embarrassing, or confidential information risk legal liability for invasion of privacy and other claims. Federal and state laws grant employees some protection against disclosure of personnel and medical records, and a common-law right to privacy protects against the public disclosure of private facts. However, in some circumstances employers are allowed to disclose confidential information, and at other times employers may be required to reveal confidential personnel information. In particular, public employers are subject to federal and state freedom-of-information laws and public records acts.

STATUTORY PROTECTIONS

The federal Privacy Act of 1974[3] significantly limits the disclosure of records relating to individuals that would otherwise be accessible through the policies and practices of government agencies or under the Freedom of Information Act of 1966 (FOIA).[4] The Privacy Act applies only to federal government agencies in the executive branch and to independent regulatory agencies. The act covers all records maintained on federal employees, including employment records. It generally prohibits the disclosure of personal information without the employee's consent, with several exemptions.[5] The major exemption affecting federal employees is that agencies are allowed to disclose records to those officers and employees of the unit that maintains the records who need the records to do their jobs. This exception was applied in a case in which an employee's personnel records were disclosed to agency attorneys and a personnel specialist who were gathering information about a sex discrimination complaint that had been filed against the agency by the employee. The court held that this disclosure did not violate the Privacy Act because the investigating attorneys needed the information.[6] The act gives employees access to their records; allows them to ask that information which they think is false or misleading be corrected

or amended; and allows them to include in their files statements of any disagreement they have with the content of their
records.[7]

The Privacy Act does not cover private employers. Instead,
Congress established the Privacy Protection Study Commission
to recommend guidelines and possible legislation on personnel
records of private employers. The commission's report, issued
in 1977, suggested that private employers voluntarily adopt its
recommendations on protecting the confidentiality of
employee records. No subsequent federal legislation on this
subject was enacted. The commission's report is outlined later
in this chapter.

Many states have privacy protection laws that protect state
government employees, or include exceptions in their public
disclosure laws that would otherwise cover employee records.
These laws vary significantly, and some courts have held that
certain governmental employee records are not protected from
public disclosure. The Supreme Court of Florida found in one
case that employee records kept as part of a tax-supported
hospital's files were not exempted from the public records act
by an exemption for public records "which are presently
provided by law to be confidential."[8] A New York law has
been held not to provide a private right of action to a police
officer whose personnel records were disclosed to third parties.[9]

A built-in tension exists between the anti-disclosure mandate of the federal and state privacy laws and the pro-dis-
closure mandates of the federal Freedom of Information Act
and its state counterparts. On the one hand, the government is
expected to operate in the open and allow the public access to
public records. On the other hand, the government is expected
to protect the privacy of its employees. This tension has been
most clearly focused in many cases where members of the
public or the press have sought access to the personnel or
employment records of public employees. For example, the
Washington Public Disclosure Act limits the disclosure of per-

sonnel records to the extent that disclosure would violate personal privacy or a vital governmental interest. As part of an ongoing study, a researcher in one case sought access to personnel records regarding fire fighters and police officers who were receiving disability pay and/or retirement. The court ruled that disclosure by the state government did not violate the employees' right to privacy because the information released pertained only to injuries that would not be highly offensive to reasonable people, and the records were of legitimate interest to the public.[10]

Many states have laws regulating access to and inspection of employee personnel files maintained by both public and private employers. Some state laws grant employees the right to correct or explain any inaccurate data in their personnel files.[11] Michigan's law, one of the most comprehensive, requires that certain investigative files be maintained separately, and that no records be gathered or maintained on employees' associations, political activities, or non-employment activities outside the workplace.[12] Massachusetts' law allows employees to inspect their personnel records. If any disagreement exists regarding any items in the personnel record, the employer and employee may arrange for removal or correction of any inaccurate information. If the parties cannot agree to a mutual correction of any alleged inaccurate data, the employee may submit a written statement explaining his or her position and such statements are put in the personnel file.[13]

Other states have enacted "service-letter" laws. Nebraska, for example, requires all employers to provide, at former employees' requests, a letter that describes the nature and duration of services rendered by the employee and includes a statement describing why the employee quit or was discharged. An employer that willfully or negligently fails to furnish the required information is subject to a fine and imprisonment.[14]

Even when no specific law provides for the correction of inaccurate information, courts have recognized that public employees have an interest in preventing the disclosure of inaccurate information maintained in their files. In *Perri v. Aytch*,[15] a public employee was suspended without a hearing following her arrest for possession of a controlled substance. Although the charge was subsequently dismissed, she was denied reinstatement to her job and discharged. The U.S. Court of Appeals for the Third Circuit held that the employee was entitled to a pre-termination hearing as a necessary procedural safeguard to protect against the disclosure to future employers of the dismissed charges of illegal conduct that were part of her personnel file.

COMMON LAW PRIVACY CLAIMS

Private sector employees are not protected under most state privacy protection laws, but they can use common law privacy torts to protect the expectations of privacy they have in certain types of confidential information maintained by their employers. Most common law privacy cases have involved disclosure of confidential medical information, but the position taken by the courts in these cases would apply to other types of personal, confidential information. In *Levias v. United Airlines*,[16] a flight attendant sought a waiver from the airline's medical examiner of the weight limit imposed by the airline for appearance purposes. Her private physician gave the airline's medical examiner confidential medical information regarding the employee's gynecological problems, other physical problems, and information regarding the contraceptive methods she used. The medical examiner disclosed much of this information to the attendant's male flight supervisor and made other comments regarding the medical information in front of another supervisor. A jury found that these disclosures were an invasion of the flight attendant's right of privacy and granted her $14,000 in compensatory damages and $20,000 in punitive damages. An appellate court upheld the finding of compensatory damages, stating that no employment privilege was involved because the flight attendant's supervisors did not have a real need to know the disclosed data; only the medical examiner needed the information in deciding whether to grant the requested waiver. The court reversed the award of punitive damages, however, finding no malice, hostility, or prolonged indifference by the employer to the adverse consequences from the disclosure of the information.

REQUIRED DISCLOSURE

Policies or laws often require employers to disclose confidential information regardless of the employee's interest in confidentiality. Employers can be compelled to disclose information if an employee's privacy right is outweighed by the needs of the government, the rights of a union, or the needs of a third party. In these instances courts balance the asserted need for information against the privacy rights of the individual. In *U.S. v. Westinghouse Electric Corp.*,[17] an employer refused to produce medical records of past and present employees in response to a request from the National Institute for Occupational Safety and Health (NIOSH), which was conducting a health hazard evaluation at one of the employer's plants. The employer insisted that it would disclose such records only if the employee authorized the disclosure and NIOSH agreed not to share the records with other parties. The court held that the strong public interest in facilitating research and investigations by NIOSH justified "the minimal intrusion into the privacy which surrounds the employee's medical records." The court stated, however, that because those records contained information that the employees might consider highly sensitive, NIOSH was required to give prior notice to affected employees and to allow them to assert their own personal privacy claims. In *Andrews v. Veterans Administration*,[18] the U.S. Court of Appeals for the 10th Circuit found important policy reasons why the Privacy Act should not bar disclosure of relevant information to unions. It found, however, that if disclosure would constitute a clearly unwarranted invasion of privacy, within the meaning of FOIA, the Privacy Act would prohibit disclosure to unions, unless the employees concerned consented. Employers also have been required to turn over personnel files to administrative agencies, such as federal and state equal employment opportunity commissions investigating allegations of discrimination. Human rights commissions and the Equal Employment Opportunity Commission (EEOC) routinely reject employer's claims of confidentiality. In *Redmond v. City of Overland Park*,[19] a court found that the interests of a police department in determining a probationary police officer's fitness to serve as an officer outweighed the officer's interest in preventing a psychiatrist's disclosure of personal information to the department.

Several cases have involved unions' requests for information to assist in their organizing campaigns, negotiations, or representation of employees. In *Detroit Edison v. NLRB*,[20] a case decided in 1979 by the U.S. Supreme Court, the National Labor Relations Board (NLRB) ordered Detroit Edison to supply a union with information pertaining to its employee psychological aptitude testing program, specifically, the test questions, the filled-out employee answer sheets, and the score of each employee, by name. The union claimed it needed the information in connection with arbitration of a grievance. The court, balancing the needs of the union with the privacy rights of the employees, determined that the employees' rights were stronger and that any impairment of the function of the union in processing the grievances of employees was more than justified by the interest served in conditioning the disclosure of the test scores on the consent of the very employees whose grievances were being processed. The court concluded that the burden on the union in this instance is minimal, while the company's interest in preserving employee confidence in the testing program was well-founded.

Each of these cases illustrates these two important principles:

- Employers have "standing" to raise the privacy interests of their employees when confidential or personal information is sought by third parties — government agencies, unions, the press, or private litigants; and
- Privacy rights are not absolute.

As the Supreme Court noted in *Whalen v. Roe*, the process of deciding cases involving the involuntary disclosure of personal information involves a balancing of interests.[21]

GUIDELINES FOR CONFIDENTIAL INFORMATION

In many situations supervisors or other company employees can discuss confidential information without being subjected to liability, especially when they act in good faith and for a legitimate business reason. However, considerations of liability and prudent management suggest strongly that employers should establish comprehensive policies governing access to employee records and dissemination of them. Information should be disclosed only to those with an absolute need to know, with the employee's consent, if possible.

The Privacy Protection Study Commission, following extensive testimony on employer's practices and concerns, issued recommendations in 1977 designed to balance the concerns of employers and employees in three areas: 1) access to records; 2) correction of records; and 3) internal disclosures of information.[22]

Employees' Access to Their Records

Although the commission found fairness demands that job applicants or employees be allowed to see and copy records employers maintain on them, it also recognized employers' general reluctance to allow access to test scores, records that require professional interpretation, and information supplied by confidential sources, such as references. Accordingly, the commission recommended that:

- Employers designate clearly which records on applicants, employees, and former employees to which they will and will not allow access;

- Employers allow employees to see evaluations of their performance or job potential that can be used for promotion and placement;

- Employees be allowed to see records of security investigations, if those records become a part of the employee's file when investigations are completed;

- Employees be allowed to examine, copy, correct, amend, or dispute the contents of all investigative reports maintained by a consumer reporting agency or the employer requesting the report. (The Fair Credit Reporting Act requires only that employers notify individuals when such reports are used.)

Correction of Records

The commission recommended that employees who question the accuracy, timeliness, or thoroughness of records should be allowed to correct, amend, or explain those records. When a correction or amendment is made, the employer should include it in any subsequent disclosure. When an employer rejects the change requested by the employee, the commission recommended that the employee's description of the dispute be put in the record and included when the record is disclosed.

Internal Disclosure of Documents

The commission concluded that employers have a duty to see that information generated as one part of the employer-employee relationship not be disclosed to others in the organization in ways that are unfair to the employee. The commission recommended that:

- Personnel and payroll records be available internally only to authorized users on a need-to-know basis; and
- Security records or records relating to security investigations be maintained apart from other records, and that no access be given to employees unless the information is put in their personnel files or is used for discipline, termination, promotion, or evaluation.

(The Commission's recommendations on medical and insurance records are discussed in Chapter XIV.)

In the report on his survey, Linowes, the former Privacy Commission chairman, made the following additional recommendations regarding disclosures of employment data, individual access, and informing the individual:

- Employers should limit external disclosures of information in records kept on individual employees, former employees, and job applicants; they also should limit the internal use of such records;
- Employers should explain to all of their employees and to any job applicant who asks, the types of disclosures the employer might make of information in the records it maintains on them, including disclosures of information to be used in directories, and its procedures for involving them in each type of disclosure; and
- Employers should notify job applicants, employees, and others before they collect the type of information usually collected about such individuals in connection with employment decisions.

This notification should include:

(1) the types of information the employer expects to collect;

(2) the techniques that may be used to collect such information;

(3) the types of sources that are expected to be contacted;

(4) the types of organizations and people to whom information about the individuals may be disclosed and the circumstances under which this may be done, without their authorization, and the types of information that may be disclosed;

(5) the procedures established by law by which individuals may gain access to any resulting record about themselves; and

(6) the procedures under which individuals may correct, amend, or dispute any resulting records about themselves.

Although federal and state laws vary significantly on the degree of restrictions governing personnel data, employers should use care and discretion when they disclose and provide access to employees' confidential information and documents. Employers should restrict the disclosure of these records and access to them to people who have a direct and legitimate need to know the information, unless they are required by government agencies, the courts, or federal or state statutes such as freedom-of-information laws to provide greater access. In most instances, obtaining the employee's consent to disclose information will protect the employer from liability.

ILLUSTRATIONS

Employer's Disclosure Of Loan To Employee By Credit Union Was Not Actionable Invasion Of Privacy

Vicinanza, a route salesman for Houston Coca-Cola Bottling Co. for 3 years, left the firm and opened Downtown Distributing and Vending, which competed with Houston Coca-Cola Bottling. For several months after he left Houston Coca-Cola, certain employees of that firm told Vicinanza's customers and prospects that he was unreliable, dishonest, and incompetent. Vicinanza sued Houston Coca-Cola under theories of slander and tortious interference, claiming damages for lost profits. He also claimed actual and punitive damages for past and future mental anguish under the invasion of privacy tort resulting from Houston Coca-Cola credit union's disclosure of a loan made to him. He claimed mere disclosure and dissemination of any type of confidential information concerning his private life gives rise to a cause of action for invasion of privacy.

A trial court awarded damages of more than $1.3 million for slander, tortious interference, and invasion of privacy. The Texas Court of Appeals upheld some of the claims for liable and tortious interference but rejected the claim based on invasion of privacy. The court found that Vicinanza did not satisfy the element of the tort of privacy which says that the publication of the material would be highly offensive to a reasonable person of ordinary sensibilities. The appeals court said information disclosed about the loan did not "contain highly intimate or embarrassing facts about a person's private affairs, such that its publication would be highly objectionable to a person of ordinary sensibilities." [*Houston Coca-Cola Bottling Co. v. Vicinanza*, 1988 WL 54573 (Tex. App. Houston 1988).]

Discussions Between A Manager And A Co-Worker Concerning The Reasons For An Employee's Discharge Did Not Violate The Terminated Employee's Privacy

Arnold was fired by Diet Center after working there for a year, because his employer believed Arnold was discussing confidential company business with outsiders. One of Arnold's managers later discussed the reasons for Arnold's discharge with one of his co-workers. When Arnold sued for wrongful discharge based on a violation of implied contract, he added tort claims for invasion of privacy and defamation based on the manager's conversation with the co-worker.

All of Arnold's claims were dismissed before trial. An appeals court upheld the dismissal, finding that a "qualified privilege" would protect the communications from defamation and privacy claims because Diet Center had a legitimate interest in stressing to employees the importance of complying with their agreement to maintain confidentiality. The court found that the privilege was not abused because only one disclosure by the company concerning Arnold's communication had occurred; all other disclosures were by Arnold himself. [*Arnold v. Diet Center, Inc.*, 113 Idaho 581, 746 P.2d 1040, 2 IER 1531 (1987).]

Disclosure By Employer Of An Employee's Criminal Record Was Not Actionable Invasion Of Privacy Because Disclosure Was Of Public, Not Private, Facts

Baker was fired by Burlington Northern for giving false information on his employment application regarding criminal convictions. The letter advising him of the termination stated that he had answered "no" to the question "Have you ever been convicted of a crime?" But an investigation by the company showed that Baker had pled guilty to two counts of first degree burglary and was placed on probation with the sentence withheld for two years.

A copy of the letter was put in Baker's file, and copies were sent to five supervisors who needed to be informed of the termination, to the Idaho Department of Employment in response to a query about why Baker was fired, and to a union official investigating the dismissal. Baker sued for libel and invasion of privacy based on the distribution of the letter containing allegedly libelous and embarrassing private facts.

The Supreme Court of Idaho rejected Baker's charges, finding that the employer's letter was an accurate recitation of the public record of the employee's criminal record. On the invasion of privacy claim, the court found that the disclosure by the employer was of public, not private, facts and as such was not an actionable invasion of privacy. [*Baker v. Burlington Northern, Inc.*, 587 P.2d 829 (1978).]

Absolute Safeguards Must Be Provided To Protect Confidentiality Of Applicants' Records

Martin and Stretton applied to the New Jersey Casino Control Commission for licenses to work as casino dealers in Atlantic City. They refused to answer several questions on the application forms and sought to limit the scope of a release authorization that empowered various institutions, such as banks, to release confidential information about the applicants to the commission. Their applications were rejected because they were incomplete. They sued, alleging that the commission's conditioning the application for licensing on disclosure of personal information to the government infringed on their constitutional right to privacy. They also alleged that New Jersey could not require disclosure of personal information to the government unless it had taken adequate steps to ensure that the information would not be disclosed to the public.

The Supreme Court of New Jersey rejected the applicants' privacy claim, finding that the governmental interest in having applicants furnish information to enable the commission to enforce the requirements of the Casino Control Act outweighs the applicants' right to privacy, especially since most of the information is of public record. The court found, however, that the state had not instituted adequate procedures to prevent disclosure of the confidential information. It ordered the commission to promulgate regulations that would include guidelines on the storage of information and access to it, including the circumstances under which files could be removed from government offices. [*In re Martin*, 447 A.2d 1290 (1982).]

ENDNOTES

[1] *Resource*, Vol. 8, No. 6, American Society for Personnel Administration (June 1989).

[2] D. Linowes, *A Research Survey of Individual Privacy Protection in Big Business* at 3-5 (Univ. of Ill. 1989); D. Linowes, *Privacy In America* at 41

(Univ of Ill. Press 1989); "As Firms' Personnel Files Grow, Worker Privacy Falls,"*Wall Street Journal*, April 19, 1989.

[3] 5 USC 552a.

[4] *See* 5 USC 552.

[5] 5 USC 552a(b).

[6] *Howard v. Marsh*, 785 F.2d 645 (8th Cir.), *cert. denied*, 479 U.S. 988, 107 S.Ct. 581, 42 FEP Cases 560 (1986).

[7] 5 USC 552a(d).

[8] *Michel v. Douglas*, 464 So.2d 545 (Fla. 1985).

[9] *Carpenter v. City of Plattsburgh*, 105 A.2d 295, 484 N.Y.S.2d 284, *aff'd* 66 N.Y.2d 791, 497 N.Y.S.2d 909, 488 N.E.2d 839 (1985).

[10] *Seattle Firefighters Union Local No. 27 v. Hollister*, 737 P.2d 1302, 48 Wash. App. 129 (1987).

[11] *See, e.g.*, CONN. GEN. STAT. § 31-128b (West Supp. 1981); DEL. CODE ANN. tit. 19, 721 (1985), MICH. STAT. ANN. § 17.62 (Callaghan 1982).

[12] MICH. STAT. ANN. § 17.62 (Callaghan 1982).

[13] MASS. GEN. LAWS, ch. 149 § 52C (1988). *See also*, CONN. GEN. STAT. 31-128e (West Supp. 1980).

[14] *See* NEB. REV. STAT. § 48-211 (1984).

[15] 724 F.2d 362, 115 LRRM 2257 (3d Cir. 1983).

[16] 27 Ohio App. 3d 222, 500 N.E.2d 370 (1985). *See also, Bratt v. IBM*, 392 Mass. 508, 467 N.E.2d 126 (1984) (described in Chapter XIV).

[17] 638 F.2d 570 (3d Cir. 1980).

[18] 838 F.2d 418, 3 IER 1274 (10th Cir.), *cert. denied*, 109 S. Ct. 56 (1988).

[19] 672 F. Supp. 473, 2 IER 1439 (D. Kan. 1987).

[20] 440 U.S. 301, 99 S. Ct. 1123, 100 LRRM 2728 (1979).

[21] 429 U.S. 589, 97 S. Ct. 869 (1977).

[22] *Report of the Privacy Protection Study Commission*, U.S. Government Printing Office, July 1977.

* * *

Confidentiality of EAP
And Medical Information

For many years, employers have kept confidential medical information about their employees to help determine how well they can perform their jobs, or as part of employer-operated or employer-sponsored health insurance plans. Fifty percent of the employers contacted in one recent survey use employee medical records in making employment-related decisions, and 19 percent of them do not tell employees that they are doing this.[1] The amount of sensitive information available to employers has increased as a result of the emergence of employee assistance programs (EAPs)—operated by the employer or under contract with outside professionals—that help employees try to solve various personal problems, including substance abuse, eating disorders, stress, and financial problems.

Although employers traditionally regarded these issues as part of employees' private lives, many now help employees cope with these problems in an effort to reduce the adverse effects they have on job performance and productivity. One source estimates that these employee personal problems cost U.S. business as much as $100 billion per year in absenteeism, accidents and errors, and increased use of sick leave and health and insurance benefits.[2] Studies estimate that drug and alcohol dependency alone may cost business as much as $240 billion per year.[3] Concern about the effects of drug and alcohol abuse on employees' job performance has been a primary factor in the increased use of EAPs. A comprehensive survey conducted by the National Institute on Alcohol Abuse found that only 25 percent of Fortune 500 companies had EAPs in 1972, but the figure had risen to 57.7 percent by 1979, and approximately 80 percent had EAPs in 1987.

Employee assistance programs range from internally operated corporate counseling sessions to external programs developed and operated by outside professionals who refer employees to various services such as halfway houses, psychologists, therapists, financial and legal advisers, and such self-help groups as Alcoholics Anonymous, Gamblers Anonymous, and Overeaters Anonymous.

Because of the nature of the problems handled by EAPs, such as substance abuse and depression, employers may have access to personal and medical information that is much more sensitive than otherwise would be available to them. Many experts emphasize that assuring employees that their EAP records and their use of EAP services are confidential is a key to the programs' success. These experts stress that it is in employers' interest to consider the issues of confidentiality that arise in EAPs. Employers also need to be aware of the requirements of confidentiality imposed by a professional code of ethics and federal and state statutes.

DUTIES OF CONFIDENTIALITY

Codes of Ethics, Statutory Requirements

Confidentiality requirements for EAP records depend in part on whether the program is operated by the employer or an outside contractor. EAPs conducted by outside professionals may be subject to various professions' codes of ethics and professional organizations' rules of conduct. In these programs, employers often do not have direct access to employees' EAP records and they cannot obtain such access because of restrictions imposed by the EAP. Some independent EAPs establish their own confidentiality policies that prohibit their employees from disclosing information to employers that refer patients to the EAP.[4] Various codes of ethics that govern the professional responsibilities of psychiatrists, psychologists, social workers, and other profes-

sionals limit their activities when they work as EAP counselors.

The Employee Assistance Society of North America
(EASNA) has developed proposed ethical standards that state:

> The EAP practitioner protects the client's right to privacy with
> reference both to confidentiality and anonymity. Anonymity refers
> to nondisclosure of the *identity* of the individual. Confidentiality
> refers to the private, nondisclosable nature of *information* obtained
> in the communication between a client and a practitioner.[5]

Most therapists will not disclose their communications with
their patients to third parties without the patients' consent.
These ethical restraints often are supported by legal requirements. Many states have "privilege" laws that prevent third
parties from compelling disclosure of confidential communications between physicians and patients without the patient's
consent.[6] Some of these laws are designed to prevent
physicians from disclosing to third parties confidential information communicated by the patient or obtained through examination or treatment.[7] In many states physicians may be liable in tort for disclosing privileged communications, on the
basis of invasion of privacy, breach of a fiduciary relationship,
or violation of statutory requirements.[8] Employers that provide
medical services and operate EAPs may be covered by these
ethical restrictions. In addition, employers need to be concerned with confidentiality requirements imposed by the
federal Rehabilitation Act of 1973 and analogous state laws.
(See Chapter XIII.)

PHS Regulations

The U.S. Public Health Service (PHS) has issued regulations regarding the confidentiality of alcohol and drug abuse
patient records.[9] These regulations cover EAPs that:

- Are related to alcohol abuse or drug abuse education,
  training, treatment, rehabilitation, or research and
  are conducted in whole or in part, directly or by
  grant, by a federal agency;

- Require a license, registration or other authorization from a federal agency;
- Are assisted by federal funds, directly through grants or contracts or indirectly by funds from state or local governments; or
- Are assisted by the Internal Revenue Service through income tax deductions for contributions or by the granting of tax exempt status.[10]

These regulations govern access to and disclosure of employees' EAP records if the EAP falls within one of these categories. The regulations define the minimum requirements for the protection of confidentiality of patient records and information. Patients in treatment programs covered by the regulations may consent to disclosure of treatment information if such consent is obtained in writing and patients know that they can revoke it any time before the information is to be disclosed. The rules contain some exceptions to the consent requirement. For example, disclosure to medical personnel without the patient's consent is allowed to the extent necessary to meet a medical emergency.[11] The regulations provide for fines of not more than $500 for a first offense and not more than $5,000 for each subsequent offense.[12]

The regulations do not cover all drug programs. In *Listion v. Shelby County Civil Service*,[13] the state court rejected a discharged fire fighter's claim of breach of confidentiality when his employer discharged him on the basis of information and records concerning his cocaine addiction and involvement with an employee drug treatment program. The court found that Section 2.12 of the federal confidentiality regulations, which govern the records of state or local governments that are assisted by federal revenue-sharing or other unrestricted grants, was not applicable to the Shelby County employee drug abuse program because the program did not receive federal revenue-sharing funds.

Implied Promises of Confidentiality

Many courts recently have recognized employees' right to sue to enforce "contracts" based on employers' promises, manuals, and handbooks. (See Chapter XV.) Courts have been willing, in some circumstances, to recognize an implied promise of confidentiality to employees resulting from employers' statements or their distribution of handbooks expressing their policies on confidentiality. In these instances, courts have found that language in an employee manual is sufficient to create an implied promise of confidentiality even though confidentiality is not actually promised by the EAP counselor. For example, in *Woolley v. Hoffman-LaRoche*,[14] the court noted that when a company manual promises confidentiality, a court can find an implied promise of confidentiality in the employee's expectation that the information disclosed to an EAP counselor will remain confidential. To guard against such liability, employee handbooks, manuals, and EAP policies distributed to employees must include specific statements that no absolute confidentiality exists and that situations may arise that require disclosure.

Invasion of Privacy Claims

Some courts have found employers and counselors liable for the tort of invasion of privacy as a result of the release of confidential information or communications obtained by EAPs.

Bratt v. IBM[15] involved two disclosures of allegedly confidential information—that Bratt had used his employer's "open-door" policy to file grievances, and that after Bratt visited a physician under IBM's EAP, the physician disclosed confidential medical information. Bratt had been referred to the physician by one of his supervisors. Under IBM's extensive regulations on confidentiality, supervisors were barred from having direct contact with local physicians connected with the EAP.

After examining Bratt, the physician called Bratt's supervisor, informed her that Bratt was paranoid, and recommended that Bratt see a psychiatrist immediately. This and subsequent communications from the psychiatrist were disclosed to several other managers and supervisors at IBM. Bratt sued for breach of privacy guaranteed under the Massachusetts Constitution and IBM's policies.

In recognizing that an employee could state such a claim under Massachusetts law, the Massachusetts Supreme Judicial Court said courts should balance the employer's legitimate business interest in obtaining and publishing the information against the extent of the intrusion on the employee's privacy that resulted from the disclosure. Because the case involved an employee's right of privacy allegedly violated by a physician's disclosure of personal medical data, the court said the degree of the intrusion and the public's interest in preserving the confidentiality of the physician-patient relationship should be balanced against the employer's need for the medical information.

The U.S. Court of Appeals for the First Circuit subsequently applied this interpretation of Massachusetts law and held that it was not an unreasonable intrusion on Bratt's privacy to inform certain managers that Bratt had used the open-door process. Although that information may have had a negative connotation to some managers, it was not of such a personal nature that an intrusion on Bratt's privacy occurred.[16] The court held that the disclosure of Bratt's visit to a psychiatrist and the psychiatrist's medical conclusions could be an invasion of his privacy because of the paramount importance of confidentiality in the physician-patient relationship. The appellate court therefore held that Bratt had a right to a jury trial on the allegations that his employer breached his privacy through the doctor's actions.

Bratt is very important to employers that sponsor EAPs because when employers retain a physician to examine employees, no physician-patient relationship exists between the employees and the doctor. But the federal court of appeals in *Bratt* decided that if the patient reasonably believes the physician-patient relationship exists and the physician knew or reasonably should have known that the patient had such an expectation, the doctor owes a duty of confidentiality. When physicians retained or referred by a company owe a duty of patient confidentiality, they can be held liable for breaching that duty and the company also may be found liable if its managers induce a breach of that duty.

Not all states have extended the right of privacy as far as Massachusetts. In Oklahoma, a Texaco employee was referred by the company's physician for psychiatric evaluation. The employee's supervisor learned of the psychiatric treatment and allegedly disclosed that fact to several co-workers. The Supreme Court of Oklahoma held in *Eddy v. Brown*[17] that no invasion of the employee's right to privacy had occurred because the information contained in the employee's medical records was of legitimate concern to his supervisor. The court also found that no unreasonable publicity of the employee's private life had occurred because only a few co-workers knew of the psychiatric treatment.

REQUIRED DISCLOSURE OF MEDICAL DATA

Disclosure of confidential information obtained through EAPs is sometimes required when employers or physicians learn that employees or clients are dangerous and their behavior presents an unreasonable risk of harm to others. This duty to disclose was recognized first in California in *Tarasoff v. Regents of the University of California.*[18] A graduate student confided to his psychiatrist that he intended to kill a woman who had refused his advances. The psychiatrist took no action, and the patient subsequently killed the woman. The court held that when a patient poses a serious danger of violence to another person, a therapist is obligated to use reasonable care to protect the intended victim, and this may include a duty to warn. Several other states have recognized this duty, which may apply to physicians employed by companies or retained under EAPs.

Physical examinations given by employers are another area where a duty to disclose can develop. If an employer assumes a duty to determine whether prospective employees are physically fit, it can be held liable if that duty is performed negligently. For example, if a pre-employment blood test indicates a serious abnormality and that information is not disclosed to the job applicant, the employer could be held liable.[19] This duty requires that the employer communicate the results of a medical examination only to the employee, not to third parties.

HANDLING MEDICAL INFORMATION

Employers maintain medical information in many instances because they require it as a condition of employment, placement, or certification to return to work. Additionally, many employers maintain medical records as a result of providing medical care, such as routine physicals, or because they pay for health insurance or life insurance.

Many large employers have procedures that guarantee the confidentiality of medical information in all but the most extreme circumstances. In these companies, corporate medical departments only make recommendations for work restrictions based on medical diagnoses, refraining from forwarding any diagnosis or treatment details in all but the most extreme circumstances.[20] Nevertheless, it is a duty of corporate physicians to tell their employer when they find in an individual a condition that could adversely affect the interests of the employer or other employees.[21]

Employees who use medical services offered by their employer do so at some risk to the traditional confidential relationship between physician and patient, unless the employer has insulated that relationship from the usual work-related responsibilities of the medical department. When a company's medical department provides voluntary physicals or routine medical care for employees, employers may decide to have the resulting records maintained separately from the records generated by work-related contacts, so they are not inadvertently disclosed.

The U.S. Privacy Protection Commission, established by Congress under the Privacy Act of 1974 to study privacy issues in the private sector, made these recommendations for the handling of confidential employee medical records:

- Employers that maintain employment-related medical records on individuals should assure that no diagnostic or treatment information in any such record is made available for use in any employment decision; and

- Employers that provide voluntary health-care programs for their employees assure that any medical record generated by the program is maintained apart from any employment-related medical record and not used by any physician in advising on any employment-related decision or in making any employment-related decision without the express authorization of the individual to whom the record pertains.

The Privacy Commission also urged the adoption of state laws providing employees a right to sue for access to their medical records; a right to correct or amend erroneous, misleading, or incomplete information in a medical record; and a right to hold a medical care provider responsible if it can be shown that the provider has not exercised reasonable care in protecting the confidentiality of the individual's medical records.[22]

Patient Access to Medical Records

A majority of the states have laws giving employees the right to inspect portions of their medical records and, in some instances, obtain copies of them. Colorado's law, which applies to hospital records and to records kept by private physicians, psychologists, and psychiatrists, probably is the most far-reaching. The Colorado law gives patients the right to obtain a copy of their records for a reasonable fee, without having to resort to litigation, and without the authorization of physicians or hospital officials.[23] An Oklahoma law allows patients to inspect and to copy their medical records in hospitals and the physicians' offices. Unlike Colorado, Oklahoma does not give patients access to their psychiatric records during treatment or thereafter.[24]

Other states' laws grant much narrower rights of access. Florida allows patients to obtain copies of all reports of examinations and treatment, but the law applies only to records maintained by physicians; hospital records are not mentioned.[25] Conversely, the laws of Connecticut, Indiana, Louisiana, and Massachusetts cover only hospital records, and do not mention records maintained by physicians.[26]

Although the Privacy Act of 1974 does not allow employees of government agencies access to their medical records, it does require each agency that maintains such records to promulgate rules to:

> ... establish procedures for the disclosure to an individual, on his request, of his record or information pertaining to him, including special procedures, if deemed necessary, for the disclosure to an individual of medical records, including psychological records pertaining to him.[27]

Correcting Medical Information

The Privacy Commission strongly recommended that individuals have the right to review the records made by others of information they have provided and that they have the right to correct any errors and eliminate any inadequacies in such records. Within the employee-physician relationship itself, such errors usually can be corrected before they harm anyone. However, once the information has been disclosed to someone outside the relationship, corrections or amendments are more difficult to make and it becomes increasingly difficult to avoid or reverse the consequences of errors. This creates a significant danger when offhand comments and speculations that are irrelevant to a patient's medical history, diagnosis, condition, treatment, or evaluation are included in medical records that become available for use in making non-medical decisions about the employee. The Privacy Commission recommended that when individuals ask to correct or amend their medical records or information, the physician should, within a reasonable period, make the correction or amendment requested, or inform the individual of the refusal to do so and provide the reasons that support such a refusal.

Exceptions to Duties of Confidentiality

Although courts have found the disclosure of confidential medical information to be actionable in some cases, they also have held consistently that such disclosures are justifiable if they are made in the best interest of the patient or to foster a supervening societal interest. Moreover, employees cannot rely on an expectation of confidentiality in any record-keeping relationship unless they are told of restraints on disclosures. If the people who maintain the records have complete discretion in making disclosures, the individual can have no basis for an expectation of confidentiality.

Other well-recognized exceptions to the duty of confidentiality exist, such as the disclosure of medical records and information between and among medical care providers. The Privacy Commission concluded that disclosure is appropriate, without the patient's authorization, if the recipient of the information is directly involved in the diagnosis and treatment of the patient. In those circumstances, the patient's authorization can be assumed. A second exception to the duty of confidentiality is the disclosure of medical records and information about a patient when necessary to alleviate a serious threat to an individual's health or safety.

A third exception is the disclosure of information pursuant to state laws that requires the reporting of specific diagnoses to public health authorities of communicable diseases, and environmentally or occupationally related diseases.

INSURANCE RECORDS AND INFORMATION

Insurance claims records often contain information about medical diagnosis and treatment. The employer receives this information to meet several needs of employees, such as protecting them against the loss of pay due to illness or arranging for medical bills to be paid. Thus, employers that self-insure or self-administer a health insurance plan necessarily maintain a significant amount of information about employees and their families.

Corporate physicians sometimes are involved in processing claims of employment-related insurance, such as disability or sick pay, because it is their function to evaluate the medical evidence on which the claim is based. A privacy issue arises if employers want to use insurance-related information in making decisions that are unrelated to the claim, such as promotions and transfers.

The Privacy Commission offered these recommendations relating to access to and use of insurance records:

- Employers that provide life or health insurance to their employees should assure that individually identifiable insurance records are maintained separately from other records and are not available to use in making employment decisions; and,

- Employers that provide work-related insurance for employees, such as worker's compensation, voluntary sick pay, or short-term or long-term disability insurance, assure that individually identifiable records pertaining to such insurance are available internally only to authorized recipients and on a need-to-know basis.

ILLUSTRATIONS

HIV Test Result Disclosure Did Not Violate Privacy Right

Plowman, a civilian employee of the Department of the Army, sued his former supervisor, Col. Isbell, claiming that Isbell violated his constitutional right of privacy by disclosing the results of a positive human immunodeficiency virus (HIV) test to four people in Isbell's command. After learning of the positive test, Isbell consulted with the chief of the Office of Civilian Personnel and three other senior officers in his command about the appropriate action to take with Plowman. At a meeting with the five Army officials, Plowman was told he should resign.

A U.S. district court did not decide whether an individual's medical condition carries a privacy right protected by the U.S. Constitution. Rather, the court found that any such right is not absolute or unqualified. Circumstances may exist where limited disclosure is permissible and does not violate the right.

In this case, the court found that the government needed to disclose the information so that a decision could be made on how to proceed in a sensitive situation. Isbell's disclosure of confidential information was no broader than reasonably necessary to make this decision. He did not give Plowman's medical files to someone outside his command, and he did not make that information public. Rather, the disclosure was designed to help him make a difficult decision. [*Plowman v. Dept. of the Army*, 3 IER 1665 (E.D. Va. 1988).]

No Liability For Invasion Of Privacy Where Employer And Counselor Had A Duty To Disclose Information

A chemical plant employee contacted a counseling service provided by his employer. The therapist concluded that the employee was dangerous to the point of being suicidal to himself and homicidal toward others. The counseling service contacted the employee's supervisor, who, in turn, spoke with a

plant manager and union representatives to discuss removing
the employee from his job and placing him on disability leave.
The employee soon retired and sued for invasion of privacy.
His claims were rejected. The court held that the limited disclosures did not constitute "publication" of private facts and
were privileged because they were made to protect the plant
and its employees from danger. [*Davis v. Monsanto*, 627 F.
Supp. 418, 121 LRRM 2698 (S.D. W.Va. 1986).]

*Doctor Paid By Company May Be Liable In Tort For Disclos-
ing Results Of A Positive Drug Test To A Patient's Supervisor*

Crocker went to a first aid station where he worked complaining of a job-related back injury. The nurse on duty
referred him to the office of Hanby, a physician under contract
with Crocker's employer and two other companies. Johnson,
the manager of safety where Crocker worked, had observed
Crocker before he went to the doctor's office. Hanby said
when Crocker came to him, Crocker was "zonked out on
something." Johnson called Hanby and asked that Crocker be
given a urine drug screen test, and a urine specimen was obtained by the nurse. The test revealed traces of marijuana.
Crocker resigned rather than being fired.

The court rejected Crocker's claim of wrongful discharge,
finding that his only remedy was under the collective bargaining agreement. However, the court agreed that issues of fact
existed on Crocker's tort claim against Hanby for breach of the
physician-patient privilege. The court found that Crocker did
not give a separate release allowing the doctor to release any
confidential information to his employer concerning the
urinalysis, and that Crocker may not have been aware that he
was consenting to a drug test. Under established standards, the
physician-patient relationship is a confidential relationship, and
communications obtained in that relationship are not intended
to be discussed with third parties. The court held that Crocker
could present his tort claim against Hanby to a jury. [*Crocker v.
Synpol, Inc.*, 732 S.W.2d 429 (Tex. Ct. App., Beaumont, 1987).]

ENDNOTES

[1] D. Linowes, "A Research Survey of Individual Privacy Protection in Big Business" (Univ. of Ill. 1989).

[2] 42 DLR C-1 (BNA) (March 5, 1987) and 26 DLR A-8 (Feb. 9, 1988).

[3] 176 DLR A-3 (BNA) (Sept. 12, 1988).

[4] *Phillips v. City of Seattle*, 754 P.2d 116, 117 (Wash. Ct. App. 1988), *aff'd*, 766 P.2d 1099 (Wash. 1989).

[5] *Employee Assistance Programs: Benefits, Problems, and Prospects* (BNA 1987) at 42.

[6] 81 Am. Jur. 2d, *Witnesses*, § 230 *et seq.* (2d ed. 1976).

[7] 61 Am. Jur. 2d, *Physicians, Surgeons, etc.*, § 169 (2d ed. 1981).

[8] 61 Am. Jur. 2d, *Physicians, Surgeons, etc.*, § 172-173 (2d ed. 1981); *Annot.*, "Physician's tort liability for unauthorized disclosure of confidential information about plaintiff," 48 ALR 4th 668.

[9] 42 CFR 2.1, *et seq.*

[10] 29 CFR 2.12(b).

[11] 29 CFR 2.51, *et seq.*

[12] 29 CFR 2.4.

[13] 1987 WL 18785, ON WESTLAW (Tenn. Ct. App. 1987).

[14] 491 A.2d 1257 (N.J. 1985).

[15] 392 Mass. 508, 467 N.E.2d 126 (1984) (answering certified questions from the U.S. Court of Appeals for the First Circuit).

[16] *Bratt v. International Business Machine Corp.*, 785 F.2d 352, 359 (1st Cir. 1986).

[17] 715 P.2d 74 (Okla. 1986).

[18] 13 Cal. 3d 177, 529 P.2d 553, 118 Cal. Rptr. 129 (1974). *See also McIntosh v. Milano*, 403 A.2d 500 (N.J. 1979); *Hedlund v. Superior Court of Orange County*, 699 P.2d 41 (Cal. 1983).

[19] *See Coffee v. McDonnell-Douglas Corp.*, 8 Cal.3d 551, 503 P.2d 1366, 105 Cal. Rptr. 358 (1972). *See also, Betesh v. United States*, 400 F. Supp. 238 (D.D.C. 1974) (applying Maryland law); *Wojick v. Aluminum Co. of America*, 183 N.Y.S.2d 351, 18 Misc.2d 740 (1959).

[20] *Report of the Privacy Protection Study Commission*, U.S. Government Printing Office, at 266-267 (July 1977).

[21] *Id.*

[22] *Report of The Privacy Protection Study Commission*, at 291-94.

[23] COLO. REV. STAT. § 25-1-801.

[24] OKLA. STAT. ANN. tit. 76, § 19.

[25] FLA. STAT. ANN. § 458.16.

[26] CONN. GEN. STAT. ANN. § 4.104; IND. CODE ANN. § 34-3-15.5-4; LA. REV. STAT. ANN. § 44.31; MASS. GEN. LAWS ANN. ch. 111, § 70.

[27] 5 USC 552a(f)(3).

* * *

Wrongful Discharge

Although personal privacy concerns employees throughout their employment, lawsuits involving workplace privacy issues usually arise when employees are terminated. Employees sometimes allege that the reasons their employers give for firing them—off-duty drug use or dating a competitor—infringed on their personal privacy rights. In other cases, employees are discharged for refusing to take drug or polygraph tests that they believe infringe on their personal privacy. Many sexual harassment cases involve an actual or constructive discharge. When these privacy issues arise, employees often file suit for wrongful discharge under statutory or common law exceptions to the employment-at-will doctrine.

Damages in wrongful discharge cases can include back pay, lost future earnings, emotional distress, and punitive damages, depending on the state where the case occurs and the theory of recovery. Awards often are large. The average jury award for discharged employees between January 1986 and October 1988 was $602,303, and the median verdict was $158,800.[1]

Wrongful discharge is a complex subject and many differences exist among the states in the theories of recovery, the types of damages available, and employers' defenses. This chapter comprises a brief overview of wrongful discharge, outlining some of the basic theories that discharged employees have used.[2]

English common law has traditionally presumed that unless a hiring was for a specified term, it was for one year, and an employee could not be discharged without good cause during that time.[3] Courts in the United States initially adopted this rule and held that an employer must hire an employee for a specified or implied term of service. This common law rule was modified during the Industrial Revolution, and by 1900 courts in the United States almost universally had adopted the rule that an indefinite hiring was an employment that was terminable at any time at the will of either party. In short, an employee who did not have a fixed-term contract could leave the employment at any time without liability, and the employer could fire the employee at any time, without notice, "for good cause, for no cause, or even for cause morally wrong, without being thereby guilty of legal wrong." This concept is known as "employment at will."[4]

Over the past 25 years, the federal government and many states have enacted laws creating exceptions to the employment-at-will doctrine. In addition, three common-law (court-made) exceptions—public policy, implied contract, and the covenant of good faith and fair dealing—have been used to expand employee rights and enforce privacy interests. All but three states—Georgia, Louisiana, and Mississippi—now recognize one or more of these exceptions. Although the scope of each exception varies significantly among the states, they all provide additional theories under which an employee can challenge a termination or discharge that is perceived to be an infringement on employees' expectations of privacy.

STATUTORY EXCEPTIONS

Most employers and employees are familiar with the myriad of federal and state statutory restrictions on employers' power to discharge, notably Title VII of the Civil Rights Act of 1964, the Age Discrimination In Employment Act (ADEA), the Rehabilitation Act of 1973, and their state counterparts. Previous chapters have explained how these laws can affect privacy issues, including testing, no-spouse rules, polygraph use, and sexual harassment. In several other areas these and other laws restrict discharges based on employees' off-the-job activities. One obvious example is employees' religious activities. Many Title VII cases involve employees fired for refusing to work on their Sabbath. Equal Employment Opportunity Commission (EEOC) regulations require that employers make reasonable accommodations for employees' religious preferences.[5] While the extent of this obligation has been extensively litigated,[6] recognized limits exist on discrimination based on religion or religious practices. In one case involving a claim for unemployment compensation by an employee who was fired for refusing to work on her Sabbath, the U.S. Supreme Court found that the decision of a state agency to deny the employee benefits violated constitutional guarantees of free exercise of religion and privacy.[7]

Many states also have adopted laws that grant employees protection from interference with certain protected activities. The most prevalent examples are laws protecting political expression or the filing of workers' compensation claims. Many states have laws prohibiting employers from influencing or coercing their employees' political beliefs or from interfering with the exercise of those beliefs. Employees in California enjoy strong protection against employers' interference with their political activities.[8] In Colorado, it is unlawful for employers to adopt a rule or policy forbidding employees from engaging in political activities.[9] The definition of "political activity" in these states can be extremely broad, encompassing not only involvement in political campaigns, but lobbying, or protesting on social or religious issues. For example, employees who lobby for nuclear power or for stringent environmental laws, or march for gay rights might be viewed as engaging in political activities. Several other states prohibit employers from hindering employees who have been appointed to a political office from performing their duties.[10]

Many of these state law provisions could support wrongful discharge suits. *Davis v. Louisiana Computing Corp.*[11] involved a state law that prohibited employers from forbidding employees to run for public office or from discharging them for doing so.[12] An employee who ran for city council against a candidate supported by his employer was fired after refusing his employer's request that he withdraw from the race. A trial court award of $24,000 in damages was sustained. In other states, courts have refused to find that such statutory protections provide a private right of action for damages, and have held that the only penalty is that expressly stated in the law.[13] In these states, employees still may be able to sue under a public policy theory.

PUBLIC POLICY CLAIMS

The most widely applied common law exception to employment-at-will is the public policy exception. This theory provides a cause of action for wrongful discharge, usually as a tort claim, where the reason for the discharge violates public policy. Courts in at least 39 states and the Virgin Islands have recognized a common law wrongful discharge claim if a discharge violates public policy, but these states differ significantly in how they define "public policy." Some states limit the exception to cases where an employee refuses to perform illegal acts, such as giving perjured testimony,[14] or exercises a statutory right, such as filing a workers' compensation claim.[15] Courts in other states have indicated that public policy can be defined by laws, court decisions, or the federal or state constitution.[16] In these states, courts have broad discretion in deciding whether a particular claim of "public policy" should be recognized.

Where a law that limits an employer's ability to fire employees does not specifically provide a cause of action for wrongful discharge, the public policy exception has been used to provide a remedy. In Pennsylvania, the law regulating the use of polygraphs in the workplace does not contain an express private right of action allowing employees to sue their employers for violations of the law or for discharges relating to refusal to take a polygraph examination. Pennsylvania courts have applied the public policy exception and determined that there is an implied right of action under the polygraph law.

They have stated that considerations of public policy can restrict and limit arbitrary discharge decisions by employers where the discharge contravenes or undermines an important public policy, and that Pennsylvania's anti-polygraph law is such a policy. Pennsylvania courts have therefore held that if employees can establish a causal connection between their polygraph examination or their refusal to take such a test and their dismissal, they have a tort action against their employer.[17]

As discussed throughout this report, the public policy exception has been used by private employees in wrongful discharge claims involving speech and association, searches (including drug testing), personal relationships, and off-duty conduct.

The public policy exception to the general rule of at-will employment is still novel enough in most states that courts have hesitated to expand the tort of wrongful discharge beyond discharges for refusing to do something that violates an expressed law or other public policy, or for exposing an employer's failure to comply with the law. It is highly unlikely that courts will soon move in the direction implied by *Novosel v. Nationwide Insurance Co.*, applying the various constitutional protections afforded public employees to private employees. However, if the public policy exception is to expand in any areas, it probably will be in those of freedom of expression and the personal rights of privacy involved in marriage and procreation.

CONTRACT EXCEPTIONS

The second common law exception to the employment-at-will doctrine is based on contract law. Where an employer and an employee agree on specific terms and conditions of employment or conditions for termination, the relationship is contractual in nature, and not at-will. This is the case with almost all union contracts, which usually provide that employees will not be terminated without just cause. Most non-union employees do not have specific written employment contracts, or, if they do, a term of employment is seldom specified. However, many promises are made by employers that are relied on by applicants and employees. These promises may be made orally, included in a written offer of employment, or embodied in employee handbooks and personnel manuals.

The various contract exceptions to the at-will rule address the enforceability of employer promises and statements regarding the employment relationship. Two most common examples are:

- Claims that applicants were told prior to accepting a job that they would be employed for as long as they performed satisfactorily (a promise of lifetime employment); and

- Statements in employee handbooks that employees would be terminated only for good cause.

Courts in several states have recognized that an oral promise of employment may be enforceable without running afoul of the statute of frauds (a rule of contract law requiring that a contract which cannot be performed in one year must be in writing). In 36 states and the District of Columbia, courts have held that under certain circumstances statements contained in written employee handbooks, personnel manuals, or other written personnel policies may be binding on employers. Damages for breach of these "implied contracts" usually are limited to lost pay, but in some states emotional distress damages and punitive damages are available if the contract was breached with malice or in bad faith.

These contractual restrictions can affect privacy rights. For example, if a personnel handbook states, as it did in *Weiner v. McGraw-Hill, Inc.,*[18] that "the company will resort to dismissal for just and sufficient cause only, and only after all practical steps towards rehabilitation or salvage of the employee have been taken and failed," employee discharges will be examined under that "just cause" standard as if they were contained in a union contract. An employee discharged for refusing to take a random drug test could argue just cause did not exist because the employer had no reasonable suspicion of drug use or no basis for random testing.[19] Under this provision, employees might have an additional implied contract right not to be discharged based on drug use until after they had an opportunity to complete a rehabilitation program.

Employee handbooks can limit employers' rights in other ways. Where the handbook lists reasons for discharge, an employee can argue that the handbook's list is exclusive and that a previously unannounced policy cannot be grounds for discipline. In almost any case in which the discharge is based on an employee's off-duty activities, the absence of a written policy could be the key factor to a jury trying to determine the "terms" of the employment "contract."

Employers' written policies also can create a legitimate expectation of privacy that is enforceable through contract law, as occurred in *Rulon-Miller v. IBM.*[20] The U.S. Supreme Court also recognized in *O'Connor v. Ortega* that public employers can create an expectation of privacy through their policies, procedures, guidelines, or practices. Thus, employers who develop and implement personnel policies and procedures should assume that in most states those procedures may be binding on the company as well as the employees.

GOOD FAITH AND FAIR DEALING

The third major exception to the employment-at-will doctrine is the implied covenant of good faith and fair dealing. According to some courts, this doctrine is merely a contract principle implied into employment contracts. But a few courts have gone further and created a new common law tort of wrongful discharge, including an implied-in-law obligation not to discharge employees without good cause.

The implied covenant of good faith is the most rapidly changing exception to employment-at-will. Courts in nine states and the Virgin Islands have said they recognize the doctrine in one form or another in the employment relationship. Courts in seven other states have said a limited implied covenant might be recognized in some circumstances. But the vast majority of the states that have considered the issue have rejected any form of the implied covenant in the employment relationship.

The duty of good faith and fair dealing is well-established in the law of contracts. According to the *Restatement (Second) of Contracts,* Section 205, "every contract imposes on each party a duty of good faith and fair dealing in its performance and its enforcement." The commentary to that section defines the contractual obligation as "honesty in fact in the conduct of the transaction concerned" and states that "good faith performance or enforcement of a contract emphasizes faithfulness to an agreed common purpose and consistency with the justified expectations of the other party."[21]

The seminal case on the implied covenant of good faith and fair dealing in the employment context is *Cleary v. American Airlines, Inc..*[22] In *Cleary,* an 18-year employee alleged that he had been wrongfully and without just cause suspended from his employment for alleged theft without a fair, complete, and honest investigation. Cleary also alleged that his employer had failed to afford him a fair, impartial, and objective hearing on his suspension and discharge, as provided by his employer's regulations. The employee alleged two causes of action, one sounding in contract and the other in tort. A California appeals court noted that termination of employment without legal cause after a long period of service offends the implied-in-law covenant of good faith and fair dealing in all contracts. The court also noted that the employer's policies supported the court's conclusion that the employer had recognized its responsibility to engage in good faith and fair dealing rather than arbitrary conduct with respect to all of its employees.

Prior to December 1988, the California courts were divided on the application of *Cleary.* Several California appellate court decisions construed *Cleary* strictly and stated that the availability of a tort action for violation of the implied covenant in the context of an employment relationship depends on the factors of longevity of employment and the express policies of the employer that were allegedly breached. Several other California appellate cases held that the factors discussed in *Cleary* did not define the tort. In *Khanna v. Microdata Corp.*,[23] the court concluded that a breach of the implied covenant of good faith and fair dealing in employment contracts is established when an employer engages in "bad faith action extraneous to the contract, combined with the obligor's intent to frustrate the employee's enjoyment of contract rights." Another appellate court stated that if an employer asserts in bad faith and without probable cause that good cause existed for discharge, the employer has tortiously attempted to deprive the employee of the benefits of the contract.[24] This difference of opinion was resolved by the California Supreme Court in *Foley v. Interactive Data Corp.*[25]

In *Foley*, the court ruled that the covenant of good faith and fair dealing applies to employment contracts, but does not give rise to tort damages. The court stated that the purpose of the implied covenant was to protect:

> ... the interest in having promises performed .... An allegation of breach of the implied covenant of good faith and fair dealing is an allegation of a breach of an 'ex contractu' obligation, namely one arising out of the contract itself.

In rejecting the extension of tort remedies for breach of the implied covenant of good faith and fair dealing in employment contracts, the majority opinion in *Foley* stated that the holdings in *Khanna* and similar cases were flawed because any ordinary contract breach could give rise to a bad faith action, and that under these decisions an implied covenant would provide greater protection than an implied-in-fact promise, depending on the employer's motive, while the breaching party's motive traditionally has had no effect on the scope of the damages.

The court also rejected the request of the plaintiff to carve out a new bad faith tort of wrongful discharge. In addition, the court favorably quoted a decision of the Arizona Supreme Court that summarized its view of the implied covenant:

> [t]he implied-in-a covenant of good faith and fair dealing protects the right of the parties to an agreement to receive the benefits of the agreement that they have entered into. The denial of a party's rights to those benefits, whatever they are, will breach the duty of good faith implicit in the contract. Thus, the relevant inquiry always will focus on the contract itself, to determine what the parties did agree to.

Montana courts had adopted the most expansive view of the implied covenant of good faith and fair dealing outside of California. The Montana Supreme Court concluded that the covenant is implied as a matter of law, based on the public policy of the state, and it is not dependent on contractual terms for its existence. The court also ruled that the covenant of good faith and fair dealing is not subject to contractual waiver and exists apart from and in addition to any terms agreed on by the parties. The question of whether the covenant is implied in a particular case will depend on objective manifestations by the employer giving rise to the employee's reasonable belief that he or she had job security and would be treated fairly. This broad interpretation prompted Montana employers to seek legislation limiting their liability in wrongful discharge cases.[26]

Several courts that have recognized the implied covenant of good faith and fair dealing and have applied it to the employment relationship recently have articulated limitations on this doctrine. Some courts have limited the applicability of the doctrine to conduct that goes well beyond a mere breach of contract. Alaska, like California, recently held that a breach of the implied covenant does not constitute a tort. The Supreme Court of Alaska held that when a party's conduct in breaching a contract rises to the level of a traditionally recognized tort, such as intentional infliction of emotional distress, an employee can sue in tort and recover punitive damages. However, punitive damages are not favored as a matter of law, and no justification existed for converting every breach of contract into an independent tort action.[27]

Despite the attention paid to the implied covenant of good faith and fair dealing, as of December 1988 courts in 27 states and the District of Columbia had rejected efforts to imply into all employment relationships a covenant of good faith and fair dealing or a duty to terminate in good faith. As the Supreme Court of Washington stated in *Thompson v. St. Regis Paper Co.*[28]:

> [w]e do not adopt this exception. An employer's interest in running his business as he sees fit must be balanced against the interest of the employee in maintaining his employment and this exception does not strike the proper balance. We believe that to imply into each employment contract a duty to terminate in good faith would ... subject each discharge to judicial incursions into the amorphous concept of bad faith.[29]

ENDNOTES

[1]Shepard, Heylman and Duston, *Without Just Cause: An Employer's Practical and Legal Guide to Wrongful Discharge* (BNA 1989).

[2] For a thorough discussion of wrongful discharge *see Ibid.*

[3] Murray and Scharman, "Employment At Will: Do The Exceptions Overwhelm The Rule?" 23 B.C.L. REV. 329, 332 (1982).

[4] Blades, "Employment At Will v. Individual Freedom: On Limiting The Abusive Exercise of Employer Power," 67 COLUM. L. REV. 1404, 1405 (1967), *quoting Payne v. Western Allegheny Railroad Co.*, 81 Tenn. (13 lea) 507, 519-20 (1884), *overruled on other grounds by Hutton v. Walters*, 132 Tenn. 327, 179 S.W. 134 (1915).

[5] 29 C.F.R. § 1605.

[6] *See TransWorld Airlines, Inc. v. Hardison*, 432 U.S. 63 14 FEP Cases 1697 (1977); *Mann v. Milgram Food Stores*, 730 F.2d 1186 (8th Cir. 1984); 34 FEP Cases 735 *Turpen v. Missouri-Kansas-Texas R.R.*, 573 F. Supp. 820, *aff'd*, 736 F.2d 1022 35 FEP Cases 492 (5th Cir. 1984).

[7] *Hobbie v. Unemployment Appeals Comm. of Fla.*, U.S. 480 US 136, 43 FEP Cases 21, 107 S.Ct. 1046 (1987).

[8] CAL. LAB. CODE § 1101 (West 1971).

[9] COLO. REV. STAT. § 8-2-108 (1986).

[10] *See, e.g.,* DEL. CODE ANN. tit. 15, § 5161 (1981).

[11] 394 So.2d 678 (La. App.), *cert. denied,* 400 So.2d 668 (La. 1981).

[12] LA. REV. STAT. ANN. § 23 961 (West 1964).

[13] *See Bell v. Faulkner,* 79 S.W.2d 612 (Mo. App. 1934).

[14] *Petemann v. International Brotherhood of Teamsters,* 174 Cal. App. 2d 184, 344 P2d 29, 1 IER Cases 5 (1959).

[15] *Frampton v. Central Indiana Gas Co.,* 297 N.E.2d 425 115 LRRM 4611 (Ind. 1973).

[16] *Palmateer v. International Harvester Co.,* 85 Ill. 2d 124, 421 N.E.2d 876, 115 LRRM 4165 (1981).

[17] *Perks v. Firestone Tire & Rubber Co.,* 611 F.2d 1363 115 LRRM 4592 (3d Cir. 1979); *Molush v. Orkin Exterminating Company, Inc.,* 547 F. Supp. 54 115 LRRM 4940 (E.D. Pa. 1982).

[18] 57 N.Y.2d 458, 457 N.Y.S.2d 193 443 N.E.2d 441, 118 LRRM 2689 (1982).

[19] This is one of the claims being made in several pending lawsuits. *See* Chapter III.

[20] 162 Cal. App.3d 241, 208 Cal. Rptr. 524 IER Cases: 405 (1984), discussed in Chapter XI.

[21] *Restatement (Second) of Contracts* 205 (1979), comment a.

[22] 111 Cal. App. 3d 443, 168 Cal. Rptr. 722 1IER 122 (1980).

[23] 170 Cal. App. 3d 250, 215 Cal. Rptr. 860, 1 IER 1854 (1985), *rev. granted by Foley,* 222 Cal. Rptr. 740, 712 P.2d 891 2 IER 167 (1986).

[24] *Koehrer v. Superior Court,* 181 Cal. App. 3d 1155, 226 Cal. Rptr. 820 (1986).

[25] *Daily Labor Report* (BNA) No. 2, Jan. 2, 1989, at D-1.

[26] This law was recently upheld as constitutional by the Montana Supreme Court. *Meech v. Hillhaven West, Inc.* Semingson 1989 WL 71666 (Mont. 1989).

[27] *Arco Alaska, Inc. v. Akera,* 753 P.2d 1150, 3 IER 808 (Alaska 1988); *see also Martin v. Federal Life Ins. Co.,* 109 Ill. App. 2d 596, 440 N.E.2d 998, 1006, 115 LRRM 4524 (1982).

[28] 102 Wash. 2d 219, 685 P.2d 108, 1 IER 392 (1984).

[29] *Id., citing, Parnar v. Americana Hotels, Inc.,* 65 Hawaii 370, 377, 652 P.2d 625, 629, 115 LRRM 4817 (1982).

* * *

Defamation

Terminations for cause, including poor performance, misconduct, and insubordination, involve employers' conclusions concerning employees' abilities, integrity, or behavior. Employees often dispute the truth or accuracy of these evaluations. When former employees look for a new job they must explain why they were fired. That is why many wrongful discharge suits include claims for defamation and related torts such as false light invasion of privacy or public disclosure of private facts. Such tort claims can expose employers to the risk of compensatory and punitive damages. Because these theories are well established, courts are more likely to allow such claims to be decided by a jury than novel wrongful discharge theories.

Most employers know that they can face liability for defamation. That threat is the reason many employers give for their refusal to provide comprehensive employment references. Most employers try to verify resume information on job applicants, but most of those same employers will not provide such information to other employers out of fear of defamation claims. Nevertheless, little evidence exists that fear of defamation claims has changed the way employers handle discharges or how firings are communicated to the fired employees' co-workers. The focus of employers on job references as the greatest source of potential liability obscures the fact that employers could be liable for many other intra-company communications. It also obscures the fact that employers defeat defamation claims far more often than they are found liable. Although a few juries have awarded discharged employees large sums for defamatory remarks made by supervisors in references or statements to co-workers, these well-publicized cases are far outnumbered by the decisions in which employee defamation claims are dismissed before trial.

ELEMENTS OF DEFAMATION

Defamation is one of several tort theories that protect a person's reputation. Defamation law has developed in a somewhat haphazard manner. It varies among the states and it is characterized by what one legal authority calls a "set of arbitrary and illogical rules."[1] The two types of defamation are libel (defamation by writing) and slander (defamation by speech).

The elements of a defamation claim are:

- allegedly defamatory information about the plaintiff,
- that is communicated or "published" to a third party,
- is false, and
- damages the plaintiff's reputation.

Defamatory "communications" are ones that harm their subjects' reputation in a way that lowers the community's estimation of them or deters other people from associating with them. The defamatory statement must be communicated to a third person. Except under the theory of "compelled self-disclosure," discussed below, traditional defamation principles hold that derogatory words and insults made only to the plaintiff, and not communicated to another person, do not provide a basis for defamation.[2]

The general rule is that people do not have an action for defamation unless their reputation is damaged. In the employment setting, two exceptions overwhelm the rule, so that damages are presumed. They are:

- Comments that impute criminal behavior to another person if the crime is punishable by imprisonment or is a crime involving "moral turpitude," such as theft or fraud;[3] and

- Any communication that ascribes to another person conduct or characteristics that adversely affect his fitness for proper conduct of a business or profession.

Criticism of a single mistake or one act of misconduct may or may not be included in the second exception, depending on the nature of the business.[4] In the employment setting almost any comment critical of an employee's skills, abilities, performance, and fitness for work can be considered defamatory.

Taken together, these two exceptions classify as "defamatory" almost every negative employment reference or comment to co-workers regarding a discharge for cause. This means that former employees need not show any actual damage to their reputation, because damages are presumed by law. However, only "reputational" injuries are presumed. If an employee wants to recover economic damages, such as the loss of a job or loss of prospective employment, it is the employee's burden to show that the defamatory remark was a substantial factor in bringing about the harm. Under normal principles governing damages, the amount of any economic injury must be proven by the plaintiff with reasonable certainty.[5]

Another element of defamation is that the statements in question must be "published," that is, communicated to at least one other person. Because of this, employers are frequently advised to limit job references to avoid "publication" outside the company. However, when a statement is communicated to other employees, even within the company, the element of publication usually is established. In defamation law, a publication may be to any third person, including a defendant's own agent, employee, or officer, even when the defendant is a corporation.[6] Because of this, any defamatory statement can be the basis for a lawsuit. If a defamatory statement has been communicated to supervisors or co-workers, then communicating that statement to prospective employers in a reference increases only the size of potential compensatory damages, not the risk of being sued.

Moreover, a small but growing number of states have recognized an exception to the requirement that the publication must be made by the defendant to a third person. These courts, recognizing the doctrine of "compelled self-publica-

tion," have held that where employers intend or have reason to
suppose that a statement they make to an employee will be
communicated to some other party in the ordinary course of
events, it is not necessary that the employer communicate
those reasons to some other person to satisfy the requirement
of publication. This exception has been applied where discharged employees have alleged that their employers gave
them false and defamatory reasons for the discharge, which
they were then forced to repeat during questioning by prospective employers. Although the most publicized of these cases is
a 1986 Minnesota decision, _Lewis v. Equitable Life Assurance
Society of the United States,_[7] similar cases have existed since
1980.[8]

For many years courts required that plaintiffs prove another
element—some degree of negligence or "fault" by the defendant—to recover for defamation.[9] This rule, which was established by the U.S. Supreme Court, is now in doubt. In 1964,
the court ruled in _New York Times Co. v. Sullivan_[10] that the
First Amendment limits the reach of state defamation laws.
Noting that freedom of expression on public questions is
secured by the First Amendment, the court held that a public
official could not recover damages for defamatory falsehood
unless he could prove that the false statement was made with
"actual malice." Actual malice means that the statement was
made with knowledge that it was false, or with reckless disregard as to whether it was false. Subsequent decisions, notably
Gertz v. Robert Welch, Inc.,[11] applied this rule to private figures
as well as public figures. It thus became the established standard in all states that, to prove defamation, a plaintiff had to
show that the defendant knew the statement was false and that
the defendant acted in reckless disregard of its falsity, or acted
negligently in failing to assert the truth of the matter.[12]

This scope of the rule was curtailed by the Supreme Court
in _Dun & Bradstreet v. Greenmoss Builders._[13] Dun & Bradstreet
provides subscribers with financial and related information
about businesses. It sent a report indicating that Greenmoss

had filed a voluntary petition for bankruptcy. That statement was false. It was determined at trial that the mistake was made by a 17-year-old high school student paid by Dun & Bradstreet to review bankruptcy pleadings. The company had failed to check with Greenmoss to see if the information was true before the report was distributed. The court found that this speech was on matters of private concern, which is entitled to less First Amendment protection than matters of public concern. The court then concluded that the state interest in protecting defamation supported an award of $50,000 for compensatory or presumed damages and $300,000 in punitive damages, even absent a showing of actual malice. *Dun & Bradstreet* suggests that state courts are not constitutionally required, under the First Amendment, to insist that a plaintiff prove that the defendant acted negligently or with actual malice in every case.[14]

Once the element of "fault" is removed, the traditional common law principles apply. To establish a prima facie case of defamation, former employees need only show that some comment critical of their performance or implying criminal misconduct was made by an agent or manager of their former employer and communicated to some other person, such as a co-worker or prospective employer.

EMPLOYER DEFENSES

The number and types of defenses employers have depends on the facts of the particular case, the damages sought, and the jurisdiction involved. For example, claims can be pre-empted by the National Labor Relations Act (NLRA), the Employee Retirement Income Security Act (ERISA), a state discrimination law, or worker's compensation laws. For claims that are not pre-empted, employers have three primary defenses to avoid liability—truth, qualified privilege, and consent.

Truth

It is often said that truth is an absolute defense to defamation. Under the common law rule, truth was an affirmative defense that the defendant was required to plead and prove. All defamatory statements were presumed to be false unless the defendant proved they were true. In every state, employers can escape liability by showing that the statement was true. In one Texas case, a customer reportedly saw a salesman stealing dairy products. The allegation was then investigated by the company and communicated to the salesman, who was then fired. A jury awarded the salesman $500,000 in actual damages and $500,000 in punitive damages for slander. Subsequently, a Texas court of appeals found that the allegations made by the company were true, and reversed the jury verdict.[15]

After the *Gertz* decision, many states held that the plaintiff, not the defendant, had to prove that statements were false, as part of the burden of proving actual malice. The issue of whether the U.S. Constitution requires plaintiffs to prove that the statement was false in employment cases and other disputes between private individuals relating to private matters is unsettled. The latest Supreme Court pronouncement on this issue, *Philadelphia Newspapers, Inc. v. Hepps*,[16] concluded that a private-figure plaintiff must prove falsity as well as fault in cases concerning speech of public concern. In an aside, the court noted that:

> [W]hen the speech is of exclusively private concern and the plaintiff is a private figure, as in *Dun & Bradstreet*, the constitutional requirements do not necessarily force any change in at least some of the features of the common law landscape.

This 5-4 decision leaves open the question of whether all private plaintiffs must prove falsity or whether truth is a defense, that must be proven by the defendant in cases involving private concerns.

The question of which side bears the burden of proof is most significant in motions for summary judgment or in post-trial proceedings, where the employer seeks to have the case dismissed because the plaintiff cannot produce evidence that the statements were false. The question also can be significant in any case where the evidence is inconclusive or has been lost. As a practical matter, employers always should plead the defense of truth and try to show that the statements were true. The best evidence to support the defense of truth is a prior decision by a separate fact-finding body. For example, if an employee has been convicted of theft, that is conclusive evidence that the defamatory statements or accusations were true.

Consent

The law recognizes that the consent of a person to the publication of defamatory remarks is a complete defense to defamation.[17] This defense has been raised in several cases involving employment references, with mixed results. Consent to publish defamatory remarks may occur when a discharged employee directly requests that a former employer provide a reference, or when the applicant gives a prospective employer permission to contact references. Consent can be given at the time of the discharge or on applying for new employment. Courts disagree on the extent to which a former employee has to know or anticipate that a reference will be defamatory in order to consent to the statements.

The U.S. Court of Appeals for the 11th Circuit has held that under Florida law, a discharged employee who gave a prospective employer " ... a complete right to check on anything [the employee] did in the past" consented to the publication of defamatory remarks by a former employer. The court noted that the plaintiff knew at the time he gave this permission that his former employer criticized his performance when he was terminated, and the employer provided only negative information in response to a direct question from a prospective employer.[18] However, the appeals court did not make clear whether the employee's knowledge of what position his former employer might take was necessary to show consent.

Some courts have found that when a prospective employer asks on a job application whether it can contact an applicant's former employers, and the applicant says "yes," this is consent to any defamatory reference.[19] Other courts have looked more carefully at the circumstances of the alleged consent, and have found that consent does not exist if plaintiffs could not reasonably be expected to know that their employer's response would be defamatory.[20] One Florida court has ruled that an authorization and release in an employment application is not enforceable, concluding that releases of liability for intentional torts violate public policy.[21]

These cases demonstrate that releases in an employment application comprise successful defenses against defamation in some jurisdictions. Even in the absence of a release, consent may be a viable defense, depending on the facts. It is perhaps the most under-utilized defense available to employers who are sued for negative references.

Privilege

The most frequently litigated issue in defamation claims brought by former employees is whether the statement was privileged. The law of defamation recognizes a variety of situations where a speaker is free to make statements without fear of liability. In certain circumstances an absolute privilege exists; the speech is protected regardless of the speaker's motives. In many states, all comments made during criminal prosecutions and hearings on unemployment compensation, worker's compensation, or other issues are accorded an absolute privilege due to the judicial or quasi-judicial nature of the proceedings. Where an absolute privilege exists, the employee cannot recover for defamatory remarks that are made in a privileged setting. But the absolute privilege does not protect employers that repeat those same remarks outside the privileged context.

Intra-company communications and references provided to prospective employers fall within the scope of "qualified" business privileges. A qualified privilege exists where the statement:

- Is made in good faith;
- Concerns a subject in which the person making the statement has an interest or duty; and
- Is made to a person having a corresponding interest or duty.

A qualified privilege can be lost if it is "abused," including situations where the speaker acted with malice or excessively publicized the statement. Qualified privileges can be raised when a claim of defamation is based on statements communicated during an evaluation or investigation when a company communicates the reason for a plaintiff's termination to co-workers, and always when a former employer gives a reference to a prospective employer.

Defamation claims sometimes arise during investigations of allegations of misconduct. Investigations are likely to include accusations of wrongdoing made to or about an employee; discussions among managers of the accusations; and other communications that on their face are defamatory if they are untrue. The common business-concern privilege has been uniformly applied to these intra-company "investigative" communications.[22] To preserve the privilege, accusations should be confined to the decisionmakers involved in the investigation and disciplinary process. Fact-finding interviews with other employees should be conducted in ways that avoid making defamatory accusations which may not be privileged. For example, employers might say, "We're investigating an accusation of misconduct involving John Doe. The accusation may not be true, and we just want to determine the facts. Do you know anything about this situation?"

The states are divided on the extent to which telling co-workers why employees are fired is covered by a qualified business privilege. Some courts hold that a qualified privilege can be lost through excessive publication to co-workers who do not have an interest in the matter, such as the publication of an employee's termination in a company newspaper.[23] Other courts have held that discussions concerning discharge of employees are protected and that widespread communication within the company did not destroy the privilege. *Gonzalez v. Avon Products, Inc.*[24] involved eight employees who were fired after an investigation into theft from the company. A few days after these discharges the plant manager gave a speech to all 900 employees at the plant to explain his decision to fire the eight workers and to reassert the company's policy of terminating employees only for just cause. In a subsequent defamation action, the court held that the employees' termination was a matter of common interest for the employees in the plant who heard the speech, and the speech was not motivated by spite or ill will.[25]

A qualified privilege also extends to references given to present or prospective employers to protect the interests of the company that receives the reference. The law recognizes that giving accurate references is accepted conduct that is desirable to encourage, so former employers are conditionally privileged to make a defamatory communication about the character or conduct of an employee when asked by a prospective employer for a reference.[26] If the employer tries to ensure that the person to whom the reference is given is in fact a present or prospective employer of the subject of the reference, excessive publication is not a factor.

Without evidence of excessive publication, plaintiffs can show the qualified privilege was abused only if the speaker acted with malice. The law varies among the states on what constitutes malice for the purpose of loss of a qualified privilege. In some states, the employer must have acted out of spite or ill will toward the former employee. Jury verdicts finding that employers acted with spite tend to be upheld where the employer makes an accusation of criminal activity without trying to learn the facts, and where evidence indicates the speaker harbored animosity toward the plaintiff.[27] The other definition of malice that is sometimes used, adopted in *New York Times v. Sullivan*, is evidence that the defendant spoke knowing that the statement was false or with reckless disregard to the truth or falsity of the statement.[28]

These two concepts meld in many situations. Juries and courts often look more harshly on employers who do not undertake a reasonable investigation of employees' alleged misconduct before making a defamatory statement. In reference cases, jury verdicts finding that former employers acted with actual malice tend to be affirmed where the former employer made inconsistent statements, lied about significant facts, or had made threats toward the plaintiff.[29] Without evidence of actual malice or ill will, jury verdicts will be reversed.[30]

The existence of a qualified privilege usually is a question of law for the court to decide, with the issue of malice treated as a question of fact frequently left to a jury.[31] Nevertheless, a surprisingly large number of reported cases over the last several years have involved either summary judgments in favor of an employer, directed verdicts at trial, or reversals on appeal of jury verdicts favoring the plaintiff, based on a lack of evidence of malice. A review of reported federal and state cases from January 1985 to May 1988 by the authors revealed 37 cases involving in-house communications or references where the employer was granted summary judgment or an adverse jury verdict was reversed on appeal because no evidence of malice existed. Of the 15 reported decisions against employers, five were denials of summary judgment on the grounds that questions of fact existed on the issue of malice and in one case the employer had failed to plead privilege as an affirmative defense.[32]

This trend is likely to continue based on the U.S. Supreme Court's rearticulation of the standards for summary judgment in *Celotex v. Cattrett*[33] and *Anderson v. Liberty Lobby*.[34] Because the plaintiff must prove malice where a qualified privilege exists, in federal court the plaintiff must present facts from which a jury could determine that the element of malice is satisfied. For example, in *McKinney v. K-Mart Corp.*,[35] an audit of the lay-away department showed that $19,000 was missing. The plaintiff, a senior employee in the department, was interviewed by local officials and by senior company management. During one of these interviews, she became upset and resigned. In her subsequent lawsuit, the employee identified several defamatory statements that were made by various managers. The district court granted summary judgment in favor of the company, finding that the plaintiff had failed to produce any evidence of malice or ill will, as required by *Celotex.*

The theme of these and many other recent cases is that if an employer acts reasonably in evaluating performance problems or investigating and subsequently discharging employees for misconduct, documents these reasons, and truthfully responds to a prospective employer that asks why it terminated the employee, the employee will have to produce specific evidence of spite or ill will before the case can go to a jury.

The authors' review of defamation cases brought against employers between 1985 and 1988 also revealed that:

- Most defamation actions are brought in conjunction with other tort claims and wrongful discharge allegations. Refusing to provide references will not eliminate other claims arising from a discharge for cause.

- Many more defamation claims are included in complaints based on statements made to co-workers than on negative references. This may be because fired employees are more likely to learn, usually from co-workers, about statements made by the company at or near the time they are discharged than they are about a negative reference. Former employees find out about negative references only if they are refused employment and thereafter ask the firm that turns

them down if their previous employer provided a
negative reference, and the prospective employer
tells them it did. Mere suspicion that a former
employer is giving negative references is not enough
to show that a defamatory statement has been
published.

- Where employers are held liable for defamation and
  the claims are sustained on appeal, liability usually is
  based on facts that also support other causes of
  action, such as wrongful discharge or intentional
  infliction of emotional distress.

- The same facts that defeat a wrongful discharge
  action or discrimination action usually are sufficient
  to establish that the employer did not abuse the
  qualified business privilege.

PRACTICAL GUIDELINES

The risk of a defamation action based on statements to co-
workers or job references cannot be eliminated. However,
several ways exist to reduce the risk of liability:

- When employees are terminated, make sure they
  know why they were discharged and explain company
  policy on providing references.

- Obtain written, signed consents from employees that
  authorize the company to disclose relevant
  information to potential employers.

- Ask employers seeking references to obtain written
  consent from the employee if they have not done so.
  Make sure that consents are up-to-date.

- Ask prospective employers for written requests for
  references as a condition for your answering any
  questions. All employers know it is easier to call
  former employers without advance notice when
  checking references, but this creates the risk that the
  caller is not a prospective employer.

- If your firm provides more reference information than name and job title, the person providing the reference should be truthful and should provide whatever explanation is necessary about the circumstances of the discharge to minimize the possibility that the reasons are misunderstood. The reference giver should distinguish opinions from facts or other observations, and should explain any other factors, such as personal problems between the employee and a manager, that may have contributed to the discharge.

- When answering questions from prospective employers, confine statements to those related to the job involved.

- Confine comments to facts that are easily documented. This is easier where the former employer can point to past performance reviews. In employee misconduct cases, this may involve descriptions of information provided to the employer and what investigation was conducted prior to firing the employee for misconduct.

- Most important of all, be fair and impartial. Where possible, point out the employee's good qualities. A balanced reference is evidence that the employer did not act with malice.

Employers that provide more detailed references than name, job title, and dates of employment must decide whether to do so orally or in writing. Telephone or in-person discussions are more helpful to the prospective employer, and they may be more beneficial to firms that provide references because such forums enable them to limit their responses to inquiries to which qualified privilege attaches. Written references could be interpreted as providing information that was not sought, and is therefore not entitled to the same protection as information that is requested.

ILLUSTRATIONS

Employer Recklessly Disregarded The Truthfulness Of Statement Made To Prospective Employer Of Why Employee Had Been Discharged

Burger, a discharged funeral home embalmer, sued his former employer for slander as a result of a statement the employer made to a prospective employer of the embalmer. His former employer said it discharged Burger for working for a competitor on the employer's time. The evidence at trial revealed that this statement was false and had been contrived after Burger was fired. Burger proved that the employer never told him why he was fired, that he previously worked for other funeral homes when he was off duty with the employer's knowledge and consent, and that such conduct during off-duty hours did not violate company policy. The evidence also showed that the employer threatened witnesses so they would not testify for the plaintiff.

On the basis of this evidence, a jury awarded the employee $1.00 in actual damages and $85,000 in punitive damages. The trial court ordered the jury verdict on the punitive damages award dismissed. The U.S. Court of Appeals for the Eighth Circuit reversed this order, finding that ample evidence existed to demonstrate the employer falsely made the statement or recklessly disregarded the truthfulness of it. [*Burger v. McGilley Memorial Chapels*, 856 F.2d 1046, 47 FEP 1290 (8th Cir. 1988).]

Employer Held Not Liable For Statement Made By Manager Outside Scope Of His Employment

Newberry, a T-Bird store manager, was terminated in December 1984 for failing twice, in violation of company policy, to fill out the appropriate charge slips for merchandise he purchased from T-Bird. Newberry sued for two alleged acts of defamation. The first act allegedly occurred after the discharge when Newberry's supervisor said in a loud voice on the store floor, "I don't trust you." The second act occurred in May 1985, when the supervisor allegedly told another manager's spouse at a dinner that Newberry had been fired "for stealing." A jury entered a verdict in favor of Newberry on both of the defamation claims and awarded him $36,818 for compensatory damages and $5,000 in punitive damages.

The New Mexico Supreme Court found that the statement "I don't trust you" was an expression of opinion, not of existing fact, and thus was not actionable defamation. As for the statement that Newberry was fired for stealing, the court held that the company was not liable for damages for the supervisor's defamatory statement, because it was made outside the scope of his employment. The court also noted that when the dinner took place in May 1985 Newberry was gainfully employed elsewhere, and little evidence existed that the statement caused actual injury to Newberry's reputation. [*Newberry v. Allied Stores*, 4 IER Cases 562 (N.M. 1989).]

$250,000 Defamation Award Upheld For Discharged Salesman

Brannon, who had worked 18 years as a pharmaceutical salesman for Wyeth Laboratories, was terminated for allegedly falsifying his sales calls. He sued for breach of an oral employment contract and defamation, alleging that after he was fired Wyeth employees told members of the pharmaceutical industry, including several doctors, that Brannon had been fired for not working, for falsifying reports, and for pursuing personal activities on company time. A jury awarded him $300,000 for breach of contract and $250,000 for defamation.

The appeals court upheld both awards. The court found that Wyeth officials' statements had the tendency to deprive Brannon of the public's confidence, to injure him in his occupation, and/or injure his reputation. The court also found that the jury did not abuse its discretion in awarding $250,000 to the employee because the charges of dishonesty were severe, the motives of the employer were suspicious, the publication was extensive, and Brannon had enjoyed a reputation for trustworthiness in the industry prior to the defamation. [*Brannon v. Wyeth Laboratories, Inc.*, 8 IER Cases 61 (La. Ct. App. 1987).]

Escorting Employee Off Premises After Termination Does Not Constitute Defamatory Publication

Gay, a nurses' aide at William Hill Manor Nursing Home, was discharged for placing a pillow over a patient's face to keep her from shouting. She was escorted to her locker and then through the nursing home to her car by the home's administrator, assistant administrator, and director of nursing. Gay filed a defamation claim alleging her reputation was harmed by being escorted out of the home. She also alleged that a report submitted to the state Employment Security Administration (ESA), which gave "physical mistreatment of a resident" as the reason for termination, was a defamatory publication that fell outside the scope of the nursing home's qualified privilege.

The court noted that to prove that one's reputation has been harmed a person must show that the defamatory statement or action was published to a third party who must reasonably recognize its defamatory nature. In this case, the court found that the nursing home's action in escorting Gay to her locker and then to her car did not constitute defamatory publication because Gay did not show that the action was in any way unusual or that other employees or patients perceived it as unusual.

The court also found that a qualified privilege protected the statement submitted to the ESA when Gay applied for unemployment benefits and that the statement was not submitted with malice. [*Gay v. William Hill Manor, Inc.*, 3 IER Cases 744, (Md. Ct. Spec. App. 1988).]

ENDNOTES

[1] *Prosser and Keeton on Torts* § 111 at 772 (5th ed. 1984).

[2] *See Wyant v. SCM Corp.*, 692 S.W.2d 814 (Ky. Ct. App. 1985).

[3] *Restatement (Second) of Torts* § 571 (1977).

[4] *Restatement (Second) of Torts* § 573 (1977).

[5] *Restatement (Second) of Torts* §§ 575, 622 and 622A (1977).

[6] *Prosser & Keeton on Torts* § 113 at 798 (5th ed. 1984).

[7] 389 N.W.2d 876, 1 IER Cases 1269 (Minn. 1986) (employer's statement made directly to plaintiff).

[8] *Neighbors v. Kirksville College of Osteopathic Medicine*, 694 S.W.2d 822 (Mo. Ct. App. 1985) (allegation that defendant knew that a service letter sent to the plaintiff providing reasons for termination would be seen by prospective employers stated cause of action); *McKinney v. County of Santa Clara*, 110 Cal. App. 3d 787, 168 Cal. Rptr. 89 (1980); *First State Bank of Corpus Christi v. Ake*, 606 S.W.2d 696 (Tex. Ct. App. 1980); *Belcher v. Little*, 315 N.W.2d 734 (Iowa 1982).

[9] *See Restatement (Second) of Torts* § 580B (1977).

[10] 376 U.S. 254, 84 S. Ct. 710 (1964).

[11] 418 U.S. 323, 94 S. Ct. 2997 (1974).

[12] *Restatement (Second) of Torts* § 580B (1977).

[13] 472 U.S. 749, 105 S. Ct. 2939 (1985).

[14] 105 S. Ct. at 2946. *See also Philadelphia Newspapers, Inc. v. Hepps*, 475 U.S. 767, 106 S. Ct. 1558, 1563 (1986); *Blue Ridge Bank v. Veribanc Inc.*, 866 F.2d 681 (4th Cir. 1989) (private figure was not required to show actual malice to recover).

[15] *Borden, Inc. v. Wallace*, 570 S.W.2d 445 (Tex. Ct. App. 1978).

[16] 475 U.S. 767, 106 S. Ct. 1558 (1986).

[17] *Restatement (Second) of Torts*, § 583C (1977).

[18] *Litman v. Massachusetts Mutual Life Ins. Co.*, 739 F.2d 1549, 1560 (11th Cir. 1984).

[19] *Gengler v. Phelps*, 92 N.M. 465, 589 P.2d 1056, 1058 (1978). *See also Turner v. Halliburton*, 240 Kan. 1, 722 P.2d 1106, 1114-15 (1986); 50 Am. Jur. 2d, *Libel and Slander* § 149 (1970).

[20] *Exxon Corp. v. Schoene*, 67 Md. App. 412, 508 A.2d 142, 147 (1986).

[21] *Kellums v. Freight Sales Centers, Inc.*, 467 So. 2d 816, 817 (Fla. Dist. Ct. App. 1985).

[22] *See Pappas v. Air France*, 652 F. Supp. 198, 202 (E.D.N.Y. 1986); *Chapman v. Atlantic Zayre, Inc.*, 2 IER Cases 1255, 1258 (Ga. Sup. Ct. 1987).

[23] *Zinda v. Louisiana Pacific Corp.*, 140 Wis. 2d 277, 409 N.W.2d 436 (Wis. Ct. App. 1987), *aff'd in part, rev'd in part*, 440 N.W.2d 548 (1989).

[24] 648 F. Supp. 1404 (D. Del. 1986), *aff'd*, 822 F.2d 53 (3d Cir. 1987).

[25] *See also Gordon v. Tenneco Retail Service Co.*, 666 F. Supp. 908, 2 IER Cases 1027 (N.D. Mass. 1987).

[26] *See Restatement (Second) of Torts* § 595, comments i and j.

[27] *See Frank B. Hall & Co. v. Buck*, 678 S.W.2d 612, *cert. denied*, 472 U.S. 1009, 105 S. Ct. 2704 (1984).

[28] *See Babb v. Minder*, 806 F.2d 749 (7th Cir. 1986) (applying Illinois law).

[29] *See, e.g., Becker v. Alloy Hardfacing & Engineering Co.*, 401 N.W.2d 655 (Minn. 1987); *DiBiasio v. Brown & Sharpe Manufacturing*, 525 A.2d 489 (R.I. 1987).

[30] *Turner v. Halliburton Co.*, 722 P.2d 1106 (Kan. 1986); *Haldeman Petroleum, Inc.*, 376 N.W.2d 98 (Iowa 1985); *see also Dalton v. Herbruck Egg Sales Corp.*, 164 Mich. App. 543, 417 N.W.2d 496, 2 IER 1729 (1987) (summary judgment for employer where no evidence existed that the reference was made with malice).

[31] *But see Vandergrift v. American Brands Corp.*, 572 F.Supp 496, 115 LRRM 2317 (D.N.H. 1983) (existence of privilege is for the jury).

[32] Shepard and Duston, *Thieves at Work* at 259 (BNA 1988).

[33] 477 U.S. 317, 106 S. Ct. 2548 (1986).

[34] 477 U.S. 242, 106 S. Ct. 2505 (1986).

[35] 649 F. Supp. 1217, 2 IER Cases 529 (S.D.W. Va. 1986).

* * *

APPENDIX A

State-By-State Survey
Workplace Privacy Law
A-3

STATE-BY-STATE SURVEY
WORKPLACE PRIVACY LAW

As the cases in the text demonstrate, workplace privacy issues have been addressed by different states in widely divergent ways. Although every state recognizes some privacy rights, the extent to which the right exists from state to state can mean the difference between no liability and very substantial liability for employers, depending on where the employee is located and where the case is brought.

The following chart describes the status of employee privacy rights in the nation's 50 states, the District of Columbia, Puerto Rico, and the Virgin Islands as of July 1989. It focuses on statutes and court decisions affecting the general rights of all employees. Several points should be kept in mind in using the chart as a guide. This chart is not intended to encompass all the possible constitutional privacy and due process protections accorded public employees. It does not cover all of the wrongful discharge and common law tort theories that could apply in a particular state; it only includes decisions that already have applied those theories in workplace privacy cases. Federal statutes also are omitted.

This survey is not intended as a substitute for obtaining competent legal advice in this sensitive and dynamic area of employee relations. The case law in this area is changing rapidly, and this survey can only serve as an initial research guide. The chart is intended to provide managers and employees with an overview of the breadth and variety of state responses to privacy concerns, and to increase awareness of some of the legislative and judicial decisions affecting workplace privacy issues. It is absolutely essential that managers consult counsel before privacy-related litigation arises, develop preventive programs of policy formation, and disseminate such policies to supervisory personnel.

STATE / ISSUE	STATUTE/ CASE LAW	DISCUSSION
ALABAMA		
Right to Privacy	Phillips v. Smalley Maintenance Serv., Inc., 435 So. 2d 705 (Ala. 1983).	Adopts Restatement (Second) of Torts definition; female employee recovers damages for sexual harassment.
Polygraphs	Smith v. American Cast Iron Pipe Co., 370 So. 2d 283 (Ala. 1979).	An employee who refused to take a polygraph test during an internal plant investigation was properly discharged for "failing to cooperate with the investigation." [Note: federal polygraph law may supersede.]
Employee Records	Horne v. Patton, 291 Ala. 701, 287 So. 2d 824 (1973).	Physician's release of confidential medical information to the patient's employer constituted an invasion of the patient's privacy.
ALASKA		
Right to Privacy	Alaska Const. art. I, § 22.	"The right of the people to privacy is recognized and shall not be infringed upon. The legislature shall implement this section."
Speech/ Political Activities	Alaska Stat. § 24.20.050 (1986); State v. Haley, 687 P.2d 305 (Alaska 1984).	Statute prohibiting members of the legislative professional staff from joining any "partisan" political organization that would tend to undermine the essential nonpartisan nature of their functions refers exclusively to activities on behalf of political parties and does not extend to every cause that might express a view on any issue of public concern.
Polygraphs	Alaska Stat. § 23.10.037 (1986).	An employer or his agent may not "request," "suggest," or "require" that an employee or applicant submit to a polygraph or lie

detector examination. This section does not apply to police officers or police officer applicants.

Topic	Citation	Description
Personal Relationships	Conway, Inc. v. Ross, 627 P.2d 1029 (Alaska 1981).	After being hired as a "topless stripper," an employee was fired for engaging in an act of prostitution on her own time. The court found that the employee had not breached the express terms of the contract, and that her extra-curricular activities had not so injured the employer's business reputation as to give good cause for her discharge.
Employee Records	Alaska Stat. § 23.10.430 (1989)	Employers must grant current and former employees access to their personnel files. The law does not supersede the terms of a collective bargaining agreement.

ARIZONA

Topic	Citation	Description
Right to Privacy	Ariz. Const. art. II § 8 (1982).	"No person shall be disturbed in his private affairs, or his home invaded, without authority of law."
Speech/ Political Activities	Ariz. Rev. Stat. Ann. § 16-1012 (1984).	It is unlawful for any employer to make any threat intended or calculated to influence the political opinions of his employees within 90 days of an election.
Polygraphs	Valley Vendors, Inc. v. Jamieson, 129 Ariz. 238, 630 P.2d 61 (Ariz. Ct. App. 1981).	The refusal of an employee to submit to a polygraph examination did not constitute willful or negligent misconduct connected with his employment and therefore did not bar his right to unemployment insurance benefits.

Employee Records	Ariz. Rev. Stat. Ann. § 44-1691 to 44-1693 (1986); Valencia v. Duval Corp., 132 Ariz. 348, 645 P.2d 1262 (Ariz. Ct. App. 1982).	This law governs the actions of consumer reporting agencies in compiling, maintaining, and disseminating information regarding employees. The conduct of company personnel supervisor and company designated physician who telephoned employee's physician to obtain medical information was not sufficiently "extreme and outrageous" conduct so as to entitle the employee to prevail on an invasion of privacy claim.

ARKANSAS

Right to Privacy	Dodrill v. Arkansas Democrat Co., 265 Ark. 628, 590 S.W.2d 840 (1979), cert. denied, 444 U.S. 1076, 100 S. Ct. 1024 (1980).	Adopts definition in the Restatement (Second) of Torts, § 652 (1977).
Polygraphs	Jackson v. Kinark Corp., 282 Ark. 548, 669 S.W.2d 898 (1984).	Summary judgment was not proper where an employee claimed that his discharge for refusing to take a polygraph was in breach of a contract set out in his employee handbook.
Employee Records	Ark. Stat. Ann. § 12-2804 (1979).	All employee evaluation or job performance records of public employees shall be open to public inspection only upon final administrative resolution of any suspension or termination proceeding if there is a compelling public interest in their disclosure.
Sexual Harassment	Ark. Stat. Ann. § 81-405 (1976).	Prohibits in employment "any influence, practices, or conditions calculated to injuriously affect the morals of the female employees."

CALIFORNIA

Right to Privacy	Cal. Const. art. I, § 1 (1972).	"All people are by nature free and independent and have inalienable rights. Among these are enjoying and defending life and liberty, acquiring, possessing and protecting property, and pursuing and attaining safety, happiness, and privacy."
	Porten v. Univ. of San Francisco, 64 Cal. App. 3d 825, 134 Cal. Rptr. 839 (1976).	California's constitutional right to privacy is an inalienable right that may not be violated by anyone, and may be enforced through a private right of action.
	Garrett v. Los Angeles City Unified School Dist., 116 Cal. App. 3d 472, 172 Cal. Rptr. 170 (1981).	A claim of "invasion of bodily privacy" may not be based on the requirement that a teacher submit to a chest x-ray prior to her initial employment.
Speech/ Political Activities	Cal. Lab. Code § 1101 (West 1972).	No employer shall make, adopt, or enforce any rule forbidding or preventing an employee from engaging or participating in politics.
Drug/ Alcohol Testing	Wilkinson, et al. v. Times-Mirror Books and Matthew Bender & Co., et al., No. 636361-3 (Cal. Super. Ct.), rev'd, (Cal. Ct. App. June 1988).	Superior court found state constitutional protection of privacy applies to the private sector as well as to government action and enjoined company from conditioning any employment decisions on drug tests. Appellate court overturned preliminary injunction.
Polygraphs	Cal. Lab. Code § 432.2 (West Supp. 1987).	An employer or his agent cannot "demand" or "require" employees or applicants to submit to a polygraph examination.

Topic	Citation	Description
	Long Beach City Employees Ass'n v. City of Long Beach, 41 Cal. 3d 937, 227 Cal. Rptr. 90, 719 P.2d 660, 1 IER Cases 465 (1986).	Public employer's orders to its public safety officers to submit to a polygraph examination as a condition of their employment intruded upon the employees' privacy rights.
AIDS Testing	Cal. Health & Safety Code, §§ 199.20 and 199.21(f) (West Supp. 1987).	These sections protect the privacy of individuals subject to AIDS testing and prohibits employers from testing for AIDS or using the test results in making employment decisions.
Medical Screening	Sienkiewicz v. Santa Cruz County, 195 Cal. App. 3d 134, 240 Cal. Rptr. 451 (1987).	Public employer may require an employee to meet physical or mental standards reasonably related to duties required by job and health and safety of employee or others.
Monitoring/ Surveillance	Robinson v. Hewlett-Packard Corp., 183 Cal. App. 3d 1108, 228 Cal. Rptr. 591, 48 FEP Cases 819 (1986).	Former employee's allegation that his discharge was based on an invasion of his privacy was not supported by sufficient evidence demonstrating actual surveillance.
Personal Relationships	Thorne v. City of El Segundo, 802 F.2d 1131, 3 IER Cases 657 (9th Cir. 1986).	Police officials violated applicant's constitutional rights of privacy and free association by conducting broad and unregulated inquiry into her off-duty sexual activity and by relying on information concerning such activities when reviewing her employment application.
	Rulon-Miller v. Int'l Business Machines Corp., 162 Cal. App. 3d 241, 208 Cal. Rptr. 524, 1 IER Cases 405 (1984).	An employee's right to privacy was violated where the employer discharged the employee because of her romantic involvement with a manager from a rival company.

Crosier v. United Parcel Serv., Inc., 150 Cal. App. 3d 1132, 198 Cal. Rptr. 361 (1983).

Upholding summary judgment for the employer against the employee's wrongful discharge claim, the court noted that the employer was legitimately concerned with appearances of favoritism, possible claims of sexual harass- ment, and employee dissension created by romantic relationships between management and non-management employees.

Employee Records

Cal. Lab. Code § 432.7 (West Supp. 1987).

Applicants cannot be asked to disclose information regarding arrests that do not result in conviction unless trial is pending for that arrest.

Cal. Lab. Code § 1198.5 (West Supp. 1987).

Every employer shall, at reasonable times and at reasonable intervals, allow an employee, upon request, to inspect such personnel files that are used or have been used to determine the employee's qualifications.

Board of Trustees v. Superior Court, 119 Cal. App. 3d 516, 174 Cal. Rptr. 160 (1981).

Statutory right of employee to inspect personnel file used to determine his qualifi- cations, which explicitly did not apply to letters of reference, was not in contravention of constitutional right of privacy.

Cal. Civil Code § 56.20 (West 1982).

Each employer who receives medical information shall establish private procedures to ensure the confidentiality and protection from unauthorized use and disclosure of that information.

Cal. Civil Code § 1798 (West 1985).

The Informational Practices Act of 1977 limits the maintenance and dissemination of personal confidential information by state agencies.

Johnson v. Winter, 127 Cal. App. 3d 435, 179 Cal. Rptr. 585 (1982).

Sheriff's department applicant was entitled to access to the investigation file, but the department could lawfully withhold any matters obtained with an implicit or explicit understanding that they would be kept confidential.

Sexual Harassment

Cal. Gov't. Code § 12940(i) (West Supp. 1984).

It is unlawful for an employer to fail to take all reasonable steps necessary to prevent discrimination and harassment from occurring.

COLORADO

Speech/ Political Activities

Colo. Rev. Stat. § 80-2-108 (1986).

It shall be unlawful for any corporation, company, or any employer of labor to adopt a rule forbidding an employee from engaging in political activities.

Personal Relation- ships

Butero v. Dept. of Highways, 772 P.2d 633, 3 IER Cases 1797 (Colo. Ct. App. 1988).

Colorado State Personnel Board upheld appointing authority's refusal to promote employee to higher position with Dept. of Highways, where he would have been directly supervised by his father.

Employee Records

Colo. Rev. Stat. § 24-72- 308(3)(f)(I)(1983).

An employer may not require an applicant to describe any information contained in "sealed" arrest records.

Wells v. Premier Indus. Corp., 691 P.2d 765 (Colo. Ct. App. 1984).

An employer did not violate an employee's right to privacy where, after notifying the employee of its intention to comply with an I.R.S. summons, the employer produced the employee's records.

Defamation	Churchey v. Adolph Coors Co., 759 P.2d 1336, 3 IER Cases 1032 (Colo. 1988); Patane v. Broadmoor Hotel, Inc., 708 P.2d 473 (Colo. Ct. App. 1985)	An employer can be liable in defamation for foreseeable self-publication if it had reason to believe that employee would be under strong compulsion to inform third person of contents of defamatory statement. However, an employer's privilege to inform other employees of reason for a change in personnel is not abused as a matter of law when reasons are communicated to employees other than those involved in the personnel decision.

CONNECTICUT

Right to Privacy	Jonap v. Silver, 1 Conn. App. 550, 474 A.2d 800 (1984).	An employer invaded an employee's right to privacy where the employer wrongfully credited the employee with writing and publishing a letter, which the employee claimed harmed his reputation and possible business opportunities.
Drug/ Alcohol Testing	1987 Conn. Legis. Serv. P.A. 87-551 (West).	A positive urinalysis drug test cannot be used by an employer to determine an employee's eligibility for promotion, termination, or any adverse personnel action unless confirmation tests were performed and confirmed the initial test.
Polygraphs	Conn. Gen. Stat. Ann. § 31-51g (West 1987).	An employer or his agent may not "request" or "require" an employee or applicant to submit to a polygraph examination as a condition of employment. An employer may not dismiss or discipline an employee for failure to take a polygraph examination.
Medical Screening	Conn. Gen. Stat. Ann. §§ 46a-60(a)(7) to -60(a)(10).	Requires employers to give employees notice if they are working with reproductive hazards,

Monitoring/ Surveil- lance	Conn. Gen. Stat. Ann. § 31- 48b(b) (West 1987).	and to use reasonable effort to temporarily transfer pregnant employees.

No employer shall operate any "electronic surveillance device or system," including sound or voice recording or closed circuit system to record or monitor employees in areas designed for the health and comfort of the employees or for safeguarding their persons, such as rest rooms, locker rooms, or lounges. |
Employee Records	Conn. Gen. Stat. Ann. § 31- 128b and c (West Supp. 1987).	Provides for inspection by an employee of personnel and medical files maintained by an employer. An employer is required to keep personnel files for at least one year following termination of an employee.
	Conn. Gen. Stat. Ann. § 31- 128f (West Supp. 1987)	Provides the procedure and conditions for disclosure of information within an employee's personnel file and medical record. Subject to certain exceptions, information from an employee's personnel file or medical record may not be disclosed without written authorization of the employee.
	Conn. Gen. Stat. Ann. § 31- 51i (West 1987).	The portion of a job application containing information concerning the arrest record of a job applicant shall not be available to any member of the firm interviewing the applicant except the personnel department.
Sexual Harassment	Conn. Gen. Stat. Ann. § 46a- 60(a)(8) (West Supp. 1984).	Prohibits harassment of any employee on the basis of sex. "Harassment" includes any unwelcome sexual advances.

DELAWARE

Right to Privacy	Avallone v. Wilmington Medical Center, Inc., 553 F. Supp. 931 (D. Del. 1982).	The fact that a former head nurse was asked by others why she left her place of employment is insufficient, as a matter of law, to constitute an action against her former employer for invasion of privacy.
Polygraphs	Del. Code Ann. tit. 19, § 704 (1985).	An employer or his agent may not "require" or "suggest" that an employee or applicant submit to a polygraph examination.
AIDS Testing	Del. Code Ann. tit. 16, § 1201 (1988).	Prohibits discrimination against individuals with AIDS and requires confidentiality of test results and consent to AIDS test.
Employee Records	Del. Code Ann. tit. 19, § 721 (1985).	An employee has a right to inspect his or her personnel file. An employer may require a written request from the employee.

DISTRICT OF COLUMBIA

Right to Privacy	Flake v. Bennett, 611 F. Supp. 70 (D.D.C. 1985).	Government agencies may not require full security investigations for positions that do not affect national security of the United States because it violates employees' right to privacy.
Speech/ Political Activities	Clark v. Library of Congress, 750 F.2d 89 (D.C. Cir. 1984).	Employer failed to demonstrate any legitimate or compelling justification for investigation into the political beliefs and associations of the plaintiff, whose position was classified as non-sensitive to security interests.

Topic	Citation	Description
Polygraphs	D.C. Code Ann. § 36-801 to 36-803 (1981).	An employer may not "administer," "have administered," "accept," or "use" the results of a polygraph examination in connection with employment or an application for employment.
Personal Relationships	D.C. Code Ann. § 1-2502 (1981 & Supp. 1985).	Protects against discrimination in employment, including discharge of an employee, on the basis of sexual orientation.
Employee Records	D.C. Code Ann. § 1-632.1 (1981).	Public employee personnel files are to be established, maintained, and disposed of in a manner designed to ensure the "greatest degree of privacy."

FLORIDA

Topic	Citation	Description
Right to Privacy	Fla. Const. art. I, § 23 (1980).	"Every natural person has the right to be left alone and free from governmental intrusion into his private life except as otherwise provided herein. This section shall not be construed to limit the public's right of access to public records and meetings as provided by law."
Drug Testing	City of Palm Bay v. Bauman, 475 So. 2d 1322 (Fla. Dist. Ct. App. 1985).	Prohibited random testing of police officers and fire fighters, holding that drug tests are only permissible where there is a reasonable suspicion that the person is using drugs.
Polygraphs	Farmer v. City of Ft. Lauderdale, 427 So.2d 187 (Fla.), cert. denied, 464 U.S. 816, 104 S. Ct. 74 (1983). Contra, State Dept. of Highway Safety v. Zimmer,	The polygraph is sufficiently unreliable that a police officer cannot be ordered to take a polygraph test and his refusal is not a sufficient basis for dismissal.

Category	Citation	Description
	398 So. 2d 463 (Fla. Dist. Ct. App. 1981).	No person shall be compelled to identify characteristics that, if disclosed, would identify any individual who receives or has received a serological test; prohibits employers from using the results of a serological test for AIDS in employment decisions.
AIDS Testing	Fla. Stat. Ann. § 381.606 (West 1986).	
Medical Screening	Fla. Stat. Ann. §§ 448.075-76, 228.201 (West 1984 & Supp. 1986).	Prohibits employers from requiring testing of employees for sickle-cell trait or the discharge of an employee solely because he has the trait.
Personal Relation- ships	National Indus., Inc. v. Comm'n on Human Relations, 527 So. 2d 894 (Fla. Dist. Ct. App. 1988).	Former employee filed suit alleging wrongful discharge because of her marriage to a former employee accused of misconduct. Employer's termination of employee to keep her husband off the premises was not discrimination based on marital status.
Employee Records	Fla. Stat. § 943.058 (1988).	Employers may not inquire about an applicant's arrest records or expunged convictions.
	Michel v. Douglas, 464 So. 2d 545 (Fla. 1985); Forsberg v. Housing Authority of Miami Beach, 455 So. 2d 373 (Fla. 1984).	Tax-supported hospital's employee records were not exempted from the Florida Public Records Act by exemption provided for public records "which are presently provided by law to be confidential or which are prohibited from being inspected by the public," or by exemption for "any information revealing surveillance techniques or procedures or personnel," and no federal or state right of disclosure privacy exists.

A-16

WORKPLACE PRIVACY

GEORGIA

Right to
Privacy

Cummings v. Walsh Const.
Co., 561 F. Supp. 872, 31
FEP Cases 930 (S.D. Ga.
1983).

There was no intrusion on a female employee's
seclusion or solitude where she agreed to
engage in sex with her supervisor, and her own
disclosure of this fact negated the supervisor's public disclosures. The employee was
permitted to proceed with her sexual
harassment and emotional distress claims.

Polygraphs

Ga. Code Ann. § 43-36-14
(Supp. 1986).

Restricts the questions that may be asked by a
polygraph examiner during a polygraph
examination.

Hester v. City of
Milledgeville, 777 F.2d 1492
(1985), reh. denied, 782
F.2d 180 (11th Cir. 1986).

Proper use of control questions in polygraph
examinations did not violate fire fighters'
privacy rights.

AIDS
Testing

Ga. Code Ann. §§ 24-9-40.1
and 24-9-47 (1988).

Limits disclosure of AIDS test results but may
allow AIDS tests required by insurance
companies.

Monitoring/
Surveil-
lance

Ellenberg v. Pinkerton's,
Inc., 130 Ga. App. 254, 202
S.E.2d 701 (1973).

Employer hired detective agency to conduct
surveillance of an employee who sued the
company for a work-related injury. The court
held that reasonable surveillance, not
designed to frighten or torment plaintiff, is
a lawful method of obtaining evidence, where
detective merely watched plaintiffs house and
followed plaintiff's car.

Awbrey v. Great Atlantic &
Pacific Tea Co., 505 F.
Supp. 604 (N.D. Ga. 1980).

The Georgia wiretap statute, Ga. Code Ann.
§ 26-3004(1), contains an implied cause of
action under which employee could sue his

Fowler v. Southern Bell Tel. & Tel. Co., 343 F.2d 150 (5th Cir. 1965).

employer for a wiretap allegedly placed on telephones at employer's premises.

Employee Records

Ga. Code Ann. § 35-3-34 (1982).

Georgia recognizes a cause of action for invasion of privacy through wiretapping irrespective of whether the information obtained is published or disclosed.

Information gathered on applicants and current employees relating to "records of guilt" may be revealed to employer by the Georgia Crime Information Center where the employee has access to cash or valuable items or when the employee must ensure the security or safety of property or persons.

Kobeck v. Nabisco, Inc., 166 Ga. App. 652, 305 S.E.2d 183, 1 IER Cases 200 (1983).

An employee did not state a claim for intrusion where her employer revealed her attendance records to her husband (who subsequently committed suicide after concluding that her frequent absences from work were because she had been seeing another man) because there was no physical intrusion upon the employee's privacy.

HAWAII

Right to Privacy

Hawaii Const. art. I, § 6.

"The right of the people to privacy is recognized and shall not be infringed without the showing of a compelling state interest. The legislature shall take affirmative steps to implement this right."

Nakano v. Matayoshi, 68 Haw. 140, 706 P.2d 814 (1985).

Financial disclosure requirements of the county's ethics code did not violate the state's constitutionally protected privacy

Speech/ Political Activities	Pagdilao v. Maui Intercontinental Hotel, 703 F. Supp. 863, 3 IER Cases 1628 (D. Haw. 1988).	rights where disclosure requirements paralleled those of the constitution's ethics provision, and were thus consistent with reasonable expectations of privacy. The values of freedom of speech and privacy are not promoted by plaintiff's shouting of profane comments at a company official, so defendant did not violate public policy by terminating plaintiff for profanity and insubordination.
Polygraphs	Haw. Rev. Stat. § 378-21 (1985).	It shall be unlawful for any employer to require a prospective employee or employee to submit to a lie detector test as a condition of employment or continued employment.
AIDS Testing	1988 Haw. Sess. Laws 290 (1988).	Requires confidentiality of test results.
Employee Records	Haw. Rev. Stat. § 831-3.1(b)(1976).	The state may not give out information of arrests that are not followed by convictions in connection with applications for employment.

IDAHO

Polygraphs	Idaho Code § 44-903 to § 44-904 (1977).	No person, firm, or corporation shall "require" an applicant or employee to take a polygraph examination as a condition of employment.
Employee Records	Baker v. Burlington Northern, Inc., 99 Idaho 688, 587 P.2d 829 (1978).	The employer's publication of the employee's recent criminal activity was a disclosure of public facts and thus not an actionable invasion of privacy.

ILLINOIS

Right to Privacy	Ill. Const. art. I, § 6.	"The people shall have the right to be secure in their persons, houses, papers, and other possessions against unreasonable searches, seizures, invasion of privacy, or interceptions of communications by eavesdropping devices or other means."
Speech/ Political Activities	Barr v. Kelso-Burnett Co., 106 Ill. 2d 520, 478 N.E.2d 1354 (1985).	In an action for retaliatory discharge from employment in violation of the employee's free speech rights, the court held that the complaint, which cited statutory and constitutional provisions relating only to the power of government, not individuals, failed to state a cause of action.
Drug Testing	Chappelle v. Rice, 3 IER Cases 1372 (N.D. Ill. 1988); Taylor v. O'Grady, 669 F. Supp. 1422, 2 IER Cases 897 (N.D. Ill. 1987); Railway Labor Executives Ass'n v. Norfolk & Western Ry. Co., 659 F. Supp. 325 (N.D. Ill.), aff'd, 833 F.2d 700 (7th Cir. 1987); Div. 241, Amalgamated Transit Union v. SUSCY, 538 F.2d 1264 (7th Cir.), cert. denied, 429 U.S. 1029, 97 S. Ct. 653 (1976).	Compulsory drug urinalysis of probationary police officers constitutes a reasonable search and seizure within the Fourth Amendment where there is a reasonable, individualized suspicion of illegal drug use, or impairment on the job. The state's interest in protecting the public can outweigh an individual's expectation of privacy with regard to blood and urine tests.
Polygraphs	Ill. Rev. Stat. ch. 111 § 2401 to § 2432 (Smith-Hurd	Polygraph examination evidence is too unreliable to form the basis for the just

1978); Kaske v. City of Rockford, 96 Ill. 2d 298, 450 N.E.2d 314, cert. denied, 464 U.S. 960, 104 S. Ct. 391 (1983).

cause dismissal of a public employee or civil servant, and a city police officer cannot be disciplined for refusing to take a polygraph.

But see Cipov v. Int'l Harvester Co., 134 Ill. App. 3d 522, 481 N.E.2d 22 (1985); Rozier v. St. Mary's Hosp., 88 Ill. App. 3d 994, 411 N.E.2d 50 (1980).

There is no "public policy" shielding at-will employees from polygraph examinations.

Applicant Investigations — Ill. Rev. Stat. ch. 68, para. 2-103 (Smith-Hurd Supp. 1987).

It is a civil rights violation for any employer to inquire on an employment application whether a job applicant has ever been arrested.

Oden v. Cahill, 79 Ill. App. 3d 768, 398 N.E.2d 1061 (1979).

The Illinois Civil Service Commission did not invade a police applicant's right to privacy by utilizing information that was ordered expunged from the applicant's record in its hiring decision. The court recognized no right of privacy in information that "already is, or can legally be made public."

AIDS Testing — Ill. Rev. Stat. ch. 111.5, para. 7308.1 (1988).

Permits physicians to administer a blood test for AIDS without informing the patient if the patient has authorized general medical treatment.

Personal Relation- ships	McCluskey v. Clark Oil & Refining Corp., 147 Ill. App. 3d 822, 498 N.E.2d 559 (1986).	Termination of an employee because she was married to a co-worker did not violate public policy.
Employee Records	Ill. Rev. Stat. ch. 48, para. 2002 (Smith-Hurd 1986).	Every employer shall, upon an employee's request, which the employer may require to be in writing, permit the employee to inspect his personnel documents.
	Illinois State Employees Ass'n v. Walker, 57 Ill. 2d 512, 315 N.E.2d 9, cert. denied, 419 U.S. 1058, 95 S. Ct. 642 (1974).	Financial disclosures required of state employees do not deprive them of their right to privacy under either the state or federal constitution.
Defamation	Jones v. Britt Airways, Inc., 622 F. Supp. 389 (N.D. Ill. 1985).	An employee's allegations that on several occasions her employer had stated to other employees that she had been dismissed for embezzling company funds satisfied the publication requirement for defamation.

INDIANA

| Speech/ Political Activities | Ind. Code Ann. § 3-4-7-3 (Burns 1982). | It is a misdemeanor for an employer to threaten an employee to influence the employee's political opinions or actions. |
| Drug Testing | Graphic Comm. Union v. Stone Container Corp., 3 IER Cases 261 (S.D. Ind. 1988). | Mandatory drug testing program is enjoined until arbitrator determines whether unilaterally imposed change can be implemented, since injury to employees from program that requires testing, disclosure, and property searches without reasonable cause cannot be remedied by arbitrator's prohibition of future testing. |

Employee Records	Ind. Code Ann. § 4-1-6 (Burns 1986).	Governs the maintenance and disclosure of personal information by state agencies.
Defamation	Lawson v. Howmet Aluminum Corp., 449 N.E.2d 1172 (Ind. Ct. App. 1983).	Statement made to the employment security division about the plaintiff is, by statute (Ind. Code § 22-4-17-9 (Burns 1976)), protected by a qualified privilege. The protection of a qualified privilege, however, may be lost if the privilege was abused by excessive publication of the defamatory statement.
Reasons for Termination	Ind. Code Ann. § 22-6-3-1 (Burns 1986).	Former employer of discharged employee must give the employee a letter confirming past employment.
IOWA		
Right to Privacy	Winegard v. Larsen, 260 N.W.2d 816 (Iowa 1977).	Cause of action for invasion of privacy, whether under false light theory or any other, was not shown by evidence that attorneys made slightly inaccurate statements of fact concerning marriage dissolution proceeding.
Drug Testing	Iowa Code Ann. § 730.5 (1987).	An employer shall not require or request employees or applicants for employment to submit to a drug test as a condition of employment, pre-employment or promotion except in cases of peace and correctional officers of the state.
	Bhd. of Maintenance of Way Employees, Lodge 16 v.	A railroad can unilaterally administer chemical drug tests to all employees who

	appear to be impaired or are involved in any accident.
Burlington Northern Ry. Co., 802 F.2d 1016, 1 IER Cases 789 (8th Cir. 1986).	
McDonell v. Hunter, 612 F. Supp. 1122 (S.D. Iowa 1985), aff'd as modified, 809 F.2d 1302, 1 IER Cases 1297 (8th Cir. 1987).	State correctional facility personnel may be held liable for invasion of an employee's right to privacy where a facility demands a blood or urine sample of an employee without "reasonable suspicion."
Polygraphs	Iowa Code §§ 730.4(1)- § 730.4(3) (West Supp. 1987).
	An employer shall not "require" an applicant for employment to take a lie detector test as a condition of employment.
AIDS Testing	Iowa Code §§ 601 A.2 and 601 A.6 (1988).
	Prohibits discrimination and requires confidentiality of results. Employers may not require testing.
Monitoring/ Surveil- lance	McDonell v. Hunter, 612 F. Supp. 1122 (S.D. Iowa 1985), aff'd as modified, 809 F.2d 1302, 1 IER Cases 1297 (8th Cir. 1987).
	State correctional facility personnel may be held liable for invasion of an employee's right to privacy where a facility (1) does not utilize a reasonable method for searching employees, such as "pat-downs" or inspection of persons or packages, (2) conducts a strip search of employees without "reasonable suspicion," (3) conducts a search of an employee's vehicle that is not within the confines of the correctional facility.
Defamation	Haldeman v. Total Petroleum, Inc., 376 N.W.2d 98 (Iowa 1985).
	A qualified privilege exists for an employer to make statements regarding the reasons for a former employee's discharge to a potential employer.
	Anderson v. Low Rent Housing Comm'n, 304 N.W.2d 239 (Iowa
	An individual does not consent to an invasion of her privacy by going to the media in

response to publication of the reasons for her termination.

KANSAS

Topic	Citation	Description
	1981), cert. denied, 454 U.S. 1086, 102 S. Ct. 645 (1981).	
Right to Privacy	Johnson v. Boeing Airplane Co., 175 Kan. 275, 262 P.2d 808 (1953).	An employee waived his right to privacy by voluntarily posing for a picture that was subsequently published by the company in an advertisement for the equipment that the company manufactured.
Drug Testing	Kan. Gen. Stat. Ann. § 75-4362 (1988).	The state has the authority to implement a drug screening program for persons holding the office of governor, lieutenant governor, and attorney general or any safety sensitive position in state government based upon reasonable suspicion of drug use.
AIDS Testing	Kan. Stat. § 65-108 (1988).	One may not use AIDS test results to discriminate.
Monitoring/ Surveillance	Gretencord v. Ford Motor Co., 538 F. Supp. 331 (D. Kan. 1982).	The court held that the employee failed to state a cause of action for invasion of privacy as a result of the employer's policy to randomly search vehicles prior to their exit from the employer's property.
Employee Records	Atchison, Topeka, and Santa Fe Ry. Co. v. Lopez, 216 Kan. 108, 531 P.2d 455, 14 FEP Cases 111 (1975).	Enforcement of a Railway Commission subpoena requiring production of arrest and conviction records of all employees was not deemed to be an invasion of the employees' privacy.
Reasons for Termination	Kan. Stat. Ann. § 44-808(3) (1986).	Employers are required to furnish discharged employees who so request a service letter setting forth the tenure of employment,

KENTUCKY

Polygraphs	Douthitt v. Kentucky Unemployment Ins. Comm'n, 676 S.W.2d 472 (Ky. Ct. App. 1984).	The claimant's refusal to submit to polygraph tests was not sufficient misconduct to deny employment compensation benefits in light of the unreliability of such examinations.
Personal Relation- ships	Grzyb v. Evans, 700 S.W.2d 399, 1 IER Cases 1125 (Ky. 1985).	Discharge of employee allegedly for fraternizing with a female employee does not violate the public policy against sex discrimination and the freedom of association.

LOUISIANA

Right to Privacy	La. Const. art. I, § 5 (1975).	"Every person shall be secure in his person, property, communications, houses, papers, and effects against unreasonable searches, seizures, or invasions of privacy."
	Public Employees Ass'n of New Orleans, Inc. v. City of New Orleans, 404 So. 2d 537 (La. Ct. App. 1981); Cangelosi v. Schwegmann Bros. Giant Super Markets, 379 So. 2d 836 (La. Ct. App.), aff'd 390 So. 2d 196 (La. 1980).	There is no invasion of privacy where an employer reasonably and in good faith questions an employee about potential conflicts of interest.
Speech/ Political Activities	La. Rev. Stat. Ann. § 23:961 (West 1985).	No employer having more than 20 employees shall adopt or enforce any rule forbidding or preventing any employee from engaging or

Topic	Citation	Description
Polygraphs	Ballaron v. Equitable Shipyards, Inc., 521 So. 2d 481, 3 IER Cases 520 (La. Ct. App.), cert. denied, 522 So. 2d 571 (La. 1988).	Consent forms for a polygraph test that an employer required employees to sign did not violate their right to privacy.
AIDS Testing	Leckelt v. Bd. of Comm'rs, 4 IER Cases 383, 49 FEP Cases 541 (E.D. La. 1989).	Licensed practical nurse had no reasonable expectation of privacy regarding his HIV status where hospital had long-standing infection control procedures which precluded testing for suspected infection to protect patients and employees and employee had long-term relationship with individual with AIDS. Limited intrusion on privacy outweighed by hospital's interest in knowing the result of an AIDS test voluntarily taken.
Medical Screening	La. Rev. Stat. Ann. § 23-1002 (1985).	Provides that an employer may not discharge an employee on the basis of the sickle cell trait.
Monitoring/ Surveillance	Love v. Southern Bell Tel. and Tel. Co., 263 So. 2d 460 (La. Ct. App.), writ denied, 262 La. 1117, 266 So. 2d 429 (1972).	Employer found liable for invading a former employee's right to privacy where the employer utilized information in his disciplinary proceeding acquired when other employees entered the former employee's trailer and found him intoxicated. Louisiana courts require employers to stay within proper legal limits in investigating employees.
Defamation	Thibodeaux v. Southwest Louisiana Hosp. Ass'n, 488	An employer may be liable for defamation where it publishes it discharged an employee for

(preceding text, top of page) participating in politics or becoming a candidate for public office.

theft; however, statements made in good faith and for legitimate reasons are conditionally privileged.

MAINE

Right to Privacy	Hudson v. S.D. Warren Co., 608 F. Supp. 477 (D. Me. 1985).	No invasion of privacy existed where an employee alleged the employer discharged him after an undercover police agent falsely reported to his employer that he consumed alcohol on the job and offered the agent a drink. There was no public disclosure because the statements were made to a small group of persons, and the recipients had a legitimate interest in it.
Drug Testing	Me. Rev. Stat. Ann. tit. 26, §§ 681-690 (1989).	Allows drug testing of job applicants only after they have been offered a job or placed on a waiting list, where "probable cause" exists, and restricts random or arbitrary testing to safety sensitive jobs, unless otherwise agreed under a labor contract. Before testing, employers must participate in an employee assistance plan. Employers must also offer rehabilitation before firing employees. Positive tests must be confirmed. Blood tests are prohibited and urine test subjects must be allowed to remain clothed and unobserved.

So. 2d 743 (La. Ct. App. 1986); Farria v. La Bonne Terrebonne of Houma, Inc., 476 So. 2d 474 (La. Ct. App. 1985); Alford v. Georgia-Pacific Corp., 331 So. 2d 558 (La. Ct. App.), writ denied, 334 So. 2d 427 (La. 1976).

Polygraphs	Me. Rev. Stat. Ann. tit. 32, § 7166(1)-(3) (Supp. 1986).	An employer may not directly or indirectly "require," "request," or "suggest" that any applicant or employee submit to a polygraph examination as a condition of employment.
AIDS Testing	Me. Rev. Stat. Ann. tit. 5 § 19204-B(1) (1989).	No health care facility may require that an employee or applicant for employment submit to a HIV test . . . except when based on a BFOQ.
	Me. Rev. Stat. Ann. tit. 5 § 19203 (1988).	Results of AIDS test may not be disclosed except to (1) the subject; (2) authorized persons; (3) designated health care provider; (4) blood or organ donees; and (5) state agencies responsible for custodial care of subject.
Medical Screening	Me. Human Rights Commission Guide to Pre-employment Inquiries, FEP Manual (BNA) 455:545 (1988).	Pre-employment pelvic exams are unlawful. Questions regarding pregnancy are unlawful if used to deny or limit employment opportunities.
Employee Records	Me. Rev. Stat. Ann. tit. § 26, § 631 (Supp. 1986).	Provides for the right of employees or former employees to review their personnel files.
	Me. Rev. Stat. Ann. tit. 30 § 64 and § 2257 (Supp. 1986).	The county commission shall, on written request from an employee, or former employee, provide the employee or his duly authorized representative with an opportunity to review his personnel file.
Defamation	Saunders v. VanPelt, 497 A.2d 1121 (Me. 1985).	A pediatrician's false statements about an employee's inability to perform psychological testing upon children were actionable per se because they related to the employee's profession.

	Tucci v. Guy Gannett Pub. Co., 464 A.2d 161 (Me. 1983).	Public employer found not liable for defamation when the city manager wrote newspaper articles describing a cheating incident on a police promotional examination in which an employee allegedly participated.
MARYLAND		
Right to Privacy	*Hollander v. Lubow*, 277 Md. 47, 351 A.2d 421, *cert. denied*, 426 U.S. 936, 96 S. Ct. 2651 (1976).	Employer found not liable for invasion of privacy when it disclosed that its former employee operated a competing business while he worked for the employer.
Speech/ Political Activities	Md. Ann. Code art. 33, § 26-16 (6) (Michie 1986).	An employer is prohibited from influencing through coercion an employee's political opinions or actions within 90 days of election.
	De Bleecker v. Montgomery County, 292 Md. 498, 438 A.2d 1348 (1982).	A Roman Catholic priest who was discharged from his at-will public employment as a teacher in a county detention center, allegedly in violation of his right to free speech because of comments to inmates stated a claim.
Drug Testing	*United Food and Commercial Workers, Local 400 v. Callahan*, 3 IER Cases 1495 (Md. 1988).	Mandatory urinalysis testing for illegal drugs, as part of police officer's and firefighter's routine periodic physical exam constitutes unreasonable search and seizure under Fourth Amendment since there is no evidence of drug problem within the department or of any suspicion of individual drug use.
Polygraphs	Md. Ann. Code art. 100, § 95 (Supp. 1975).	No employer may demand or require an employee or applicant to submit to a polygraph, lie detector, or similar test or examination.

	Moniodis v. Cook, 64 Md. App. 1, 494 A.2d 212, 1 IER Cases 441, cert. denied, 304 Md. 631, 500 A.2d 649 (1985).	A former employee's discharge for refusing to submit to a polygraph examination clearly violated the mandate of the statute prohibiting lie detector tests as a condition of employment.
Medical Screening	Md. Ann. Code art. 100, § 95(A) (Supp. 1986).	An employer may not require an applicant to answer, orally or in writing, "questions pertaining to any physical, psychological, or psychiatric illness, disability, or treatment which did not bear a direct material and timely relationship to the applicant's fitness or competency to properly perform the activities of the desired position."
Monitoring/ Surveil- lance	Pemberton v. Bethlehem Steel Corp., 66 Md. App. 133, 502 A.2d 1101 (1985), cert. denied, 306 Md. 289, 508 A.2d 488, cert. denied, 479 U.S. 984, 107 S. Ct. 571 (1986).	Surveillance, consisting of observing a union business agent outside his residence, and in other public places, which was conducted in such a way that the subject was unaware of the surveillance, was not an intrusion upon seclusion.
	Md. Ann. Code art. 27, § 740(a)-(b) (1982).	An employer may not, in any application, interview, or otherwise, require an applicant for employment or admission to disclose information concerning criminal charges against him that have been expunged.
Personal Relation- ships	Maryland Comm'n on Human Relations v. Baltimore Gas & Electric Co., 296 Md. 46, 459 A.2d 205 (Md. Ct. App. 1983).	Utility company's policy of refusing to hire spouses of employees was held to violate state statutes governing employment practices, unless justified as business necessity.

Defamation	Adler v. American Standard Corp., 538 F. Supp. 572 (D. Md. 1982).	An employee's complaint alleging that plaintiff's former employers made statements in connection with discharge of plaintiff that were not true and were maliciously and recklessly made would not be dismissed for failure to reproduce exact words alleged to have been defamatory.
	Gay v. William Hill Manor, Inc., 74 Md. App. 51, 536 A.2d 690, 3 IER Cases 744, cert. denied, 312 Md. 601, 541 A.2d 964 (1988).	Nursing home's action in escorting employee through halls to her locker and then to her car after it discharged her did not constitute defamatory publication, where there was no testimony from employee that such action was unusual.
MASSACHU-SETTS		
Right to Privacy	Mass. Ann. Laws ch. 214, § 1B (West Supp. 1987)	Protects persons against unreasonable, substantial, or serious interference with his/her privacy.
	Cort v. Bristol-Myers Co., 385 Mass. 300, 431 N.E.2d 908 (1982).	Where employees declined to provide any information they regarded as confidential or personal in employees' questionnaires, the employer was not liable to the employees for invasion of privacy because the employer's attempt at invasion of privacy, if it was one, failed.
	Bratt v. Int'l Business Machines Corp., 785 F.2d 352 (1st Cir. 1986).	Employer's distribution of memos regarding employee's mental health problem was an invasion of his privacy.

Drug Testing	Bally v. Northeastern Univ., 403 Mass. 713, 532 N.E.2d 49 (1989).	Massachusetts State Civil Rights Act was not violated by private university's drug testing program for student athletes on its intercollegiate athletic teams. Nor did the drug testing violate Massachusetts' right of privacy statute, absent public disclosure of confidential information.
Polygraphs	Mass. Gen. Laws Ann. ch. 149, § 19B (1989).	No employer shall request any employee, including police officers, to submit to a polygraph examination as a condition of employment.
Applicant Investigations	Mass. Gen. Laws Ann. ch. 276, § 100A (West Supp. 1987).	Employment applications must notify applicants that they may answer "no record" to inquiries regarding prior arrest records if their criminal records have been "sealed."
Honesty Testing	Mass. Gen. Laws Ann. ch. 149, § 19B (1989).	Prohibits employers from using as a condition of employment any device, mechanism, instrument or written examination, which is operated, or the results of which are used or interpreted by an examiner for the purpose of purporting to assist in or enable the detection of deception, the verification of truthfulness, or the rendering of a diagnostic opinion regarding the honesty of an individual.
AIDS Testing	Mass. Gen. Laws Ann. ch. 111, § 70F (West Supp. 1987).	No health care facility shall disclose the results of an AIDS test to any person other than the subject thereof without first obtaining the subject's written, informed consent, or identify the subject of such tests. No employer shall require an AIDS test as a condition for employment.

Cronan v. New England Telephones, 1 IER Cases 658 (D. Mass. 1986).	State law breach of privacy complaint alleging that the employer forced the employee to disclose that he had been diagnosed as having ARC, a form of AIDS, and then revealed his medical condition to other employees was based upon a statutory right to privacy independent of private agreements.
Medical Screening	Mass. Gen. Laws Ann. ch. 149, § 19A (1988).	"Any employer requiring a physical examination shall, upon request, cause said person to be furnished with a copy of the medical report following the . . . examination."
Employee Records	Mass. Gen. Laws Ann. ch. 149 § 52C (West Supp. 1987).	Any employer receiving a written request from an employee shall provide the employee with an opportunity to review his personnel records.
	Pottle v. School Comm. of Braintree, 395 Mass. 861, 482 N.E.2d 813 (1985).	The disclosure of the names and addresses of public school employees to labor unions does not constitute invasion of personal privacy because school employees, by virtue of their public employment, have diminished expectations of privacy, and the names and addresses are available from other sources.
	Alberts v. Devine, 395 Mass. 59, 479 N.E.2d 113, cert. denied, 474 U.S. 1013, 106 S. Ct. 546 (1985).	When aspects of employee's health could affect employee's ability effectively to perform job duties physician may disclose to patient's employer whatever information might bear on employee's ability effectively to perform job duties.
Defamation	Stepanischen v. Merchants Despatch Transp. Corp., 722	The employer's conditional privilege to communicate adverse information about the

MICHIGAN

Right to Privacy

F.2d 922, 1 IER Cases 309 (1st Cir. 1983); Arsenault v. Allegheny Airlines, Inc., 485 F. Supp. 1373 (D. Mass.), aff'd, 636 F.2d 1199, (1st Cir. 1980).

Cole v. Dow Chemical Co., 112 Mich. App. 198, 315 N.W.2d 565 (1982).

employee would be actionable if the employee was able to show actual malice.

Employees sought relief based on constitutional right to privacy for sterility caused by exposure to a chemical during employment. The privacy claim could not be maintained since there was no state action.

Speech/ Political Activities

Mich. Stat. Ann. § 17.62(7) (Callaghan 1982).

An employer shall not gather or keep a record of employee's associations, political activities, publications, or communications of non-employment activity unless authorized by the employee, occur on the employer's premises, or during working hours, and disrupt the duties of the employee or other employees.

Drug Testing

DiTomaso v. Electronic Data Systems, 3 IER Cases 1700 (E.D. Mich. 1988).

Security officers failed to state a claim for invasion of privacy by intrusion based on workplace drug test that uncovered their off-duty use of marijuana, since the employer had significant interest in assuring that officers were drug-free prior to formation of any reasonable suspicion, and reasonable person would not find method of securing urine objectionable.

Polygraphs

Mich. Comp. Laws § 32.203 (1985).

Employers may not require their employees to take lie detector tests as a condition of

AIDS Testing	Mich. Comp. Laws §§ 5131 & 5133 (1989).	continued employment. Employees who are discharged for refusal to take such a test may recover double the wages lost.
Medical Screening	Mich. Civil Rights Commission Pre-Employment Inquiry Guide, FEP Manual (BNA) 455:1185 (1982).	Requires written informed consent prior to AIDS testing and provides for confidentiality of test results containing any information regarding any communicable disease or infection. It is unlawful to make any inquiries regarding an applicant's physical or mental health which are not directly related to the requirement of a specific job.
Monitoring/ Surveil- lance	Mich. Comp. Laws Ann. § 37.2205a (West 1985).	Employers are forbidden to make inquiries of their employees concerning prior arrests that did not result in a conviction.
	Mich. Stat. Ann. § 17.62(9) (Callaghan 1982).	If an employer has reasonable cause to believe an employee is engaged in certain criminal activities he may keep a separate file on the investigation. Upon completion of the investigation, the employee must be notified that an investigation was conducted. If no disciplinary action was taken, the file and all copies must be destroyed.
Personal Relation- ships	Briggs v. North Muskegon Police Dep't., 563 F. Supp. 585, 1 IER Cases 195 (W.D. Mich. 1983), aff'd, 746 F.2d 1475, 1 IER Cases 1136 (6th Cir. 1984).	Dismissal of a married, part-time officer for cohabiting with a woman who was not his wife violated the officer's right to privacy.

Forced resignation of employee due to management disapproval of her social relationships with co-employee was neither sex discrimination nor discrimination on the basis of "marital status" under the state civil rights statute.

Sears v. Ryder Truck Rental, Inc., 596 F. Supp. 1001, 41 FEP Cases 1347 (E.D. Mich. 1984).

Anti-nepotism policies which include co-workers who are married did not directly and substantially infringe on the right to marry.

Miller v. C.A. Muer Corp., 420 Mich. 355, 362 N.W.2d 650, 43 FEP Cases 1195 (1984).

Employee Records

An employer, upon written request that describes the personnel record, shall provide to the employee an opportunity to periodically review at reasonable intervals the employee's personnel record. Employees who disagree with information in a personnel file may include a statement of the disagreement. Exceptions include employee references, materials affecting other employees, private information about others, and separately maintained grievance and criminal investigations.

Mich. Stat. Ann. § 17.62(1) - (5) (Callaghan 1982).

An employer shall not divulge a disciplinary report, letter, or reprimand to a third party without written notice.

Mich. Stat. Ann. § 17.62(6) (Callaghan 1982).

An employer shall not, in connection with an application for employment, personnel, or membership, request or maintain a record of information regarding an arrest.

Mich. Comp. Laws Ann. § 37.2205a (West 1985).

Defamation

The communication of an allegedly libelous statement concerning an employee within the

Brantley v. Zantop Int'l Airlines, Inc., 617 F. Supp.

MINNESOTA

	1032 (E.D. Mich. 1985); Harrison v. Arrow Metal Products Corp., 20 Mich. App. 590, 174 N.W.2d 875 (1969).	corporation itself constitutes publication for purposes of a defamation action.
Drug Testing	Minn. Stat. Ann. § 181.951 (1988).	An employer is permitted to conduct drug and alcohol testing under very strict conditions where the employer has reasonable suspicion to believe that the employee is under the influence of drugs or alcohol.
Polygraphs	Minn. Stat. Ann. § 181.75 (West Supp. 1987); Gawel v. Two Plus Two, Inc., 309 N.W.2d 746 (Minn. 1981).	An employer may not, directly or indirectly, "solicit" or "require" a polygraph examination of an employee or applicant. If the employee requests a polygraph examination, the employer must inform the employee that the test is voluntary. The court upheld the constitutionality of the statute.
	Minn. Stat. Ann. § 181.76 (West Supp. 1987); Jeffers v. Convoy Co., 636 F. Supp. 1337, 1 IER Cases 919 (D. Minn. 1986); Kamrath v. Suburban Nat. Bank, 363 N.W.2d 108 (Minn. Ct. App. 1985).	If an employee requests and submits to a polygraph examination, the results of the examination may only be distributed to those persons who are authorized by the employee to receive the results. An employee may bring an action under Minn. Stat. Ann. § 181.76 for civil damages and equitable relief if an employer forces or attempts to force an employee to submit to a polygraph examination.
Personal Relationships	State v. Porter Farms, Inc., 382 N.W.2d 543 (Minn. Ct. App. 1986).	Statutory prohibition against discharging employee because of "marital status" extends to refusing to hire and firing individuals

Employee Records	1989 Minn. Sess. Law Serv. 349 (West).	living with but not married to persons of the opposite sex.
	Minn. Stat. Ann. § 364.04 (West Supp. 1987).	Allows employee access to records. Disputed information can be removed or corrected. Retaliation prohibited.
		The State of Minnesota may not use, distribute, or disseminate the following in connection with an application for public employment: arrest records not followed by conviction, conviction that has been annulled or expunged, or misdemeanor offenses for which no jail sentence has been imposed.
Defamation	Frankson v. Design Space Int'l., 380 N.W.2d 560 (Minn. Ct. App.), aff'd in part, rev'd in part, 394 N.W.2d 140 (Minn. 1986).	The court upheld a damage award against an employer predicated upon in-house statements made by corporate employees and officials regarding the alleged reason for the employee's discharge. There was sufficient evidence that the statements were made with actual malice.
	Lee v. Metropolitan Airport Comm'n, 428 N.W.2d 815, 3 IER Cases 1152 (Minn. Ct. App. 1988).	The court held that employer was not liable for defamation for discussing fact that employee made harassing phone calls while on duty as a dispatcher. Employer's discussion with co-worker was qualified privileged statement made without malice and regularly scheduled dispatcher's meeting was proper occasion to discuss allegation.

MISSISSIPPI

Speech/Political Activities — Miss. Code Ann. 79-1-9 (1972). — Provides a fine of $250 against a corporation for every unlawful interference with the social, civil, or political rights of any of its agents or employees.

Defamation — Hooks v. McCall, 272 So. 2d 925 (Miss. 1973). — A discharged employee may not base a slander claim upon another employee's statement to a superior that the discharged employee stole equipment belonging to the employer where there was no showing that the statements were made with malice.

MISSOURI

Right to Privacy — Haith v. Model Cities Health Corp., 704 S.W.2d 684 (Mo. Ct. App. 1986); Sullivan v. Pulitzer Broadcasting Co., 709 S.W.2d 475 (Mo. 1976). — Plaintiffs could bring an invasion of privacy claim based on allegations that the defendant wrongfully misappropriated their names in seeking additional grant money. Missouri law, however, does not recognize a tort claim for false light invasion of privacy.

Speech/Political Activities — Mo. Stat. Ann. § 578.115 (Vernon 1979). — Provides that no employee may be denied employment or advancement because of his refusal to work on his normal day of worship.

Mo. Stat. Ann. § 115.637(6) (Vernon Supp. 1987). — An employer who makes or enforces any order, rule, or regulation to prevent an employee from engaging in political activities has committed a misdemeanor.

Polygraphs — Gibson v. Hummel, 688 S.W.2d 4 (Mo. Ct. App. 1985). — Conduct of convenience store operator in requiring an employee to take a polygraph examination and subsequently terminating her based on results of that examination did not amount to outrageous conduct sufficient to render the operator liable where more than one half of inventory shortages at the store were due to employee theft.

Topic	Citation	Description
AIDS Testing	Mo. Rev. Stat. §§ 191.650-191.695 (1988).	Prohibits discrimination against AIDS patients and requires confidentiality of test results.
Personal Relationships	Lile v. Hancock Place School Dist., 701 S.W.2d 500 (Mo. Ct. App. 1985).	No violation of teacher's right of privacy where the teacher was terminated for alleged "immoral conduct" committed in his home involving two school-aged daughters of the woman with whom he lived.
	Duckworth v. Sayad, 670 S.W.2d 88 (Mo. Ct. App. 1984).	Police department's termination of a police officer who allegedly engaged in sexual misconduct in a room, which was visible only by standing in a particular spot on a balcony, constituted an invasion of the officer's privacy.
Employee Records	Howard v. Marsh, 785 F.2d 645, 40 FEP Cases 433 (8th Cir.), cert. denied, 479 U.S. 988, 107 S. Ct. 581, 42 FEP Cases 560 (1986).	The Privacy Act was not violated by the disclosure of records concerning a civilian employee of the military when the records were used by military officials in drafting a rebuttal to the employee's charges of sex discrimination.
Reasons for Termination	Mo. Stat. Ann. § 290.140 (Vernon Supp. 1986).	A private employer must upon written request by the discharged employee provide a service letter written a year after leaving the job.
	Eib v. Federal Reserve Bank, 633 S.W.2d 432 (Mo. Ct. App. 1982).	The court interpreted the service letter statute as requiring only that the reason stated in the letter be the true reason for

MONTANA

Right to Privacy

Mont. Const. art. II § 10.

"The right of the individual privacy is essential to the well-being of a free society and shall not be infringed without the showing of a compelling state interest."

Speech/ Political Activities

Mont. Code Ann. §§ 13-35-226, 228 (1985).

Implied or expressed threats by employers or promises calculated to influence the political opinions or actions of their employees are not permitted.

Drug/AIDS Testing

Mont. Code Ann. § 39-2-304 (1987).

No employer shall require any person to submit to a blood or urine test, except for employment in hazardous work environments or in jobs the primary responsibility of which is security, public safety, or fiduciary responsibility; or unless the employer has reason to believe the employee's faculties are impaired on the job.

Polygraphs

Mont. Code Ann. § 39-2-304 (1986).

No person, firm, or corporation shall require any person to take a polygraph test or any form of mechanical lie detector test. This section does not apply to public law enforcement agencies.

Personal Relation-ships

Storch v. Board of Directors, 169 Mont. 176, 545 P.2d 644 (1976).

No invasion of privacy found where a drug consultant was discharged based upon his "personal lifestyle." Since the employee counseled people with personal problems, his personal lifestyle was relevant to his job performance.

discharge; the reason itself need not be justified.

Hulett v. Bozeman School
Dist. No. 7, 740 P.2d 1132,
49 FEP Cases 456 (Mont.
1987).

Anti-nepotism policy which prohibited employment of spouses is discriminatory since marital status is recognized as a protected class in Montana.

Reasons for Termination

Mont. Code Ann. § 39-2-801 (1985).

A discharged employee must be furnished a written reason for his discharge if he requests. Failure to do so precludes an employer from thereafter furnishing any statement of the reason for discharge to another potential employer.

NEBRASKA

Speech/ Political Activities

Neb. Rev. Stat. § 32-1223 (1984).

It shall be unlawful for any person to coerce or attempt to coerce any voter in his voting or other political action.

Drug Testing

Neb. Rev. Stat. Ann. § 48-1901-1910 (1988).

An employer may not deny any continued employment or take any disciplinary action on the basis of a drug test unless a positive finding of drugs was subsequently confirmed by gas chromatography, mass spectrometry, or other scientific testing techniques.

Rushton v. Nebraska Public
Power Dist., 844 F.2d 562, 3
IER Cases 257 (8th Cir.
1988).

A drug testing program that requires public utility employees with access to protected areas of a nuclear power plant to submit to drug screening at least once a year does not violate the employee's constitutional rights. Individualized suspicion of drug use is not a prerequisite to search where state interest is so great and private interest is so diminished.

Polygraphs	Neb. Rev. Stat. § 81-1932 (1981).	An employer may not "require" an employee or applicant to submit to a "truth & deception" examination unless such employment involves law enforcement.
	Collins v. Baker's Supermarkets, Inc., 223 Neb. 365, 389 N.W.2d 774 (1986).	Requiring a worker who took a lie detector test to work for a lesser salary did not constitute termination of employment in violation of a statute.
AIDS Testing	Glover v. Eastern Nebraska Community Office of Retardation, 686 F. Supp. 243, 3 IER Cases 135 (D. Neb. 1988), aff'd, 867 F.2d 461, 41 IER Cases 65 (8th Cir. 1989).	Mandatory blood testing for AIDS is not justified for public employees, even if they have extensive contact with mentally retarded clients.
Medical Screening	Neb. Rev. Stat. §§ 48-1901– 48-1910 (1988).	Regulates "chemical tests" of employees. Employees have a right to a re-test and disclosure of results is limited.
Personal Relation- ships	Voichahoske v. City of Grand Island, Hall County, 194 Neb. 175, 231 N.W.2d 124 (1975).	Employer must show that its refusal to hire the spouse of a current employee is justified by a compelling governmental interest.
Defamation	White v. Ardan, Inc., 230 Neb. 11, 430 N.W.2d 27, 3 IER Cases 1640 (1988).	Security executive's written statements to employer's supervisory personnel regarding discharges of employees were privileged, and security executive did not act with malice, where it was security executive's responsibility to give employer that information, each allegedly defamatory statement was true, and there was no evidence reflecting malice on his part.

	Reasons for Termination	Neb. Rev. Stat. §§ 48-209; 48-211 (1984).	At the end of his employment an employee is entitled to a service letter.

NEVADA

Right to Privacy	Kemp v. Block, 607 F. Supp. 1262 (D. Nev. 1985).	An employee had no reasonable expectation that his argument in the work area with a foreman would be private since the argument took place in loud voices, the co-worker who recorded the conversation was in a place where he had a right to be, and the employee had no right to prevent other persons from entering the work area while the argument ensued.
Speech/ Political Activities	Nev. Rev. Stat. § 613.040 (1986).	It is unlawful for an employer to prohibit an employee from engaging in politics or becoming a candidate for public office.
Polygraphs	Nev. Rev. Stat. § 648.183 and § 648.193 (1985).	Sets forth standards applicable to the administration and utilization of polygraph examination results. An examiner is prohibited from inquiring into the religion, political affiliations, affiliations with other labor organizations, or sexual activities of the person examined.
Medical Screening	Nev. Equal Rights Commission Pre-employment Inquiry Guide (1986).	It is unacceptable for a prospective employer to ask any questions regarding an applicant's general medical condition, state of health, or illnesses.
Monitoring/ Surveillance	Nev. Rev. Stat. § 613.160 (1985).	It is unlawful for an employer to discipline or discharge an employee based upon the report of a special agent, detective, or spotter, involving a question of integrity, honesty, or

		breach of rules, unless the employer gives notice and a hearing to the employee, and the employee may confront the person making the report at the hearing.
Employee Records	Nev. Rev. Stat. 613.075 (1985).	Employee has the right to inspect records retained on the employee.
	Dunphy v. Sheehan, 92 Nev. 259, 549 P.2d 332 (1976).	The financial disclosure provisions of an ethics in government law requiring public officers to make certain financial disclosures were found to be unconstitutionally vague and an overbroad intrusion upon the right to privacy of public officers.
Defamation	Circus Circus Hotels, Inc. v. Witherspoon, 57 P.2d 101 (Nev. 1983).	Employer's letter to state administrative agency reviewing employee claim for unemployment compensation was absolutely privileged. Former employer had a qualified privilege to make statements about the character or conduct of former employees to present or prospective employers.
NEW HAMPSHIRE		
Polygraphs	O'Brien v. Papa Gino's of America, Inc., 780 F.2d 1067, 1 IER Cases 458 (1st Cir. 1986).	Employer's policy, which included employee's submission to a polygraph when he was suspected of using drugs outside the work-place, violated an employee's common law right to privacy.
AIDS Testing	N.H. Rev. Stat. Ann. §§ 141-F:5 & 141-F:8 (1988).	Informed consent must be obtained before an individual may be tested for AIDS. Results must be kept confidential.

| Employee Records | N.H. Rev. Stat. Ann. § 275.56 (Supp. 1986). | Every employer shall provide a reasonable opportunity for any employee who so requests to inspect such employee's personnel file and further, upon request, provide employer with a copy of all or part of such file. |

NEW JERSEY

| Right to Privacy | Devlin v. Greiner, 147 N.J. Super. 446, 371 A.2d 380 (1977). | New Jersey permits common law privacy actions recognized in the Restatement (Second) of Torts, § 652 (1977). |

| Polygraphs | N.J. Stat. Ann. § 2C:40A-1 (West Supp. 1987). | Protects employees from being discharged for refusing to take lie detector tests required as a condition of their employment (with certain exceptions for employers involved in the manufacture of drugs). |
| | State v. Vornado, Inc., 155 N.J. Super. 354, 382 A.2d 945 (1978); State v. Berkey Photo, Inc., 150 N.J. Super. 56, 374 A.2d 1226 (1977); State v. Community Distrib., Inc., 64 N.J. 479, 317 A.2d 697 (1974). | An employer may not unlawfully "influence" an employee to take a polygraph test. |

| Medical Screening | N.J. Stat. Ann. § 10:5-12a (West Supp. 1986); McKenna v. Fargo, 451 F. Supp. 1355 (D.N.J. 1978), aff'd, 601 F.2d 575 (3d Cir. 1979). | An employer is prohibited from refusing to employ or from discharging from employment any individual because of an atypical cellular blood trait. The interest of the city in screening out applicants who would not be able to handle the psychological pressures of the job was sufficient to justify an intrusion into the applicant's privacy by requiring psychological testing. |

Personal Relation- ships	Slohoda v United Parcel Serv., Inc., 193 N.J. Super. 586, 475 A.2d 618 (1984).	An employer's policy of discharging a married employee who engages in adultery, but not an unmarried employee who has an illicit sexual relationship, is based in significant part on the employee's marital status, in violation of state law.
	Greenberg v. Kimmelman, 99 N.J. 552, 494 A.2d 294 (1985).	Casino ethics amendment prohibiting employment to any member of the immediate family of any state officer or employee was held to be constitutional.
Defamation	Rogozinski v. Airstream By Angell, 152 N.J. Super. 133, 377 A.2d 807 (1977), modified, 164 N.Y. Super., 397 A.2d 334 (1979).	Employer had a qualified privilege to make statements concerning employees to the unemployment compensation commission. Absent malice, employer is not liable for defamation.

NEW MEXICO

Speech/ Political Activities	N.M. Stat. Ann. § 1-20-13 (1985).	Prohibits an employer from threatening to discharge or actually discharging an employee because of their political opinions or beliefs.
AIDS Testing	N.M. Stat. Ann. ch. 228 and 227, L. 1989 §§ 1-8.	Prohibits use of AIDS test as a condition of employment, and requires informed consent and confidentiality for all AIDS tests.
Defamation	Gengler v. Phelps, 92 N.M. 465, 589 P.2d 1056 (N.M. Ct. App. 1978), cert. denied, 92 N.M. 353, 588 P.2d 554 (1979).	A former employee could not base a slander action upon his former employer's giving of a "less than desirable reference" to a potential employer. An absolute privilege also exists where the former employee consents to the

NEW YORK

Right to Privacy

McKinney's N.Y. Comp. Laws § 51 (West 1976).

Every person shall have the right of privacy to be secure from an appropriation of one's name.

Caesar v. Chemical Bank, 66 N.Y.2d 698, 487 N.E.2d 275, 496 N.Y.S.2d 418 (1985).

Oral or implied consent is a complete defense to a privacy action under the civil rights law.

Speech/Political Activities

N.Y. Elec. Law § 17-150, 17-154 (McKinney 1978).

It is a misdemeanor for an employer to make threats calculated to influence the political opinions or actions of employees.

Socialist Workers Party v. Attorney General of the United States, 642 F. Supp. 1357 (S.D.N.Y. 1986).

The FBI's use of informants in the Socialist Workers Party organization constituted an invasion of privacy, where the program was designed to ferret out private matters rather than information of a public nature.

Drug Testing

Caruso v. Ward, 72 N.Y.2d 432, 530 N.E.2d 850, 534 N.Y.S.2d 142, 3 IER Cases 1537 (1988).

Police department order requiring periodic, random drug urinalysis testing of present and future voluntary members of elite organized crime control bureau constitutes reasonable search and seizure under New York and federal constitutions. Privacy interests of officers are minimized due to their pursuit of service in bureau whose integrity the state has crucial interest in maintaining.

Patchogue-Medford Congress of Teachers v. Board of Education, 70 N.Y.2d 57, 510

Blanket drug testing of teachers being considered for tenure is unconstitutional in the absence of reasonable suspicion based on

publication by permitting her references to be contacted.

supportable objective facts and established administrative standards.

	N.E.2d 325, 517 N.Y.S.2d 456, 2 IER Cases 198 (1987).	
Polygraphs	N.Y. Lab. Law § 735 (McKinney Supp. 1987).	No employer or his agent will "require," "suggest," or "knowingly" permit any employee or applicant to submit to a "psychological stress evaluator" and no employer shall administer or utilize the results of such test for any reason whatsoever.
	People v. Hamilton, 125 A.2d 1000, 511 N.Y.S.2d 190, 42 FEP Cases 1069 (1986).	Penalty imposed against an employer for incidents of sexual harassment of female job applicants during pre-employment lie detector tests.
Applicant Investigations	N.Y. Exec. Law § 296(16) (McKinney Supp. 1987).	Prohibits an employer from making inquiries or acting adversely against a person on the basis of an arrest or criminal accusation that was terminated in favor of that person.
AIDS Testing	N.Y. Pub. Health Law, ch. 45, art. 27-F, § 2780 (McKinney 1989).	Prohibits AIDS testing without the informed consent of the individual to be tested. Results must be kept confidential.
Medical Screening	New York State Dep't. of Civil Service "Guide To Job Interviewing," FEP Manual (BNA) 455:3171 (1982).	Consideration of I.Q. in hiring is illegal. One cannot refuse to hire on the grounds that an individual is or was under the care of a doctor for physical or psychological therapy.
Monitoring/ Surveillance	Chenkin v. Bellevue Hosp. Center, 479 F. Supp. 207 (S.D.N.Y. 1979).	A public hospital's policy of conducting random spot inspections of employees' packages as employees are leaving the building does not violate the Fourth Amendment despite an employee's actual subjective expectation of

privacy in his knapsack and contents, and the hospital announcement of the inspection policy does not render such expectation of privacy unreasonable.

N.Y. Lab. Law § 201-a (McKinney 1986).

No person may be required to be fingerprinted as a job prerequisite or as a condition of continued employment. The statute excludes public employees.

DeLury v. Kretchmer, 66 Misc. 2d 897, 322 N.Y.S.2d 517 (1971).

Sanitation employees' rights to privacy were not invaded where pictures of them are taken without their permission to be shown to witnesses who claimed that sanitation employees are collecting waste from commercial enterprises for their own remuneration.

Personal Relationships

Campbell Plastics, Inc. v. N.Y. State Human Rights Appeal Bd., 81 A.D.2d 991, 440 N.Y.S.2d 73 (1981).

Employer's refusal to hire an applicant because her husband is already an employee was lawful and does not constitute discrimination based upon marital status.

Employee Records

N.Y. Exec. Law § 296(16) (McKinney Supp. 1987).

It shall be an unlawful discriminatory practice for any person, agency, bureau, or association to make any inquiry about any arrest or criminal accusation of such individual not then pending against the individual.

Carpenter v. City of Plattsburgh, 105 A.D. 295, 484 N.Y.S.2d 284, appeal denied, 64 N.Y.2d 1012, 478 N.E.2d 204, 489 N.Y.S.2d 63 (1985).

New York civil rights law, which protects confidentiality of personnel records of law enforcement officers, creates no private right of action.

Defamation	Loughry v. Lincoln First Bank, N.A., 67 N.Y.2d 369, 494 N.E.2d 70, 502 N.Y.S.2d 965 (1986).	Statements of four security officers alleging that employee used and sold cocaine made in a confidential meeting may be qualifiedly privileged but the privilege was lost because the statements were made with malice. Employer was liable for compensatory damages for slander by its agents, but not for punitive damages because neither employee was a "superior officer" of the company.
	Mandelblatt v. Perelman, 683 F. Supp. 379, 3 IER Cases 857 (S.D.N.Y. 1988).	No claim for defamation may be predicated on letters to discharged employee containing notice of termination and stating management view that employee had engaged in specified misconduct where letters were published only to persons with legitimate job-related interest in receiving them.

NORTH CAROLINA

Polygraphs	Truesdale v. Univ. of North Carolina, 91 N.C. App. 186, 371 S.E.2d 503, 3 IER Cases 1268 (1988), rev. denied, 323 N.C. 706, 377 S.E.2d 229 (1989); Atkins v. City of Greensboro, 39 FEP Cases 424 (M.D.N.C. 1985).	Requiring as a condition of employment that probationary campus security officer answer polygraph examination questions addressing homosexual activity, sexual arousal by viewing children and other unnatural sexual acts would not have violated her right to privacy since named sexual activities are not entitled to protection.
Medical Screening	N.C. Gen. Stat. § 95-28.1 (1985).	Prohibits discrimination against, or the discharge of, any person from employment for having sickle cell anemia.
Employee Records	N.C. Gen. Stat. § 126-23 (1986).	Subject only to rules and regulations for safekeeping of the records adopted by the

state personnel commission, every person having custody of such records shall permit them to be inspected and examined and copies thereof made by any person during regular business hours.

A discharged hospital employee had no claim against the hospital or other employees for invasion of privacy based upon public disclosure of private facts where the other hospital employees stated in an employee meeting that the discharged employee's reason for termination was "lack of credibility."

Nothing shall prevent a public employee from engaging in political activities while not on duty or in uniform.

A state agency may not discriminate against an employee or applicant for employment merely because the spouse of that employee or applicant is also an employee of that state agency. This prohibition does not apply to employment of the spouse of a person who has the power to hire, fire, or make performance evaluations with respect to the position involved.

A former chief of police's personnel file, maintained by the city's director of personnel, was subject to disclosure because it constituted a "public record" within the meaning of article XI, § 6 of the North Dakota

Reasons for Termination	Trought v. Richardson, 78 N.C. App. 758, 338 S.E.2d 617, 1 IER Cases 750, rev. denied, 316 N.C. 557, 344 S.E.2d 18, 1 IER Cases 1040 (1986).

NORTH
DAKOTA

Speech/ Political Activities	N.D. Cent. Code § 44-08-19 (Allen-Smith 1978).
Personal Relation- ships	N.D. Cent. Code ch. 34-11-.111, § 1 (1987).
Employee Records	City of Grand Forks v. Grand Forks Herald, Inc., 307 N.W.2d 572 (N.D. 1981).

Constitution and § 44-04-18 of the North Dakota Century Code.

OHIO

Applicant Investiga-tions	Ohio Rev. Code Ann. § 2953.43(A)-(B) (Anderson 1982).	Applicants for employment may respond to inquiries regarding expunged arrest records as if the arrest did not occur. State officers and employees may not make available for employment purposes any information regarding expunged arrest records.
Employee Records	Ohio Rev. Code Ann. § 4113.23(A) (Anderson 1973).	No employer or physician shall refuse upon written request of an employee to furnish the employee or former employee or their designated representative a copy of any medical report pertaining to the employee.
	Dispatch Printing Co. v. Wells, 18 Ohio St. 3d 382, 481 N.E.2d 632 (1985).	A newspaper was entitled to reasonable access to all information contained in a former police chief's personnel files following his demotion to detective, which could be released under a statute governing public records.
	Levias v. United Airlines, 27 Ohio App. 3d 222, 500 N.E.2d 370 (1985).	Airline's medical examiner wrongfully disclosed medical information regarding the reasons for a flight attendant's waiver of weight limits to a male supervisor who had no compelling reason to know that information, in breach of the flight attendant's right of privacy.
Defamation	Rady v. Forest City Enter., Inc., 489 N.E.2d 1090 (Ohio Com. Pl. 1986).	Sufficient evidence supported jury's conclusion that the employer's defamatory statements regarding a former employee were motivated by actual malice.

OKLAHOMA

Right to   Okla. Stat. Ann. tit. 21   Any person, firm, or corporation that uses for
Privacy   § 839.1 (West 1983).   the purposes of advertising for the sale of
                                                    any goods, wares, or merchandise, or for the
                                                    solicitation of patronage by any business
                                                    enterprise, the name, portrait, or picture of
                                                    any person, without having obtained the
                                                    consent of such person, is guilty of a
                                                    misdemeanor.

                  Eddy v. Brown, 715 P.2d 74   The fact that limited numbers of co-workers
                  (Okla. 1986).   heard that employee was undergoing psychiatric
                                                    treatment did not amount to publicity in sense
                                                    of disclosure to general public, and thus the
                                                    employer's disclosures were not actionable.

Monitoring/   Simmons v. Southwestern Bell   An employer did not invade a former employee's
Surveil-   Tel. Co., 452 F. Supp. 392   constitutional right to privacy where the
lance   (W.D. Okla. 1978), aff'd,   employer monitored employee's telephone
                  611 F.2d 342 (10th Cir.   conversations at a "test desk" telephone where
                  1979).   the employee was informed that the telephones
                                                    would be monitored.

Personal   Okla. Stat. Ann. tit. 70,   Oklahoma law prohibiting teachers from
Relation-   § 6-103.15 (West Supp.   advocating public or private homosexual
ships   1987); Board of Education v.   activity was unconstitutional. Oklahoma law
                  Nat'l Gay Task Force, 470   now authorizes the dismissal of teachers and
                  U.S. 903, 105 S. Ct. 1858,   school personnel who have engaged in sodomy,
                  37 FEP Cases 505 (1985).   or who solicit or impose sodomy during school,
                                                    if this activity "has impeded the
                                                    effectiveness" of the teacher's work
                                                    performance.

Reasons for Termination	Okla. Stat. Ann. tit. 40, § 171 (West 1986).	Public service corporations and their contractors are required to provide a discharged employee with a service letter stating the duration and nature of their services.

OREGON

Right to Privacy	Bodewig v. K-Mart, Inc., 54 Or. App. 480, 635 P.2d 657 (1981), rev. denied, 292 Or. 450, 644 P.2d 1128 (1982).	An applicant could submit to the jury the question of whether the conduct of an employer's manager exceeded the bounds of social tolerance when the manager, a 32-year-old male who after concluding that the employee did not take the customer's money, put her through a degrading and humiliating experience of submitting to a strip search in order to satisfy a customer.
Drug Testing	Ass'n of Western Pulp and Paper Workers v. Boise Cascade Corp., 644 F. Supp. 183, 1 IER Cases 1072 (D. Ore. 1986).	Court upheld an employer's program requiring employees involved in on-the-job accidents to submit to drug and alcohol testing when reporting an injury on a worker's compensation claim, despite a contention that such requirements violate an Oregon statute forbidding discrimination against workers who apply for benefits or invoke the procedures of the statute.
Polygraphs	Or. Rev. Stat. § 659.225 (1985).	No person shall require a a condition for employment or continuation of employment any person or employee to take a breathalyzer test, polygraph test, or any other form of lie detection test.
AIDS Testing	Or. Admin. R. 333-12-265(1); 333-12-265(3) (1988).	Requires confidentiality of AIDS test results as well as consent before testing.

Monitoring/ Surveil- lance	Or. Rev. Stat. § 181.555 (1985).	Describes the procedures governing disclosure by the state of criminal offender information regarding any conviction or arrests less than one year old on which there has been no acquittal or dismissal.
	Hall v. May Dep't. Stores Co., 292 Or. 131, 637 P.2d 126 (1981).	A department store employee, accused of theft by her employer, was threatened and interrogated in an attempt to force a confession from the employee of stealing. The court found that the "cold-blooded tactic of interrogation upon scanty evidence" could support a recovery for the tort of outrage.
	McLain v. Boise Cascade Corp., 271 Or. 549, 533 P.2d 343 (1975).	An employee seeking worker's compensation waives his right of privacy to the extent of a reasonable investigation by employer or his agents regarding the employee's alleged injury. Any surveillance by the employer or his agents must be conducted in a reasonable and unobtrusive manner.
Personal Relation- ships	Or. Rev. Stat. § 659.340 (1981).	It is an unlawful employment practice for an employer to refuse to hire or employ an individual solely because another member of an individual's family works or has worked for that employer.
	Patton v. J.C. Penney Co., 301 Or. 117, 719 P.2d 854 (1986); Karren v. Far West Fed. Savings, 79 Or. App. 131, 717 P.2d 1271, rev. denied, 301 Or. 666, 725 P.2d 1293 (1986).	The employer was not liable for infliction of emotional distress, when the employer fired the employee for refusing to discontinue a relationship with a female co-worker.

Employee Records	Or. Rev. Stat. § 652.750(2) (1981).	At the request of an employee, his employer shall provide a reasonable opportunity for the employee to inspect those personnel records of the employee that are used or have been used to determine the employee's qualifications for employment, promotion, additional compensation, or employment termination.
Defamation	Walsh v. Consolidated Freightways, Inc., 278 Or. 347, 563 P.2d 1205 (1977).	A former employer has a qualified privilege to make statements about the character or conduct of his employees to present or prospective employers. However, this privilege is not absolute.

PENNSYLVANIA

Right to Privacy	Wells v. Thomas, 569 F. Supp. 426 (E.D. Pa. 1983).	Alleged disclosure of terms of plaintiff's separation agreement, entered into between personnel director and university hospital, to other hospital employees did not constitute requisite level of publicity required to state a valid claim for invasion of privacy by publicity given to private life.
Speech/ Political Activities	Novosel v. Nationwide Ins. Co., 721 F.2d 894, 1 IER Cases 286 (3d Cir. 1983).	Former employee's allegation of discharge for refusal to participate in former employer's lobbying effort and his privately stated opposition to company's political stand stated a claim for wrongful discharge.
Drug Testing	Amalgamated Transit Union, Div. 1279 v. Cambria Transit Auth., 691 F. Supp. 898, 4 IER Cases 22 (W.D. Pa. 1988).	City bus drivers and mechanics are denied preliminary injunctions as to mandatory drug testing during annual physical exams. Additional intrusion is minimal and does not affront any reasonable expectation of bodily

		integrity since examinations already included blood and urine testing and government's interest in public safety justified this intrusion.
Polygraphs	Pa. Stat. Ann. tit. 18 § 7321 (Purdon 1983 & Supp. 1987); Pa. Stat. Ann. tit. 18 § 7507 (Purdon 1983); Anderson v. Philadelphia, 845 F.2d 1216, 3 IER Cases 353 (3d Cir. 1988); Smith v. Greyhound Lines, Inc., 614 F. Supp. 558 (W.D. Pa. 1984), aff'd, 800 F.2d 1139 (3d Cir. 1986); Molush v. Orkin Exterminating Co., 547 F. Supp. 54 (E.D. Pa. 1982); Polsky v. Radio Shack, 666 F.2d 824 (3d Cir. 1981); Perks v. Firestone Tire & Rubber Co., 611 F.2d 1363 (3d Cir. 1979).	An employer, public or private, may not "require" an employee or other individual to submit to a lie detector test as a condition of employment, with a few exceptions, e.g., public law enforcement or employees who dispense or have access to narcotics and dangerous drugs. The statute embodies a recognized facet of public policy and provides a wrongful discharge tort cause of action for at-will employees.
Applicant Investigations	Pa. Stat. Ann. tit. 18 § 9125 (Purdon 1983).	Whenever an employer is in receipt of information that is part of an employment applicant's criminal history record information file, it may use that information for the purposes of deciding whether to hire the applicant.
	Fraternal Order of Police, Lodge No. 5 v. City of Philadelphia, 812 F.2d 105, 1 IER Cases 1496 (3d Cir. 1987).	Questions in application for police department's special investigation unit pertaining to applicant's physical and mental condition, financial status, gambling habits, and alcohol consumption, and arrest records

Monitoring/ Surveil- lance	did not unconstitutionally infringe upon applicant's privacy interest.
Spencer v. General Tel. Co., 551 F. Supp. 896 (M.D. Pa. 1982).	Public telephone company's policy requiring employees to sign a form consenting to investigations to screen out security risks did not constitute common law tort of invasion of privacy.
Rogers v. Int'l Business Machines Corp., 500 F. Supp. 867 (W.D. Pa. 1980).	Where the employer's decision to terminate is based on the rationale that the employee's relationship with another employee exceeds reasonable business associations, the employer's investigation (including examination of company records and interviews of employees) does not violate the employee's privacy expectations.
Shuman v. City of Philadelphia, 470 F. Supp. 449 (E.D. Pa. 1979).	In the absence of a showing that a policeman's private, off-duty personal activities have an impact upon his on-the-job performance, the court found that inquiry into those activities violates the constitutionally protected right of privacy.
Vernars v. Young, 539 F.2d 966 (3d Cir. 1976).	The opening of a co-employee's mail and reading it without authority, like intentionally overhearing the telephone conversation of another, is an intrusion on the right to privacy.
Marks v. Bell Tel. Co., 460 Pa. 73, 331 A.2d 424 (1975).	No tort of invasion of privacy is committed in the absence of an intentional overhearing of a private conversation during a wire tap.

Personal Relation- ships	Turner v. Letterkenny Fed. Credit Union, 351 Pa. Super 51, 505 A.2d 259 (1985).	An employee is not wrongfully discharged after warnings from the board that his relationship with his subordinates is extremely disappointing.
	Staats v. Ohio Nat'l Life Ins. Co., 620 F. Supp. 118 (W.D. Pa. 1985).	The court found that the right to associate with a non-spouse at an employer's convention is hardly the kind of threat to "some recognized facet of public policy" viewed by Pennsylvania courts as sufficient to support the tort of wrongful discharge.
Employee Records	Pa. Stat. tit. 43, § 1322 (Purdon Supp. 1986).	An employer shall, at reasonable times, upon request of an employee permit that employee to inspect his or her own personnel files.
	Patton v. Federal Bureau of Investigation, 626 F. Supp. 445 (M.D. Pa. 1985), aff'd, 782 F.2d 1030 (3d Cir. 1986).	Information from a rejected employment applicant's file, which contained material that would not have been revealed where there was a promise of confidentiality, was exempted from disclosure by the Privacy Act, which exempts disclosure of information that reveals the identity of the source who expressly promised that the identity would be held in confidence.
	Duquesne Light Co. v. Commonwealth Unemployment Compensation Bd. of Review, 82 Pa. Commw. 34, 474 A.2d 407 (1984).	An employee's exercise of his legally protected right under the Federal Privacy Act not to disclose medical information required for renewal of his nuclear control operator's license cannot disqualify the employee for unemployment compensation benefits where the employer discharged rather than transferred him to another position.

Defamation	Geyer v. Steinbronn, 351 Pa. Super. 536, 506 A.2d 901 (1986).	Employer's statements about a former employee were defamatory because the employer acted with malice.
	Krochalis v. Insurance Co. of North America, 629 F. Supp. 1360 (E.D. Pa. 1985).	Employer's statements to co-workers that employee was terminated for fraudulent activity were subject to qualified privilege. Employer and co-workers had common business interest in insuring propriety in the conduct of employer's affairs.
	Elbeshbeshy v. Franklin Inst., 618 F. Supp. 170 (E.D. Pa. 1985).	Employee who sued for defamation, after employer cited "lack of cooperation" as the reason for his termination on employee's record, has stated viable cause of action.

PUERTO RICO

Speech/ Political Activities	P.R. Laws Ann. tit. 29, §§ 146, 136 (1985).	Prohibits the discharge of an employee because of political beliefs and political affiliation. The aggrieved employee can sue for double damages, in addition to reinstatement.
Defamation	Vargas v. Royal Bank of Canada, 604 F. Supp. 1036 (D.P.R. 1985).	The bank's communication to other employees to the effect that the employees had been indefinitely suspended was held to be privileged, since the communication had been made to persons within the business association.

RHODE ISLAND

Right to Privacy	R.I. Gen. Laws § 9-1-28.1 (Michie Supp. 1983).	It is the policy of this state that every person shall have the right to privacy, which includes the right to be secure from

Speech/ Political Activities	R.I. Gen. Laws § 17-23-6 (1981).	unreasonable intrusion upon one's physical solitude, the right to be secure from an appropriation of one's name, the right to be secure from unreasonable publicity, and the right to be secure from publicity that reasonably places another in a false light. It is a felony for an employer to attempt to influence the political actions or opinions of employees by threats, arguments, or statements.
Polygraphs	R.I. Gen. Laws § 28-6.1-1 (1986).	No employer or agent shall request, require, or subject any employee or person applying for employment to any lie detector tests as a condition of employment or continued employment.
Applicant Investiga- tions	R.I. Gen. Laws § 28-5-7G (Supp. 1985).	An employer may not inquire about information regarding an applicant's prior arrests or criminal charges. An employer may ask an applicant about criminal convictions.
Honesty Testing	R.I. Stat. § 28-6.1-1 (1986).	Prohibits any employer from using any lie detector tests as a condition of employment. "Lie detector test" includes any device, mechanism, instrument or written examination which is operated, or the results of which are used or interpreted by an examiner for the purpose of purporting to assist in or enable the detection of deception, the verification of truthfulness, or the rendering of a diagnostic opinion regarding the honesty of an individual.

AIDS Testing	R.I. Gen. Laws § 23-6-12 (1989).	Permits testing without consent if result is not identified with a particular individual.
Monitoring/ Surveillance	R.I. Gen. Laws § 28-7-13(1) (1986). A	It is an unfair labor practice for an employer to spy upon or keep under surveillance employees or their representatives in exercise of their rights and to engage in connected activities under § 28-7-17 to self-organization collective bargaining.
Employee Records	R.I. Gen. Laws § 28-6.4-1 (1986).	Every employer shall, after a written, seven days advance notice, permit an employee to inspect his personnel files.
	R.I. Gen. Laws § 5-37.3-4 (Supp. 1986).	Except as otherwise provided in this act, a patient's confidential health care information shall not be released or transferred without the written consent of such patient.
Defamation	Swanson v. Speidel Corp., 110 R.I. 335, 293 A.2d 307 (1972).	A qualified privilege protects intra-company communications, including a written termination notice sent by plaintiff's superiors to the personnel department. The same qualified privilege extends to communications to prospective employers.

SOUTH CAROLINA

Right to Privacy	S.C. Const. art. I, § 10 (1971).	"The right of the people to be secure in their houses, persons, papers, and offices against unreasonable searches and seizures and unreasonable invasions of privacy shall not be violated."

Corder v. Champion Road Machinery Int'l Corp., 283 S.C. 520, 324 S.E.2d 79 (S.C. Ct. App. 1984), cert. denied, 286 S.C. 126, 332 S.E.2d 533 (1985).

Alleged threats of discharge did not constitute a cause of action for the invasion of an employee's privacy.

Todd v. South Carolina Farm Bureau Mutual Ins. Co., 276 S.C. 284, 278 S.E.2d 607 (S.C. 1981).

Allegations by former employee that defendants wrongfully accused former employee of leaking information from an investigation of fire loss claims to an arsonist, supported former employee's cause of action against defendants for invasion of his right of privacy.

Speech/Political Activities

S.C. Code of Laws § 16-17-560 (Law. Co-Op. 1985).

Whosoever shall assault or intimidate any citizen because of political opinion or the exercise of political rights and privileges guaranteed to every citizen of the United States by the Constitution and laws thereof shall be guilty of a misdemeanor.

Drug Testing

Satterfield v. Lockheed Missiles and Space Co., 617 F. Supp. 1359 (D.S.C. 1985).

An employer did not invade an at-will employee's right to privacy when the employee was terminated based on a positive urinalysis to detect drug use. The only publication of the test results and the reason for termination were made by the employee.

Personal Relationships

Hamilton v. Bd. of Trustees, 282 S.C. 519, 319 S.E.2d 717 (S.C. Ct. App. 1984).

Former school teacher failed to show that nepotism policy substantially interfered with her right to marry and lost her suit seeking to be rehired.

Defamation

Tyler v. Macks Stores, 275 S.C. 456, 272 S.E.2d 633 (1980).

Employee who was discharged after he submitted to a polygraph test can allege sufficient legal basis for defamation suit based on the

SOUTH DAKOTA

Employee Records

S.D. Codified Laws Ann. § 3-6A-31 (1985).

Any records required or maintained by the bureau of personnel that pertain to an employee must be available and open to inspection by an employee during normal business working hours.

Defamation

Ruple v. Weinaug, 328 N.W.2d 857 (S.D. 1983).

A communication sent by a city manager to a mayor with respect to a finance officer's problems was privileged.

TENNESSEE

Drug Testing

Tenn. Code Ann. tit. 41, ch. 1, § 1 (1988).

The Commissioner of Correction shall have the authority to require security personnel employed by the Dept. of Corrections to submit to drug tests where there is a reasonable suspicion based upon specific objective facts that the employee is under the influence of drugs.

Polygraphs

Tenn. Code Ann. § 62-27-123 (Supp. 1986).

Limits the scope of polygraph examinations by making it unlawful for the examiner to inquire into the examinee's beliefs or opinions regarding religion, politics, racial or union matters, or his sexual preference or activities, unless the examination is given as the result of an investigation into the examinee's illegal activity in one of those areas.

possibility that other fellow employees might infer he was discharged for a wrongful activity.

Tenn. Code Ann. § 62-27-125 (1986).

Each prospective polygraph examinee shall be required to sign a notification prior to the examination that acknowledges his or her consent to the examination and his or her knowledge of the right to refuse testing.

Tenn. Code Ann. § 62-27-128 (Michie 1986).

Provides that no employer may take any adverse personnel action based solely on the results of a polygraph examination.

Int'l Union v. Garner, 601 F. Supp. 187 (M.D. Tenn. 1985); Beard v. Akzona, Inc., 517 F. Supp. 128 (E.D. Tenn. 1981).

Employees, who were also union organizers, unsuccessfully brought an action for invasion of privacy alleging that their managers and police officers engaged in surveillance of union meetings and conveyed information regarding identity of persons attending meetings to their employers.

Employee Records

Tenn. Code Ann. § 8-50-108 (1981).

Any state employee is entitled access, at any reasonable time, to his personnel files.

TEXAS

Drug Testing

Texas Employment Comm'n v. Hughes Drilling Fluids, 746 S.W.2d 796, 3 IER Cases 451 (Tex. Ct. App. 1988).

Employer's mandatory urine drug screening policy does not violate employee's right of privacy under Texas common law because employee, by remaining on the job, consented to screening, thereby forfeiting his "right to be let alone" in the workplace.

Polygraphs

Tex. Civ. Stat. art. 4413 (29cc) (Vernon Supp. 1987).

A polygraph examiner must inform an employee that a test is voluntary.

Talent v. City of Abilene, 508 S.W.2d 592 (Tex. 1974); Gulden v. McCorkle, 680 F.2d

Court reversed and reinstated a fireman who was dismissed for failure to submit to polygraph after he was charged with a crime

Category	Citation	Description
	1070 (5th Cir. 1982), cert. denied, 459 U.S. 1206, 103 S. Ct. 1194 (1983).	not relating to the performance of a fireman's official duties or to his accounting for his public trust.
	Texas State Employees Union v. Texas Dept. of Mental Health, 746 S.W.2d 303, 2 IER Cases 1077 (Tex. 1987).	Privacy rights protected by the constitution barred the Texas Department of Mental Health and Mental Retardation from administering mandatory polygraph tests to employees during the investigation of drug and alcohol charges.
Applicant Investigations	Tex. Rev. Civ. Stat. art. 6252-17a (Vernon Supp. 1987).	Any institution of higher education is entitled to obtain criminal history record information pertaining to an applicant for a security-sensitive position.
AIDS Testing	Tex. Stat. Ann. art. 44196-1, §§ 9.01-9.06 (1987).	A person may not require another person to undergo any medical procedure or test for AIDS unless it is necessary as a bona fide occupational qualification and there exists no less discriminatory means of satisfying the occupational qualification.
Monitoring/ Surveillance	K-Mart Corp. Store No. 7441 v. Trotti, 677 S.W.2d 632 (Tex. Ct. App. 1984).	An employer had created a legitimate expectation of privacy in the locker assigned to an employee, even though employee used his own lock, and thus was not liable for an unconsented-to search of the employee's purse in the locker.
Personal Relationships	Tex. Stat. Ann. art. 5996a, § 1 (1987).	No officer of this state shall appoint, or vote for, or confirm the appointment to any office of any person related within the second degree by affinity or within the third degree by consanguinity to the person so appointing or voting.

Collier v. Civil Serv. Comm'n, 764 S.W.2d 364 (Tex. Ct. App. 1989).

Summary judgment denied to city fire department in suit challenging city's "nepotism rule" which precluded any person from being employed if any member of that person's immediate family was already a member of the department.

Defamation — Frank B. Hall & Co. v. Buck, 678 S.W.2d 612 (Tex. Ct. App. 1984), cert. denied, 472 U.S. 1009, 105 S. Ct. 2704 (1985).

After termination, former employee brought defamation action claiming his reputation had been injured when the employer made derogatory statements to the investigator. The court concluded there was ample evidence of ill will toward the former employee, from which the jury concluded that the statements were made in reckless disregard of the truth.

Reasons for Termination — Tex. Rev. Civ. Stat. Ann. art. 5196f (1987).

Provides that a corporate employee who is discharged is entitled to a service letter from the employer stating the reasons for the discharge, but the contents of this letter cannot be made the basis of a libel claim against the employer furnishing it.

UTAH

Right to Privacy — Utah Code Ann. § 45-33 (Allen-Smith 1982).

The personal identity of an individual has been abused if an advertisement is published in which the personal identity of that individual is used in a manner that implies the individual endorses the product, and consent has not been obtained for such use from the individual.

Speech/Political Activities — Utah Code Ann. § 20-13-6 (1984).

It is a misdemeanor for an employer to make threats in order to influence an employee's political opinions or actions.

Topic	Citation	Description
Drug Testing	Utah Code Ann. § 34-38-1 (Supp. 1987).	The legislature finds that fair and equitable testing for drug and alcohol in the workplace is in the best interests of all parties.
Polygraphs	Utah Code Ann. § 34-37-16 (Supp. 1986).	An employee's refusal to take a deception detection test cannot be the basis for an employer's decision to terminate.
Personal Relation- ships	Utah Code Ann. § 52-3-1 (1987).	No public officer may employ, appoint, or vote for a relative to any position when the salary, wages, pay, or compensation of the appointee will be paid from public funds and the appointee will be directly supervised by a relative except in limited circumstances.
Employee Records	Utah Code Ann. § 67-18-1 (1977).	Public employees have the right to examine and make copies of documents in their personnel files. Documents classified as "confidential" may not be copied or examined.
	KUTV, Inc. v. Utah State Bd. of Educ., 689 P.2d 1357 (Utah 1984).	The results of a survey administered to school personnel, which were designed to elicit responses concerning discrimination in high school, were considered "public records" and therefore subject to disclosure.

VERMONT

Topic	Citation	Description
Drug Testing	Vt. Stat. Ann. tit. 21 §§ 511-520 (1987).	An employer shall not as a condition of employment, promotion, or change of status of employment request or require that an employee or applicant for employment take or submit to a drug test unless statutory exception applies.

Polygraphs	Vt. Stat. Ann. tit. 21, § 494b (Supp. 1986).	Employers may not require employees to take a polygraph as a condition of employment or change in status of employment. Exemption for police and sheriff departments, any employer authorized or required by federal law or regulations to administer polygraph examinations.
AIDS Testing	Vt. Stat. Ann. tit. 18, § 1128 (1988).	It shall be an unfair labor practice for an employer to request or require an applicant or employee to have an HIV-related blood test as a condition of employment.
	Vt. Stat. Ann. tit. 21, § 495 (1988).	Prohibits AIDS testing as a condition of employment.
Employee Records	Vt. Stat. Ann. tit. 1, § 317(b)(7) (1985).	Personnel files are not considered "public records" and are therefore not subject to inspection by any person other than the employee to which the files pertain or his or her designated representative.
VIRGINIA		
Right to Privacy	Va. Code Ann. § 8.01-40 (1984); Brown v. American Broadcasting Co., 704 F.2d 1296 (4th Cir. 1983).	Prohibits the use of a person's name, portrait, or picture without his consent, for commercial purposes.
	Ponton v. Newport News School Bd., 632 F. Supp. 1056, 42 FEP Cases 83 (E.D. Va. 1986).	School district's interest in protecting children from exposure to an unmarried, pregnant teacher does not outweigh the teacher's privacy interest in exercising her constitutional right to bear children out of wedlock, even if school district's interest was legitimate.

Topic	Citation	Description
Polygraphs	Va. Code Ann. § 40.1-51.4:3 (1981).	No employer shall require a prospective employee to answer questions in a polygraph test concerning the prospective employee's sexual activities unless such sexual activity has resulted in a conviction of a violation of the criminal laws of Virginia.
Applicant Investigations	Va. Code Ann. § 19.2-392.4 A and B (1983).	An employer shall not in any application or investigation require an applicant for employment to disclose information concerning an arrest or criminal charge against him that has been expunged.
AIDS Testing	Core v. United States Postal Serv., 730 F.2d 964 (4th Cir. 1984).	Freedom of Information Act required release of requested information about successful applicants, but exemption for personnel, medical, and similar files precluded disclosure of information about other applicants.
	Plowman v. Dept of Army, 698 F. Supp. 627, 3 IER Cases 1665 (E.D. Va. 1988).	Army colonel who disclosed to federal officials that civilian employee he supervised had tested positive for HIV did not violate employee's constitutional right to privacy since officer's limited disclosure to Army personnel with responsibility for employee's health was no broader than reasonably necessary to determine how to proceed in sensitive situation.
Employee Records	Va. Code Ann. § 6.1-377 (1983).	Provides rules for maintenance, use, and dissemination of personal information.

Defamation	Great Coastal Express, Inc. v. Ellington, 230 Va. 142, 334 S.E.2d 846 (1985).	Employer's statement that it discharged employee for bribery constituted slander per se because the employer accused the employee of an offense involving moral turpitude.

VIRGIN ISLANDS

Polygraphs	Robinson v. Hess Oil Virgin Islands Corp., 19 V.I. 106 (1982).	An employee may file a wrongful discharge action claiming his employer fired him based on the results of a negligently administered polygraph examination.
Employee Records	V.I. Code Ann. tit. 24, § 422 (Supp. 1985).	Upon request, an employer is required to make an employee's personnel file available to him for inspection at reasonable times.

WASHINGTON

Right to Privacy	Wash. Const. art. I, § 7.	"No person shall be disturbed in his private affairs, or have his home invaded, without authority of law."
	Eastwood v. Cascade Broadcasting Co., 106 Wash. 2d 466, 722 P.2d 1295 (1986).	A plaintiff need not be defamed in order to bring a false light invasion of privacy action. It is enough that he is given unreasonable and highly objectionable publicity that attributes to him characteristics, conduct, or beliefs that are false, thereby placing him before the public in a false position.
Drug Testing	Alverado v. Washington Public Power Supply System, 111 Wash. 2d 424, 759 P.2d 427, 3 IER Cases 769 (1988),	In industries that are subject to extensive government regulation, employees have a diminished expectation of privacy and may be tested for drugs and alcohol despite the

absence of a reasonable basis for individualized suspicion.

cert. denied, 109 S. Ct. 1637, 4 IER Cases 352 (1989).

Polygraphs

Wash. Rev. Code Ann. § 49.44.120 and § 49.44.130 (Supp. 1987).

Employers are prohibited from requiring that employees take a lie detector test as a condition of employment. The statute does not apply to applicants for law enforcement jobs or to employees who manufacture, distribute, or dispense controlled substances or who have sensitive positions directly involving national security.

Stone v. Chelan County Sheriff's Dept., 110 Wash. 2d 806, 756 P.2d 736, 3 IER Cases 793 (1988).

city jailor who requested transfer to county sheriff's office after his job was terminated is "making initial application for employment" so as to fall within exception to Washington law that prohibits requiring polygraph test as condition of employment.

AIDS Testing

Wash. Rev. Code § 49.60.172 (1988).

Prohibits AIDS testing as a condition of employment or termination of an employee based on results of HIV test unless absence of HIV virus is a bona fide occupational qualification.

Personal Relation-ships

Trumbauer v. Group Health Co-op., 635 F. Supp. 543 (W.D. Wash. 1986).

Employer that allegedly knew about probationary employee's relationship with his supervisor when the employee was hired and that allegedly had not enforced its anti-nepotism policy against other employees was not estopped from discharging the probationary employee based upon his relationship with the supervisor, where employee was terminable at will.

| Employee Records | Wash. Rev. Code. § ch. 49.12.240 (West Supp. 1987). | Every employer shall, at least annually, permit the requesting employee to inspect any or all of his or her own personnel files. |
| | *Jeffers v. City of Seattle,* 23 Wash. App. 301, 597 P.2d 899 (1979). | A former police officer, by requesting a disability pension and its continuation, waived his right of privacy pertaining to his medical condition, providing investigation was of such condition as carried out in a reasonable manner. |

WEST VIRGINIA

Speech/ Political Activities	W. Va. Code § 3-8-11 (1987).	It is a misdemeanor for an employer to threaten an employee intending to influence the employee's political views or actions.
Polygraphs	W. Va. Code § 21-5-5b (1985).	No public or private employer can require an employee to submit to a polygraph test. This prohibition does not apply to employers who are law enforcement agencies or state military forces, or who manufacture or distribute drugs.
	Cordle v. General Hugh Mercer Corp., 325 S.E.2d 111 (W. Va. 1984).	It is contrary to the public policy of West Virginia for an employer to require or request that an employee submit to a polygraph test or similar test as a condition of employment.
AIDS Testing	W. Va. Code §§ 16-3C-1 to 16-3C-4 (1988).	Provides for mandatory testing under enumerated circumstances and requires confidentiality of test results.
Employee Records	*Davis v. Monsanto,* 627 F. Supp. 418 (S.D. W. Va. 1986).	The employer's limited disclosure of confidential information concerning an employee's psychiatric condition was

privileged where the safety of other employees was involved. There was also insufficient publicity to establish cause of action for public disclosure of private facts.

W. Va. Code § 29B-1-4(3) (1988).

Records of law enforcement agencies are exempt from the state Freedom of Information Act.

WISCONSIN

Right to Privacy

Wis. Stat. Ann. § 895.50 (West 1983).

Provides a statutory right to privacy, as stated in Restatement (Second) of Torts § 652 (1977) and sets forth the relief available when the right to privacy is violated.

Hirsch v. S.C. Johnson & Son, Inc., 90 Wis. 2d 379, 280 N.W.2d 129 (1979).

A cause of action for appropriation of a person's name for commercial use exists as a matter of Wisconsin common law.

Speech/ Political Activities

Bushko v. Miller Brewing Co., 134 Wis. 2d 136, 396 N.W.2d 167 (1986); Schultz v. Industrial Coils, Inc., 125 Wis. 2d 520, 373 N.W.2d 74 (Wis. Ct. App. 1985); Harman v. La Crosse Tribune, 117 Wis. 2d 448, 344 N.W.2d 536 (Wis. Ct. App.), cert. denied, 469 U.S. 803, 105 S. Ct. 58 (1984).

Terminated employee did not have wrongful discharge cause of action against employer merely because discharge may have been attributable to employee's complaints concerning public policy matters; employee conceded that employer had not required him to violate any constitutional or statutory provision.

Polygraphs

Wis. Stat. Ann. § 942.06 (West 1982).

An employer may not "require" or "administer" a polygraph examination or any similar test to detect honesty without prior written and informed consent of the subject.

Wis. Stat. Ann. § 111.37(1)(a),(b) (West Supp. 1986).

An employer may not subject an employee or prospective employee to honesty-testing devices such as polygraph, voice stress analysis, or psychological stress evaluations. The use of devices that can record a person's cardiovascular or respiratory pattern is permissible, however, for the purposes of verifying truthfulness or detecting deception.

AIDS Testing

Wis. Stat. Ann. § 103.15(2)(a) (West Supp. 1986).

No employer may, directly or indirectly, solicit or require as a condition of employment of any employee or prospective employee to submit to a test to discover the presence of HIV-III.

Personal Relation- ships

Wis. Stat. Ann. § 111.321 (West Supp. 1986).

Prohibits the termination of an employee on the basis of sexual orientation.

Ward v. Frito-Lay, Inc., 95 Wis. 2d 372, 290 N.W.2d 536 (Wis. Ct. App. 1980).

A male employee was fired because his relationship with a female employee, with whom he was living, was resulting in employee comment, insubordination, and the filing of a grievance at the employer's plant. In characterizing the discharge as a "business judgment," the court found that there was no intimidation by the employer, nor did the employer act in bad faith.

Employee Records

Wis. Stat. Ann. § 103.13(2) (West Supp. 1986).

Provides an employee the right to inspect personnel documents.

WYOMING

Speech/Political Activities

Wyo. Stat. § 22-26-112; § 22-26-116 (1977).

It is a misdemeanor for an employer to interfere with the "political rights" of employees, or to discharge an employee because of his nomination for or election to political office.

Personal Relationships

Board of Trustees v. Holso, 584 P.2d 1009 (Wyo.), reh. denied, 587 P.2d 203 (Wyo. 1978).

A school superintendent's recommendation to terminate a teacher because of the teacher's alleged immorality violated the teacher's constitutional right to privacy.

Employee Records

Wyo. Stat. Ann. § 7-19-101 (1988).

The Wyoming Criminal History Records Act applies to records of any criminal justice agency. Information may be disclosed to other criminal justice agencies, other governmental agencies as authorized by law or executive order, or to the person who is the subject of the record. Records may also be released upon satisfactory proof that the subject consents to the release and the application is made through a criminal justice agency. Such requests must be accompanied by the subject's fingerprints.

APPENDIX B

SELECTED CASES

Skinner v. Railway Labor Executives' Association
B-3

National Treasury Employees Union v. Von Raab
B-23

Consolidated Rail Corp. v. Railway Labor Executives' Association
B-35

SKINNER v. RLEA

Supreme Court of the United States

SKINNER, Secretary of Transportation, et al. v. RAILWAY LABOR EXECUTIVES' ASSOCIATION, et al., No. 87-1555, March 21, 1989

Before REHNQUIST, Chief Justice, and BRENNAN, WHITE, MARSHALL, BLACKMUN, STEVENS, O'CONNOR, SCALIA, and KENNEDY, Justices.

Full Text of Opinion

JUSTICE KENNEDY delivered the opinion of the Court.

The Federal Railroad Safety Act of 1970 authorizes the Secretary of Transportation to "prescribe, as necessary, appropriate rules, regulations, orders, and standards for all areas of railroad safety." 84 Stat. 971, 45 U.S.C. §431(a). Finding that alcohol and drug abuse by railroad employees poses a serious threat to safety, the Federal Railroad Administration (FRA) has promulgated regulations that mandate blood and urine test of employees who are involved in certain train accidents. The FRA also has adopted regulations that do not require, but do authorize, railroads to administer breath and urine tests to employees who violate certain safety rules. The question presented by this case is whether these regulations violate the Fourth Amendment.

I

A

The problem of alcohol use on American railroads is as old as the industry itself, and efforts to deter it by carrier rules began at least a century ago. For many years, railroads have prohibited operating employees from possessing alcohol or being intoxicated while on duty, and from consuming alcoholic beverages while subject to being called for duty. More recently, these proscriptions have been expanded to forbid possession or use of certain drugs. These restrictions are embodied in "Rule G," an industry-wide operating rule promulgated by the Association of American Railroads, and are enforced, in various formulations, by virtually every railroad in the country. The customary sanction for Rule G violations is dismissal.

In July 1983, the FRA expressed concern that these industry efforts were not adequate to curb alcohol and drug abuse by railroad employees. The Agency pointed to evidence indicating that on-the-job intoxication was a significant problem in the railroad industry.[1] The Agency also found, after a review of accident investigation reports, that from 1972 to 1983 "the nation's railroads experienced at least 21 significant train accidents involving alcohol or drug use as a probable cause or contributing factor," and that these accidents "resulted in 25 fatalities, 61 non-fatal injuries, and property damage estimated at $19 million (approximately $27 million in 1982 dollars)." 48 Fed. Reg. 30726 (1983). The FRA further identified "an additional 17 fatalities to operating employees working on or around rail rolling stock that involved alcohol or drugs as a contributing factor." *Ibid.* In light of these problems, the Agency solicited comments from interested parties on various regulatory approaches to the problems of alcohol and drug abuse throughout the Nation's railroad system.

Comments submitted in response to this request indicated that railroads were able to detect a relatively small number of Rule G violations, owing, primarily, to their practice of relying on observation by supervisors and co-workers to enforce the rule. 49 Fed. Reg. 24266-24267 (1984). At the same time, "industry participants ... confirmed that alcohol and drug use [did] occur on the railroads with unacceptable frequency," and available information from all sources "suggest[ed] that the problem includ[ed] 'pockets' of drinking and drug use involving multiple crew members (before and during work), sporadic cases of individuals reporting to work impaired, and repeated drinking and drug use by individual employees who are chemically or psychologically dependent on those substances." *Id.*, at 24253-24254. "Even without the benefit of regular post-accident testing," the Agency "identified 34 fatalities, 66 injuries and over $28 million in property damage (in 1983 dollars) that resulted from the errors of alcohol and drug-impaired employees in 45 train accidents and train incidents during the period 1975 through 1983." *Id.*, at 24254. Some of these accidents resulted in the release of hazardous materials and, in one case, the ensuing pollution required

[1] The FRA noted that a 1979 study examining the scope of alcohol abuse on seven major railroads found that "[a]n estimated one out of every eight railroad workers drank at least once while on duty during the study year." 48 Fed. Reg. 30724 (1983). In addition, "5% of workers reported to work 'very drunk' or got 'very drunk' on duty at least once in the study year," and "13% of workers reported to work at least 'a little drunk' one or more times during that period." *Ibid.* The study also found that 23% of the operating personnel were "problem drinkers," but that only 4% of these employees "were receiving help through an employee assistance program, and even fewer were handled through disciplinary procedures." *Ibid.*

the evacuation of an entire Louisiana community. *Id.,* at 24254, 24259. In view of the obvious safety hazards of drug and alcohol use by railroad employees, the Agency announced in June 1984 its intention to promulgate federal regulations on the subject.

B

After reviewing further comments from representatives of the railroad industry, labor groups, and the general public, the FRA, in 1985, promulgated regulations addressing the problem of alcohol and drugs on the railroads. The final regulations apply to employees assigned to perform service subject to the Hours of Service Act of 1907, ch. 2939, 34 Stat. 1415, 45 U.S.C. §61 *et seq.* The regulations prohibit covered employees from using or possessing alcohol or any controlled substance. 49 CFR §219.101(a)(1) (1987). The regulations further prohibit those employees from reporting for covered service while under the influence or impaired by alcohol, or while having a blood alcohol concentration of .04 or more, or while under the influence of or impaired by any controlled substance. §219.101(a)(2). The regulations do not restrict, however, a railroad's authority to impose an absolute prohibition on the presence of alcohol or any drug in the body fluids of persons in its employ, §219.101(c), and, accordingly, they do not "replace Rule G or render it unenforceable." 50 Fed. Reg. 31538 (1985).

To the extent pertinent here, two subparts of the regulations relate to testing. Subpart C, which is entitled "Post-Accident Toxicological Testing," is mandatory. It provides that railroads "shall take all practicable steps to assure that all covered employees of the railroad directly involved ... provide blood and urine samples for toxicological testing by FRA," §219.203(a), upon the occurrence of certain specified events. Toxicological testing is required following a "major train accident," which is defined as any train accident that involves (i) a fatality, (ii) the release of hazardous material accompanied by an evacuation or a reportable injury, or (iii) damage to railroad property of $500,000. §219.201(a)(1). The railroad has the further duty of collecting blood and urine samples for testing after an "impact accident," which is defined as a collision that results in reportable injury, or in damage to railroad property of $50,000 or more. §219.201(a)(2). Finally, the rail-

road is also obligated to test after "[a]ny train incident that involves a fatality to any on-duty railroad employee." §219.201(a)(3).

After occurrence of an event which activates its duty to test, the railroad must transport all crew members and other covered employees directly involved in the accident or incident to an independent medical facility, where both blood and urine samples must be obtained from each employee.[2] After the samples have been collected, the railroad is required to ship them by prepaid air freight to the FRA laboratory for analysis. §219.205(d). There, the samples are analyzed using "state-of-the-art equipment and techniques"[3] to detect and measure alcohol and drugs.[3] The FRA proposes to place primary reliance on analysis of blood samples, as blood is "the only available body fluid ... that can provide a clear indication not only of the presence of alcohol and drugs but also their current impairment effects." 49 Fed. Reg. 24291 (1984). Urine samples are also necessary, however, because drug traces remain in the urine longer than in blood, and in some cases it will not be possible to transport employees to a medical facility before the time it takes for certain drugs to be eliminated from the bloodstream. In those instances, a "positive urine test, taken with specific information on the pattern of elimination for the particular drug and other information on the behavior of the employee and the circumstances of the accident, may be crucial to the determination of" the cause of an accident. *Ibid.*

The regulations require that the FRA notify employees of the results of the tests and afford them an opportunity to respond in writing before preparation of any final investigative report. See §219.211(a)(2). Employees who

---

[2] The regulations provide a limited exception from testing "if the railroad representative can immediately determine, on the basis of specific information, that the employee had no role in the cause(s) of the accident/incident." 49 CFR 219.203(a)(3)(i) (1987). No exception may be made, however, in the case of a "major train accident." *Ibid.* In promulgating the regulations, the FRA noted that, while it is sometimes possible to exonerate crew members in other situations calling for testing, it is especially difficult to assess fault and degrees of fault in the aftermath of the more substantial accidents. See 50 Fed. Reg. 31544 (1985).

[3] See Federal Railroad Administration, United States Dept. of Transportation Field Manual: Control of Alcohol and Drug Use in Railroad Operations B-12 (1986) (Field Manual). Ethyl alcohol is measured by gas chromatography. *Ibid.* In addition, while drug screens may be conducted by immunoassays or other techniques, "[p]ositive drug findings are confirmed by gas chromatography/mass spectrometry." *Ibid.* These tests, if properly conducted, identify the presence of alcohol and drugs in the biological samples test with great accuracy.

refuse to provide required blood or urine samples may not perform covered service for nine months, but they are entitled to a hearing concerning their refusal to take the test. §219.213.

Subpart D of the regulations, which is entitled "Authorization to Test for Cause," is permissive. It authorizes railroads to require covered employees to submit to breath or urine tests in certain circumstances not addressed by Subpart C. Breath or urine tests, or both, may be ordered (1) after a reportable accident or incident, where a supervisor has a "reasonable suspicion" that an employee's acts or omissions contributed to the occurrence or severity of the accident or incident, §219.301(b)(2); or (2) in the event of certain specific rule violations, including noncompliance with a signal and excessive speeding, §219.301(b)(3). A railroad also may require breath tests where a supervisor has a "reasonable suspicion" that an employee is under the influence of alcohol, based upon specific, personal observations concerning the appearance, behavior, speech, or body odors of the employee. §219.301(b)(1). Where impairment is suspected, a railroad, in addition, may require urine tests, but only if two supervisors make the appropriate determination, §219.301(c)(2)(i), and, where the supervisors suspect impairment due to a substance other than alcohol, at least one of those supervisors must have received specialized training in detecting the signs of drug intoxication. §219.301(c)(2)(ii).

Subpart D further provides that whenever the results of either breath or urine tests are intended for use in a disciplinary proceeding, the employee must be given the opportunity to provide a blood sample for analysis at an independent medical facility. §219.303(c)(1). If an employee declines to give a blood sample, the railroad may presume impairment, absent persuasive evidence to the contrary, from a positive showing of controlled substance residues in the urine. The railroad must, however, provide detailed notice of this presumption to its employees, and advise them of their right to provide a contemporaneous blood sample. As in the case of samples procured under Subpart C, the regulations set forth procedures for the collection of samples, and require that samples "be analyzed by a method that is reliable within known tolerances." §219.307(b).

C

Respondents, the Railway Labor Executives' Association and various of its member labor organizations, brought the instant suit in the United States District Court for the Northern District of California, seeking to enjoin the FRA's regulations on various statutory and constitutional grounds. In a ruling from the bench, the District Court granted summary judgment in petitioners' favor. The court concluded that railroad employees "have a valid interest in the integrity of their own bodies" that deserved protection under the Fourth Amendment. App. to Pet. for Cert. 53a. The court held, however, that this interest was outweighed by the competing "public and governmental interest in the . . . promotion of . . . railway safety, safety for employees, and safety for the general public that is involved with the transportation." Id., at 52a. The District Court found respondents' other constitutional and statutory arguments meritless.

A divided panel of the Court of Appeals for the Ninth Circuit reversed. 839 F.2d 575 [2 IER Cases 1601] (1988). The court held, first, that tests mandated by a railroad in reliance on the authority conferred by Subpart D involve sufficient government action to implicate the Fourth Amendment, and that the breath, blood, and urine tests contemplated by the FRA regulations are Fourth Amendment searches. The court also "agre[ed] that the exigencies of testing for the presence of alcohol and drugs in blood, urine or breath require prompt action which precludes obtaining a warrant." id., at 583. The court further held "that accommodation of railroad employees' privacy interest with the significant safety concerns of the government does not require adherence to a probable cause requirement," and, accordingly, that the legality of the searches contemplated by the FRA regulations depends on their reasonableness under all the circumstances. Id., at 587.

The court concluded, however, that particularized suspicion is essential to a finding that toxicological testing of railroad employees is reasonable. Ibid. A requirement of individualized suspicion, the court stated, would impose "no insuperable burden on the government," id., at 588, and would ensure that the tests are confined to the detection of current impairment, rather than to the discovery of "the metabolites of various drugs, which are not evidence of current intoxication and may remain in the body for days or weeks after the ingestion of the drug." Id., at 588-589. Except for the provisions authorizing breath and urine tests on a "reasonable suspicion" of drug or alcohol impairment, 49 CFR §219.301(b)(1) and (c)(2) (1987), the FRA regulations did not require a showing of individualized suspicion, and, accordingly, the court invalidated them.

Judge Alarcon dissented. He criticized the majority for "fail[ing] to engage in [a] balancing of interests" and for focusing instead "solely on the degree of impairment of the workers' privacy interests." 839 F.2d, at 597. The dissent would have held "that the government's compelling need to assure railroad safety by controlling drug use among railway personnel outweighs the need to protect privacy interests." *Id.*, at 596.

We granted the Government's petition for a writ of certiorari, 486 U.S. — (1988), to consider whether the regulations invalidated by the Court of Appeals violate the Fourth Amendment. We now reverse.

II

The Fourth Amendment provides that "[t]he right of the people to be secure in their persons, houses, papers, and effects, against unreasonable searches and seizures, shall not be violated...." The Amendment guarantees the privacy, dignity, and security of persons against certain arbitrary and invasive acts by officers of the Government or those acting at their direction. *Camara* v. *Municipal Court*, 387 U.S. 523, 528 (1967). See also *Delaware* v. *Prouse*, 440 U.S. 648, 653-654 (1979); *United States* v. *Martinez-Fuerte*, 428 U.S. 543, 554 (1976). Before we consider whether the tests in question are reasonable under the Fourth Amendment, we must inquire whether the tests are attributable to the Government or its agents, and whether they amount to searches or seizures. We turn to those matters.

A

[1] Although the Fourth Amendment does not apply to a search or seizure, even an arbitrary one, effected by a private party on his own initiative, the Amendment protects against such intrusions if the private party acted as an instrument or agent of the Government. See *United States* v. *Jacobsen*, 466 U.S. 109, 113-114 (1984); *Coolidge* v. *New Hampshire*, 403 U.S. 443, 487 (1971). See also *Burdeau* v. *McDowell*, 256 U.S. 465, 475 (1921). A railroad that complies with the provisions of Subpart C of the regulations does so by compulsion of sovereign authority, and the lawfulness of its acts is controlled by the Fourth Amendment. Petitioners contend, however, that the Fourth Amendment is not implicated by Subpart D of the regulations, as nothing in Subpart D compels any testing by private railroads.

[2] We are unwilling to conclude, in the context of this facial challenge, that breath and urine tests required by private railroads in reliance on Subpart D will not implicate the Fourth Amendment. Whether a private party should be deemed an agent or instrument of the Government for Fourth Amendment purposes necessarily turns on the degree of the Government's participation in the private party's activities, cf. *Lustig* v. *United States*, 338 U.S. 74, 78-79 (1949) (plurality opinion); *Byars* v. *United States*, 273 U.S. 28, 32-33 (1927), a question that can only be resolved "in light of all the circumstances." *Coolidge* v. *New Hampshire*, 403 U.S. at 443. The fact that the Government has not compelled a private party to perform a search does not, by itself, establish that the search is a private one. Here, specific features of the regulations combine to convince us that the Government did more than adopt a passive position toward the underlying private conduct.

The regulations, including those in Subpart D, pre-empt state laws, rules, or regulations covering the same subject matter, 49 CFR §219.13(a) (1987), and are intended to supersede "any provision of a collective bargaining agreement, or arbitration award construing such an agreement." 50 Fed. Reg. 31552 (1985). They also confer upon the FRA the right to receive certain biological samples and test results procured by railroads pursuant to Subpart D. §219.11(c). In addition, a railroad may not divest itself of, or otherwise compromise by contract, the authority conferred by Subpart D. As the Agency explained, such "authority ... is conferred for the purpose of promoting the public safety, and a railroad may not shackle itself in a way inconsistent with its duty to promote the public safety." 50 Fed. Reg. 31552 (1985). Nor is a covered employee free to decline his employer's request to submit to breath or urine tests under the conditions set forth in Subpart D. See §219.11(b). An employee who refuses to submit to the tests must be withdrawn from covered service. See 4 App. to Field Manual 18.

In light of these provisions, we are unwilling to accept petitioners' submission that tests conducted by private railroads in reliance on Subpart D will be primarily the result of private initiative. The Government has removed all legal barriers to the testing authorized by Subpart D, and indeed has made plain not only its strong preference for testing, but also its desire to share the fruits of such intrusions. In addition, it has mandated that the railroads not bargain away the authority to perform tests granted by Subpart D. These are clear indices of the Government's encouragement, endorsement, and participation, and suffice to implicate the Fourth Amendment.

B

Our precedents teach that where, as here, the Government seeks to obtain physical evidence from a person, the Fourth Amendment may be relevant at several levels. See, e.g., *United States* v. *Dionisio*, 410 U.S. 1, 8 (1973). The initial detention necessary to procure the evidence may be a seizure of the person, *Cupp* v. *Murphy*, 412 U.S. 291, 294-295 (1973); *Davis* v. *Mississippi*, 394 U.S. 721, 726-727 (1969), if the detention amounts to a meaningful interference with his freedom of movement. *INS* v. *Delgado*, 466 U.S. 210, 215 (1984); *United States* v. *Jacobsen*, 466 U.S., at 113, n.5. Obtaining and examining the evidence may also be a search, see *Cupp* v. *Murphy, supra*, at 295; *United States* v. *Dionisio, supra*, at 8, 13-14, if doing so infringes an expectation of privacy that society is prepared to recognize as reasonable. See, e.g., *California* v. *Greenwood*, 486 U.S. ——, —— (1988); *United States* v. *Jacobsen, supra*, at 113.

[3] We have long recognized that a "compelled intrusio[n] into the body for blood to be analyzed for alcohol content" must be deemed a Fourth Amendment search. See *Schmerber* v. *California*, 384 U.S. 757, 767-768 (1966). See also *Winston* v. *Lee*, 470 U.S. 753, 760 (1985). In light of our society's concern for the security of one's person, see, e.g., *Terry* v. *Ohio*, 392 U.S. 1, 9 (1968), it is obvious that this physical intrusion, penetrating beneath the skin, infringes an expectation of privacy that society is prepared to recognize as reasonable. The ensuing chemical analysis of the sample to obtain physiological data is a further invasion of the tested employee's privacy interests. Cf. *Arizona* v. *Hicks*, 480 U.S. 321, 324-325 (1987). Much the same is true of the breath-testing procedures required under Subpart D of the regulations. Subjecting a person to a breathalyzer test, which generally requires the production of alveolar or "deep lung" breath for chemical analysis, see, e.g., *California* v. *Trombetta*, 467 U.S. 479, 481 (1984), implicates similar concerns about bodily integrity and, like the blood-alcohol test we considered in *Schmerber*, should also be deemed a search. See 1 W. LaFave, Search and Seizure §2.6(a), p. 463

(1987). See also *Burnett* v. *Municipality of Anchorage*, 806 F.2d 1447, 1449 (CA9 1986); *Shoemaker* v. *Handel*, 795 F.2d 1136, 1141 [1 IER Cases 814] (CA3), cert. denied, 479 U.S. 986 [1 IER Cases 1136] (1986).

[4] Unlike the blood-testing procedure at issue in *Schmerber*, the procedures prescribed by the FRA regulations for collecting and testing urine samples do not entail a surgical intrusion into the body. It is not disputed, however, that chemical analysis of urine, like that of blood, can reveal a host of private medical facts about an employee, including whether she is epileptic, pregnant, or diabetic. Nor can it be disputed that the process of collecting the sample to be tested, which may in some cases involve visual or aural monitoring of the act of urination, itself implicates privacy interests. As the Court of Appeals for the Fifth Circuit has stated:

"There are few activities in our society more personal or private than the passing of urine. Most people describe it by euphemisms if they talk about it at all. It is a function traditionally performed without public observation; indeed, its performance in public is generally prohibited by law as well as social custom." *National Treasury Employees Union* v. *Von Raab*, 816 F.2d 170, 175 [2 IER Cases 15] (1987).

Because it is clear that the collection and testing of urine intrudes upon expectations of privacy that society has long recognized as reasonable, the Federal Courts of Appeals have concluded unanimously, and we agree, that these intrusions must be deemed searches under the Fourth Amendment.[*]

In view of our conclusion that the collection and subsequent analysis of

---

[*] See, e. g., *Lovvorn* v. *City of Chattanooga*, 846 F.2d 1539, 1542 [3 IER Cases 673] (CA6 1988); *Copeland* v. *Philadelphia Police Dept.*, 840 F.2d 1139, 1143 [2 IER Cases 1825] (CA3 1988), cert. pending No. 88-66; *Railway Labor Executives Association* v. *Burnley*, 839 F.2d 575, 580 [2 IER Cases 1601] (CA9 1988) (case below); *Everett* v. *Napper*, 833 F.2d 1507, 1511 [2 IER Cases 1377] (CA11 1987); *Jones* v. *McKenzie*, 266 U.S. App. D. C. 85, 88, 833 F.2d 335, 338 [2 IER Cases 1121] (1987); *National Treasury Employees Union* v. *Von Raab*, 816 F.2d 170, 176 [2 IER Cases 15] (CA5 1987); *McDonell* v. *Hunter*, 809 F.2d 1302, 1307 [1 IER Cases 1297] (CA8 1987); *Division 241 Amalgamated Transit Union* v. *Suscy*, 538 F.2d 1264, 1266-1267 (CA7), cert. denied, 429 U.S. 1029 (1976). See also *Alverado* v. *Washington Public Power Supply System*, 111 Wash.2d 424, 434, 759 P.2d 427, 432-433 [3 IER Cases 769] (1988), cert. pending, No. 88-645.

Taking a blood or urine sample might also be characterized as a Fourth Amendment seizure, since it may be viewed as a meaningful interference with the employee's possessory interest in his bodily fluids. Cf. *United States* v. *Jacobsen*, 466 U.S. 109, 113 (1984). It is not necessary to our analysis in this case, however, to characterize the taking of blood or urine samples as a seizure of those bodily fluids, for the privacy expectations protected by this characterization are adequately taken into account by our conclusion that such intrusions are searches.

the requisite biological samples must be deemed Fourth Amendment searches, we need not characterize the employer's antecedent interference with the employee's freedom of movement as an independent Fourth Amendment seizure. As our precedents indicate, not every governmental interference with an individual's freedom of movement raises such constitutional concerns that there is a seizure of the person. See *United States* v. *Dionisio*, 410 U.S. at 9–11 (grand jury subpoena, though enforceable by contempt, does not effect a seizure of the person); *United States* v. *Mara*, 410 U.S. 19, 21 (1973) (same). For present purposes, it suffices to note that any limitation on an employee's freedom of movement that is necessary to obtain the blood, urine, or breath samples contemplated by the regulations must be considered in assessing the intrusiveness of the searches effected by the Government's testing program. Cf. *United States*, v. *Place*, 462 U.S. 696, 707–709 (1983).

III

A

To hold that the Fourth Amendment is applicable to the drug and alcohol testing prescribed by the FRA regulations is only to begin the inquiry into the standards governing such intrusions. *O'Connor* v. *Ortega*, 480 U.S. 709, 719 [1 IER Cases 1617] (1987) (plurality opinion); *New Jersey* v. *T. L. O.*, 469 U.S. 325, 337 (1985). For the Fourth Amendment does not proscribe all searches and seizures, but only those that are unreasonable. *United States* v. *Sharpe*, 470 U.S. 675, 682 (1985); *Schmerber* v. *California*, 384 U.S., at 768. What is reasonable, of course, "depends on all the circumstances surrounding the search or seizure and the nature of the search or seizure itself." *United States* v. *Montoya de Hernandez*, 473 U.S. 531, 537 (1985). Thus, the permissibility of a particular practice "is judged by balancing its intrusion on the individual's Fourth Amendment interests against its promotion of legitimate governmental interests." *Delaware* v. *Prouse*, 440 U.S. at 654; *United States* v. *Martinez-Fuerte*, 428 U.S. 543 (1976).

In most criminal cases, we strike this balance in favor of the procedures described by the Warrant Clause of the Fourth Amendment. See *United States* v. *Place, supra*, at 701, and n.2; *United States* v. *United States District Court*, 407 U.S. 297, 315 (1972). Except in certain well-defined circumstances, a search or seizure in such a case is not reasonable unless it is accomplished pursuant to a judicial warrant issued upon probable cause. See, *e.g., Payton* v. *New York*, 445 U.S. 573, 586 (1980); *Mincey* v. *Arizona*, 437 U.S. 385, 390 (1978). We have recognized exceptions to this rule, however, "when 'special needs, beyond the normal need for law enforcement, make the warrant and probable-cause requirement inpracticable.'" *Griffin* v. *Wisconsin*, 483 U.S. ——, —— (1987), quoting *New Jersey* v. *T. L. O.*, 469 U.S. at 351 (BLACKMUN. J., concurring in judgment). When faced with such special needs, we have not hesitated to balance the governmental and privacy interests to assess the practicality of the warrant and probable cause requirements in the particular context. See, *e.g., Griffin* v. *Wisconsin, supra*, at —— —— (search of probationer's home): *New York* v. *Burger*, 482 U.S. 691, 699–703 (1987) (search of premises of certain highly regulated businesses); *O'Connor* v. *Ortega*, 480 U.S., at 721–725 (work-related searches of employees' desks and offices); *New Jersey* v. *T. L. O.*, 469 U.S., at 337–342 (search of student's property by school officials); *Bell* v. *Wolfish*, 441 U.S. 520, 558–560 (1979) (body cavity searches of prison inmates).

The Government's interest in regulating the conduct of railroad employees to ensure safety, like its supervision of probationers or regulated industries, or its operation of a government office, school, or prison, "likewise presents 'special needs' beyond normal law enforcement that may justify departures from the usual warrant and probable-cause requirements." *Griffin* v. *Wisconsin*, 483 U.S., at ——. The Hours of Service employees covered by the FRA regulations include persons engaged in handling orders concerning train movements, operating crews, and those engaged in the maintenance and repair of signal systems. 50 Fed. Reg. 31511 (1985). It is undisputed that these and other covered employees are engaged in safety-sensitive tasks. The Agency so found, and respondents conceded the point at oral argument. Tr. of Oral Arg. 46–47. As we have recognized, the whole premise of the Hours of Service Act is that "[t]he length of hours of service has direct relation to the efficiency of the human agencies upon which protection [of] life and property necessarily depends." *Baltimore & Ohio R. Co.* v. *ICC*, 221 U.S. 612, 619 (1911). See also *Atchison, T. & S.F.R. Co.* v. *United States*, 244 U.S. 336, 342 (1917) ("it must be remembered that the purpose of the act was to prevent the dangers which must necessarily arise to the employee and to the public from continuing men in a dangerous and hazardous business for periods so long as to render them unfit to give that service which is essential to the protection of themselves and those entrusted to their care").

The FRA has prescribed toxicological tests, not to assist in the prosecution of employees but rather "to prevent accidents and casualties in railroad operations that result from impairment of employees by alcohol or drugs." 49 CFR §219.1(a) (1987).[5] This governmental interest in ensuring the safety of the traveling public and of the employees themselves plainly justifies prohibiting covered employees from using alcohol or drugs on duty, or while subject to being called for duty. This interest also "require[s] and justif[ies] the exercise of supervision to assure that the restrictions are in fact observed." Griffin v. Wisconsin, 483 U.S., at ——. The question that remains, then, is whether the Government's need to monitor compliance with these restrictions justifies the privacy intrusions at issue absent a warrant or individualized suspicion.

B

An essential purpose of a warrant requirement is to protect privacy interests by assuring citizens subject to a search or seizure that such intrusions are not the random or arbitrary acts of government agents. A warrant assures the citizen that the intrusion is authorized by law, and that it is narrowly limited in its objectives and scope. See, e.g., New York v. Burger, 482 U.S., at 703; United States v. Chadwick, 433 U.S. 1, 9 (1977); Camara v. Municipal Court, 387 U.S., at 532. A warrant also provides the detached scrutiny of a neutral magistrate, and thus ensures an objective determination whether an intrusion is justified in any given case. See United States v. Chadwick, supra, at 9. In the present context, however, a warrant would do little to further these aims. Both the circumstances justifying toxicological testing and the permissible limits of such intrusions are defined narrowly and specifically in the regulations that authorize them, and doubtless are well known to covered employees. Cf. United States v. Biswell, 406 U.S. 311, 316 (1972). Indeed, in light of the standardized nature of the tests and the minimal discretion vested in those charged with administering the program, there are virtually no facts for a neutral magistrate to evaluate. Cf. Colorado v. Bertine, 479 U.S. 367, 376 (1987) (BLACKMUN, J., concurring).[6]

We have recognized, moreover, that the Government's interest in dispensing with the warrant requirement is at its strongest when, as here, "the burden of obtaining a warrant is likely to frustrate the governmental purpose behind the search." Camara v. Municipal Court, 387 U.S., at 533. See also New Jersey v. T. L. O., 469 U.S. at 340; Donovan v. Dewey, 452 U.S. 594, 603 (1981). As the Agency recognized, alcohol and other drugs are eliminated from the bloodstream at a constant rate, see 49

---

[5] The regulations provide that "[e]ach sample provided under [Subpart C] is retained for not less than six months following the date of the accident or incident and may be made available to . . . a party in litigation upon service of approximate compulsory process on the custodian . . . ." 49 CFR §219.211(d) (1987). The Agency explained, when it promulgated this provision, that it intends to retain such samples primarily "for its own purposes (e. g., to permit reanalysis of a sample if another laboratory reported detection of a substance not tested for in the original procedure)." 50 Fed. Reg. 31545 (1985). While this provision might be read broadly to authorize the release of biological samples to law enforcement authorities, the record does not disclose that it was intended to be, or actually has been, so used. Indeed, while respondents aver generally that test results might be made available to law enforcement authorities, Brief for Respondents 24, they do not seriously contend that this provision, or any other part of the administrative scheme, was designed as "a 'pretext' to enable law enforcement authorities to gather evidence of penal law violations." New York v. Burger, 482 U.S. 691, 716–717, n. 27 (1987). Absent a persuasive showing that the FRA's testing program is pretextual, we assess the FRA's scheme in light of its obvious administrative purpose. We leave for another day the question whether routine use is criminal prosecutions of evidence obtained pursuant to the administrative scheme would give rise to an inference of pretext, or otherwise impugn the administrative nature of the Agency's program.

[6] Subpart C of the regulations, for example, does not permit the exercise of any discretion in choosing the employees who must submit to testing, except in limited circumstances provided only if warranted by objective criteria. See ante at 5, n. 2. Subpart D, while conferring some discretion to choose those who may be required to submit to testing, also imposes specific constraints on the exercise of that discretion. Covered employees may be required to submit to breath or urine tests only if they have been directly involved in specified rule violations or errors, or if their acts or omissions contributed to the occurrence or severity of specified accidents or incidents. To be sure, some discretion necessarily must be used in determining whether an employee's acts or omissions contributed to the occurrence or severity of an event, but this limited assessment of the objective circumstances surrounding the event does not devolve unbridled discretion upon the supervisor in the field. Cf. Marshall v. Barlow's, Inc., 436 U.S. 307, 323 (1978).

In addition, the regulations contain various safeguards against any possibility that discretion will be abused. A railroad that requires post-accident testing in bad faith, 49 CFR §219.201(c) (1987), or that willfully imposes a program of authorized testing that does not comply with Subpart D, §219.9(a)(3), or that otherwise fails to follow the regulations, §219.9(a)(5), is subject to civil penalties, see pt. 219. App. A. p. 105, in addition to whatever damages may be awarded through the arbitration process.

Fed. Reg. 24291 (1984), and blood and breath samples taken to measure whether these substances were in the bloodstream when a triggering event occurred must be obtained as soon as possible. See *Schmerber* v. *California*, 384 U.S. at 770-771. Although the metabolites of some drugs remain in the urine for longer periods of time and may enable the Agency to estimate whether the employee was impaired by those drugs at the time of a covered accident, incident, or rule violation, 49 Fed. Reg. 24291 (1984), the delay necessary to procure a warrant nevertheless may result in the destruction of valuable evidence.

The Government's need to rely on private railroads to set the testing process in motion also indicates that insistence on a warrant requirement would impede the achievement of the Government's objective. Railroad supervisors, like school officials, see *New Jersey* v. *T. L. O.*, 469 U.S. at 339-340, and hospital administrators, see *O'Connor* v. *Ortega*, 480 U.S. at 722, are not in the business of investigating violations of the criminal laws or enforcing administrative codes, and otherwise have little occasion to become familiar with the intricacies of this Court's Fourth Amendment jurisprudence. "Imposing unwieldy warrant procedures . . . upon supervisors, who would otherwise have no reason to be familiar with such procedures, is simply unreasonable." *Ibid.*

[5] In sum, imposing a warrant requirement in the present context would add little to the assurances of certainty and regularity already afforded by the regulations, while significantly hindering, and in many cases frustrating, the objectives of the Government's testing program. We do not believe that a warrant is essential to render the intrusions here at issue reasonable under the Fourth Amendment.

C

[6] Our cases indicate that even a search that may be performed without a warrant must be based, as a general matter, on probable cause to believe that the person to be searched has violated the law. See *New Jersey* v. *T. L. O.*, 469 U.S., at 340. When the balance of interests precludes insistence on a showing of probable cause, we have usually required "some quantum of individualized suspicion" before concluding that a search is reasonable. See, *e.g.*, *United States* v. *Martinez-Fuerte*, 428 U.S., at 560. We made it clear, however, that a showing of individualized suspicion is not a constitutional floor, below which a search

must be presumed unreasonable. *Id.*, at 561. In limited circumstances, where the privacy interests implicated by the search are minimal, and where an important governmental interest furthered by the intrusion would be placed in jeopardy by a requirement of individualized suspicion, a search may be reasonable despite the absence of such suspicion. We believe that is true of the intrusions in question here.

By and large, intrusions on privacy under the FRA regulations are limited. To the extent transportation and like restrictions are necessary to procure the requisite blood, breath, and urine samples for testing, this interference alone is minimal given the employment context in which it takes place. Ordinarily, an employee consents to significant restrictions in his freedom of movement where necessary for his employment, and few are free to come and go as they please during working hours. See, *e.g.*, *INS* v. *Delgado*, 466 U.S. at 218. Any additional interference with a railroad employee's freedom of movement that occurs in the time it takes to procure a blood, breath, or urine sample for testing cannot, by itself, be said to infringe significant privacy interests.

Our decision in *Schmerber* v. *California*, 384 U.S. 757 (1966), indicates that the same is true of the blood tests required by the FRA regulations. In that case, we held that a State could direct that a blood sample be withdrawn from a motorist suspected of driving while intoxicated, despite his refusal to consent to the intrusion. We noted that the test was performed in a reasonable manner, as the motorist's "blood was taken by a physician in a hospital environment according to accepted medical practices." *Id.*, at 771. We said also that the intrusion occasioned by a blood test is not significant, since such "tests are a commonplace in these days of periodic physical examinations and experience with them teaches that the quantity of blood extracted is minimal, and that for most people the procedure involves virtually no risk, trauma, or pain." *Ibid. Schmerber* thus confirmed "society's judgment that blood tests do not constitute an unduly extensive imposition on an individual's privacy and bodily integrity." *Winston* v. *Lee*, 470 U.S. at 762. See also *South Dakota* v. *Neville*, 459 U.S. 553, 563 (1983) ("The simple blood-alcohol test is . . . safe, painless, and commonplace"); *Breithaupt* v. *Abram*, 352 U.S. 432, 436 (1957) ("The blood test procedure has become routine in our everyday life").

[7] The breath tests authorized by Subpart D of the regulations are even

less intrusive than the blood tests prescribed by Subpart C. Unlike blood tests, breath tests do not require piercing the skin and may be conducted safely outside a hospital environment and with a minimum of inconvenience or embarrassment. Further, breath tests reveal the level of alcohol in the employee's bloodstream and nothing more. Like the blood-testing procedures mandated by Subpart C, which can be used only to ascertain the presence of alcohol or controlled substances in the bloodstream, breath tests reveal no other facts in which the employee has a substantial privacy interest. Cf. *United States* v. *Jacobsen*, 466 U.S., at 123; *United States* v. *Place*, 462 U.S., at 707. In all the circumstances, we cannot conclude that the administration of a breath test implicates significant privacy concerns.

[8] A more difficult question is presented by urine tests. Like breath tests, urine tests are not invasive of the body and, under the regulations, may not be used as an occasion for inquiring into private facts unrelated to alcohol or drug use.[7] We recognize, however, that the procedures for collecting the necessary samples, which require employees to perform an excretory function traditionally shielded by great privacy, raise concerns not implicated by blood or breath tests. While we would not characterize these additional privacy concerns as minimal in most contexts, we note that the regulations endeavor to reduce the intrusiveness of the collection process. The regulations do not require that samples be furnished under the direct observation of a monitor, despite the desirability of such a procedure to ensure the integrity of the sample. See 50 Fed. Reg. 31555 (1985). See also Field Manual B-15; *id.*, at D-1. The sample is also collected in a medical environment, by personnel unrelated to the railroad employer, and is thus not unlike similar procedures encountered often in the context of a regular physical examination.

[9] More importantly, the expectations of privacy of covered employees are diminished by reason of their participation in an industry that is regulated pervasively to ensure safety, a goal dependent, in substantial part, on the health and fitness of covered employees. This relation between safety and employee fitness was recognized by Congress when it enacted the Hours of Service Act in 1907, *Baltimore & Ohio R. Co.* v. *ICC*, 221 U.S., at 619, and also when it authorized the Secretary to "test . . . railroad facilities, equipment, rolling stock, operations, *or persons*, as he deems necessary to carry out the provisions" of the Federal Railroad Safety Act of 1970. 45 U.S.C. §437(a) (emphasis added). It has also been recognized by state governments,[8] and has long been reflected in industry practice, as evidenced by the industry's promulgation and enforcement of Rule G. Indeed, the Agency found, and the Court of Appeals acknowledged, see 839 F.2d, at 585, that "most railroads require periodic physical examinations for train and engine employees and certain other employees." 49 Fed. Reg. 24278 (1984). See also *Railway Labor Executives Assn.* v. *Norfolk & Western R. Co.*, 833 F.2d 700, 705–706 [126 LRRM 3121] (CA7 1987); *Brotherhood of Maintenance of Way Employees, Lodge 16* v. *Burlington Northern R. Co.*, 802 F.2d 1016, 1024 [1 IER Cases 789] (CA8 1986).

We do not suggest, of course, that the interest in bodily security enjoyed by those employed in a regulated industry must always be considered minimal. Here, however, the covered employees have long been a principal focus of regulatory concern. As the dissenting judge below noted, "[t]he reason is obvious. An idle locomotive, sitting in the round-house, is harmless. It becomes lethal when operated negligently by persons who are under the influence of alcohol or drugs." 839 F.2d, at 593. Though some of the priva-

---

[7] When employees produce the blood and urine samples required by Subpart C they are asked by medical personnel to complete a form stating whether they have taken any medications during the preceding 30 days. The completed forms are shipped with the samples to the FRA's laboratory. See Field Manual B-15. This information is used to ascertain whether a positive test result can be explained by the employee's lawful use of medications. While this procedure permits the Government to learn certain private medical facts that an employee might prefer not to disclose, there is no indication that the Government does not treat this information as confidential, or that it uses the information for any other purpose. Under the circumstances, we do not view this procedure as a significant invasion of privacy. Cf. *Whalen* v. *Roe*, 429 U.S. 589, 602 (1977).

[8] See, *e.g.*, Ala. Code §37-2-85 (1975) (requiring that persons to be employed as dispatchers, engineers, conductors, brakemen, and switchmen be subjected to a "thorough examination" respecting, *inter alia*, their skill, sobriety, eyesight, and hearing); Mass. Gen. Laws, ch. 160, §§178-181 (1979) (prescribing eyesight and experience requirements for railroad engineers and conductors); N.Y.R.R. Law §63 (McKinney 1952) (requiring that all applicants for positions as motormen or gripmen "be subjected to a thorough examination . . . as to their habits, physical ability, and intelligence"). See also *Nashville, C. & S.L.R. Co.* v. *Alabama*, 128 U.S. 96, 98-99 (1888) (noting, in upholding a predecessor of Alabama's fitness-for-duty statute against a Commerce Clause challenge, that a State may lawfully require railway employees to undergo eye exams in the interests of safety).

cy interests implicated by the toxicological testing at issue reasonably might be viewed as significant in other contexts, logic and history show that a diminished expectation of privacy attaches to information relating to the physical condition of covered employees and to this reasonable means of procuring such information. We conclude, therefore, that the testing procedures contemplated by Subparts C and D pose only limited threats to the justifiable expectations of privacy of covered employees.

[10] By contrast, the government interest in testing without a showing of individualized suspicion is compelling. Employees subject to the tests discharge duties fraught with such risks of injury to others that even a momentary lapse of attention can have disastrous consequences. Much like persons who have routine access to dangerous nuclear power facilities, see, *e.g.*, *Rushton* v. *Nebraska Public Power Dist.*, 844 F.2d 562, 566 [3 IER Cases 257] (CA8 1988); *Alverado* v. *Washington Public Power Supply System*, 111 Wash.2d, at 436, 759 P.2d, at 433–434, employees who are subject to testing under the FRA regulations can cause great human loss before any signs of impairment become noticeable to supervisors or others. An impaired employee, the Agency found, will seldom display any outward "signs detectable by the lay person or, in many cases, even the physician." 50 Fed. Reg. 31526 (1985). This view finds ample support in the railroad industry's experience with Rule G, and in the judgment of the courts that have examined analogous testing schemes. See, *e.g.*, *Brotherhood of Maintenance Way Employees, Lodge 16* v. *Burlington Northern R. Co.*, 802 F.2d, at 1020. Indeed, while respondents posit that impaired employees might be detected without alcohol or drug testing,[*] the premise of respon-

dents' lawsuit is that even the occurrence of a major calamity will not give rise to a suspicion of impairment with respect to any particular employee.

While no procedure can identify all impaired employees with ease and perfect accuracy, the FRA regulations supply an effective means of deterring employees engaged in safety-sensitive tasks from using controlled substances or alcohol in the first place. 50 Fed. Reg. 31541 (1985). The railroad industry's experience with Rule G persuasively shows, and common sense confirms, that the customary dismissal sanction that threatens employees who use drugs or alcohol while on duty cannot serve as an effective deterrent unless violators know that they are likely to be discovered. By ensuring that employees in safety-sensitive positions know they will be tested upon the occurrence of a triggering event, the timing of which no employee can predict with certainty, the regulations significantly increase the deterrent effect of the administrative penalties associated with the prohibited conduct, cf. *Griffin* v. *Wisconsin*, 483 U.S., at ——, concomitantly increasing the likelihood that employees will forgo using drugs or alcohol while subject to being called for duty.

The testing procedures contemplated by Subpart C also help railroads obtain invaluable information about the causes of major accidents, see 50 Fed. Reg. 31541 (1985), and to take appropriate measures to safeguard the general public. Cf. *Michigan* v. *Tyler*, 436 U.S. 499, 510 (1978) (noting that prompt investigation of the causes of a fire may uncover continuing dangers and thereby prevent the fire's recurrence); *Michigan* v. *Clifford*, 464 U.S. 287, 308 (19840 (REHNQUIST, J., dissenting) (same). Positive test results would point toward drug or alcohol impairment on the part of members of the crew as a possible cause of an accident, and may help to establish whether a particular accident, otherwise not drug related, was made worse by the inability of impaired employees to respond appropriately. Negative test results would likewise furnish invaluable clues, for eliminating drug impairment as a potential cause or contributing factor would help establish the significance of equipment failure, inadequate training, or other po-

---

[*] Respondents offer a list of "less drastic and equally effective means" of addressing the Government's concerns, including reliance on the private proscriptions already in force, and training supervisory personnel "to effectively detect employees who are impaired by drug or alcohol use without resort to such intrusive procedures as blood and urine tests." Brief for Respondents 40–43. We have repeatedly stated, however, that "[t]he reasonableness of any particular government activity does not necessarily or invariably turn on the existence of alternative 'less intrusive' means." *Illinois* v. *Lafayette*, 462 U.S. 640, 647 (1983). See also *Colorado* v. *Bertine*, 479 U.S. 367, 373–374 (1987). It is obvious that "[t]he logic of such elaborate less-restrictive-alternative arguments could raise insuperable barriers to the exercise of virtually all search-and-seizure powers," *United States* v. *Martinez-Fuerte*, 428 U.S., at 556–557, n.12, because judges engaged in *post hoc* evaluations of government conduct " 'can almost always imagine some alternative means by which the objectives of the [Government] might have been accomplished.' " *United States* v. *Montoya de Hernandez*, 473 U.S. 531, 542 (1985), quoting *United*

States v. *Sharpe*, 470 U.S. 675, 686–687 (1985). Here, the FRA expressly considered various alternatives to this drug-screening program and reasonably found them wanting. At bottom, respondents' insistence on less drastic alternatives would require us to second-guess the reasonable conclusions drawn by the FRA after years of investigation and study. This we decline to do.

tential causes and suggest a more thorough examination of these alternatives. Tests performed following the rule violations specified in Subpart D likewise can provide valuable information respecting the causes of those transgressions, which the Agency found to involve "the potential for a serious train accident or grave personal injury, or both." 50 Fed. Reg. 31553 (1985).

A requirement of particularized suspicion of drug or alcohol use would seriously impede an employer's ability to obtain this information, despite its obvious importance. Experience confirms the Agency's judgment that the scene of a serious rail accident is chaotic. Investigators who arrive at the scene shortly after a major accident has occurred may find it difficult to determine which members of a train crew contributed to its occurrence. Obtaining evidence that might give rise to the suspicion that a particular employee is impaired, a difficult endeavor in the best of circumstances, is most impracticable in the aftermath of a serious accident. While events following the rule violations that activate the testing authority of Subpart D may be less chaotic, objective indicia of impairment are absent in these instances as well. Indeed, any attempt to gather evidence relating to the possible impairment of particular employees likely would result in the loss or deterioration of the evidence furnished by the tests. Cf. *Michigan* v. *Clifford*, 464 U.S., at 293, n.4 (plurality opinion); *Michigan* v. *Tyler*, 436 U.S., at 510. It would be unrealistic, and inimical to the Government's goal of ensuring safety in rail transportation, to require a showing of individualized suspicion in these circumstances.

Without quarreling with the importance of these governmental interests, the Court of Appeals concluded that the post-accident testing regulations were unreasonable because "[b]lood and urine tests intended to establish drug use other than alcohol . . . cannot measure current drug intoxication or degree of impairment." 839 F.2d, at 588. The court based its conclusion on its reading of certain academic journals that indicate that the testing of urine can disclose only drug metabolites, which "may remain in the body for days or weeks after the ingestion of the drug." *Id.*, at 589. We find this analysis flawed for several reasons.

As we emphasized in *New Jersey* v. *T. L. O.*, "it is universally recognized that evidence, to be relevant to an inquiry, need not conclusively prove the ultimate fact in issue, but only have 'any tendency to make the existence of any fact that is of consequence to the determination [of the point in issue] more probable or less probable than it would be without the evidence.' " 469 U.S., at 345, quoting Fed. Rule Evid. 401. Even if urine test results disclosed nothing more specific than the recent use of controlled substances by a covered employee, this information would provide the basis for further investigative work designed to determine whether the employee used drugs at the relevant times. See Field Manual B-4. The record makes clear, for example, that a positive test result, coupled with known information concerning the pattern of elimination for the particular drug and information that may be gathered from other sources about the employee's activities, may allow the Agency to reach an informed judgment as to how a particular accident occurred. See *ante*, at 5.

More importantly, the Court of Appeals overlooked the Agency's policy of placing principal reliance on the results of blood tests, which unquestionably can identify very recent drug use, see, *e.g.*, 49 Fed. Reg. 24291 (1984), while relying on urine tests as a secondary source of information designed to guard against the possibility that certain drugs will be eliminated from the bloodstream before a blood sample can be obtained. The court also failed to recognize that the FRA regulations are designed not only to discern impairment but also to deter it. Because the record indicates that blood and urine tests, taken together, are highly effective means of ascertaining on-the-job impairment and of deterring the use of drugs by railroad employees, we believe the Court of Appeals erred in concluding that the post-accident testing regulations are not reasonably related to the Government objectives that support them.[10]

We conclude that the compelling government interests served by the FRA's regulations would be significantly hindered if railroads were required to point to specific facts giving rise to a reasonable suspicion of impairment before testing a given employee. In view of our conclusion that,

---

[10] The Court of Appeals also expressed concern that the tests might be quite unreliable, and thus unreasonable. 839 F.2d, at 589. The record compiled by the Agency after years of investigation and study does not support this conclusion. While it is impossible to guarantee that no mistakes will ever be made in isolated cases, respondents have challenged the administrative scheme on its face. We deal therefore with whether the tests contemplated by the regulations can *ever* be conducted. Cf. *Bell* v. *Wolfish*, 441 U.S. 520, 560 (1979). Respondents have provided us with no reason for doubting the Agency's conclusion that the tests at issue here are accurate in the overwhelming majority of cases.

on the present record, the toxicological testing contemplated by the regulations is not an undue infringement on the justifiable expectations of privacy of covered employees, the Government's compelling interests outweigh privacy concerns.

IV

The possession of unlawful drugs is a criminal offense that the Government may punish, but it is a separate and far more dangerous wrong to perform certain sensitive tasks while under the influence of those substances. Performing those tasks while impaired by alcohol is, of course, equally dangerous, though consumption of alcohol is legal in most other contexts. The Government may take all necessary and reasonable regulatory steps to prevent or deter that hazardous conduct, and since the gravamen of the evil is performing certain functions while concealing the substance in the body, it may be necessary, as in the case before us, to examine the body or its fluids to accomplish the regulatory purpose. The necessity to perform that regulatory function with respect to railroad employees engaged in safety-sensitive tasks, and the reasonableness of the system for doing so, have been established in this case.

Alcohol and drug tests conducted in reliance on the authority of Subpart D cannot be viewed as private action outside the reach of the Fourth Amendment. Because the testing procedures mandated or authorized by Subparts C and D effect searches of the person, they must meet the Fourth Amendment's reasonableness requirement. In light of the limited discretion exercised by the railroad employers under the regulations, the surpassing safety interests served by toxicological tests in this context, and the diminished expectation of privacy that attaches to information pertaining to the fitness of covered employees, we believe that it is reasonable to conduct such tests in the absence of a warrant or reasonable suspicion that any particular employee may be impaired. We hold that the alcohol and drug tests contemplated by Subparts C and D of the FRA's regulations are reasonable within the meaning of the Fourth Amendment. The judgment of the Court of Appeals is accordingly reversed.

It is so ordered.

Concurring Opinion

JUSTICE STEVENS, concurring in part and concurring in the judgment.

In my opinion the public interest in determining the causes of serious railroad accidents adequately supports the validity of the challenged regulations. I am not persuaded, however, that the interest in deterring the use of alcohol or drugs is either necessary or sufficient to justify the searches authorized by these regulations.

I think it a dubious proposition that the regulations significantly deter the use of alcohol and drugs by Hours of Service employees. Most people — and I would think most railroad employees as well — do not go to work with the expectation that they may be involved in a major accident, particularly one causing such catastrophic results as loss of life or the release of hazardous material requiring an evacuation. Moreover, even if they are conscious of the possibilities that such an accident might occur and that alcohol or drug use might be a contributing factor, if the risk of serious personal injury does not deter their use of these substances, it seems highly unlikely that the additional threat of loss of employment would have any effect on their behavior.

For this reason, I do not join the portions of Part III of the Court's opinion that rely on a deterrence rationale; I do, however, join the balance of the opinion and the Court's judgment.

Dissenting Opinion

JUSTICE MARSHALL, with whom JUSTICE BRENNAN joins, dissenting.

The issue in this case is not whether declaring a war on illegal drugs is good public policy. The importance of ridding our society of such drugs is, by now, apparent to all. Rather, the issue here is whether the Government's deployment in that war of a particularly draconian weapon — the compulsory collection and chemical testing of railroad workers' blood and urine — comports with the Fourth Amendment. Precisely because the need for action against the drug scourge is manifest, the need for vigilance against unconstitutional excess is great. History teaches that grave threats to liberty often come in times of urgency, when constitutional rights seem too extravagant to endure. The World War II relocation-camp cases, *Hirabayashi* v. *United States*, 320 U.S. 81 (1943); *Korematsu* v. *United States*, 323 U.S. 214 (1944), and the Red Scare and McCarthy-Era internal subversion cases, *Schenck* v. *United States*, 249 U.S. 47 (1919); *Dennis* v. *United States*, 341 U.S.

494 (1951), are only the most extreme reminders that when we allow fundamental freedoms to be sacrificed in the name of real or perceived exigency, we invariably come to regret it.

In permitting the Government to force entire railroad crews to submit to invasive blood and urine tests, even when it lacks any evidence of drug or alcohol use or other wrongdoing, the majority today joins those shortsighted courts which have allowed basic constitutional rights to fall prey to momentary emergencies. The majority holds that the need of the Federal Railroad Administration (FRA) to deter and diagnose train accidents outweighs any "minimal" intrusions on personal dignity and privacy posed by mass toxicological testing of persons who have given no indication whatsoever of impairment. *Ante,* at 19. In reaching this result, the majority ignores the text and doctrinal history of the Fourth Amendment, which require that highly intrusive searches of this type be based on probable cause, not on the evanescent cost-benefit calculations of agencies or judges. But the majority errs even under its own utilitarian standards, trivializing the raw intrusiveness of, and overlooking serious conceptual and operation flaws in, the FRA's testing program. These flaws cast grave doubts on whether that program, though born of good intentions, will do more than ineffectually symbolize the Government's opposition to drug use.

The majority purports to limit its decision to postaccident testing of workers in "safety-sensitive" jobs, *ante,* at 15, much as it limits its holding in the companion case to testing of transferees to jobs involving drug interdiction or the use of firearms. *National Treasury Employees Union* v. *Von Raab* [4 IER Cases 247], *post,* at 6. But the damage done to the Fourth Amendment is not so easily cabined. The majority's acceptance of dragnet blood and urine testing ensures that the first, and worst, casualty of the war on drugs will be the precious liberties of our citizens. I therefore dissent.

I

The Court today takes its longest step yet toward reading the probable-cause requirement out of the Fourth Amendment. For the fourth time in as many years, a majority holds that a "special nee[d], beyond the normal need for law enforcement," makes the "requirement" of probable cause "impracticable." *Ante,* at 14 (citations omitted). With the recognition of "[t]he Government's interest in regulating the conduct of railroad employ-

ees to ensure safety" as such a need, *ante,* at 15, the Court has now permitted "special needs" to displace constitutional text in each of the four categories of searches enumerated in the Fourth Amendment: searches of "persons," *ante,* p. ——; "houses," *Griffin* v. *Wisconsin,* 483 U.S. 868 (1987); "papers," *O'Connor* v. *Ortega,* 480 U.S. 709 [1 IER Cases 1617] (1987); and "effects," *New Jersey* v. *T. L. O.,* 46 U.S. 325 (1985).

The process by which a constitutional "requirement" can be dispensed with as "impracticable" is an elusive one to me. The Fourth Amendment provides that "[t]he right of the people to be secure in their persons, houses, papers, and effects, against unreasonable searches and seizures, shall not be violated; and no Warrants shall issue, but upon probable cause, supported by Oath or affirmation, and particularly describing the place to be searched, and the persons or things to be seized." The majority's recitation of the Amendment, remarkably, leaves off after the word "violated," *ante,* at 9, but the remainder of the Amendment — the Warrant Clause — is not so easily excised. As this Court has long recognized, the Framers intended the provisions of that Clause — a warrant and probable cause — to "provide the yardstick against which official searches and seizures are to be measured." *T. L. O., supra,* at 359–360 (opinion of BRENNAN, J.). Without the content which those provisions give to the Fourth Amendment's overarching command that searches and seizures be "reasonable," the Amendment lies virtually devoid of meaning, subject to whatever content shifting judicial majorities, concerned about the problems of the day, choose to give to that supple term. See *Dunaway* v. *New York,* 442 U.S. 200, 213 (1979) ("[T]he protections intended by the Framers could all too easily disappear in the consideration and balancing of the multifarious circumstances presented by different cases"). Constitutional requirements like probable cause are not fair-weather friends, present when advantageous, conveniently absent when "special needs" make them seem not.

Until recently, an unbroken line of cases had recognized probable cause as an indispensable prerequisite for a full-scale search, regardless whether such a search was conducted pursuant to a warrant or under one of the recognized exceptions to the warrant requirement. *T. L. O., supra,* at 358 and 359, n.3 (opinion of BRENNAN, J.); see also *Chambers v. Maroney,* 399 U.S. 42, 51 (1970). Only where the Government action in question had a "substantially less intrusive" impact on privacy, *Dunaway, supra*, at 210. and thus clearly fell short of a full-scale search, did we relax the probable cause standard. *Id.*, at 214 ("For all but those narrowly defined intrusions, the requisite 'balancing'. . . is embodied in the principle that seizures are 'reasonable' only if supported by probable cause"); see also *T. L. O., supra*, at 360 (opinion of BRENNAN, J.). Even in this class of cases, we almost always required the Government to show some individualized suspicion to justify the search.[1] The few searches which we upheld in the absence of individualized justification were routinized, fleeting, and nonintrusive encounters conducted pursuant to regulatory programs which entailed no contact with the person.[2]

In the four years since this Court, in *T. L. O.*, first began recognizing "special needs" exceptions to the Fourth Amendment. the clarity of Fourth Amendment doctrine has been badly distorted, as the Court has eclipsed the probable-cause requirement in a patchwork quilt of settings: public school principals' searches of students' belongings, *T. L. O.*; public employers' searches of employees' desks. *O'Connor*; and probation officers' searches of probationers' homes, *Griffin*.[3] Tell-

ingly, each time the Court has found that "special needs" counseled ignoring the literal requirements of the Fourth Amendment for such full-scale searches in favor of a formless and unguided "reasonableness" balancing inquiry, it has concluded that the search in question satisfied that test. I have joined dissenting opinions in each of these cases, protesting the "jettison[ing of] . . . the only standard that finds support in the text of the Fourth Amendment" and predicting that the majority's "Rohrschach-like 'balancing test' " portended "a dangerous weakening of the purpose of the Fourth Amendment to protect the privacy and security of our citizens." *T. L. O., supra*, at 357–358 (opinion of BRENNAN, J.).

The majority's decision today bears out that prophecy. After determining that the Fourth Amendment applies to the FRA's testing regime, the majority embarks on an extended inquiry into whether that regime is "reasonable," an inquiry in which it balances " 'all the circumstances surrounding the search or seizure and the nature of the search or seizure itself.' " *Ante*, at 14, quoting *United States* v. *Montoya de Hernandez*, 473 U.S. 531, 537 (1985). The result is "special needs" balancing analysis' deepest incursion yet into the core protections of the Fourth Amendment. Until today, it was conceivable that, when a Government search was aimed at a person and not simply the person's possessions, balancing analysis had no place. No longer: with nary a word of explanation or acknowledgment of the novelty of its approach, the majority extends the "special needs" framework to a regulation involving compulsory blood withdrawal and urinary excretion, and chemical testing of the bodily fluids collected through these procedures. And until today, it was conceivable that a prerequisite for surviving "special needs" analysis was the existence of individualized suspicion. No longer: in contrast to the searches in *T. L. O.*, *O'Connor*, and *Griffin*, which were supported by individualized evidence suggesting the culpability of the persons whose property was searched,[4] the regulatory regime upheld today requires the post accident collection and testing of the blood and urine of *all* covered em-

---

[1] The first, and leading, case of a minimally intrusive search held valid when based on suspicion short of probable cause is *Terry* v. *Ohio*, 392 U.S. 1, 30 (1968). where we held that a police officer who observes unusual conduct suggesting criminal activity by persons he reasonably suspects are armed and presently dangerous may "conduct a carefully limited search of the outer clothing of such persons." See also *United States* v. *Hensley*, 469 U.S. 221 (1985) (upholding brief stop of person described on wanted flyer while police ascertain if arrest warrant has been issued); *Delaware* v. *Prouse*, 440 U.S. 648 (1979) (invalidating discretionary stops of motorists to check licenses and registrations when not based on reasonable suspicion that the motorist is unlicensed, the automobile is unregistered, or that the vehicle or an occupant should otherwise be detained); *Pennsylvania* v. *Mimms*. 434 U.S. 106 (1977) (upholding limited search where officers who had lawfully stopped car saw a large bulge under the driver's jacket); *United States* v. *Brignoni-Ponce*, 422 U.S. 873 (1975) (upholding brief stops by roving border patrols where officers reasonably believe car may contain illegal aliens); *Adams* v. *Williams*, 407 U.S. 143 (1972) (upholding brief stop to interrogate suspicious individual believed to be carrying narcotics and gun).

[2] See, *e.g.*, *United States* v. *Martinez-Fuerte*, 428 U.S. 543 (1976) (brief interrogation stop at permanent border checkpoint to ascertain motorist's residence status); *Camara* v. *Municipal Court*, 387 U.S. 523 (1967) (routine annual inspection by city housing department).

[3] The "special needs" the Court invoked to justify abrogating the probable-cause requirement were, in *New Jersey* v. *T. L. O.*, 469 U.S. 325, 341 (1985), "the substantial need of teachers and administrators for freedom to maintain order in the schools"; in *O'Connor* v. *Ortega*, 480 U.S. 709, 725 [1 IER Cases 1617] (1987), "the efficient and proper operation of the workplace"; and in *Griffin* v. *Wisconsin*, 483 U.S. 868, 878 (1987), the need to preserve "the deterrent effect of the supervisory arrangement" of probation.

[4] See, *T. L. O. supra*, at 346 (teacher's report that student had been smoking provided reasonable suspicion that purse contained cigarettes); *O'Connor, supra*, at 726 (charges of specific financial improprieties gave employer individualized suspicion of misconduct by employee); *Griffin, supra*, at —— (tip to police officer that probationer was storing guns in his apartment provided reasonable suspicion).

ployees — even if every member of this group gives every indication of sobriety and attentiveness.

In widening the "special needs" exception to probable cause to authorize searches of the human body unsupported by *any* evidence of wrongdoing, the majority today completes the process begun in *T. L. O.* of eliminating altogether the probable-cause requirement for civil searches — those undertaken for reasons "beyond the normal need for law enforcement." *Ante,* at 14 (citations omitted). In its place, the majority substitutes a manipulable balancing inquiry under which, upon the mere assertion of a "special need," even the deepest dignitary and privacy interests become vulnerable to governmental incursion. See *ante,* at 14-15 (distinguishing criminal from civil searches). By its terms, however, the Fourth Amendment — unlike the Fifth and Sixth — does not confine its protections to either criminal or civil actions. Instead, it protects generally "[t]he right of the people to be secure." '

The fact is that the malleable "special needs" balancing approach can be justified only on the basis of the policy results it allows the majority to reach. The majority's concern with the railroad safety problems caused by drug and alcohol abuse is laudable; its cavalier disregard for the text of the Constitution is not. There is no drug exception to the Constitution, any more than there is a communism exception or an exception for other real or imagined sources of domestic unrest. *Coolidge* v. *New Hampshire,* 403 U.S. 443, 455 (1971). Because abandoning the explicit protections of the Fourth Amendment seriously imperils "the right to be let alone — the most comprehensive of rights and the right most valued by civilized men," *Olmstead* v. *United States,* 277 U.S. 438, 478 (1928) (Brandeis, J., dissenting), I reject the majority's "special needs" rationale as unprincipled and dangerous.

II

The proper way to evaluate the FRA's testing regime is to use the same analytic framework which we have traditionally used to appraise Fourth Amendment claims involving full-scale searches, at least until the recent "special needs" cases. Under that framework, we inquire, serially, whether a search has taken place, see, *e.g., Katz* v. *United States,* 389 U.S. 347, 350-353 (1967); whether the search was based on a valid warrant or undertaken pursuant to a recognized exception to the warrant requirement, see, *e.g., Welsh* v. *Wisconsin,* 466 U.S. 740, 748-750 (1984); whether the search was based on probable cause or validly based on lesser suspicion because it was minimally intrusive, see, *e.g., Dunaway,* 442 U.S., at 208-210; and, finally, whether the search was conducted in a reasonable manner, see, *e.g., Winston* v. *Lee,* 470 U.S. 753, 763-766 (1985). See also *T. L. O.,* 469 U.S., at 354-355 (opinion of BRENNAN, J.) (summarizing analytic framework).

The majority's threshold determination that "covered" railroad employees have been searched under the FRA's testing program is certainly correct. *Ante,* at 11-14. Who among us is not prepared to consider reasonable a person's expectation of privacy with respect to the extraction of his blood, the collection of his urine, or the chemical testing of these fluids? *United States* v. *Jacobsen,* 466 U.S. 109, 113 (1984).⁶ The majority's ensuing conclusion that the warrant requirement may be dispensed with, however, conveniently overlooks the fact that there are three distinct searches at issue. Although the importance of collecting blood and urine samples before drug or alcohol metabolites disappear justifies waiving the warrant requirement for those two searches under the narrow "exigent circumstances" exception, see *Schmerber* v. *California,* 384 U.S. 757, 770 (1966) ("[T]he delay necessary to obtain a warrant... threaten[s] 'the destruction of evidence'"), no such exigency prevents railroad officials from securing a warrant before chemically testing the samples they obtain. Blood and urine do not spoil if properly collected and preserved, and there is no reason to doubt the ability of railroad officials to grasp the relatively simple procedure of obtaining a warrant authorizing, where appropriate, chemical analysis of the extracted fluids. It is therefore wholly unjustified to dispense with the warrant requirement for this final search. See *Chimel* v.

That the Fourth Amendment applies equally to criminal and civil searches was emphasized, ironically enough, in the portion of *T. L. O.* holding the Fourth Amendment applicable to schoolhouse searches. 469 U.S., at 335. The malleability of "special needs" balancing thus could not be clearer: the majority endorses the applicability of the Fourth Amendment to civil searches in determining whether a search has taken place, but then wholly ignores it in the subsequent inquiry into the validity of that search.

' The FRA's breath-testing procedures also constitute searches subject to constitutional safeguards. See *ante,* at 12 (reaching same conclusion). I focus my discussion on the collection and testing of blood and urine because those more intrusive procedures better demonstrate the excesses of the FRA's scheme.

California, 395 U.S. 752, 761-764 (1969) (exigency exception permits warrantless searches only to the extent that exigency exists).

It is the probable-cause requirement, however, that the FRA's testing regime most egregiously violates, a fact which explains the majority's ready acceptance and expansion of the countertextual "special needs" exception. By any measure, the FRA's highly intrusive collection and testing procedures qualify as full-scale personal searches. Under our precedents, a showing of probable cause is therefore clearly required. But even if these searches were viewed as entailing only minimal intrusions on the order, say, of a police stop-and-frisk, the FRA's program would still fail to pass constitutional muster, for we have, without exception, demanded that even minimally intrusive searches of the person be founded on individualized suspicion. See *supra*, at 4, and n. 1. The Government concedes it does not satisfy this standard. Brief for Petitioners 18. Only if one construes the FRA's collection and testing procedures as akin to the routinized and fleeting regulatory interactions which we have permitted in the absence of individualized suspicion, see *supra*, n. 2, might these procedures survive constitutional scrutiny. Presumably for this reason, the majority likens this case to *United States* v. *Martinez-Fuerte*, 428 U.S. 543 (1976), which upheld brief automobile stops at the border to ascertain the validity of motorists' residence in the United States. *Ante*, at 19. Case law and common sense reveal both the bankruptcy of this absurd analogy and the constitutional imperative of adhering to the textual standard of probable cause to evaluate the FRA's multifarious full-scale searches.

Compelling a person to submit to the piercing of his skin by a hypodermic needle so that his blood may be extracted significantly intrudes on the "personal privacy and dignity against unwarranted intrusion by the State" against which the Fourth Amendment protects. *Schmerber, supra*, at 767. As we emphasized in *Terry*, "[e]ven a limited search of the outer clothing . . . constitutes a severe, though brief, intrusion upon cherished personal security, and it must surely be an annoying, frightening, and perhaps humiliating experience," 392 U.S., at 24-25. We have similarly described the taking of a suspect's fingernail scraping as a " 'severe, though brief, intrusion upon cherished personal security.' " *Cupp* v. *Murphy*, 412 U.S. 291, 295 (1973) (quoting *Terry, supra*, at 24-25,

and upholding this procedure upon a showing of probable cause). The government-compelled withdrawal of blood, involving as it does the added aspect of physical invasion, is surely no less an intrusion. The surrender of blood on demand is, furthermore, hardly a quotidian occurrence. Cf. *Martinez-Fuerte, supra*, at 557 (routine stops involve "quite limited" intrusion).

In recognition of the intrusiveness of this procedure, we specifically required in *Schmerber* that police have evidence of a drunk-driving suspect's impairment before forcing him to endure a blood test:

"The interest in human dignity and privacy which the Fourth Amendment protects forbid any such intrusions on the mere chance that desired evidence might be obtained. In the absence of a clear indication that in fact such evidence will be found, these fundamental human interests require law officers to suffer the risk that such evidence may disappear. . . ." 384 U.S., at 769-770.

Schmerber strongly suggested that the "clear indication" needed to justify a compulsory blood test amounted to a showing of probable cause, which "plainly" existed in that case. *Id.*, at 768. Although subsequent cases interpreting *Schmerber* have differed over whether a showing of individualized suspicion would have sufficed, compare *Winston*, 470 U.S., at 760 (*Schmerber* "noted the importance of probable cause"), with *Montoya de Hernandez*, 473 U.S., at 540 (*Schmerber* "indicate[d] the necessity for particularized suspicion"), by any reading, *Schmerber* clearly forbade compulsory blood tests on any lesser showing than individualized suspicion. Exactly why a blood test which, if conducted on one person, requires a showing of at least individualized suspicion may, if conducted on many persons, be based on no showing whatsoever, the majority does not — and cannot — explain.[1]

_____
[1] The majority, seeking to lessen the devastating ramifications of *Schmerber* v. *California*, 384 U.S. 757 (1966) and to back up its assertion that Government-imposed blood extraction does not "infringe significant privacy interests," *ante*, at 20, emphasizes *Schmerber's* observation that blood tests are commonplace and can be performed with " 'virtually no risk, trauma, or pain.' " *Ibid.*, quoting 384 U.S., at 771. The majority, however, wrenches this statement out of context. It made this statement only *after* the Court established that the blood test fell within the exigent circumstances exception to the warrant requirement, *and* that the test was supported by probable cause. Indeed, the statement was made only in the context of the separate inquiry into whether the compulsory blood test was conducted in a reasonable manner. 384 U.S., at 768-772; see also *Winston* v. *Lee*, 470 U.S. 753, 760-761 (1985) ("*Schmerber* recognized that the ordinary requirements of the Fourth Amendment would be the *threshold requirements* for conducting this kind of surgical search and seizure. . . . Beyond these standards, *Schmerber's* inquiry considered a number of other factors in determining the 'reasonableness' of the

Compelling a person to produce a urine sample on demand also intrudes deeply on privacy and bodily integrity. Urination is among the most private of activities. It is generally forbidden in public, eschewed as a matter of conversation, and performed in places designed to preserve this tradition of personal seclusion. Cf. *Martinez-Fuerte, supra,* at 560 (border-stop questioning involves no more than "some annoyance" and is neither "frightening" nor "offensive"). The FRA, however, gives scant regard to personal privacy, for its Field Manual instructs supervisors monitoring urination that railroad workers must provide urine samples *"under direct observation* by the physician/technician." Federal Railroad Administration, United States Dept. of Transportation, Field Manual: Control of Alcohol and Drug Use in Railroad Operations (D-5) (1986) (emphasis added).[8] That the privacy interests offended by compulsory and supervised urine collection are profound is the overwhelming judgment of the lower courts and commentators. As Professor — later Solicitor General — Charles Fried has written:

"[I]n our culture the excretory functions are shielded by more or less absolute privacy, so much so that situations in which this privacy is violated are experienced as extremely distressing, as detracting from one's dignity and self esteem." Fried, Privacy, 77 Yale L.J. 475, 487 (1968).[9]

The majority's characterization of the privacy interests implicated by urine collection as "minimal," *ante,* at 21, is nothing short of startling. This

---

blood test") (emphasis added). The majority also cites *South Dakota* v. *Neville,* 459 U.S. 553 (1983), and *Breithaupt* v. *Abram,* 352 U.S. 432 (1957) for the proposition that blood tests are commonplace. *Ante,* at 20. In both those cases, however, the police officers who attempted to impose blood tests on drunk-driving suspects had exceptionally strong evidence of the driver's inebriation. 459 U.S., at 554-556; 352 U.S., at 433.

[8] The majority dismisses as nonexistent the intrusiveness of such "direct observation," on the ground that FRA regulations state that such observation is not require[d]." 50 Fed. Reg. 31555 (1985), cited *ante,* at 22. The majority's dismissal is too hasty, however, for the regulations — in the very same sentence — go on to state: "but observation is the most effective means of ensuring that the sample is that of the employee and has not been diluted." 50 Fed. Reg. 31555 (1985). Even if this were not the case, the majority's suggestion that officials monitoring urination will disregard the clear commands of the Field Manual with which they are provided is dubious, to say the least.

[9] See, *e.g., National Treasury Employees Union* v. *Von Raab,* 816 F.2d 170, 175 [2 IER Cases 15] (CA5 1987), aff'd in part, *post,* p. —— [4 IER Cases 247]; *Taylor v. O'Grady,* 669 F.Supp. 1422, 1433-1434 [2 IER Cases 897] (ND Ill. 1987); *Feliciano v. City of Cleveland,* 661 F.Supp. 578, 586 [2 IER Cases 419] (ND Ohio 1987); *American Federation of Government Employees, AFL-CIO* v. *Weinberger,* 651 F.Supp. 726, 732-733 [1 IER Cases 1137] (SD Ga. 1986); *Capua v. City of Plainfield,* 643 F.Supp. 1507, 1514 [1 IER Cases 625] (NJ 1986).

characterization is, furthermore, belied by the majority's own prior explanation of why compulsory urination constitutes a search for the purpose of the Fourth Amendment:

" 'There are few activities in our society more personal or private than the passing of urine. Most people describe it by euphemisms if they talk about it at all. It is a function traditionally performed without public observation; indeed, its performance in public is generally prohibited by law as well as social custom.' " *Ante,* at 12, quoting *National Treasury Employees Union* v. *Von Raab,* 816 F.2d 170, 175 [2 IER Cases 15] (CA5 1987).

The fact that the majority can invoke this powerful passage in the context of deciding that a search has occurred, and then ignore it in deciding that the privacy interests this search implicates are "minimal," underscores the shameless manipulability of its balancing approach.

Finally, the chemical analysis the FRA performs upon the blood and urine samples implicates strong privacy interests apart from those intruded upon by the collection of bodily fluids. Technological advances have made it possible to uncover, through analysis of chemical compounds in these fluids, not only drug or alcohol use, but also medical disorders such as epilepsy, diabetes, and clinical depression. Cf. *Martinez-Fuerte,* 428 U.S. at 558, quoting *United States* v. *Brignoni-Ponce,* 442 U.S. 873, 880 (1975) (check-point inquiry involves only " 'a brief question or two' " about motorist's residence). As the Court of Appeals for the District of Columbia has observed: "such tests may provide Government officials with a periscope through which they can peer into an individual's behavior in her private life, even in her own home." *Jones* v. *McKenzie,* 266 U.S. App. D.C. 85, 89, 833 F.2d 335, 339 [2 IER Cases 1121] (1987); see also *Capua v. City of Plainfield,* 643 F.Supp. 1507, 1511 [1 IER Cases 625] (NJ 1986) (urine testing is "form of surveillance" which "reports on a person's off-duty activities just as surely as someone had been present and watching"). The FRA's requirement that workers disclose the medications they have taken during the 30 days prior to chemical testing further impinges upon the confidentiality customarily attending personal health secrets.

By any reading of our precedents, the intrusiveness of these three searches demands that they — like other full-scale searches — be justified by probable cause. It is no answer to suggest, as does the majority, that railroad workers have relinquished the protection afforded them by this Fourth Amendment requirement, either by "participat[ing] in an industry that is regulated pervasively to ensure safety" or by undergoing periodic fitness tests pursuant to state law or to collective-bargaining agreements. *Ante,* at 22.

Our decisions in the regulatory search area refute the suggestion that the heavy regulation of the railroad industry eclipses workers' rights under the Fourth Amendment to insist upon a showing of probable cause when their bodily fluids are being extracted. This line of cases has exclusively involved searches of employer *property,* with respect to which "[c]ertain industries have such a history of government oversight that no reasonable expectation of privacy could exist for a *proprietor* over the *stock* of such an enterprise." *Marshall* v. *Barlow's, Inc.,* 436 U.S. 307, 313 (1978) (emphasis added) (citation omitted), quoted in *New York* v. *Burger,* 482 U.S. 691, 700 (1987). Never have we intimated that regulatory searches reduce employees' rights of privacy in their *persons.* See *Camara,* 387 U.S., at 537 "[T]he inspections are [not] personal in nature"); cf. *Donovan* v. *Dewey,* 452 U.S. 594, 598-599 (1981); *Marshall, supra* at 313. As the Court pointed out in *O'Connor,* individuals do not lose Fourth Amendment rights at the workplace gate, 480 U.S., at 716-718; see also *Oliver* v. *United States,* 466 U.S. 170, 178 n.8 (1984), any more than they relinquish these rights at the schoolhouse door, *T. L. O.,* 469 U.S., at 333, or the hotel room threshold. *Hoffa* v. *United States,* 385 U.S. 293, 301 (1966). These rights mean little indeed if, having passed through these portals, an individual may remain subject to a suspicionless search of his person justified solely on the grounds that the Government already is permitted to conduct a search of the inanimate contents of the surrounding area. In holding that searches of persons may fall within the category of regulatory searches permitted in the absence of probable cause or even individualized suspicion, the majority sets a dangerous and ill-conceived precedent.

The majority's suggestion that railroad workers' privacy is only minimally invaded by the collection and testing of their bodily fluids because they undergo periodic fitness tests, *ante,* at 22-23, is equally baseless. As an initial matter, even if participation in these fitness tests did render "minimal" an employee's "interest in bodily security," *ante,* at 23 such minimally intrusive searches of the person require, under our precedents, a justificatory showing of individualized suspicion. See *supra,* at 4. More fundamentally,

railroad employees are *not* routinely required to submit to blood or urine tests to gain or to maintain employment, and railroad employers do not ordinarily have access to employees' blood or urine, and certainly not for the purpose of ascertaining drug or alcohol usage. That railroad employees sometimes undergo tests of eyesight, hearing, skill, intelligence, and agility, *ante,* at 22, n. 8, hardly prepares them for Government demands to submit to the extraction of blood, to excrete under supervision, or to have these bodily fluids tested for the physiological and psychological secrets they may contain. Surely employees who release basic information about their financial and personal history so that employers may ascertain their "ethical fitness" do not, by so doing, relinquish their expectations of privacy with respect to their personal letters and diaries, revealing though these papers may be of their character.

I recognize that invalidating the full-scale searches involved in the FRA's testing regime for failure to comport with the Fourth Amendment's command of probable cause may hinder the Government's attempts to make rail transit as safe as humanly possible. But constitutional rights have their consequences, and one is that efforts to maximize the public welfare, no matter how well-intentioned, must always be pursued within constitutional boundaries. Were the police freed from the constraints of the Fourth Amendment for just one day to seek out evidence of criminal wrongdoing, the resulting convictions and incarcerations would probably prevent thousands of fatalities. Our refusal to tolerate this spectre reflects our shared belief that even beneficent governmental power — whether exercised to save money, save lives, or make the trains run on time — must always yield to "a resolute loyalty to constitutional safeguards." *Almeida-Sanchez* v. *United States,* 413 U. S. 266, 273 (1973). The Constitution demands no less loyalty here.

III

Even accepting the majority's view that the FRA's collection and testing program is appropriately analyzed under a multifactor balancing test, and not under the literal terms of the Fourth Amendment, I would still find the program invalid. The benefits of suspicionless blood and urine testing are far outstripped by the costs imposed on personal liberty by such sweeping searches. Only by erroneously deriding as "minimal" the privacy and dignity interests at stake, and by uncritically inflating the likely efficacy of the FRA's testing program, does the majority strike a different balance.

For the reasons stated above, I find nothing minimal about the intrusion on individual liberty that occurs whenever the Government forcibly draws and analyzes a person's blood and urine. Several aspects of the FRA's testing program exacerbate the intrusiveness of these procedures. Most strikingly, the agency's regulations not only do not forbid, but, in fact, appear to invite criminal prosecutors to obtain the blood and urine samples drawn by the FRA and use them as the basis of criminal investigations and trials. See 49 CFR §219.211(d) (1987) ("Each sample . . . may be made available to . . . a party in litigation upon service of appropriate compulsory process on the custodian of the sample . . ."). This is an unprecedented invitation, leaving open the possibility of criminal prosecutions based on suspicionless searches of the human body. Cf. *National Treasury Employees Union,* post, at 7 (Customs Service drug-testing program prohibits use of test results in criminal prosecutions); *Camara,* 387 U.S., at 537.

To be sure, the majority acknowledges, in passing, the possibility of criminal prosecutions, ante, at 16, n.5, but it refuses to factor this possibility into its Fourth Amendment balancing process, stating that "the record does not disclose that [49 CFR §219.211(d)] was intended to be, or actually has been, so used." *Ibid.* This demurrer is highly disingenuous. The Government concedes that it finds "no prohibition on the release of FRA testing results to prosecutors." Brief for Petitioners 10, n. 15. The absence of prosecutions to date — which is likely due to the fact that the FRA's regulations have been held invalid for much of their brief history — hardly proves that prosecutors will not avail themselves of the FRA's invitation in the future. If the majority really views the impact of FRA testing on privacy interests as minimal even if these tests generate criminal prosecutions, it should say so. If the prospect of prosecutions would lead the majority to reassess the validity of the testing program with prosecutions as part of the balance, it should say so, too, or condition its approval of that program on the nonrelease of test results to prosecutors. In ducking this important issue, the majority gravely disserves both the values served by the Fourth Amendment and the rights of those persons whom the FRA searches. Furthermore, the majority's refusal to restrict the release of

test results casts considerable doubt on the conceptual basis of its decision — that the "special need" of railway safety is one "beyond the normal need for law enforcement." *Ante,* at 14 (citations omitted).[10]

The majority also overlooks needlessly intrusive aspects of the testing process itself. Although the FRA requires the collection and testing of both blood and urine, the agency concedes that mandatory urine tests — unlike blood tests — do not measure current impairment and therefore cannot differentiate on-duty impairment from prior drug or alcohol use which has ceased to affect the user's behavior. See 49 CFR §219.309(2) (1987) (urine test may reveal use of drugs or alcohol as much as 60 days prior to sampling). Given that the FRA's stated goal is to ascertain current impairment, and not to identify persons who have used substances in their spare time sufficiently in advance of their railroad duties to pose no risk of on-duty impairment, §219.101(a), mandatory urine testing seems wholly excessive. At the very least, the FRA could limit its use of urinalysis to confirming findings of current impairment suggested by a person's blood tests. The additional invasion caused by automatically testing urine as well as blood hardly ensures that privacy interests "will be invaded no more than is necessary." *T. L. O.,* 469 U.S., at 343.

The majority's trivialization of the intrusions on worker privacy posed by the FRA's testing program is matched at the other extreme by its blind acceptance of the Government's assertion that testing will "dete[r] employees engaged in safety-sensitive tasks from using controlled substances or alcohol," and "help railroads obtain invaluable information about the causes of major accident[s]." *Ante,* at 25. With respect, first, to deterrence, it is simply implausible that testing employees *after* major accidents occur, 49 CFR §219.201(a)(1) (1987), will appreciably discourage them from using drugs or alcohol. As JUSTICE STEVENS observes in his concurring opinion:

"Most people — and I would think most railroad employees as well — do not go to

_____

[10] As a result of the majority's extension of the regulatory search doctrine to searches of the person, individuals the FRA finds to have used drugs may face criminal prosecution, even if their impairment had nothing to do with causing an accident. The majority observes that evidence of criminal behavior unearthed during an otherwise valid regulatory search is not excludible unless the search is shown to be a "pretext" for obtaining evidence for a criminal trial, ante, at 16, n. 5, citing *New York* v. *Burger,* 482 U.S. 691, 716, 717, n. 27 (1987) — a defense the majority belittles but, mercifully, preserves for another day.

work with the expectation that they may be involved in a major accident, particularly one causing such catastrophic results as loss of life or the release of hazardous material requiring an evacuation. Moreover, even if they are conscious of the possibilities that such an accident might occur and that alcohol or drug use might be a contributing factor, if the risk of serious personal injury does not deter their use of these substances, it seems highly unlikely that the additional threat of loss of employment would have any effect on their behavior." *Ante,* at 1.

Under the majority's deterrence rationale, people who skip school or work to spend a sunny day at the zoo will not taunt the lions because their truancy or absenteeism might be discovered in the event they are mauled. It is, of course, the fear of the accident, not the fear of a postaccident revelation, that deters. The majority's credulous acceptance of the FRA's deterrence rationale is made all the more suspect by the agency's failure to introduce, in an otherwise ample administrative record, *any* studies explaining or supporting its theory of accident deterrence.

The poverty of the majority's deterrence rationale leaves the Government's interest in diagnosing the causes of major accidents as the sole remaining justification for the FRA's testing program. I do not denigrate this interest, but it seems a slender thread from which to hang such an intrusive program, particularly given that the knowledge that one or more workers were impaired at the time of an accident falls far short of proving that substance abuse caused or exacerbated that accident. See 839 F.2d 575, 587 [2 IER Cases 1601] (CA9 1988). Some corroborative evidence is needed: witness or co-worker accounts of a worker's misfeasance, or at least indications that the cause of the accident was within a worker's area of responsibility. Such particularized facts are, of course, the very essence of the individualized suspicion requirement which the respondent railroad workers urge, and which the Court of Appeals found to "pos[e] no insuperable burden on the government." *Id.,* at 588. Furthermore, reliance on the importance of diagnosing the causes of an accident as a critical basis for upholding the FRA's testing plan is especially hard to square with our frequent admonition that the interest in ascertaining the causes of a criminal episode does not justify departure from the Fourth Amendment's requirements. "[T]his Court has never sustained a search upon the sole ground that officers reasonably expected to find evidence of a particular crime . . . ." *Katz,* 389 U.S., at 356. Nor should it here.

IV

In his first dissenting opinion as a Member of this Court, Oliver Wendell Holmes observed:

"Great cases, like hard cases, make bad law. For great cases are called great, not by reason of their real importance in shaping the law of the future, but because of some accident of immediate overwhelming interest which appeals to the feelings and distorts the judgment. These immediate interests exercise a kind of hydraulic pressure which makes what previously was clear seem doubtful, and before which even well settled principles of law will bend." *Northern Securities Co.* v. *United States,* 193 U.S. 197, 400-401 (1904).

A majority of this Court, swept away by society's obsession with stopping the scourge of illegal drugs, today succumbs to the popular pressures described by Justice Holmes. In upholding the FRA's plan for blood and urine testing, the majority bends time-honored and textually-based principles of the Fourth Amendment — principles the Framers of the Bill of Rights designed to ensure that the Government has a strong and individualized justification when it seeks to invade an individual's privacy. I believe the Framers would be appalled by the vision of mass governmental intrusions upon the integrity of the human body that the majority allows to become reality. The immediate victims of the majority's constitutional timorousness will be those railroad workers whose bodily fluids the Government may now forcibly collect and analyze. But ultimately, today's decision will reduce the privacy all citizens may enjoy, for, as Justice Holmes understood, principles of law, once bent, do not snap back easily. I dissent.

TREASURY EMPLOYEES v. VON RAAB

Supreme Court of the United States

NATIONAL TREASURY EMPLOYEES UNION, et al. v. VON RAAB, Commissioner, U.S. Customs Service, No. 86-1879, March 21, 1989

Before REHNQUIST, Chief Justice, and BRENNAN, WHITE, MARSHALL, BLACKMUN, STEVENS, O'CONNOR, SCALIA, and KENNEDY, Justices.

Full Text of Opinion

JUSTICE KENNEDY delivered the opinion of the Court.

We granted certiorari to decide whether it violates the Fourth Amendment for the United States Customs Service to require a urinalysis test from employees who seek transfer or promotion to certain positions.

I

A

The United States Customs Service, a bureau of the Department of the Treasury, is the federal agency responsible for processing persons, carriers, cargo, and mail into the United States, collecting revenue from imports, and enforcing customs and related laws. See Customs USA, Fiscal Year 1985, p.4. An important responsibility of the Service is the interdiction and seizure of contraband, including illegal drugs. *Ibid.* In 1987 alone, Customs agents seized drugs with a retail value of nearly 9 billion dollars. See Customs USA, Fiscal Year 1987, p. 40. In the routine discharge of their duties, many Customs employees have direct contact with those who traffic in drugs for profit. Drug import operations, often directed by sophisticated criminal syndicates, *United States* v. *Mendenhall*, 446 U.S. 544, 561-562 (1980) (Powell, J., concurring), may be effected by violence or its threat. As a necessary response, many Customs operatives carry and use firearms in connection with their official duties. App. 109.

In December 1985, respondent, the Commissioner of Customs, established a Drug Screening Task Force to explore the possibility of implementing a drug screening program within the Service. *Id.*, at 11. After extensive research and consultation with experts in the field, the Task Force concluded "that drug screening through urinalysis is technologically reliable, valid and accurate." *Ibid.* Citing this conclusion, the Commissioner announced his in-

tention to require drug tests of employees who applied for, or occupied, certain positions within the Service. *Id.*, at 10-11. The Commissioner stated his belief that "Customs is largely drug-free," but noted also that "unfortunately no segment of society is immune from the threat of illegal drug use." *Id.*, at 10. Drug interdiction has become the agency's primary enforcement mission, and the Commissioner stressed that "there is no room in the Customs Service for those who break the laws prohibiting the possession and use of illegal drugs." *Ibid.*

In May 1986, the Commissioner announced implementation of the drug-testing program. Drugs tests were made a condition of placement or employment for positions that meet one or more of three criteria. The first is direct involvement in drug interdiction or enforcement of related laws, an activity the Commissioner deemed fraught with obvious dangers to the mission of the agency and the lives of customs agents. *Id.*, at 17, 113. The second criterion is a requirement that the incumbent carry firearms, as the Commissioner concluded that "[p]ublic safety demands that employees who carry deadly arms and are prepared to make instant life or death decisions be drug free." *Id.*, at 113. The third criterion is a requirement for the incumbent to handle "classified" material, which the Commissioner determined might fall into the hands of smugglers if accessible to employees who, by reason of their own illegal drug use, are susceptible to bribery or blackmail. *Id.*, at 114.

After an employee qualifies for a position covered by the Customs testing program, the Service advises him by letter that his final selection is contingent upon successful completion of drug screening. An independent contractor contacts the employee to fix the time and place for collecting sample. On reporting for the test, the employee must produce photographic identification and remove any outer garments, such as a coat or a jacket, and personal belongings. The employee may produce the sample behind a partition, or in the privacy of a bathroom stall if he so chooses. To ensure against adulteration of the specimen, or substitution of a sample from another person, a monitor of the same sex as the employee remains close at hand to listen for the normal sounds of urination. Dye is added to the toilet water to prevent the employee from using the water to adulterate the sample.

Upon receiving the specimen, the monitor inspects it to ensure its proper temperature and color, places a tamper-proof custody seal over the container, and affixes an identification label indicating the date and the individual's specimen number. The employee signs a chain-of-custody form, which is initialed by the monitor, and the urine sample is placed in a plastic bag, sealed, and submitted to a laboratory.[1]

The laboratory tests the sample for the presence of marijuana, cocaine, opiates, amphetamines, and phencyclidine. Two tests are used. An initial screening test uses the enzyme-multiplied-immunoassay technique (EMIT). Any specimen that is identified as positive on this initial test must then be confirmed using gas chromatography/mass spectrometry (GC/MS). Confirmed positive results are reported to a "Medical Review Officer," "[a] licensed physician ... who has knowledge of substance abuse disorders and has appropriate medical training to interpret and evaluate the individual's positive test result together with his or her medical history and any other relevant biomedical information." HHS Reg. §1.2, 53 Fed. Reg. 11980 (1988); HHS Reg. §2.4(g), id., at 11983. After verifying the positive result, the Medical Review Officer transmits it to the agency.

---

[1] After this case was decided by the Court of Appeals. 816 F.2d 170 [2 IER Cases 15] (CA5 1987), the United States Department of Health and Human Services, in accordance with recently enacted legislation. Pub. L. 100–71. §503, 101 Stat. 468–471, promulgated regulations (hereinafter HHS Regulations or HHS Reg.) governing certain federal employee drug testing programs. 53 Fed. Reg. 11979 (1988). To the extent the HHS Regulations add to, or depart from, the procedures adopted as part of a federal drug screening program covered by Pub. L. 100–71, the HHS Regulations control. Pub. L. 100–71, §503(b)(2)(B), 101 Stat. 470. Both parties agree that the Customs Service's drug testing program must conform to the HHS Regulations. See Brief for Petitioners 6, n. 8; Brief for Respondents 4–5. and n.4. We therefore consider the HHS Regulations to the extent they supplement or displace the Commissioner's original directive. See California Bankers Assn. v. Shultz, 416 U.S. 21, 53 (1974); Thorpe v. Housing Authority, 393 U.S. 268, 281–282 (1969).

One respect in which the original Customs directive differs from the now-prevailing regime concerns the extent to which the employee may be required to disclose personal medical information. Under the Service's original plan, each tested employee was asked to disclose, at the time the urine sample was collected, any medications taken within the last 30 days, and to explain any circumstances under which he may have been in legitimate contact with illegal substances within the last 30 days. Failure to provide this information at this time could result in the agency not considering the effect of medications or other licit contacts with drugs on a positive test result. Under the HHS Regulations, an employee need not provide information concerning medications when he produces the sample for testing. He may instead present such information only after he is notified that his specimen tested positive for illicit drugs, at which time the Medical Review Officer reviews all records made available by the employee to determine whether the positive indication could have been caused by lawful use of drugs. See HHS Reg. §2.7, 53 Fed. Reg. 11985–11986 (1988).

Customs employees who test positive for drugs and who can offer no satisfactory explanation are subject to dismissal from the Service. Test results may not, however, be turned over to any other agency, including criminal prosecutors, without the employee's written consent.

B

Petitioners, a union of federal employees and a union official, commenced this suit in the United States District Court for the Eastern District of Louisiana on behalf of current Customs Service employees who seek covered positions. Petitioners alleged that the Custom Service drug-testing program violated, inter alia, the Fourth Amendment. The District Court agreed. 649 F.Supp. 380 [1 IER Cases 945] (1986). The court acknowledged "the legitimate governmental interest in a drug-free work place and work force," but concluded that "the drug testing plan constitutes an overly intrusive policy of searches and seizures without probable cause or reasonable suspicion, in violation of legitimate expectations of privacy." Id., at 387. The court enjoined the drug testing program, and ordered the Customs Service not to require drug tests of any applicants for covered positions.

A divided panel of the United States Court of Appeals for the Fifth Circuit vacated the injunction. 816 F.2d 170 [2 IER Cases 15] (1987). The court agreed with petitioners that the drug screening program, by requiring an employee to produce a urine sample for chemical testing, effects a search within the meaning of the Fourth Amendment. The court held further that the searches required by the Commissioner's directive are reasonable under the Fourth Amendment. It first noted that "[t]he Service has attempted to minimize the intrusiveness of the search" by not requiring visual observation of the act of urination and by affording notice to the employee that he will be tested. Id., at 177. The court also considered it significant that the program limits discretion in determining which employees are to be tested, ibid., and noted that the tests are an aspect of the employment relationship. Id., at 178.

The court further found that the Government has a strong interest in detecting drug use among employees who meet the criteria of the Customs program. It reasoned that drug use by covered employees casts substantial doubt on their ability to discharge their duties honestly and vigorously, undermining public confidence in the integrity of the Service and concomitantly impairing the Service's efforts to enforce the drug laws. *Id.*, at 178. Illicit drug users, the court found, are susceptible to bribery and blackmail may be tempted to divert for their own use portions of any drug shipments they interdict, and may, if required to carry firearms, "endanger the safety of their fellow agents, as well as their own, when their performance is impaired by drug use." *Ibid.* "Considering the nature and responsibilities of the jobs for which applicants are being considered at Customs and the limited scope of the search," the court stated, "the exaction of consent as a condition of assignment to the new job is not unreasonable." *Id.*, at 179.

The dissenting judge concluded that the Customs program is not an effective method for achieving the Service's goals. He argued principally that an employee "given a five day notification of a test date need only abstain from drug use to prevent being identified as a user." *Id.*, at 184. He noted also that persons already employed in sensitive positions are not subject to the test. *Ibid.* Because he did not believe the Customs program can achieve its purposes, the dissenting judge found it unreasonable under the Fourth Amendment.

We granted certiorari. 485 U.S. —— (1988). We now affirm so much of the judgment of the court of appeals as upheld the testing of employees directly involved in drug interdiction or required to carry firearms. We vacate the judgment to the extent it upheld the testing of applicants for positions requiring the incumbent to handle classified materials, and remand for further proceedings.

II

[1] In *Skinner* v. *Railway Labor Executives Assn.* [4 IER Cases 224], *ante* at 11-14, decided today, we hold that federal regulations requiring employees of private railroads to produce urine samples for chemical testing implicate the Fourth Amendment, as those tests invade reasonable expectations of privacy. Our earlier cases have settled that the Fourth Amendment protects individuals from unreasonable searches conducted by the Government, even when the Government acts as an employer, *O'Connor* v. *Ortega*, 480 U.S. 709, 717 [1 IER Cases 1617] (1987) (plurality opinion); see *id.*, at 731 (SCALIA, J., concurring in judgment), and, in view of our holding in *Railway Labor Executives* that urine tests are searches, it follows that the Customs Service's drug testing program must meet the reasonableness requirement of the Fourth Amendment.

While we have often emphasized, and reiterate today, that a search must be supported, as a general matter, by a warrant issued upon probable cause, see, *e.g.*, *Griffin* v. *Wisconsin*, 483 U.S. 868, —— (1987); *United States* v. *Karo*, 468 U.S. 705, 717 (1984), our decision in *Railway Labor Executives* reaffirms the longstanding principle that neither a warrant nor probable cause, nor, indeed, any measure of individualized suspicion, is an indispensable component of reasonableness in every circumstance. *Ante*, at 14-19. See also *New Jersey* v. *T.L.O.*, 469 U.S. 325, 342, n. 8 (1985); *United States* v. *Martinez-Fuerte*, 428 U.S. 543, 556-661 (1976). As we note in *Railway Labor Executives*, our cases establish that where a Fourth Amendment intrusion serves special governmental needs, beyond the normal need for law enforcement, it is necessary to balance the individual's privacy expectations against the Government's interests to determine whether it is impractical to require a warrant or some level of individualized suspicion in the particular context. *Ante*, at 14-15.

It is clear that the Customs Service's drug testing program is not designed to serve the ordinary needs of law enforcement. Test results may not be used in a criminal prosecution of the employee without the employee's consent. The purposes of the program are to deter drug use among those eligible for promotion to sensitive positions within the Service and to prevent the promotion of drug users to those positions. These substantial interests, no less than the Government's concern for safe rail transportation at issue in *Railway Labor Executives*, present a special need that may justify departure from the ordinary warrant and probable cause requirements.

A

[2] Petitioners do not contend that a warrant is required by the balance of privacy and governmental interests in this context, nor could any such contention withstand scrutiny. We have recognized before that requiring the Government to procure a warrant for every work-related intrusion "would conflict with 'the common-sense realization that government offices could not function if every employment decision became a constitutional matter.'" *O'Connor* v. *Ortega, supra*, at 722, quoting *Connick* v. *Myers*, 461 U.S. 138, 143 [1 IER Cases 178] (1983). See also *id.*, at 732 (SCALIA, J., concurring in judgment); *New Jersey* v. *T.L.O., supra*, at 340 (noting that "[t]he warrant requirement . . . is unsuited to the school environment: requiring a

teacher to obtain a warrant before searching a child suspected of an infraction of school rules (or of the criminal law) would unduly interfere with the maintenance of the swift and informal disciplinary procedures needed in the schools"). Even if Customs Service employees are more likely to be familiar with the procedures required to obtain a warrant than most other Government workers, requiring a warrant in this context would serve only to divert valuable agency resources from the Service's primary mission. The Customs Service has been entrusted with pressing responsibilities, and its mission would be compromised if it were required to seek search warrants in connection with routine, yet sensitive, employment decisions.

Furthermore, a warrant would provide little or nothing in the way of additional protection of personal privacy. A warrant serves primarily to advise the citizen that an intrusion is authorized by law and limited in its permissible scope and to interpose a neutral magistrate between the citizen and the law enforcement officer "engaged in the often competitive enterprise of ferreting out crime." *Johnson v. United States*, 333 U.S. 10, 14 (1948). But in the present context, "the circumstances justifying toxicological testing and the permissible limits of such intrusions are defined narrowly and specifically . . . , and doubtless are well known to covered employees." *Ante*, at 17. Under the Customs program, every employee who seeks a transfer to a covered position knows that he must take a drug test, and is likewise aware of the procedures the Service must follow in administering the test. A covered employee is simply not subject "to the discretion of the official in the field." *Camara* v. *Municipal Court*, 387 U.S. 523, 532 (1967). The process becomes automatic when the employee elects to apply for, and thereafter pursue, a covered position. Because the Service does not make a discretionary determination to search based on a judgment that certain conditions are present, there are simply "no special facts for a neutral magistrate to evaluate." *South Dakota* v. *Opperman*, 428 U.S. 364, 383 (1976) (POWELL, J., concurring).

B

[3, 4] Even where it is reasonable to dispense with the warrant requirement in the particular circumstances, a search ordinarily must be based on probable cause. *Ante*, at 19. Our cases teach, however, that the probable-cause standard " 'is peculiarly related to criminal investigations.' " *Colorado* v. *Bertine*, 479 U.S. 367, 371 (1987), quoting *South Dakota* v. *Opperman*, 428 U.S. 364, 370, n.5 (1976). In particular, the traditional probable-cause standard may be unhelpful in analyzing the reasonableness of routine administrative functions, *Colorado* v. *Bertine*, *supra*, at 371; see also *O'Connor* v. *Ortega*, 480 U.S., at 723, especially where the Government seeks to *prevent* the development of hazardous conditions or to detect violations that rarely generate articulable grounds for searching any particular place or person. Cf. *Camara* v. *Municipal Court*, 387 U.S., at 535–536 (noting that building code inspections, unlike searches conducted pursuant to a criminal investigation, are designed "to prevent even the unintentional development of conditions which are hazardous to public health and safety"); *United States* v. *Martinez-Fuerte*, 428 U.S., at 557 (noting that requiring particularized suspicion before routine stops on major highways near the Mexican border "would be impractical because the flow of traffic tends to be too heavy to allow the particularized study of a given car that would enable it to be identified as a possible carrier of illegal aliens"). Our precedents have settled that, in certain limited circumstances, the Government's need to discover such latent or hidden conditions, or to prevent their development, is sufficiently compelling to justify the intrusion on privacy entailed by conducting such searches without any measure of individualized suspicion. *E.g.*, *ante*, at 19. We think the Government's need to conduct the suspicionless searches required by the Customs program outweighs the privacy interests of employees engaged directly in drug interdiction, and of those who otherwise are required to carry firearms.

The Customs Service is our Nation's first line of defense against one of the greatest problems affecting the health and welfare of our population. We have adverted before to "the veritable national crisis in law enforcement caused by smuggling of illicit narcotics." *United States* v. *Montoya de Hernandez*, 473 U.S. 531, 538 (1985). See also *Florida* v. *Royer*, 460 U.S. 491, 513 (BLACKMUN, J., dissenting). Our cases also reflect the traffickers' seemingly inexhaustible repertoire of deceptive practices and elaborate schemes for importing narcotics, *e.g.*, *United States* v. *Montoya de Hernandez*, *supra*, at 538–539; *United States* v. *Ramsey*, 431 U.S. 606, 608–609 (1977). The record in this case confirms that, through the adroit selection of source locations, smuggling routes, and increasingly elaborate methods of concealment, drug traffickers have managed to bring into this country increasingly large quantities of illegal drugs. App. 111. The record also indicates, and it is well known, that drug smugglers do not hesitate to use violence to protect their lucrative trade and avoid apprehension. *Id.*, at 109.

Many of the Service's employees are often exposed to this criminal element and to the controlled substances they seek to smuggle into the country. *Ibid.* Cf. *United States* v. *Montoya de Hernandez, supra*, at 543. The physical safety of these employees may be threatened, and many may be tempted not only by bribes from the traffickers with whom they deal, but also by their own access to vast sources of valuable contraband seized and controlled by the Service. The Commissioner indicated below that "Customs [o]fficers have been shot, stabbed, run over, dragged by automobiles, and assaulted with blunt objects while performing their duties." App. at 109-110. At least nine officers have died in the line of duty since 1974. He also noted that Customs officers have been the targets of bribery by drug smugglers on numerous occasions, and several have been removed from the Service for accepting bribes and other integrity violations. *Id.*, at 114. See also Customs USA, Fiscal Year 1987, at 31 (reporting internal investigations that resulted in the arrest of 24 employees and 54 civilians); Customs USA, Fiscal Year 1986, p.32 (reporting that 334 criminal and serious integrity investigations were conducted during the fiscal year, resulting in the arrest of 37 employees and 17 civilians); Customs USA, Fiscal Year 1985, at 32 (reporting that 284 criminal and serious integrity investigations were conducted during the 1985 fiscal year, resulting in the arrest of 15 employees and 51 civilians).

It is readily apparent that the Government has a compelling interest in ensuring that front-line interdiction personnel are physically fit, and have unimpeachable integrity and judgment. Indeed, the Government's interest here is at least as important as its interest in searching travelers entering the country. We have long held that travelers seeking to enter the country may be stopped and required to submit to a routine search without probable cause, or even founded suspicion, "because of national self protection reasonably requiring one entering the country to identify himself as entitled to come in, and his belongings as effects which may be lawfully brought in." *Carroll* v. *United States*, 267 U.S. 132, 154 (1985). See also *United States* v. *Montoya de Hernandez, supra*, at 538; *United States* v. *Ramsey, supra*, at

617-619. This national interest in self protection could be irreparably damaged if those charged with safeguarding it were, because of their own drug use, unsympathetic to their mission of interdicting narcotics. A drug user's indifference to the Service's basic mission or, even worse, his active complicity with the malefactors, can facilitate importation of sizable drug shipments or block apprehension of dangerous criminals. The public interest demands effective measures to bar drug users from positions directly involving the interdiction of illegal drugs.

The public interest likewise demands effective measures to prevent the promotion of drug users to positions that require the incumbent to carry a firearm, even if the incumbent is not engaged directly in the interdiction of drugs. Customs employees who may use deadly force plainly "discharge duties fraught with such risks of injury to others that even a momentary lapse of attention can have disastrous consequences." *Ante*, at 23. We agree with the Government that the public should not bear the risk that employees who may suffer from impaired perception and judgment will be promoted to positions where they may need to employ deadly force. Indeed, ensuring against the creation of this dangerous risk will itself further Fourth Amendment values, as the use of deadly force may violate the Fourth Amendment in certain circumstances. See *Tennessee* v. *Garner*, 471 U.S. 1, 7-12 (1985).

Against these valid public interests we must weigh the interference with individual liberty that results from requiring these classes of employees to undergo a urine test. The interference with individual privacy that results from the collection of a urine sample for subsequent chemical analysis could be substantial in some circumstances. *Ante*, at 21. We have recognized, however, that the "operational realities of the workplace" may render entirely reasonable certain work-related intrusions by supervisors and co-workers that might be viewed as unreasonable in other contexts. See *O'Connor* v. *Ortega*, 480 U.S., at 717; *id.*, at 732 (SCALIA, J., concurring in judgment). While these operational realities will rarely affect an employee's expectations of privacy with respect to searches of his person, or of personal effects that the employee may bring to the workplace, *id.*, at 716, 725, it is plain that certain forms of public employment may diminish privacy expectations even with respect to such personal searches. Employees of the United States Mint, for example, should expect to be subject to certain routine personal searches when they leave the workplace every day. Similarly, those who join our military or intelligence services may not only be required to give what in other contexts might be viewed as extraordinary assurances of trustworthiness and probity, but also may expect intrusive inquiries into their physical fitness for those special positions. Cf. *Snepp* v. *United States*, 444 U.S. 507, 509, n.3 (1980); *Parker* v. *Levy*, 417 U.S. 733, 758 (1974); *Committee for GI Rights* v. *Callaway*, 171 U.S. App. D.C. 73, 84, 518 F.2d 466, 477 (1975).

We think Customs employees who are directly involved in the interdiction of illegal drugs or who are required to carry firearms in the line of duty likewise have a diminished expectation of privacy in respect to the intrusions occasioned by a urine test. Unlike most private citizens or government employees in general, employees involved in drug interdiction reasonably should expect effective inquiry into their fitness and probity. Much the same is true of employees who are required to carry firearms. Because successful performance of their duties depends uniquely on their judgment and dexterity, these employees cannot reasonably expect to keep from the Service personal information that bears directly on their fitness. Cf. *In re Caruso* v. *Ward*, 72 N.Y.2d 433, 441, 530 N.E.2d 850, 854-855 [3 IER Cases 1537] (1988). While reasonable tests designed to elicit this information doubtless infringe some privacy expectations, we do not believe these expectations outweigh the Government's compelling interests in safety and in the integrity of our borders.[2]

[5] Without disparaging the importance of the governmental interests that support the suspicionless searches of these employees, petitioners nevertheless contend that the Service's drug testing program is unreasonable in two particulars. First, petitioners argue that the program is unjustified because it is not based on a belief that testing will reveal any drug use by covered employees. In pressing this argument, petitioners point out that the Service's testing scheme was not implemented in response to any perceived drug problem among Customs employees, and that the program actually has not led to the discovery of a significant number of drug users.

Brief for Petitioners 37, 44; Tr. of Oral Arg. 11-12, 20-21. Counsel for petitioners informed us at oral argument that no more than 5 employees out of 3,600 have tested positive for drugs. *Id.*, at 11. Second, petitioners contend that the Service's scheme is not a "sufficiently productive mechanism to justify [its] intrusion upon Fourth Amendment interests," *Delaware* v. *Prouse*, 440 U.S. at 648, 658-659, because illegal drug users can avoid detection with ease by temporary abstinence or by surreptitious adulteration of their urine specimens. Brief for Petitioners 46-47. These contentions are unpersuasive.

Petitioners' first contention evinces an unduly narrow view of the context in which the Service's testing program was implemented. Petitioners do not dispute, nor can there be doubt, that drug abuse is one of the most serious problems confronting our society today. There is little reason to believe that American workplaces are immune from this pervasive social problem, as is amply illustrated by our decision in *Railway Labor Executives*. See also *Masino* v. *United States*, 589 F.2d 1048, 1050 (Ct.Cl. 1978) (describing marijuana use by two Customs Inspectors). Detecting drug impairment on the part of employees can be a difficult task, especially where, as here, it is not feasible to subject employees and their work-product to the kind of day-to-day scrutiny that is the norm in more

___

[2] The procedures prescribed by the Customs Service for the collection and analysis of the requisite samples do not carry the grave potential for "arbitrary and oppressive interference with the privacy and personal security of individuals," *United States* v. *Martinez-Fuerte*, 428 U.S. 543, 554, (1976), that the Fourth Amendment was designed

to prevent. Indeed, these procedures significantly minimize the program's intrusion on privacy interests. Only employees who have been tentatively accepted for promotion or transfer to one of the three categories of covered positions are tested, and applicants know at the outset that a drug test is a requirement of those positions. Employees are also notified in advance of the scheduled sample collection, thus reducing to a minimum any "unsettling show of authority," *Delaware* v. *Prouse*, 440 U.S. 648, 657 (1979), that may be associated with unexpected intrusions on privacy. Cf. *United States* v. *Martinez-Fuerte, supra*, at 559 (noting that the intrusion on privacy occasioned by routine highway checkpoints is minimized by the fact that motorists "are not taken by surprise as they know, or may obtain knowledge of, the location of checkpoints and will not be stopped elsewhere"); *Wyman* v. *James*, 400 U.S. 309, 320-321 (1971) (providing a welfare recipient with advance notice that she would be visited by a welfare caseworker minimized the intrusion on privacy occasioned by the visit). There is no direct observation of the act of urination, as the employee may provide a specimen in the privacy of a stall.

Further, urine samples may be examined only for the specified drugs. The use of samples to test for any other substances is prohibited. See HHS Reg. §2.1(c), 53 Fed. Reg. 11980 (1988). And, as the court of appeals noted, the combination of EMIT and GC/MS tests required by the Service is highly accurate, assuming proper storage, handling, and measurement techniques. 816 F.2d at 181. Finally, an employee need not disclose personal medical information to the Government unless his test result is positive, and even then any such information is reported to a licensed physician. Taken together, these procedures significantly minimize the intrusiveness of the Service's drug screening program.

traditional office environments. Indeed, the almost unique mission of the Service gives the Government a compelling interest in ensuring that many of these covered employees do not use drugs even off-duty, for such use creates risks of bribery and blackmail against which the Government is entitled to guard. In light of the extraordinary safety and national security hazards that would attend the promotion of drug users to positions that require the carrying of firearms or the interdiction of controlled substances, the Service's policy of deterring drug users from seeking such promotions cannot be deemed unreasonable.

The mere circumstance that all but a few of the employees tested are entirely innocent of wrongdoing does not impugn the program's validity. The same is likely to be true of householders who are required to submit to suspicionless housing code inspections, see Camara v. Municipal Court, 387 U.S. 523 (1967), and of motorists who are stopped at the checkpoints we approved in United States v. Martinez-Fuerte, 428 U.S. 543 (1976). The Service's program is designed to prevent the promotion of drug users to sensitive positions as much as it is designed to detect those employees who use drugs. Where, as here, the possible harm against which the Government seeks to guard is substantial, the need to prevent its occurrence furnishes an ample justification for reasonable searches calculated to advance the Government's goal.[3]

[6] We think petitioners' second argument — that the Service's testing program is ineffective because employees may attempt to deceive the test by a brief abstention before the test date, or by adulterating their urine specimens — overstates the case. As the Court of Appeals noted, addicts may be unable to abstain even for a limited period of time, or may be unaware of the "fade-away effect" of certain drugs. 816 F.2d, at 180. More importantly, the avoidance techniques suggested by petitioners are fraught with uncertainty and risks for those employees who venture to attempt them. A particular employee's pattern of elimination for a given drug cannot be predicted with perfect accuracy, and, in any event, this information is not likely to be known or available to the employee. Petitioners' own expert indicated below that the time it takes for particular drugs to become undetectable in urine can vary widely depending on the individual, and may extend for as long as 22 days. App. 66. See also ante, at 26 (noting Court of Appeals' reliance on certain academic literature that indicates that the testing of urine can discover drug use " 'for . . . weeks after the ingestion of the drug' "). Thus, contrary to petitioners' suggestion, no employee reasonably can expect to deceive the test by the simple expedient of abstaining after the test date is assigned. Nor can he expect attempts at adulteration to succeed, in view of the precautions taken by the sample collector to ensure the integrity of the sample. In all the circumstances, we are persuaded that the program bears a close and substantial relation to the Service's goal of deterring drug users from seeking promotion to sensitive positions.[4]

---

[3] The point is well illustrated also by the Federal Government's practice of requiring the search of all passengers seeking to board commercial air liners, as well as the search of their carry-on luggage, without any basis for suspecting any particular passenger of an untoward motive. Applying our precedents dealing with administrative searches, see, e.g., Camara v. Municipal Court, the lower courts that have considered the question have consistently concluded that such searches are reasonable under the Fourth Amendment. As Judge Friendly explained in a leading case upholding such searches:

"When the risk is the jeopardy to hundreds of human lives and millions of dollars of property inherent in the pirating or blowing up of a large airplane, that danger alone meets the test of reasonableness, so long as the search is conducted in good faith for the purpose of preventing hijacking or like damage and with reasonable scope and the passenger has been given advance notice of his liability to such a search so that he can avoid it by choosing not to travel by air." United States v. Edwards, 498 F.2d 496, 500 (CA2 1974) (emphasis in original). See also United States v. Skipwith, 482 F.2d 1272, 1275-1276 (CA5 1973); United States v. Davis, 482 F.2d 893, 907-912 (CA9 1973).

It is true, as counsel for petitioners pointed out at oral argument, that these air piracy precautions were adopted in response to an observable national and international hijacking crisis. Tr. of Oral Arg. 13. Yet we would not suppose that, if the validity of these searches be conceded, the Government would be precluded from conducting them absent a demonstration of danger as to any particular airport or airline. It is sufficient that the Government have a compelling interest in preventing an otherwise pervasive societal problem from spreading to the particular context.

Nor would we think, in view of the obvious deterrent purpose of these searches, that the validity of the Government's airport screening program necessarily turns on whether significant numbers of putative air pirates are actually discovered by the searches conducted under the program. In the 15 years the program has been in effect, more than 9.5 billion persons have been screened, and over 10 billion pieces of luggage have been inspected. See Federal Aviation Administration, Semiannual Report to Congress on the Effectiveness of The Civil Aviation Program (Nov. 1988) (Exhibit 6). By far the overwhelming majority of those persons who have been searched, like Customs employees who have been tested under the Service's drug screening scheme, have proved entirely innocent — only 42,000 firearms have been detected during the same period. Ibid. When the Government's interest lies in deterring highly hazardous conduct, a low incidence of such conduct, far from impugning the validity of the scheme for implementing this interest, is more logically viewed as a hallmark of success. See Bell v. Wolfish, 441 U.S. 520, 559 (1979).

[4] Indeed, petitioners' objection is based on those features of the Service's program — the provision of advance notice and the failure of the sample

In sum, we believe the Government has demonstrated that its compelling interests in safeguarding our borders and the public safety outweigh the privacy expectations of employees who seek to be promoted to positions that directly involve the interdiction of illegal drugs or that require the incumbent to carry a firearm. We hold that the testing of these employees is reasonable under the Fourth Amendment.

C

[7] We are unable, on the present record, to assess the reasonableness of the Government's testing program insofar as it covers employees who are required "to handle classified material." App. 17. We readily agree that the Government has a compelling interest in protecting truly sensitive information from those who, "under compulsion of circumstances or for other reasons, ... might compromise [such] information." *Department of the Navy v. Egan,* 484 U.S. 518, —— (1988). See also *United States* v. *Robel,* 389 U.S. 258, 267 (1967) ("We have recognized that, while the Constitution protects against invasions of individual rights, it does not withdraw from the Government the power to safeguard its vital interest.... The Government can deny access to its secrets to those who would use such information to harm the Nation"). We also agree that employees who seek promotions to positions where they would handle sensitive information can be required to submit to a urine test under the Service's screening program, especially if the positions covered under this category require background investigations, medical examinations, or other intrusions that may be expected to diminish their expectations of privacy in respect of a urinalysis test. Cf. *Department of the Navy* v. *Egan, supra,* at —— (noting that the Executive branch generally subjects those desiring a security clearance to "a background investigation that varies according to the degree of adverse effect the applicant could have on the national security").

[8] It is not clear, however, whether the category defined by the Service's testing directive encompasses only those Customs employees likely to gain access to sensitive information. Employees who are tested under the Service's scheme include those holding such diverse positions as "Accountant," "Accounting Technician," "Animal Caretaker," "Attorney (All)," "Baggage Clerk," "Co-op Student (All)," "Electric Equipment Repairer," "Mail Clerk/Assistant," and "Messenger." App. 42–43. We assume these positions were selected for coverage under the Service's testing program by reason of the incumbent's access to "classified" information, as it is not clear that they would fall under either of the two categories we have already considered. Yet it is not evident that those occupying these positions likely to gain access to sensitive information, and this apparent discrepancy raises in our minds the question whether the Service has defined this category of employees more broadly than necessary to meet the purposes of the Commissioner's directive.

We cannot resolve this ambiguity on the basis of the record before us, and we think it is appropriate to remand the case to the court of appeals for such proceedings as may be necessary to clarify the scope of this category of employees subject to testing. Upon remand the court of appeals should examine the criteria used by the Service in determining what materials are classified and in deciding whom to test under this rubric. In assessing the reasonableness of requiring tests of these employees, the court should also consider pertinent information bearing upon the employees' privacy expectations, as well as the supervision to which these employees are already subject.

III.

Where the Government requires its employees to produce urine samples to be analyzed for evidence of illegal drug use, the collection and subsequent chemical analysis of such samples are searches that must meet the reasonableness requirement of the Fourth Amendment. Because the testing program adopted by the Customs Service is not designed to serve the ordinary need of law enforcement, we have balanced the public interest in the Service's testing program against the privacy concerns implicated by the tests, without reference to our usual presumption in favor of the procedures specified in the Warrant Clause, to assess whether the tests required by Customs are reasonable.

We hold that the suspicionless testing of employees who apply for promotion to positions directly involving the interdiction of illegal drugs, or to positions which require the incumbent to carry a firearm, is reasonable. The Government's compelling interests in preventing the promotion of drug us-

---

collector to observe directly the act of urination — that contribute significantly to diminish the program's intrusion on privacy. See *supra,* at 14, n.2. Thus, under petitioners' view, "the testing program would be more likely to be constitutional if it were more pervasive and more invasive of privacy." 816 F.2d, at 180.

ers to positions where they might endanger the integrity of our Nation's borders or the life of the citizenry outweigh the privacy interests of those who seek promotion to these positions, who enjoy a diminished expectation of privacy by virtue of the special, and obvious, physical and ethical demands of those positions. We do not decide whether testing those who apply for promotion to positions where they would handle "classified" information is reasonable because we find the record inadequate for this purpose.

The judgment of the Court of Appeals for the Fifth Circuit is affirmed in part and vacated in part, and the case is remanded for further proceedings consistent with this opinion.

It is so ordered.

Dissenting Opinions

JUSTICE MARSHALL, with whom JUSTICE BRENNAN joins, dissenting.

For the reasons stated in my dissenting opinion in *Skinner* v. *Railway Labor Executives Association* [4 IER Cases 224], *ante*, p. ——, I also dissent from the Court's decision in this case. Here, as in *Skinner*, the Court's abandonment of the Fourth Amendment's express requirement that searches of the person rest on probable cause is unprincipled and unjustifiable. But even if I believed that balancing analysis was appropriate under the Fourth Amendment, I would still dissent from today's judgment, for the reasons stated by JUSTICE SCALIA in his dissenting opinion, *post*, p. ——, and for the reasons noted by the dissenting judge below relating to the inadequate tailoring of the Customs Service's drug-testing plan. See 816 F.2d 170, 182–184 [2 IER Cases 15] (CA5 1987) (Hill, J.).

JUSTICE SCALIA, with whom JUSTICE STEVENS joins, dissenting.

The issue in this case is not whether Customs Service employees can constitutionally be denied promotion, or even dismissed, for a single instance of unlawful drug use, at home or at work. They assuredly can. The issue here is what steps can constitutionally be taken to *detect* such drug use. The Government asserts it can demand that employees perform "an excretory function traditionally shielded by great privacy," *Skinner* v. *Railway Labor Executives' Assn.* [4 IER Cases 224], *ante*, at 21, while "a monitor of the same sex . . . remains close at hand to listen for the normal sounds," *ante*, at 3, and that the excretion thus produced be turned over to the Government for chemical analysis. The Court agrees that this constitutes a search for purposes of the Fourth Amendment — and I think it obvious that it is a type of search particularly destructive of privacy and offensive to personal dignity.

Until today this Court had upheld a bodily search separate from arrest and without individualized suspicion of wrong-doing only with respect to prison inmates, relying upon the uniquely dangerous nature of that environment. See *Bell* v. *Wolfish*, 441 U.S. 520, 558–560 (1979). Today, in *Skinner*, we allow a less intrusive bodily search of railroad employees involved in train accidents. I joined the Court's opinion there because the demonstrated frequency of drug and alcohol use by the targeted class of employees, and the demonstrated connection between such use and grave harm, rendered the search a reasonable means of protecting society. I decline to join the Court's opinion in the present case because neither frequency of use nor connection to harm is demonstrated or even likely. In my view the Customs Service rules are a kind of immolation of privacy and human dignity in symbolic opposition to drug use.

The Fourth Amendment protects the "right of the people to be secure in their persons, houses, papers, and effects, against unreasonable searches and seizures." While there are some absolutes in Fourth Amendment law, as soon as those have been left behind and the question comes down to whether a particular search has been "reasonable," the answer depends largely upon the social necessity that prompts the search. Thus, in upholding the administrative search of a student purse in a school, we began with the observation (documented by an agency report to Congress) that "[m]aintaining order in the classroom has never been easy, but in recent years, school disorder has often taken particularly ugly forms: drug use and violent crime in the schools have become major social problems." *New Jersey* v. *T.L.O.*, 469 U.S. 325, 339 (1985). When we approved fixed checkpoints near the Mexican border to stop and search cars for illegal aliens, we observed at the outset that "the Immigration and Naturalization Service now suggests there may be as many as 10 or 12 million aliens illegally in the country," and that "[i]nterdicting the flow of illegal entrants from Mexico poses formidable law enforcement problems." *United States* v. *Martinez-Fuerte*, 428 U.S. 543, 551–552 (1976). And the substantive analysis of our opinion today in *Skinner* begins, "[t]he problem of alcohol use on American railroads is as old as the industry itself," and goes on to cite statistics concerning that problem and the accidents it causes, including a 1979 study finding that "23% of the operating personnel were 'problem drinkers.' " *Skinner, ante*, at 1, and 2, n.1.

The Court's opinion in the present case, however, will be searched in vain for real evidence of a real problem that will be solved by urine testing of Customs Service employees. Instead, there are assurances that "[t]he Customs Service is our Nation's first line of defense against one of the greatest problems affecting the health and welfare of our population," *ante*, at 10; that "[m]any of the Service's employees are often exposed to [drug smugglers] and to the controlled substances they seek to smuggle into the country," *ante*, at 11; that "Customs officers have been the targets of bribery by drug smugglers on numerous occasions, and several have been removed from the Service for accepting bribes and other integrity violations," *ibid.*; that "the Government has a compelling interest in ensuring that front-line interdiction personnel are physically fit, and have unimpeachable integrity and judgment," *ibid*; that the "national interest in self protection could be irreparably damaged if those charged with safeguarding it were, because of their own drug use, unsympathetic to their mission of interdicting narcotics," *ante*, at 12; and that "the public should not bear the risk that employees who may suffer from impaired perception and judgment will be promoted to positions where they may need to employ deadly force," *ibid*. To paraphrase Churchill, all this contains much that is obviously true, and much that is relevant; unfortunately, what is obviously true is not relevant, and what is relevant is not obviously true. The only pertinent points, it seems to me, are supported by nothing but speculation, and not very plausible speculation at that. It is not apparent to me that a Customs Service employee who uses drugs is significantly more likely to be bribed by a drug smuggler, any more than a Customs Service employee who wears diamonds is significantly more likely to be bribed by a diamond smuggler — unless, perhaps, the addiction to drugs is so severe, and requires so much money to maintain, that it would be detectable even without benefit of a urine test. Nor is it apparent to me that Customs officers who use drugs will be appreciably less "sympathetic" to their drug-interdiction mission, any more than police officers who exceed the speed limit in their private cars are appreciably less sympathetic to their mission of enforcing the traffic laws. (The only difference is that the Customs officer's individual efforts, if they are irreplaceable, can theoretically affect the availability of his own drug supply — a prospect so remote as to be an absurd basis of motivation.) Nor, finally, is it apparent to me that urine tests will be even marginally more effective in preventing gun-carrying agents from risking "impaired perception and judgment" than is their current knowledge that, if impaired, they may be shot dead in unequal combat with unimpaired smugglers — unless, again, their addiction is so severe that no urine test is needed for detection.

What is absent in the Government's justifications — notably absent, revealingly absent, and as far as I am concerned dispositively absent — is the recitation of *even a single instance* in which any of the speculated horribles actually occurred: an instance, that is, in which the cause of bribe-taking, or of poor aim, or of unsympathetic law enforcement, or of compromise of classified information, was drug use. Although the Court points out that several employees have in the past been removed from the Service for accepting bribes and other integrity violations, and that at least nine officers have died in the line of duty since 1974, *ante*, at 11, there is no indication whatever that these incidents were related to drug use by Service employees. Perhaps concrete evidence of the severity of a problem is unnecessary when it is so well known that courts can almost take judicial notice of it; but that is surely not the case here. The Commissioner of Customs himself has stated that he "believe[s] that Customs is largely drug-free," that "[t]he extent of illegal drug use by Customs employees was not the reason for establishing this program," and that he "hope[s] and expect[s] to receive reports of very few positive findings through drug screening." App. 10, 15. The test results have fulfilled those hopes and expectations. According to the Service's counsel, out of 3,600 employees tested, no more than 5 tested positive for drugs. *See ante*, at 15.

The Court's response to this lack of evidence is that "[t]here is little reason to believe that American workplaces are immune from [the] pervasive social problem" of drug abuse. *Ante*, at 15. Perhaps such a generalization would suffice if the workplace at issue could produce such catastrophic social harm that no risk whatever is tolerable — the secured areas of a nuclear power plant, for example, see *Rushton* v. *Nebraska Public Power District*, 844 F.2d 562 [3 IER Cases 257] (CA8 1988). But if such a generalization suffices to justify demeaning bodily searches, without particularized suspicion, to guard against the bribing or blackmailing of a law enforcement agent, or the careless use of a firearm, then the Fourth Amendment has become frail protection indeed. In *Skinner, Bell, T.L.O.*, and *Martinez-Fuerte*, we took pains to establish the existence of special need for the search or seizure — a need based not upon the existence of a "pervasive social problem" combined with speculation as to the effect of that problem in the field at issue, but rather upon well known or well demonstrated evils in that field, with well known or well demonstrated consequences. In *Skinner*, for example, we pointed to a long history of alcohol abuse in the railroad industry, and noted that in an 8-year period 45 train accidents and incidents had occurred because of alcohol- and drug-impaired railroad employees, killing 34 people, injuring 66, and causing more than $28 million in property damage. *Ante*, at 3. In the present case, by contrast, not only is the Customs Service thought to be "largely drug-free," but the connection between whatever drug use may exist and serious social harm is entirely speculative. Except for the fact that the search of a person is much more intrusive than the stop of a car, the present case resembles *Delaware* v. *Prouse*, 440 U.S. 648 (1979), where we held that the Fourth Amendment prohibited random stops to check drivers' licenses and motor vehicle registration. The contribution of this practice to highway safety, we concluded, was "marginal at best" since the number of licensed drivers that must be stopped in order to find one unlicensed one "will be large indeed." *Id.*, at 660.

Today's decision would be wrong, but at least of more limited effect, if its approval of drug testing were confined to that category of employees assigned specifically to drug interdiction duties. Relatively few public employees fit that description. But in extending approval of drug testing to that category consisting of employees who carry firearms, the Court exposes vast numbers of public employees to this needless indignity. Logically, of course, if those who carry guns can be treated in this fashion, so can all others whose work, if performed under the influence of drugs, may endanger others — auto-mobile drivers, operators of other potentially dangerous equipment, construction workers, school crossing guards. A similarly broad scope attaches to the Court's approval of drug testing for those with access to "sensitive information."[1] Since this category is not limited to Service employees with drug interdiction duties, nor to "sensitive information" specifically relating to drug traffic, today's holding apparently approves drug testing for all federal employees with security clearances — or, indeed, for all federal employees with valuable confidential information to impart. Since drug use is not a particular problem in the Customs Service, employees throughout the government are no less likely to violate the public trust by taking bribes to feed their drug habit, or by yielding to blackmail. Moreover, there is no reason why this super-protection against harms arising from drug use must be limited to public employees; a law requiring similar testing of private citizens who use dangerous instruments such as guns or cars, or who have access to classified information would also be constitutional.

There is only one apparent basis that sets the testing at issue here apart from all these other situations — but it is not a basis upon which the Court is willing to rely. I do not believe for a minute that the driving force behind these drug-testing rules was any of the feeble justifications put forward by counsel here and accepted by the Court. The only plausible explanation, in my view, is what the Commissioner himself offered in the concluding sentence of his memorandum to Customs Service employees announcing the program: "Implementation of the drug

---

[1] The Court apparently approves application of the urine tests to personnel receiving access to "sensitive information." *Ante*, at 19. Since, however, it is unsure whether "classified material" is "sensitive information," it remands with instructions that the court of appeals "examine the criteria used by the Service in determining what materials are classified and in deciding whom to test under this rubric." *Ante*, at 20. I am not sure what these instructions mean. Surely the person who classifies information *always* considers it "sensitive" .n some sense — and the Court does not indicate what particular sort of sensitivity is crucial. Moreover, it seems to me most unlikely that "the criteria used by the Service in determining what materials are classified" are any different from those prescribed by the President in his Executive Order on the subject, see Exec. Order No. 12356, 3 CFR 166 (1982 Comp.) — and if there is a difference it is probably unlawful, see §5.4(b)(2), id., at 177. In any case, whatever idiosyncratic standards for classification the Customs Service might have would seem to be irrelevant, inasmuch as the rule at issue here is not limited to material classified *by the Customs Service*, but includes (and may well apply principally to) material classified elsewhere in the Government — for example, in the Federal Bureau of Investigation, the Drug Enforcement Administration or the State Department — and conveyed to the Service. See App. 24-25.

screening program would set an important example in our country's struggle with this most serious threat to our national health security." App. 12. Or as respondent's brief to this Court asserted: "if a law enforcement agency and its employees do not take the law seriously, neither will the public on which the agency's effectiveness depends." Brief for United States 36. What better way to show that the Government is serious about its "war on drugs" than to subject its employees on the front line of that war to this invasion of their privacy and affront to their dignity? To be sure, there is only a slight chance that it will prevent some serious public harm resulting from Service employee drug use, but it will show to the world that the Service is "clean," and — most important of all — will demonstrate the determination of the Government to eliminate this scourge of our society! I think it obvious that this justification is unacceptable; that the impairment of individual liberties cannot be the means of making a point; that symbolism, even symbolism for so worthy a cause as the abolition of unlawful drugs, cannot validate an otherwise unreasonable search.

There is irony in the Government's citation, in support of its position, of Justice Brandeis's statement in *Olmstead* v. *United States*, 277 U.S. 438, 485 (1928) that "[f]or good or for ill, [our Government] teaches the whole people by its example." Brief for United States 36. Brandeis was there *dissenting* from the Court's admission of evidence obtained through an unlawful Government wiretap. He was not praising the Government's example of vigor and enthusiasm in combatting crime, but condemning its example that "the end justifies the means," 277 U.S. at 485. An even more apt quotation from that famous Brandeis dissent would have been the following:

"[I]t is . . . immaterial that the intrusion was in aid of law enforcement. Experience should teach us to be most on our guard to protect liberty when the Government's purposes are beneficent. Men born to freedom are naturally alert to repel invasion of their liberty by evil-minded rulers. The greatest dangers to liberty lurk in insidious encroachment by men of zeal, well-meaning but without understanding." *Id.*, at 479.

Those who lose because of the lack of understanding that begot the present exercise in symbolism are not just the Customs Service employees, whose dignity is thus offended, but all of us — who suffer a coarsening of our national manners that ultimately give the Fourth Amendment its content, and who become subject to the administration of federal officials whose respect for our privacy can hardly be greater than the small respect they have been taught to have for their own.

CONRAIL v. RLEA

Supreme Court of the United States

CONSOLIDATED RAIL CORPO-
RATION v. RAILWAY LABOR EX-
ECUTIVES' ASSOCIATION, et al.,
No. 88-1, June 19, 1989

RAILWAY LABOR ACT

1. 'Minor' and 'major' disputes ►103.305

Controversy arising from employer's
assertion of right under collective-bargaining contract to take action is "minor" dispute under RLA if action is
arguably justified by terms of contract, but dispute would be "major" if
employer's claims are frivolous or obviously insubstantial.

**2. Change in working conditions —
Adjustment board's discretion — Contractual right ►103.305 ►103.703 ►103.503**

Employer may make change in
working conditions without prior negotiations with union if employer asserts claim that collective-bargaining
contract gives it discretion to make
such change and if that claim is arguably justified by terms of contract, and
courts may defer to arbitral jurisdiction of adjustment board. Effect of this
ruling will be to delay collective bargaining in some cases until arbitration
process is exhausted, but there is no
inconsistency between that result and
RLA policies.

**3. Physical examinations — Drug-
testing program — 'Minor' dispute —
Adjustment's board's jurisdiction
►103.305 ►124.60 ►103.503**

Controversy arising from railroad's
unilateral decision to include drug
testing in periodic and return-from-
leave physical examinations of employees is "minor," rather than "major," dispute within exclusive
jurisdiction of adjustment board, since
railroad's claim that collective-bargaining contract impliedly authorizes
it to impose suspicionless drug testing
is neither frivolous nor obviously insubstantial, as interpreted in light of
past practice.

On writ of certiorari to the U.S.
Court of Appeals for the Third Circuit
(845 F2d 1187, 128 LRRM 2168). Reversed.

Dennis J. Morikawa, Philadelphia,
Pa. (Harry A. Rissetto, Washington,
D.C., Michael J. Ossip and Sarah A.
Kelly, Philadelphia, Pa., and Bruce B.

Wilson and Jeffrey H. Burton, Philadelphia, Pa., with him on brief; Mor-
gan, Lewis & Bockius, of counsel), for
petitioner.

Lawrence M. Mann, (Alper & Mann,
Washington, D.C., William G. Mahoney, John O'B. Clarke, Jr., and
Highsaw & Mahoney, P.C., Washington, D.C., with him on brief; Laurence
Gold, Washington, D.C., and Corne-
lius C. O'Brien, Jr., and O'Brien &
Davis, P.C., of counsel), for respondents.

Charles Fried, Solicitor General,
John R. Bolton, Assistant Attorney
General, Thomas W. Merrill, Deputy
Solicitor General, Lawrence S. Rob-
bins, Assistant to the Solicitor Gener-
al, Leonard Schaitman, and Jeffrey
Clair, filed brief for the United States,
as amicus curiae, urging reversal.

Richard T. Conway, Ralph J. Moore,
Jr., and D. Eugenia Langan, and Shea
& Gardner, Washington, D.C., and
David P. Lee, Washington, D.C., filed
brief for National Railway Labor Conference, as amicus curiae, urging reversal.

Martin C. Seham and Lee R.A. Seham (Seham, Klein & Zelman), New
York, N.Y. filed brief for Allied Pilots
Association, as amicus curiae, urging
affirmance.

Before REHNQUIST, Chief Justice,
and BRENNAN, WHITE, MAR-
SHALL, BLACKMUN, STEVENS,
O'CONNOR, SCALIA, and KENNE-
DY, Justices.

Full Text of Opinion

JUSTICE BLACKMUN delivered the
opinion of the Court.

In this case, we must examine the
concepts of "major" and "minor" disputes in the area of railway labor relations, articulate a standard for differentiating between the two, and apply
that standard to a drug-testing dispute.

I

Since its formation in 1976, petitioner Consolidated Rail Corporation
(Conrail), has required its employees to
undergo physical examinations periodically and upon return from leave.
These examinations include the testing of urine for blood sugar and albumin and, in some circumstances, for
drugs. On February 20, 1987, Conrail
announced unilaterally that urinalysis drug screening would be included
henceforth as part of *all* periodic and
return-from-leave physical examinations. Respondent Railway Labor Executives' Association (the Union), an
unincorporated association of chief executive officers of 19 labor organiza-

tions which collectively represent Conrail's employees, opposes this unilateral drug-testing addition.[1]

The parties agree that Conrail's inclusion of drug testing in all physical examinations has created a labor dispute the resolution of which is governed by the Railway Labor Act, 44 Stat. 577, as amended, 45 U.S.C. §151 et seq. (RLA).[2] The question presented by this case is what *kind* of labor dispute we have before us: whether Conrail's addition of a drug screen to the urinalysis component of its required periodic and return-to-duty medical examinations gives rise to a "major" or "minor" dispute under the RLA.

The United States District Court for the Eastern District of Pennsylvania agreed with Conrail that this case involves a minor dispute, because Conrail's policy of conducting physical examinations, which the parties agree is an implied term of their collective-bargaining agreement, arguably gave Conrail the discretion to include drug testing in all physical examinations. The Third Circuit reversed, ruling that "the undisputed terms of the implied agreement governing medical examinations cannot be plausibly interpreted to justify the new testing program." 845 F.2d 1187, 1193 [128 LRRM 2168] (1988). Although we find the question to be a close one, we agree with the District Court, and with those Courts of Appeals that have held, on similar facts, that disputes concerning the addition of a drug-testing component to routine physical examinations are minor disputes. See, *e.g., Railway Labor Executives Assn.* v. *Norfolk & Western R. Co.,* 833 F.2d 700, 705–706 [126 LRRM 3121] (CA7 1987); *Brotherhood of Maintenance of Way Employees* v. *Burlington Northern R. Co.,* 802 F.2d 1016, 1024 [123 LRRM 2593] (CA8 1986).

II

This Court has not articulated an explicit standard for differentiating between major and minor disputes. It adopted the major/minor terminology, drawn from the vocabulary of rail management and rail labor, as a shorthand method of describing two classes of controversy Congress had distinguished in the RLA: major disputes seek to create contractual rights, minor disputes to enforce them. *Elgin, J. & E. R. Co.* v. *Burley,* 325 U.S. 711, 723 [16 LRRM 749] (1945).

The statutory bases for the major dispute category are §2 Seventh and §6 of the RLA, 45 U.S.C. §152 Seventh and §156. The former states that no carrier "shall change the rates of pay, rules, or working conditions of its employees, as a class, as embodied in agreements except in the manner prescribed in such agreements" or through the mediation procedures established in §6. This statutory category

"relates to disputes over the formation of collective agreements or efforts to secure them. They arise where there is no such agreement or where it is sought to change the terms of one, and therefore the issue is not whether an existing agreement controls the controversy. They look to the acquisition of rights for the future, not to assertion of rights claimed to have vested in the past." *Burley,* 325 U.S., at 723.

In the event of a major dispute, the RLA requires the parties to undergo a lengthy process of bargaining and mediation.[3] §§5 and 6. Until they have exhausted those procedures, the parties are obligated to maintain the status quo, and the employer may not implement the contested change in rates of pay, rules, or working conditions. The district courts have subject matter jurisdiction to enjoin a violation of the status quo pending completion of the required procedures, without the customary showing of irreparable injury. See *Detroit & T. S. L. R. Co.* v. *Transportation Union,* 396 U.S. 142 [72 LRRM 2838] (1969) (upholding status quo injunction without discussing equitable constraints); *Divisions No. 1, Detroit, Brotherhood of Locomotive Engineers* v. *Consolidated Rail Corp.,* 844 F.2d 1218 [128 LRRM 2103] (CA6 1988). Once this protracted process ends and no agreement has been reached, the parties may resort to the use of economic force.

In contrast, the minor dispute category is predicated on §2 Sixth and §3

---

[1] The Union filed suit against Conrail on May 1, 1986, well before Conrail unilaterally added drug testing to its physical examinations. See App. 3. The Union's complaint challenged Conrail's use of drug testing to enforce its disciplinary Rule G and to comply with federal drug-testing regulations affecting the railroad industry. By the time the District Court ruled, however, the focus of the dispute had shifted to the addition of drug testing to routine physical examinations. That is the question framed by Conrail's petition for certiorari here.

[2] Cf. *Brotherhood of Locomotive Engineers* v. *Burlington Northern R. Co.,* 838 F.2d 1087, 1089–1090 [127 LRRM 2812] (CA9 1988) (employer took position that drug testing is not a mandatory subject of bargaining and thus that drug-testing disputes are not "labor disputes" subject to the dispute-resolution processes of the RLA), cert. pending, No. 87-1631.

[3] In addition, the RLA provides for arbitration of a major dispute in the event that mediation fails. Thus, the National Mediation Board is required to "endeavor . . . to induce the parties to submit their controversy to arbitration." §5 First. Participation, however, is voluntary. See Aaron, Voluntary Arbitration of Railroad and Airline Interest Disputes, in The Railway Labor Act at Fifty: Collective Bargaining in the Railroad and Airline Industries 129 (C. Rhemus ed. 1977).

First (i) of the RLA, which set forth conference and compulsory arbitration procedures for a dispute arising or growing "out of grievances or out of the interpretation or application of agreements concerning rates of pay, rules, or working conditions." This second category of disputes

"contemplates the existence of a collective agreement already concluded or, at any rate, a situation in which no effort is made to bring about a formal change in terms or to create a new one. The dispute relates either to the meaning or proper application of a particular provision with reference to a specific situation or to an omitted case. In the latter event the claim is founded upon some incident of the employment relation, or asserted one, independent of those covered by the collective agreement, e. g., claims on account of personal injuries. In either case the claim is to rights accrued, not merely to have new ones created for the future." Burley, 325 U.S., at 723.

A minor dispute in the railroad industry is subject to compulsory and binding arbitration before the National Railroad Adjustment Board, §3, or before an adjustment board established by the employer and the unions representing the employees. §3 Second.[4] The Board (as we shall refer to any adjustment board under the RLA) has exclusive jurisdiction over minor disputes. Judicial review of the arbitral decision is limited. See §3 First (q); Union Pacific R. Co. v. Sheehan, 439 U.S. 89, 93 [99 LRRM 3327] (1978). Courts may enjoin strikes arising out of minor disputes. Trainmen v. Chicago R. & I. R. Co., 353 U.S. 30 [39 LRRM 2578] (1957). Although courts in some circumstances may condition the granting of a strike injunction on a requirement that the employer maintain the status quo pending Board resolution of the dispute, see Locomotive Engineers v. Missouri-K.-T. R. Co., 363 U.S. 528, 534 [46 LRRM 2429] (1960), this Court never has recognized a general statutory obligation on the part of an employer to maintain the status quo pending the Board's decision. Cf. id., at 531, n. 3 (leaving open the question whether a federal court can require an employer to maintain the status quo during the pendency of a minor dispute at the union's inde-

pendent behest, where no strike injunction has been sought by the employer).[5]

Although experience in the rail industry suggested to Congress that the second category of disputes involved "comparatively minor" issues that seldom led to strikes, the Court recognized in Burley that this was not invariably the case. See 325 U.S., at 724; see also Trainmen, supra. Thus, the formal demarcation between major and minor disputes does not turn on a case-by-case determination of the importance of the issue presented or the likelihood that it would prompt the exercise of economic selfhelp. See National Railway Labor Conference v. International Assn. of Machinists, 830 F.2d 741, 747, n. 5 [121 LRRM 2615] (CA7 1987). Rather, the line drawn in Burley looks to whether a claim has been made that the terms of an existing agreement either establish or refute the presence of a right to take the disputed action. The distinguishing feature of such a case is that the dispute may be conclusively resolved by interpreting the existing agreement. See Garrison, The National Railroad Adjustment Board: A Unique Administrative Agency, 46 Yale L. J. 567, 568, 576 (1937).

To an extent, then, the distinction between major and minor disputes is a

---

[4] In the airline industry, also covered by the RLA, there is no national adjustment board; a minor dispute is resolved by an adjustment board established by the airline and the unions. 49 Stat. 1189, 45 U.S.C. §184. See Machinists v. Central Airlines, Inc., 372 U.S. 682 [52 LRRM 2803] (1963). In both the airline and railroad industries, the National Mediation Board has a limited role to play in resolving a minor dispute: under §5 Second, the Board may be called upon by a party to interpret "any agreement reached through mediation under the provisions of this chapter." See also 49 Stat. 1189, 45 U.S.C. §183 (applying §5 to airlines).

[5] See generally Comment, Enjoining Strikes and Maintaining the Status Quo in Railway Labor Disputes, 60 Colum. L. Rev. 381, 386–397 (1960); cf. Airline Pilots Assn. v. Eastern Air Lines Inc., —— U.S. App. D.C. ——, ——, n.2, 869 F.2d 1518, 1520, n.2 [130 LRRM 2250] (1989); International Assn. of Machinists v. Northeast Airlines, Inc., 473 F.2d 549, 555, n.7 [80 LRRM 2197] (CA1) (expressing the view that a "union [might] be able to enjoin changes in working conditions if it would be impossible otherwise later to make the workers whole"), cert. denied, 409 U.S. 845 [81 LRRM 2390] (1972); Division No. 1, Detroit, Brotherhood of Locomotive Engineers v. Consolidated Rail Corp., 844 F.2d 1218, 1224, n. 10 [128 LRRM 2103] (CA6 1988) (leaving open the question of injunction based on showing of irreparable harm). As the Union in the present case has not based its claim for injunctive relief on an allegation of irreparable injury, we decline to resolve the question whether a status quo injunction based on a claim of irreparable injury would be appropriate.

The Union suggests in passing that §2 First provides a status quo obligation applicable to all minor disputes. See Brief for Respondents 21, 30–31. It relies on Detroit & T.S.L.R. Co. v. Transportation Union, 396 U.S. 142, 151 [72 LRRM 2838] (1969), but, as we read that case, it does not support the Union's position. The language upon which the Union relies (a reference to "the implicit status quo requirement in the obligation imposed upon both parties by §2 First, 'to exert every reasonable effort' to settle disputes without interruption to interstate commerce") appears in the context of explaining that the express status quo requirements applicable to a major dispute must be broadly interpreted. It has no direct application to a minor dispute.

matter of pleading. The party who initiates a dispute takes the first step towards categorizing the dispute when it chooses whether to assert an existing contractual right to take or to resist the action in question. But the Courts of Appeals early recognized that there is a danger in leaving the characterization of the dispute solely in the hands of one party. In a situation in which the party asserting a contractual basis for its claim is "insincere" in so doing, or its "position [is] founded upon . . . insubstantial grounds," the result of honoring that party's characterization would be to undercut "the prohibitions of §2, Seventh, and §6 of the Act" against unilateral imposition of new contractual terms. *Norfolk & Portsmoth Belt Line R. Co.* v. *Brotherhood of Railroad Trainmen,* 248 F.2d 34, 43–44, n. 4 [40 LRRM 2585] (CA4 1957), cert. denied, 355 U.S. 914 [41 LRRM 2283] (1958); see also *United Industrial Workers* v. *Board of Trustees of the Galveston Wharves,* 351 F.2d 183, 188–189 [60 LRRM 2161] (CA5 1965). In such circumstances, protection of the proper functioning of the statutory scheme requires the court to substitute its characterization for that of the claimant.

To satisfy this need for some degree of judicial control, the Courts of Appeals uniformly have established some variant of the standard employed by the Third Circuit in this case:

"[I]f the disputed action of one of the parties can 'arguably' be justified by the existing agreement or, in somewhat different statement, if the contention that the labor contract sanctions the disputed action is not 'obviously insubstantial', the controversy is a [minor dispute] within the exclusive province of the National Railroad Adjustment Board." 845 F.2d, at 1190, quoting *Local 1477 United Transportation Union* v. *Baker,* 482 F.2d 228, 230 [83 LRRM 2684] (CA6 1973).

Verbal formulations of this standard have differed over time and among the Circuits; phrases such as "not arguably justified," "obviously insubstantial," "spurious," and "frivolous" have been employed.[6] See, *e.g., Brotherhood of Locomotive Engineers* v. *Burlington Northern R. Co.,* 838 F.2d 1087, 1091 [127 LRRM 2812] (CA9 1988) (review-

---

[6] See, *e.g., National Railway Labor Conference* v. *International Assn. of Machinists,* 830 F.2d 741, 746 [121 LRRM 2615] (CA7 1987) (not frivolous or obviously insubstantial); *Maine Central R. Co.* v. *United Transportation Union,* 787 F.2d 780 782 [122 LRRM 2017] (CA1) (even arguable); *International Brotherhood of Electrical Workers* v. *Washington Terminal Co.,* 154 U.S. S.App. D. C. 119, 473 F.2d 1156, 1173 [82 LRRM 2030] (1972) (reasonably susceptible), cert. denied, 411 U.S. 906 [82 LRRM 2921] (1973); *Ruby* v. *Taca International Airlines, S.A.,* 439 F.2d 1359, 1363, n. 5 [77 LRRM 2089] (CA5 1971) (wholly spurious).

ing different formulations used in the Ninth Circuit), cert. pending, No. 87-1631. "These locutions are essentially the same in their result. They illustrate the relatively light burden which the railroad must bear" in establishing exclusive arbitral jurisdiction under the RLA. *Brotherhood of Maintenance of Way Employees* v. *Burlington Northern R. Co.,* 802 F.2d 1016, 1022 [123 LRRM 2593] (CA8 1986); see also *Maine Central R. Co.* v. *United Transportation Union,* 787 F.2d 780, 783 [122 LRRM 2017] (CA1) ("The degree of scrutiny, while ill-defined, is clearly light"), cert. denied, 479 U.S. 848 [123 LRRM 2592] (1986).

[1] "To the extent that abstract words can deal with concrete cases, we think that the concept embodied in the language adopted by these . . . Courts of Appeals is correct." *Christianburg Garment Co.* v. *EEOC,* 434 U.S. 412, 421 [16 FEP Cases 502] (1978). Where an employer asserts a contractual right to take the contested action, the ensuing dispute is minor if the action is arguably justified by the terms of the parties' collective-bargaining agreement. Where, in contrast, the employer's claims are frivolous or obviously insubstantial, the dispute is major.

III

In this case, the Union appears to agree that the "arguably justified" standard generally is the appropriate one for distinguishing between major and minor disputes. Brief for Respondents 35, n. 29. But it argues that the dispute in this case, properly viewed, is neither a major dispute nor a minor dispute. According to the Union, where an employer has made a clear "change [in] . . . working conditions . . . as embodied in agreements," but asserts that it has made the change "in the manner prescribed in such agreements," §2 Seventh, because it has a contractual right to make the change, the ensuing dispute is a "hybrid dispute." Brief for Respondents 34–35, 40, n.32.

In a hybrid dispute, the Union contends, the employer may ask the Board to determine whether it has the contractual right to make a particular change, but must forgo unilateral implementation of the change until the Board reaches its decision. If the employer makes the change without establishing a clear and patent right to do so, the employer violates its statutory duty not to "change the rates of pay, rules, or working conditions of its employees, as a class, as embodied in agreements *except in the manner pre-*

scribed in such agreements or in section 6" (emphasis added). §2 Seventh. Stated more simply, the Union's position is that while a dispute over the right to make the change would be a minor dispute, the actual making of the change transforms the controversy into a major dispute.

This approach unduly constrains the freedom of unions and employers to contract for discretion. Collective-bargaining agreements often incorporate express or implied terms that are designed to give management, or the union, a degree of freedom of action within a specified area of activity. See *NLRB v. American National Insurance Co.*, 343 U.S. 395 [30 LRRM 2147] (1952); *Rutland Railway Corp. v. Brotherhood of Locomotive Engineers*, 307 F.2d 21, 35-36 [50 LRRM 2535] (CA2 1962), cert. denied, 372 U.S. 954 [52 LRRM 2704] (1963). Cf. *Steelworkers v. Warrior & Gulf Navigation Co.*, 363 U.S. 574, 580 [46 LRRM 2416] (1960); see generally Cox & Dunlop, Regulation of Collective Bargaining by the National Labor Relations Board, 63 Harv. L. Rev. 389, 401 (1950). We have held under the National Labor Relations Act (NLRA) that no principle of labor law prohibits "[b]argaining for ... flexible treatment" and requires instead that, for each working condition, the employer "agre[e] to freeze a standard into a contract." *American National Insurance Co.*, 343 U.S., at 408. We find no difference between the NLRA and the RLA in this respect. Yet the Union would subject to especially strict scrutiny the bona fides of contractual claims arising out of contract terms that grant management the power to respond flexibly to changing circumstances. The effect of a selectively heightened level of scrutiny (a "clear and patent" rather than an "arguably justified" standard) would be to limit the enforceability of such contract terms, by requiring employers rigidly to maintain the status quo pending arbitration of their right to be flexible. That result is odd in itself, cf. *Rutland Railway Corp.*, 307 F.2d, at 40 (requiring parties to negotiate over whether they have a duty to negotiate is "a solution sounding a lot like an exercise in theoretical logic"), and has unacceptable implications. To accept the bifurcated standard the Union advocates would, in effect, be impermissibly to "pass upon the desirability of the substantive terms of labor agreements," *American National Insurance Co.*, 343 U.S., at 408-409, by affording flexible terms a less favored status. Cf. *International Assn. of Machinists v. Northeast Airlines, Inc*, 473 F.2d 549, 555 [80 LRRM 2197] (CA1), cert. de-nied, 409 U.S. 845 [81 LRRM 2390] (1972).[7]

[2] Accordingly, we shall not aggravate the already difficult task of distinguishing between major disputes and minor disputes by adding a third category of hybrid disputes. We hold that if an employer asserts a claim that the parties' agreement gives the employer the discretion to make a particular change in working conditions without prior negotiation, and if that claim is arguably justified by the terms of the parties' agreement (*i.e.*, the claim is neither obviously insubstantial or frivolous, nor made in bad faith), the employer may make the change and the courts must defer to the arbitral jurisdiction of the Board.

The effect of this ruling, of course, will be to delay collective bargaining in some cases until the arbitration process is exhausted. But we see no inconsistency between that result and the policies of the RLA.[8] The core duties imposed upon employers and employees by the RLA, as set forth in §2 First, are to "make and maintain agreements" and to "settle all disputes ... in order to avoid any interruption to commerce." Referring arbitrable matters to the Board will help to "maintain agreements," by assuring that

---

[7] Even if the Union's approach had merit in the abstract, it would be unworkable in practice. As discussed below, collective-bargaining agreements often contain implied as well as express terms. The Union conceded at oral argument that an employer would have the authority, without engaging in collective bargaining or statutory mediation, to open its locker room 15 minutes later than it had in the past without first establishing its contractual right to do so through a separate arbitration proceeding. Tr. of Oral Arg. 47-48, 50. That acknowledgment stemmed from the assumption that, although a change in opening time was indeed a "change," and although access to the locker room was a "working condition," the precise time the locker room opened was not an issue of sufficient significance to have become the subject of an implied contractual agreement, even if the existence of the locker room was itself an implied term of the contract. The Union recognizes, then, that the general framework of a collective-bargaining agreement leaves some play in the joints, permitting management some range of flexibility in responding to changed conditions. The effect of adopting the Union's "hybrid dispute" proposal would be to require the trial court to make a nonexpert generalized judgment regarding the "importance" of a particular working condition, and to use that judgment as the basis for deciding whether a particular working condition is or is not within the parties' agreed range of discretion. We decline to put courts to that task.

[8] In most cases where the Board determines that the employer's conduct was not justified by the contract, the Board will be able to fashion an appropriate compensatory remedy which takes account of the delay. See, *e.g.*, Order of Conductors v. Pitney, 326 U.S. 561, 566 [17 LRRM 722] (1946); Aaxico Airlines, Inc., 47 LA 289, 316 (1966); Trans World Airlines, Inc., 34 LA 420, 425 (1959). There may be some circumstances, however, where the delay inherent in permitting the Board to consider the matter in the first instance will lead to remedial difficulties. See generally Comment, 60 Colum. L. Rev., at 394.

collective bargaining contracts are enforced by arbitrators who are experts in "the common law of [the] particular industry." *Steelworkers* v. *Warrior & Gulf Navigation Co.*, 363 U.S., at 579. Full utilization of the Board's procedures also will diminish the risk of interruptions in commerce. Failure of the "virtually endless" process of negotiation and mediation established by the RLA for major disputes, *Burlington Northern R. Co.* v. *Maintenance of Way Employees*, 481 U.S. 429, 444 [125 LRRM 2073] (1987), frees the parties to employ a broad range of economic self-help, which may disturb transportation services throughout the industry, and unsettle employer-employee relationships. *See TWA, Inc.* v. *Flight Attendants*, 489 U.S. —— [130 LRRM 2657] (1989). Delaying the onset of that process until the Board determines on the merits that the employer's interpretation of the agreement is incorrect will assure that the risks of selfhelp are not needlessly undertaken, and will aid "[t]he peaceable settlement of labor controversies." *Virginian R. Co.* v. *Railway Employees*, 300 U.S. 515, 552 [1 LRRM 743] (1937).

IV

[3] This case, then, turns on whether the inclusion of drug testing in periodic and return-from-leave physical examinations is arguably justified by the parties' collective-bargaining agreement. Neither party relies on any express provision of the agreement; indeed, the agreement is not part of the record before us. As the parties acknowledge, however, collective-bargaining agreements may include implied as well as express terms. See, *e.g., Northwest Airlines, Inc.* v. *Air line Pilots Assn.*, 442 F.2d 251, 253-254 [77 LRRM 2116] (CA8), cert. denied, 404 U.S. 871 [78 LRRM 2464] (1971). Furthermore, it is well established that the parties' "practice, usage and custom" is of significance in interpreting their agreement. See *Transportation Union* v. *Union Pacific R. Co.*, 385 U.S. 157, 161 [63 LRRM 2481] (1966). This Court has observed: "A collective bargaining agreement is not an ordinary contract for the purchase of goods and services, nor is it governed by the same old common-law concepts which control such private contracts. '. . . [I]t is a generalized code to govern a myriad of cases which the draftsmen cannot wholly anticipate. . . . The collective agreement covers the whole employment relationship. It calls into being a new common law — the common law of a particular industry or of a particular plant.' " *Id.*, at 160-161 (quot-

ing *Steelworkers* v. *Warrior & Gulf Navigation Co.*, 363 U.S., at 578-579.

In this case, Conrail's contractual claim rests solely upon implied contractual terms, as interpreted in light of past practice. Because we agree with Conrail that its contractual claim is neither frivolous nor obviously insubstantial, we conclude that this controversy is properly deemed a minor dispute within the exclusive jurisdiction of the Board.

A

The essential facts regarding Conrail's past practices — the facts in support of the positions of both Conrail and the Union — are not disputed.[*] Since its founding in 1976, Conrail routinely has required its employees to undergo physical examinations under the supervision of its Health Services Department. The parties agreed in the Court of Appeals, and the District Court found, that Conrail's authority to conduct physical examinations is an implied term of the collective-bargaining agreement, established by longstanding past practice and acquiesced in by the Union.

Conrail conducts physical examinations in three categories of cases. First, it always has required its employees to undergo *periodic* physical examinations, which have routinely included a urinalysis for blood sugar and albumin. These periodic examinations are conducted every three years for employees up to the age of 50, and every two years thereafter. Second, Conrail has required train and engine employees who have been out of service for at least 30 days due to furlough, leave, suspension, or other similar cause to undergo *return-to-duty* physical examinations. These also routinely include urinalysis. Conrail employees in other job classifications are required to undergo return-to-duty physical examinations that include urinalysis for blood sugar and albumin, but are required to submit to examinations only after absences of 90 days or more. Third, when justified by the employee's condition, Conrail has routinely

---

[*] This is not to say that the legal significance of these practices is undisputed. In particular, the parties take different views of how a court is to determine whether a particular past practice has risen to the level of an implied contractual term. Compare Brief for Respondent 42-43 with Brief for Petitioner 19. The precise definition of this standard, however, is of no particular significance to this case. As will become clear, the parties have agreed that Conrail's power to conduct physical examinations is an implied contractual term. The District Court made no factual findings that Conrail's specific practices had themselves become implied terms of the contract, and we do not suggest otherwise in the discussion that follows.

required a *follow-up* physical examination. For example, such an examination has been required for an employee who has suffered a heart attack, or has been diagnosed as having hypertension or epilepsy. Any employee who undergoes a periodic, return-to-duty, or follow-up physical examination and who fails to meet Conrail's established medical standards may be held out of service without pay until the condition is corrected or eliminated.

Conrail has implemented medical standards for all three types of physical examination. Over the years, procedures for hearing tests, lung-capacity tests, eye tests, and cardiological tests have been modified to reflect changes in medical science and technology. These changes have been made by Conrail unilaterally, without consulting the Union.

Drug testing always has had some place in Conrail's physical examinations, although its role has changed with time. Conrail has included drug testing by urinalysis as part of periodic physical examinations whenever, in the judgment of the examining physician, the employee may have been using drugs. Drug screens also routinely have been performed as part of the return-to-duty physical examination of any employee who has been taken out of service previously for a drug-related problem; in addition, drug testing is included whenever the examining physician thinks the employee may have been using drugs.

On April 1, 1984, Conrail issued a Medical Standards Manual stating that a drug screen would be included in all periodic and return-to-duty physicals. For budgetary reasons, however, this policy then was applied only in Conrail's eastern region and was discontinued after six months.

On February 20, 1987, Conrail implemented the Medical Standards Manual in all of its regions, requiring drug testing as part of its periodic and return-to-duty physicals and, in addition, requiring follow-up examinations for all employees returning to duty after disqualification for any reason associated with drug use.[10] An employee who tests positive for drugs will not be returned to service unless he provides a negative drug test within 45 days of the date he receives notice of the positive test. An employee whose first test is positive may go to Conrail's

Employee Counseling Service for evaluation. If the evaluation reveals an addiction problem, and the employee agrees to enter an approved treatment program, the employee will be given an extended period of 125 days to provide a negative test.

The problem of drug use has been addressed by Conrail not only as a medical concern, but also as a disciplinary one. This Court noted earlier in the present Term that the railroad industry has adopted operating "Rule G," which governs drug use by employees. *Skinner v. Railway Labor Executives' Assn.,* 489 U.S. ——, —— [130 LRRM 2857] (1989) (slip op. 1-2). As currently implemented by Conrail, Rule G provides: "The use of intoxicants, narcotics, amphetamines or hallucinogens by employees subject to duty, or their possession or use while on duty, is prohibited. Employees under medication before or while on duty must be certain that such use will not affect the safe performance of their duties." See App. 63. At Conrail, as elsewhere in the industry, an employee may be dismissed for violating Rule G. *Skinner,* 489 U.S. at —— (slip op. 2); Tr. of Oral Arg. 43. Conrail has relied chiefly on supervisory observation to enforce Rule G. An employee suspected of drug or alcohol use is encouraged voluntarily to agree to undergo diagnostic tests, but is not required to do so.

In addition, Conrail has implemented the Federal Railroad Administration regulations recently upheld in *Skinner* against a Fourth Amendment challenge. Since March 1986, Conrail has required all employees covered by the Hours of Service Act, 45 U.S.C. §61 *et seq.,* to undergo post-accident drug and alcohol testing, pursuant to 49 CFR §219 *et seq.* (1988).[11]

B

The dispute between the parties focuses on the meaning of these past practices. Conrail argues that adding urinalysis drug testing to its periodic and return-to-duty physicals is justified by the parties' implied agreement regarding physical examinations, as indicated by their longstanding practice of permitting Conrail unilaterally to establish and change fitness-for-duty standards, to revise testing procedures, and to remove from service employees who are deemed unfit for duty under those standards and testing pro-

---

[10] The Union suggests that Conrail's decision to implement its current drug-testing program resulted from a serious Conrail accident in January 1987, in which the engineer and conductor of the train admitted smoking marijuana in the cab just prior to the collision. Brief for Respondents 6.

[11] It was the implementation of the Federal Railroad Administration regulations that precipitated the instant lawsuit. Brief for Respondent 7, but no issue regarding Conrail's implementation of those regulations is presently before us.

cedures.[12] Conrail contends, specifically, that past practice reflects that drug
use has been deemed relevant to job
fitness, and that Conrail's physicians
have the discretion to utilize drug testing as part of their medical determination of job fitness. The expansion of
drug testing in February 1987, Conrail
argues, represents no more than a diagnostic improvement in its medical
procedures, similar to diagnostic im-
provements Conrail unilaterally made
in the past.[13]

The Union contends that, even using
the "arguably justified" standard, "it
is simply not plausible" to conclude
that the parties' agreement contemplated that Conrail had the authority
to include drug screens in all routine
physical examinations. The Union argues that Conrail has departed mate-
rially from the parties' agreement, as
reflected by Conrail's past medical
practice, in several respects. First, the
Union states that past practice limited
the use of drug testing in physical examinations to circumstances in which
there was cause to believe the employee was using drugs; the current program, on the other hand, includes testing without cause. Second, in the
Union's view, Conrail's general medical policy permits Conrail to remove
an employee from active service until
the employee's physical condition im-
proves, but does not permit Conrail to
discharge an employee for failure to
get well within a specified time; the
current drug-testing program includes a fixed time limit, and results in
discharge rather than removal from
active service. Third, the Union contends that the expansion of drug testing constitutes, for the first time, regulation by Conrail of the private, off-
duty conduct of its employees.

In addition to pointing to these asserted departures from past practice,
the Union argues that the absence of a
"meeting of the minds" on the particulars of testing and confidentiality
procedures renders untenable Conrail's claim that the parties tacitly
have agreed to Conrail's current use of
drug testing. Finally, the Union presents an alternative view of what Conrail has done: Conrail has expanded
the *disciplinary* use of drug testing to

employees not covered by the Federal
Railroad Administration regulations,
an expansion which impermissibly
adds drug testing to the list of available means for the enforcement of
Rule G.

C

In the end, the Union's arguments
distinguishing drug testing from other
aspects of Conrail's medical program,
and asserting that Conrail's true motive is disciplinary, conceivably could
carry the day in arbitration. But they
do not convince us that Conrail's contractual arguments are frivolous or insubstantial. Conrail's interpretation of
the range of its discretion as extending
to drug testing is supported by the
general breadth of its freedom of action in the past, and by its practice of
including drug testing within routine
medical examinations in some circumstances.

In the past, the parties have left the
establishment and enforcement of
medical standards in Conrail's hands.
Conrail long has treated drug use as a
matter of medical concern. Cf. American Psychiatric Association, Diagnostic and Statistical Manual of Mental
Disorders 163-179 (3d ed. 1980) (substance abuse disorders); Alcohol and
Drugs in the Workplace: Costs, Controls and Controversies 1 (1986) (disciplinary and therapeutic approaches to
drugs in the workplace); T. Denenberg
& R. Denenberg, Alcohol & Drugs: Issues in the Workplace 18 (1983) (drug
and alcohol abuse as treatable disorders); cf. *Traynor v. Turnage*, 485 U.S.
535, 562-564 (1988) (opinion concurring
in part and dissenting in part) (alcohol
dependence as medical problem). Indeed, although the scope of drug testing within physical examinations has
changed over time, drug testing has
always played some part (in appropriate circumstances) in Conrail's medical examinations. In short, there is no
established "rule" between the parties
that drug use is solely a disciplinary,
and never a medical, concern.

There need be no "meeting of the
minds" between the parties on the details of drug-testing methods or confidentiality standards for Conrail's current drug-testing program arguably to
be justified by the parties' agreement.
As we have noted, labor laws do not
require all the details of particular
practices to be worked out in advance.
Conrail's claim that drug testing is an
area in which Conrail retains a degree
of discretion finds some support in the
fact that the Union never before has
intervened in the procedural details of
Conrail's drug testing: such testing
has been performed — like other medi-

---

[12] Conrail argued in the District Court that the
parties' implied agreement regarding Rule G enforcement justified its current drug-testing practice, but abandoned that position on appeal. See
845 F.2d, at 1194.
[13] We note that Conrail does not seek to rely on
the 1984 limited implementation of routine drug
testing as evidence of a past practice acquiesced in
by the Union. See *id.*, at 1193, n.3.

cal tests — according to standards unilaterally promulgated by Conrail. Thus, the absence of a specific agreement between the parties regarding testing procedures and confidentiality does not sufficiently undermine Conrail's contractual claim to require that this dispute be classified as "major."

Conrail's well-established recognition of the relevance of drug use to medical fitness substantially weakens the Union's claim that Conrail now, for the first time, is engaging in medical testing that reveals facts about employees' private off-duty conduct. Indeed, the fact that medical testing often detects physical problems linked to off-duty behavior makes it difficult to draw a bright line for jurisdictional purposes between testing which does and that which does not reflect upon private conduct.

As to the relevance of "cause," we do not doubt that there is a difference between Conrail's past regime of limiting drug testing to circumstances in which there is cause to believe that the employee has used drugs, and Conrail's present policy of including drug tests in all routine physical examinations. Indeed, the difference between testing with and without cause perhaps could be of significance to arbitrators in deciding the merits of drug-testing disputes. See generally Denenberg & Denenberg, Drug Testing from the Arbitrator's Perspective, 11 Nova L. Rev. 371, 387-392 (1987); Veglahn, What is a Reasonable Drug Testing Program?: Insights from Arbitration Decisions, 39 Lab. L.J. 688, 689-692 (1988). But under the RLA, it is not the role of the courts to decide the merits of the parties' dispute. Our role is limited to determining where the "arguably justified" line is to be drawn. For the limited purpose of determining whether Conrail's claim of contractual right to change its medical testing procedures must be rejected as obviously insubstantial, that line cannot reasonably be drawn between testing for cause and testing without cause.

As Conrail pointed out and urged at oral argument, "particularized suspicion" is not an accepted prerequisite for medical testing. Tr. of Oral Arg. 21. A physician's decision to perform certain diagnostic tests is likely to turn not on the legal concept of "cause" or "individualized suspicion," but rather on factors such as the expected incidence of the medical condition in the relevant population, the cost, accuracy, and inherent medical risk of the test, and the likely benefits of detection. In designing diagnostic-testing programs, some employers establish a set of basic tests that are to be administered to *all* employees, see generally M. Rothstein, Medical Screening of Workers 16-19 (1984), regardless of whether there is cause to believe a particular employee will test positive. It is arguably within Conrail's range of discretion to alter its position on drug testing based on perceived changes in these variables.

We turn next to the alleged disciplinary consequences of a positive drug test. It is clear that Conrail is not claiming a right, under its medical policy, to discharge an employee because of a single positive drug test, a right many railroads assert under Rule G. See *Skinner*, 489 U.S., at —— (slip op. 2). Furthermore, an employee has the option of requesting a period of rehabilitative treatment. Thus, it is surely at least arguable that Conrail's use of drug testing in physical examinations has a medical rather than a disciplinary goal.

The fact that for drug problems, unlike other medical conditions, Conrail's standards include a fixed time period in which the employee's condition must improve, does serve to distinguish Conrail's drug policy from its response to other medical problems. Conrail has argued that it needs, for medical purposes, to require employees who deny that they are drug-dependent to demonstrate that they are capable of producing a drug-free sample at will. Tr. of Oral Arg. 13. In our view, that argument has sufficient merit to satisfy Conrail's burden of demonstrating that its claim of contractual entitlement to set a time limit for successful recovery from drug problems is not frivolous.

V

Because we conclude that Conrail's contractual arguments are not obviously insubstantial, we hold that the case before us constitutes a minor dispute that is within the exclusive jurisdiction of the Board. We make clear, however, that we go no further than to hold that Conrail has met the light burden of persuading this Court that its drug-testing practice is arguably justified by the implied terms of its collective-bargaining agreement. We do not seek to minimize any force in the Union's arguments that the discretion afforded Conrail by the parties' implied agreement, as interpreted in light of past practice, cannot be understood to extend this far. Thus, in no way do we suggest that Conrail is or is not entitled to prevail before the Board on the merits of the dispute.

The judgment is reversed.

It is so ordered.

Concurring Opinion

JUSTICE WHITE, concurring.

I join the opinion and judgment of the Court. I add these remarks only to emphasize that the parties agree and the courts below held that giving physical examinations is a matter covered by an implied agreement between the company and the unions. The company claims that although instituting drug testing is a change in conditions, the implied contract authorizes the change. I agree that this claim has substance and that the dispute is a minor one for the Adjustment Board to resolve. If the Board decides that the company is wrong about its authority under the contract, the result will be that the company has sought a change in the contract without invoking the procedures applicable to major disputes.

Dissenting Opinion

JUSTICE BRENNAN, with whom JUSTICE MARSHALL joins, dissenting.

I would affirm the judgment of the Court of Appeals for the reasons stated by that court. The routine medical examinations Conrail relies on as precedent for its drug-testing program could result, at most, in an employee being held out of service until her health improved. Conrail would have us believe that, in accepting such medical testing, the unions (arguably) agreed to testing for use of an illegal substance that could result in the employee's firing. It is unsurprising that the unions agreed to nonpunitive medical testing, and that they acquiesced in the employer making such unilateral changes in testing procedures as it determined were advisable on the basis of current medical technology. But it is inconceivable to me that in so doing the unions were also agreeing to the systematic, suspicion-less testing, on such terms and in such manner as the employer alone prescribed, of all employees for evidence of criminal activity that, under the employer's plan, could result in discharge.* Such a contention, in my view, is not "arguable" — it is frivo-

lous. I agree with the Court of Appeals that "[u]ltimately, Conrail's argument rests on the premise that testing urine for cannabis metabolites is no different in kind from testing urine for blood sugar. This ignores considerable differences in what is tested for and the consequences thereof." 845 F.2d 1187, 1194 [128 LRRM 2168] (CA3 1988).

It may be helpful to note what the General Counsel of the National Labor Relations Board had to say in addressing the somewhat similar question whether, under the National Labor Relations Act, the addition of drug testing to a previously required physical examination constitutes a "substantial change in working conditions":

"In cases where an employer has an existing program of mandatory physical examinations for employees or applicants, an issue arises as to whether the addition of drug testing constitutes a substantial change in the employees' terms and conditions of employment. In general, we conclude that it does constitute such a change. When conjoined with discipline, up to and including discharge, for refusing to submit to the test or for testing positive, the addition of a drug test substantially changes the nature and fundamental purpose of the existing physical examination. Generally, a physical examination is designed to test physical fitness to perform the work. A drug test is designed to determine whether an employee or applicant *uses* drugs, irrespective of whether such usage interferes with ability to perform work." NLRB General Counsel's Memorandum on Drug and Alcohol Testing, Memorandum GC 87-5 (Sept. 8, 1987), reprinted in BNA Daily Labor Report, No. 184, pp, D-1, D-2 (Sept. 24, 1987) (emphasis in original).

The General Counsel similarly concluded that "a union's acquiescence in a past practice of requiring applicants and/or current employees to submit to physical examinations that did not include drug testing ... does not constitute a waiver of the union's right to bargain over drug testing." *Ibid.*

Without suggesting that the NLRA question of a "substantial change in working conditions" is precisely the same as the one before us, I do think the General Counsel has a better understanding than does the Court of the relationship between drug testing and routine physical examinations. I respectfully dissent.

---

* The Court rests its holding that the purpose of Conrail' drug tests is — arguably — medical rather than disciplinary solely on the ground that Conrail will not discharge an employee on the basis of one positive drug test standing alone and that it will permit the employee "a period of rehabilitative treatment" prior to a second test. *Ante,* at 20. I do not agree that these factors even arguably bring Conrail's drug-testing program within the realm of the existing medical examinations. Beyond this, however, I note that under the Court's reasoning the outcome of the case should be different if the employer's policy were indeed "to discharge an employee because of a single positive drug test." *Ibid.*

APPENDIX C

SAMPLE COMPANY POLICIES

Major Insurance Company
C-3

Major National Hotel Chain
C-11

Major Computer and Information
Systems Manufacturer
C-15

Major Insurance Company

EMPLOYEE RECORDS

The company has long been concerned with protecting the privacy of its employees and customers, while meeting the company's need for personal information.

The company formed a Privacy Council in May 1975 to design and implement a corporate policy for collecting, retaining, using, and protecting personal information about employees and insurance customers.

The company's employee privacy policy and procedures are described in *Personnel Policies & Programs*, pages 1-61. Here are some highlights:

- In making employment decisions, the company will collect only information pertinent to the decision.

- The company will not obtain information about you from outside the company for use in making employment decisions without your written approval.

- The company will not use or permit firms representing it to use a lie detector or similar evaluators to get information from or about you in making employment decisions.

- The company will strive to make the information it collects, maintains, and uses about you as an employee accurate, timely, and complete.

- You may see and obtain a copy of most of the records the company has about you as an employee (one of the exceptions being security records maintained by Security Control/Corporate Audit). If you believe these records are wrong, you may request that they be corrected. They will either be changed or the person maintaining the records will explain why they cannot be changed. If the change cannot be made, you can then file a statement expressing your point of view.

- The company will maintain your health benefit and benefit-related medical records separately from other records, and they generally will not be used in making employment decisions about you without your permission. Medical records will be maintained in separate confidential files by Employee Health Services (EHS).

- Only authorized company employees with a valid, work-related reason may have access to records the company has about you.

- The company's records about you normally will not be disclosed in individually identifiable form to people or organizations outside the company without your written approval, unless disclosure is compelled by summons or subpoena or the records are needed for law enforcement or regulatory purposes. There are some exceptions, however. For example, the fact that you were or are a company employee, the date of your employment, and your title and position may be disclosed without your authorization in response to a request identifying you by name.

- Upon request, the company will inform you of the complete list of records maintained by the company about employees, indicating which records are available, which are not available, and why.

SEXUAL HARASSMENT

The company believes a comfortable working environment is essential to the well-being of all employees. The company will not tolerate sexual harassment of any employee by other employees, customers, or clients. Likewise, we will not tolerate the sexual harassment of customers or clients by employees.

Sexual harassment may involve a variety of unwanted, un-welcome, and repeated behaviors such as:

- Sexually suggestive statements or questions;
- Offensive jokes;
- Sexual innuendoes;
- Offensive touching or patting; and/or
- Sexual bribery;

when:

- Submitting to advances is a term or condition of employment;
- Submitting to or rejecting advances affects employment decisions; and/or
- Such conduct creates an intimidating, hostile, or offensive working environment that interferes with job performance.

As an employee, it is your responsibility to conduct yourself in a manner consistent with company policy by refraining from sexual harassment behavior. Also, you should report immediately any instance of sexual harassment to your management or divisional personnel consultant.

DRUGS AND ALCOHOL

The company is strongly committed to maintaining a workplace free from the effects of alcohol and drugs. We expect all Home Office and Field employees to report for work free from these effects and to be able to fully perform their job duties.

Selling, distributing, purchasing, possessing, or consuming alcohol or illegal drugs, and/or misusing prescribed drugs on company premises is prohibited and may be grounds for termination without prior warning. The company also discourages employees from giving out medication to other employees.

Employees whose actions suggest they are under the influence of alcohol and/or drugs will not be allowed to remain in the workplace.

Drug Testing

To emphasize our commitment to a drug-free workplace, we have instituted a drug-testing program for all Home Office employees. This means that most applicants offered jobs in Home Office facilities must pass a drug test before their job offer is finalized (former company employees are the only exception). For all employees working in Home Office facilities, it means that, if a supervisor has a reasonable suspicion that an employee is performing under the influence of drugs on the job, he or she could be tested. The individual would be sent to EHS, which would conduct an examination, assess fitness for work, and determine when and if the employee should return to work. EHS would decide whether testing is appropriate.

Employees who refuse to report to EHS or refuse to be tested could face termination. Those who test positive would be invited to enroll in appropriate medical and counseling treatment programs. If they refuse, their employment will be terminated. Employees who test positive after undergoing treatment will have their employment terminated.

Employees who may have alcohol- or drug-related problems are strongly encouraged to take advantage of the services offered by the Employee Assistance Program (EAP).

PERSONAL RELATIONSHIPS

Conflict of Interest and Personal Relationships

- No employee may report, directly or indirectly, to a relative or any individual with whom the employee maintains a personal relationship which could compromise the supervisor's ability to supervise.

- Supervisors are expected to avoid any personal relationships which might compromise their effectiveness in supervising.

LIFE-THREATENING ILLNESSES, INCLUDING AIDS

GUIDELINES: To apply the company's policies and programs to employees and applicants with life-threatening illnesses in a manner consistent with their application to employees and applicants with non-life-threatening illnesses and disabilities.

PURPOSE: The company recognizes that employees with life-threatening illnesses such as cancer, heart disease, or AIDS may wish to engage in as many of their normal activities as their condition allows, including work. The company expects supervisors to be sensitive to their condition and treat them consistently with other employees as long as they are able to meet acceptable performance standards and their conditions do not present a medical/safety threat to themselves or others.

ADMINISTRATION: The following information is intended to help supervisors apply policies and programs appropriately when they must address a situation involving an employee/applicant with a life-threatening illness.

Hiring: The company does not exclude individuals from recruitment on the basis of illness. No individual can be denied a position on the sole basis of a handicap. However, we specifically reserve the right to reject applicants or remove employees from the worksite who:

- have disabilities which prevent them from meeting job requirements;
- have disabilities which prevent them from maintaining satisfactory attendance; and/or
- have disabilities which present a health and/or safety threat to others.

Supervisors should contact divisional personnel consultants to determine an appropriate course of action.

Privacy: We do not collect information about an individual from outside the company for use in making employment decisions without the individual's written authorization.

An employee's/applicant's health condition is personal and confidential. Utmost precaution should be taken to protect such information. A supervisor should discuss an employee's health condition only with those individuals who have a business need to know and only where circumstances warrant such a discussion.

Medical records on applicants and employees are maintained in separate confidential files by EHS. None should be maintained in an employee personnel file or with the application.

With a few exceptions, information will not be disclosed to people or organizations outside the company without the individual employee's written approval.

If asked, we will neither confirm nor deny reports that an employee has a life-threatening illness to anyone either inside or outside the company.

Benefits: Employees with life-threatening illnesses are eligible for benefits on the same basis as any other employee.

Return to Work: If an employee with a life-threatening illness goes on short-term disability, he/she will be treated in accordance with the Return-to-Work Program when EHS medically certifies the employee as able to return to the job.

Termination: No employee will be terminated solely because he/she is diagnosed as, or suspected of, having a life-threatening illness.

Workplace Considerations: When dealing with situations involving employees with possible life-threatening illnesses, supervisors should:

- Contact EHS for direction if they have any medical concerns in managing a situation that involves an

employee with a life-threatening illness, e.g.,
concerns about the employee's medical fitness to
work, or concerns about the possible contagious
nature of an employee's illness.

- If warranted, make reasonable accommodations for
employees with life-threatening illnesses consistent
with the business needs of the unit by:
  □ adjusting the work schedule;
  □ providing short-term disability leave as neces-
    sary for treatment;
  □ reducing the workload or restructuring the job;
  □ adjusting the work environment or providing
    special equipment; and
  □ arranging for and allowing the employee to
    work at home.

- Refer employees with life-threatening illnesses to
EHS. If warranted, EHS will refer the employee to
an EAP counselor for information on agencies and
organizations that offer supportive services.

- Contact your divisional Human Resource
Department for guidance in responding to
co-workers' concerns.

- Refer the employee to the divisional personnel
consultant or Benefits Services for assistance in
determining available benefits.

- Be sensitive to the fact that continued employment
for an employee with a life-threatening illness may
sometimes be therapeutically important in the
individual's remission or recovery process, or may
help to prolong that person's life. Ultimately, it is the
supervisor's responsibility to determine if
accommodations (approved by EHS) can be made
based on the business needs of the unit.

Major National Hotel Chain

SEXUAL HARASSMENT

It is company policy not to discriminate against any employee or applicant with regard to sex. To further this policy, the company will not tolerate sexual harassment by or of any of its employees at the workplace.

Harassment on the basis of sex is a violation of Title VII of the 1964 Civil Rights Act and of the company Rules of Conduct. Unwelcomed sexual advances, requests for sexual favors, and other verbal or physical conduct of a sexual nature constitutes harassment when:

- submission to the conduct is made either an explicit or implicit condition of employment;
- submission to or rejection of the conduct is used as the basis for an employment decision affecting the harassed employee; or
- the harassment substantially interferes with an employee's work performance or creates an intimidating, hostile, or offensive work environment.

Employees or applicants who believe they have been discriminated against on the basis of sex should report such incidents to their supervisor, the department of Human Resources Management, or any member of management. **Confidentiality will be maintained.**

The company considers sexual harassment to be a major offense that may result in termination.

EMPLOYEE RECORDS

The Human Resource Management department and/or your supervisor should be informed of any changes affecting: name, address, telephone number, marital status, dependents, etc. It is important to keep your employee record up to date.

Periodically, personnel files will be reviewed. All job performance related materials will remain in the file. At the end of five years, material not directly pertaining to job performance will be removed.

ACCESS TO EMPLOYEE RECORDS

Access to employee records is restricted to the following:

- An employee who wishes to review his/her personal employee file.
- The direct supervisor or department head of an individual employee, if business related.

PRIVACY PROGRAM

The company endorses the President's Privacy Protection Study Commission's call to regulate and protect the collection, use, and dissemination of employee information through the adoption of the following eight principles:

- The company uses only lawful means to collect pertinent information and, to the extent possible, obtains it directly from the individual concerned.
- The company makes every reasonable effort to ensure that information collected, maintained, and acted upon is accurate, relevant, timely, and complete.
- Upon their request, the company informs individuals of the information used to make any determination adversely affecting them, to the extent permitted by legal or medical prohibitions.

- Upon their request, the company informs individuals of the uses being made of their personal information.

- The company provides the opportunity for an individual to correct or clarify personal information contained in his or her personnel file.

- The company restricts access to any personal record to those who have proper authorization or legitimate business, regulatory, or legal reason.

- Willful violation of those principles by an employee will be cause for disciplinary action which could include termination.

- The company will expect all persons acting on the company's behalf to conform to these principles regarding the confidentiality of personal information held by the company or by them. The Human Resource Management department will assume the responsibility of monitoring this privacy protection program on a continuing basis. All questions regarding the program should be referred to the Human Resource Management department.

RULES OF CONDUCT

The rules listed may result in discipline but that imposition of discipline may be based on, but not limited to, the rules as set forth.

Employees on duty must be mentally and physically alert and free from any effect produced by illegal substances or alcohol. Reporting for work under the influence of, possessing, dispensing, or using any illegal substances or alcoholic beverages while on company property is forbidden.

Conduct on or off duty that may reflect negatively on the image of the company or cause a disruption of work or company morale will be grounds for disciplinary action and may result in termination.

Major Computer and Information Systems Manufacturer

RIGHT TO PRIVACY

Employee Personal Information

It is necessary for the company to collect a certain amount of information about you — for example, payroll data, benefits and medical records, and performance evaluations.

To protect your privacy, the company has established four principles for the handling of such information. The company:

- Collects, uses, and retains only that personal information which is required for business or legal reasons.
- Provides each employee with a chance to make sure that what's in his or her personnel record is correct.
- Restricts the internal availability of personal information to those with a business need to know.
- Releases personal information outside the company only with employee approval, except to verify employment or to satisfy legitimate investigatory or legal needs.

ACCESS TO EMPLOYEE RECORDS

Personal Information and Personnel Records

You should inform your manager immediately whenever there are changes in your home address, telephone number, number of dependents, and education. You are also responsible for maintaining a current group life insurance beneficiary designation. It is important to keep this information up to date to avoid problems concerning taxes, employee benefits, and other important matters.

In response to valid requests to verify your employment for business-reference or credit purposes, the company will release, without your approval, only date(s) of employment, last work location, and last position title. With your written approval, the company will release, in addition to the above, your current or final salary and last five-year job chronology.

Personal information, as opposed to management planning and administrative data, about any employee — in his or her personnel folder, personal document file, or personnel data system — is available for review. All that is required is for an employee to ask his or her manager or Personnel.

You may review, or have a copy of, your performance plan or your employee development plan at any time. You may also have a copy of your completed performance evaluation if you wish.

On request, your medical records will be reviewed and explained to you by a company medical professional or, with your permission, medical data is available to your physician.

Many managers maintain data about their employees ranging from home telephone numbers to handwritten notes regarding performance progress or career interest. Upon request, your manager will discuss this information with you except for business confidential material such as salary forecasts.

It is a traditional company practice to publicize employee reassignments, promotions, awards, and other milestones and achievements. However, if you prefer, you can decline publicity when this does not conflict with the information needs of the business.

APPENDIX D

Selected Bibliography
D-3

Selected Bibliography

THE RIGHT TO PRIVACY

Brunn, Lisa. "Privacy and the Employment Relationship." *Houston Law Review*, Vol. 25, March 1988, p. 389.

Buskin, Arthur A., and Schaen, Samuel I. *The Privacy Act of 1974: A Reference Manual for Compliance*. Virginia: System Development Corp., 1976.

Craven. "Personhood: The Right to Be Let Alone." *Duke Law Journal*, Vol. 1976, 1976, p. 699.

Ernst, Morris L., and Schwartz, Alan U. *Privacy: The Right to Be Let Alone*. London: MacGibben & Kee, 1968.

Gerety. "Redefining Privacy." *Harvard Civil Rights — Civil Liberties Law Review*, Vol. 12, 1977, p. 233.

Lehi, Richard I., and Middlebrooks, David J. "Work-Place Privacy Issues and Employer Screening Policies." *Employee Relations Law Journal*, Vol. 11, No. 3, p. 407.

Lieberman, Jethro R. *Privacy and the Law*. New York: Lothrop, Lee & Shepard Co., 1978.

McCarthy, J. Thomas. *The Rights of Publicity and Privacy*. New York: Clark Boardman Co., Ltd., 1987.

Prosser. "Privacy." *California Law Review*, Vol. 48, 1960, p. 383.

Reiman. "Privacy, Intimacy and Personhood." *Philosophy and Public Affairs*, Vol. 6, 1976, p. 26.

Thomson. "The Right to Privacy." *Philosophy and Public Affairs*, Vol. 4, 1975, p. 295.

Tribe, Laurence H. *American Constitutional Law*. New York: The Foundation Press Inc., 1978.

Warren, Samuel D., and Brandeis, Lewis D. "The Right to Privacy." *Harvard Law Review*, Vol. 4, No. 5, 1890, p. 193.

Westin, A. *Privacy and Freedom*. London: Bodley Head, 1970.

DRUG TESTING

Alcohol and Drug Abuse in the Workplace: The Complete Resource Guide. Washington, D.C.: The Bureau of National Affairs, Inc., 1988.

Aron, Martin W. "Drug Testing: The Employer's Dilemma." *Labor Law Journal*, Vol. 38, No. 3, March 1987, p. 157.

Black, Elizabeth C. "So You Think You Have a Drug Problem: Drug Testing in the Workplace." *Employee Relations Law Journal*, Vol. 14, Winter 1988, p. 475.

Cain, Rita M. "Jar Wars: Drug Testing Advice for Private Sector Employers." *Defense Law Journal*, Vol. 37, July 1988, p. 257.

Cheever, Joan M. "Testing the Rights of Employees." *New Jersey Law Journal*, Vol. 118, August 28, 1986, p. 1.

de Bernardo, Mark A. *Drug Abuse in the Workplace: An Employer's Guide For Prevention*. U.S. Chamber of Commerce, 1987.

"Drug Testing: America's New Work Ethic? — City of Palm Bay v. Bauman." 475 So. 2d 1322 (Fla.), *Stetson Law Review*, Vol. 15, Summer 1986, p. 883.

Hartsfield, William E. "Medical Examinations as a Method of Investigating Employee Wrongdoing." *Labor Law Journal*, Vol. 37, No. 10, Oct. 1986, p. 692.

Hartstein, Barry A. "Drug Testing in the Work Place: A Primer for Employees." *Employee Relations Law Journal*, Vol. 12, Spring 1987, p. 577.

Helsky, Wayne L. "Drug Testing in the Work Place." *Florida Bar Journal*, Vol. 60, June 1986, p. 73.

Lake, Stephen F. "Unrestricted Private Employee Drug Testing Programs: An Invasion of the Worker's Right to Privacy." *California Western Law Review*, Vol. 23, Fall 1986, p. 72.

Lips, J. Alan, and Lueder, Michael C. "An Employer's Right to Test for Substance Abuse, Infectious Diseases, and Truthfulness Versus an Employee's Right to Privacy." *Labor Law Journal*, August 1988, p. 528.

Miller, David A. "Mandatory Urinalysis Testing and the Privacy Rights of Subject Employees: Toward a General Rule of Legality Under the Fourth Amendment." *University of Pittsburgh Law Review*, Vol. 48, Fall 1986, p. 201.

National Institute on Drug Abuse. *National Household Survey on Drug Abuse: Population Estimate 1985.* 1987.

O'Donnell, Michael R. "Employee Drug Testing—Balancing the Interests in the Workplace: A Reasonable Suspicion Standard." *Virginia Law Review*, Vol. 74, August 1988, p. 969.

Preer, Robert M. "The Impact of Drug Testing." *Labor Law Journal*, Jan. 1989, p. 50.

Schroeder, Elinor P. "On Beyond Drug Testing: Employee Monitoring and the Quest for the Perfect Worker." *University of Kansas Law Review*, Vol. 36, Summer 1988, p. 869.

Stern, Deborah, and Weeks, James L. "Substance Testing vs. Workers' Rights: Litigation and Collective Bargaining Strategies to Protect the Private-Sector Employee." *West Virginia Law Review*, Vol. 90, Spring 1988, p. 863.

Stille, Alexander. "Drug Testing: The Scene Is Set for a Dramatic Legal Collision Between the Rights of Employers and Workers." *National Law Journal*, Vol. 8, April 7, 1986, p. 1.

Wood, David P. "Employee Drug Testing: Practical and Legal Considerations." *Michigan Bar Journal*, Vol. 66, Feb. 1987, p. 158.

Zimmerman, Carita. "Urine Testing, Testing-Based Employment Decisions and the Rehabilitation Act of 1973." *Columbia Journal of Law and Social Problems*, Vol. 22, Spring 1989, p. 219.

POLYGRAPHS

Call, Barbara J. "Polygraph Regulations and a Trend Toward Tougher Standards." *Employee Relations Law Journal*, Vol. 11, No. 4, Spring 1986, p. 585.

Fingerhut, K.R. "Use of the Simulation Test in Pre-employment Testing." *Polygraph*, Vol. 7, 1978, pp. 185-88.

Fitzpatrick, Robert B. "Polygraph Testing of Employees in Private Industry: A Legal Overview." *Federal Bar News and Journal*, Vol. 35, March-April 1988, p. 132.

Hancock, William A. "Polygraphs and Lie Detectors in the Workplace Under the Employee Polygraph Protection Act of 1988." *Corporate Counsel's Quarterly*, Vol. 5, Jan. 1989, p. 69.

Herron, Daniel J. "Statutory Restrictions on Polygraph Testing in Employer-Employee Relations." *Labor Law Journal*, Vol. 37, No. 9, Sept. 1986, p. 632.

Hurd, Sandra N. "Use of the Polygraph in Screening Job Applicants." *American Business Law Journal*, Vol. 23, Winter 1985, p. 529.

Jacobs, Roger B., and Koch, Cora S. "Polygraph Testing: Weighing the Risks." *Employee Relations Law Journal*, Vol. 14, Autumn 1988, p. 203.

Nagle, David E. "The Polygraph in the Workplace." *University of Richmond Law Review*, Vol. 18, Fall 1983, p. 43.

Putnam, Richard L. "Polygraph Screening of Police Applicants: Necessity or Abuse?" *Polygraph*, Vol. 7(4), Dec. 1978, p. 257.

Rasnic, Carol O. "Polygraphs and Plant Closings." *Case and Comment*, Vol. 94, Jan.-Feb. 1989, p. 15.

"Regulation of Polygraph Testing in the Employment Context: Suggested Statutory Control on Test Use and Examiner Competence." *University of California at Davis Law Review*, Vol. 15, Fall 1981, p. 113.

Stack, Brian J. "Polygraphs and Privacy—Statutory Intervention Is Needed to Protect Private Worker's Rights." *Florida Bar Journal*, Vol. 59, June 1985, p. 19.

Waks, Jay W.; Brewster, Christopher R.; and Prager, David E. "Investigating Workplace Wrongdoing Under Employee Polygraph Protection Act." *New York Law Journal*, Vol. 200, Nov. 15, 1988, p. 1.

Zafran, Enid T., and Steckle, Jeffrey R. "Polygraphs in Employment: A State Survey." *Cleveland State Law Review*, Vol. 33, 1984-85, p. 751.

APPLICANT INVESTIGATIONS

"Employers Face Upsurge in Suits Over Defamation." *National Law Journal*, Vol. 9, No. 34, May 4, 1987.

Shepard, Ira M., and Duston, Robert L. *Thieves at Work: An Employer's Guide to Combating Workplace Dishonesty.* Washington, D.C.: The Bureau of National Affairs, Inc., 1988.

AIDS

"AIDS: Concern for Business." *Nation's Business*, June 1989, p. 25.

"AIDS Education: A Business Guide." American Foundation for AIDS Research, the American Council of Life Insurance, and the Health Insurance Assn. of America, Sept. 1988.

"AIDS in the Hospital Workplace." Tort and Insurance Practice Section of American Bar Association, August 1988.

AIDS in the Workplace: Resource Material (Third Edition). Washington, D.C.: The Bureau of National Affairs, Inc., 1989. (Contains information on corporate practices, legislation, litigation, guidelines, and recommendations.)

Baxley, James F. "Rehabilitating AIDS-Based Employment Discrimination: HIV Infection as a Handicap Under the Vocational Rehabilitation Act of 1973." *Seton Hall Law Review*, Vol. 19, Winter 1989, p. 23.

Bayer and Levine. "HIV Antibody Screening: An Ethical Framework for Evaluating Proposed Programs." *Journal of the American Medical Association*, Vol. 256, Oct. 3, 1986, p. 1768.

"Business Response to AIDS, a National Survey of U.S. Companies." *Fortune Magazine* and Allstate Insurance, 1988.

Centers for Disease Control. "HIV/AIDS Surveillance Report." May 1989.

Centers for Disease Control. "Human Immunodeficiency Virus Infection in the United States: A Review of Current Knowledge." *Morbidity and Mortality Weekly Report*, Vol. 36, Dec. 18, 1987, No. S-6.

Centers for Disease Control. "Recommendations for Prevention of HIV Transmission in Health Care Settings." *Mor-

bidity and Mortality Weekly Report, Vol. 36, Aug. 21, 1987, No. 2-S.

Closen, Michael L.; Connor, Susan M.; Kaufman, Howard L.; and Wojcik, Mark F. "AIDS: Testing Democracy—Irrational Responses to the Public Health Crisis and the Need for Privacy in Serologic Testing." *John Marshall Law Review*, Vol. 19, Summer 1986, p. 835.

Duffy, Jan; Pepe, Stephen P.; and Gross, Beverly. "Big Brother in the Workplace: Privacy Rights Versus Employer Needs." *Industrial Relations Law Journal*, Vol. 9, No. 1, p. 30.

Engel, Paul G. "AIDS in the Workplace." *Industry Week*, Vol. 228, No. 3, Feb. 3, 1986, p. 18.

Facilitating AIDS Education in the Work Environment. Pacific Mutual Life Insurance Co., Sept. 1987.

General Accounting Office. "AIDS Forecasting, Undercount of Cases and Lack of Key Data Weaken Existing Estimates." June 1, 1989.

Horn, Erica. "Protecting Persons With AIDS From Employment Discrimination." *The Kentucky Law Journal*, Vol. 77, Jan. 1989, p. 403.

Johnston, George W. "Coping With AIDS: Today's Major Workplace Issue." *Labor Law Journal*, May 1989, p. 302.

Kandel, William L. "AIDS in the Work Place." *Employee Relations Law Journal*, Vol. 11, No. 4, Spring 1986, p. 678.

Klein, James A. *AIDS: An Employer's Guidebook.* U.S. Chamber of Commerce, 1988.

Leonard. "AIDS, Employment and Unemployment." *Ohio State Law Journal*, Vol. 49, No. 4, 1989, p. 929.

Lotito, Michael J. "AIDS in the Workplace: A Practical Guide for Employers." *The Practical Lawyer*, Vol. 35, Jan. 1989, p. 35.

"Report of the Second Public Health Service AIDS Prevention and Control Conference," *Public Health Reports*, Vol. 103, Supp. 1, Nov. 1988.

Rothstein, Mark A. "Medical Screening of Workers: Genetics, AIDS and Beyond." *The Labor Lawyer*, Vol. 2, No. 4, Fall 1986, p. 675.

Saad, Henry. "AIDS and the Law." *Management Solutions*, Vol. 31, No. 9, Sept. 1986, p. 12.

Saad, Henry. "AIDS Discrimination in the Workplace." *Small Business Report*, Vol. 12, No. 3, March 1987, p. 79.

Schachter, V. "Legal AIDS: An Enlightened Corporate Policy." *Across the Board*, Sept. 1987, p. 12.

Schwartz, Jerry. "Mandatory AIDS Testing Draws Fire." *National Law Journal*, Vol. 9, March 9, 1987, p. 3.

Stromberg, Clifford D. "AIDS Poses Significant Legal Considerations for the Work Place." *Business and Health*, Vol. 3, No. 3, Jan.-Feb. 1986, p. 50.

Turk. "AIDS: The First Decade." *Employee Relations Law Journal*, Vol. 14, No. 4, 1989, p. 531.

Turner and Ritter. "AIDS and Employment." *The Labor Lawyer*, Vol. 5, No. 1, 1989, p. 104.

U.S. Department of Health and Human Resources. *AIDS Resource Listing: Workplace Resources*. June 1989.

HONESTY TESTING

Aiken, L. *Psychological Testing and Assessment*. Boston: Allyn and Bacon, Inc., 1976, p. 258.

Employee Testing: The Complete Resource Guide. Washington, D.C.: The Bureau of National Affairs, Inc., 1988. (Contains information on honesty testing, medical screening, substance abuse testing, and alternative methods of testing.)

Sackett, Paul. "Integrity Testing for Personnel Selection: An Update." *Personal Psychology*, 1989.

Seymour, Richard T. "Why Plaintiffs' Counsel Challenge Tests, and How They Can Successfully Challenge the Theory of 'Validity Generalization.'" *Journal of Vocational Behavior*, Vol. 33, 1988, p. 331

GENETIC TESTING AND MEDICAL SCREENING

Diamond, Anna L. "Genetic Testing in Employment Situations: A Question of Worker Rights." *Journal of Legal Medicine*, Vol. 4, No. 2, June 1983, p. 231.

Matthewman, William D. "Title VII and Genetic Testing: Can Your Genes Screen You Out of a Job?" *Howard Law Journal*, Vol. 27, Fall 1984, p. 1185.

McConnell, James G. "Genetic Testing Conflicts With Discrimination Laws." *The National Law Journal*, Vol. 9, Feb. 9, 1987, p. 14.

Paskal. "Dilemma: Save the Fetus or Sue the Employer." *Labor Law Journal*, No. 6, 1988.

Paterson. "Genetic Screening: How Much Should We Test Employees?" *Industry Week*, 1987.

Pierce, Ellen R. "The Regulation of Genetic Testing in the Workplace—A Legislative Proposal." *Ohio State Law Journal*, Vol. 46, No. 4, Fall 1985, p. 771.

Rothstein, Mark A. *Medical Screening and the Employee Health Cost Crisis*. Washington, D.C.: The Bureau of National Affairs, Inc., 1989.

Rothstein, Mark A. *Medical Screening of Workers*. Washington, D.C.: The Bureau of National Affairs, Inc., 1984.

Shapiro, Martin M.; Slutsky, Michael H.; and Watt, Richard F. "Minimizing Unnecessary Differences in Occupational

Testing." *Valparaiso University Law Review*, Vol. 23, No. 2, Winter 1989.

Sweltz, Edna L. "Genetic Testing in the Workplace: An Analysis of the Legal Implications." *Forum*, Vol. 19, Winter 1984, p. 323.

Tierney and Messing. "New Tricks for Old Dogs: Genetic Screening Makes Victim-Blaming Scientific." *Alternatives*, 1987, p. 31.

U.S. Congress, Office of Technology Assessment. *Medical Testing and Health Insurance*. Washington, D.C., August 1988.

ELECTRONIC MONITORING

Arditi, Lynn. "Is Your Boss Bugging You?" *Working Mother*, Dec. 1987.

Barba, Connie. " 'That's No "Beep," That's My Boss.' Congress Seeks to Disconnect the Secrecy of Telephone Monitoring in the Workplace." *John Marshall Law Review*, Vol. 21, Summer 1988, p. 881.

Communications Workers of America. " 'Don't Bug Me:' Consumer and Worker Action Kit to Protect Workplace Privacy." Dec. 1987.

Marx, Gary T., and Sherizen, Sanford. "Monitoring on the Job, How to Protect Privacy as Well as Property." *Technology Review*, Nov./Dec. 1986.

Reece, Laurence H. "Computer Monitoring and Privacy: Is the Orwellian Nightmare Here?" *The National Law Journal*, Vol. 10, Feb. 15, 1988, p. 20.

Susser, Peter A. "Electronic Monitoring in the Private Sector: How Closely Should Employers Supervise Their Workers?" *Employee Relations Law Journal*, Vol. 13, Spring 1988, p. 575.

U.S. Congress, Office of Technology Assessment. *The Electronic Supervisor: New Technology, New Tensions.* Washington, D.C., Sept. 1987.

PERSONAL RELATIONSHIPS

Bierman, Leonard, and Fisher, Cynthia D. "Anti-Nepotism Rules Applied to Spouses: Business and Legal Viewpoints." *Labor Law Journal*, Vol. 35, No. 10, Oct. 1984, p. 634.

Corporate Affairs: Nepotism, Office Romance, and Sexual Harassment. Washington, D.C.: The Bureau of National Affairs, Inc., 1988.

Karst. "The Freedom of Intimate Association." *Yale Law Journal*, Vol. 89, 1980, p. 624.

Kowarsky, Irving, and Hauck, Vern. "The No-Spouse Rule, Title VII and Arbitration." *Labor Law Journal*, Vol. 32, June 1981, p. 366.

Vhay. "The Harm of Asking: Towards a Comprehensive Treatment of Sexual Harassment." *University of Chicago Law Review*, Vol. 55, 1988, p. 328.

Wexler, Joan G. "Husbands and Wives: The Uneasy Case for Anti-Nepotism Rules." *Boston University Law Review*, Vol. 62, 1982, p. 75.

SEXUAL HARASSMENT

Brown, N. "*Meritor Savings Bank v. Vinson*: Clarifying the Standards of Hostile Working Environment Sexual Harassment." *Houston Law Review*, Vol. 25, March 1988, p. 444.

Kandel, William L. "Sexual Harassment: Persistent, Prevalent But Preventable." *Employee Relations Law Journal*, Vol. 14, No. 3, Winter 1988/89, p. 439.

Kennevick, J. "The Significance of the *Vinson* Decision on Corporate Employees." *Journal of Contemporary Law*, Vol. 12, No. 163, 1986.

Machlowitz, D., and Machlowitz, M. "Preventing Sexual Harassment." *A.B.A. Journal*, Vol. 73, No. 78, Oct. 1987.

CONFIDENTIALITY

Duffy, D. Jan. "Privacy vs. Disclosure: Balancing Employee and Employer Rights." *Employee Relations Law Journal*, Vol. 7, Spring 1982, p. 594.

"Employee Medical Records and the Constitutional Right to Privacy." *Washington and Lee Law Review*, Vol. 38, Fall 1981, p. 1267.

Hauselt, Denise. "Employee Privacy, Information Needs, and the Law." *Industrial and Labor Relations Review*, Vol. 14, Jan. 1980, p. 23.

Linowes, David. *Privacy in America*. Univ. of Ill. Press, 1989.

"The Union's Right to Information at the Expense of Employee's Privacy Rights." *University of Toledo Law Review*, Vol. 15, Winter 1984, p. 755.

DEFAMATION

Castagnera-Cain, James. "Defamation and Invasion of Privacy Actions in Typical Employee Relations Situations." *Lincoln Law Review*, Vol. 13, 1982, p. 1.

Duffy, D. Jan. "Defamation and Employer Privilege." *Employee Relations Law Journal*, Vol. 9, No. 3, Winter 1983-84, p. 444.

Panaro, Gerard P. *Employer's Guide to Reference Checks*. Warren, Gorham & Lamont, Inc., 1987.

EMPLOYMENT-AT-WILL

Blades, Lawrence E. "Employment-at-Will vs. Individual Freedom: On Limiting the Abusive Exercise of Employer Power." *Columbia Law Review*, Vol. 67, 1967, p. 1404.

DeGiusepe, Joseph, Jr. "The Effect of the Employment-at-Will Rule on Employee Rights to Job Security and Fringe Benefits." *Fordham Urban Law Journal*, Vol. 10, 1981, p. 1.

Gillette, Patricia K. "The Implied Covenant of Good Faith and Fair Dealing: Are Employers the Insurers of the Eighties?" *Labor Law Journal*, Vol. 3, 1985, p. 438.

Lopoitka. "The Emerging Law of Wrongful Discharge — A Quadrennial Assessment of the Labor Law Issue of the 1980s." *William and Mary Law Review*, Vol. 26, 1985, p. 449.

Mallor, Jane P. "Punitive Damages for Wrongful Discharge of At-Will Employees." *William and Mary Law Review*, Vol. 26, 1985, p. 449.

Note. "Employee Handbooks and Employment-at-Will Contracts." *Duke Law Journal*, 1985, p. 196.

Shepard, Ira M.; Heylman, Paul M.; and Duston, Robert L. *Without Just Cause: An Employer's Practical and Legal Guide on Wrongful Discharge*. Washington, D.C.: The Bureau of National Affairs, Inc., 1989.